The International Library of Sociology

THE SOCIOLOGY OF COLONIES

PART ONE

Founded by KARL MANNHEIM

The International Library of Sociology

CLASS, RACE AND SOCIAL STRUCTURE
In 21 Volumes

THE SOCIOLOGY OF COLONIES

An Introduction to the Study of
Race Contact

PART ONE

by
RENÉ MAUNIER

Translated and Edited by
E. O. LORIMER

Routledge
Taylor & Francis Group

LONDON AND NEW YORK

First published in 1949 by
Routledge

Reprinted 1998, 2002
by Routledge
2 Park Square, Milton Park, Abingdon, Oxon, OX14 4RN
711 Third Avenue, New York, NY 10017

Transferred to Digital Printing 2007

Routledge is an imprint of the Taylor & Francis Group, an informa business

First issued in paperback 2013

British Library Cataloguing in Publication Data
A CIP catalogue record for this book
is available from the British Library

The Sociology of Colonies: Part One
ISBN13: 978-0-415-17635-4 (hardback)
ISBN13: 978-0-415-86340-7 (paperback)
Class, Race and Social Structure: 21 Volumes
ISBN 0-415-17826-6
The International Library of Sociology: 274 Volumes
ISBN 0-415-17838-X

Publisher's Note
The publisher has gone to great lengths to ensure the quality of this reprint
but points out that some imperfections in the original may be apparent

CONTENTS

Part I

AN INTRODUCTION TO THE STUDY OF RACE CONTACT

Part II

PSYCHOLOGY OF EXPANSION

EDITOR'S NOTE

In rendering native names and words I have retained the French spelling where these were unfamiliar, but have substituted the accepted English spelling of familiar words. In rendering Arabic words I have normally preferred the accepted English transcription of Arabic (e.g. *waqf* rather than *ouakf*; *Jamal* rather than *Djemal*; *sharif* rather than *chérif*, and so on).

Professor Maunier frequently speaks of " the English Empire " and " the English ", where we should say " British." I have retained this wording as characteristic.

I have on occasion supplemented the author's footnotes, where a reference to French history or literature might possibly be obscure to an English reader, or where some allusion to British affairs seemed to call for comment. Such notes are enclosed in square brackets and signed EOL.

It is a pleasing duty here to acknowledge much varied help received in preparing this English Edition of Professor Maunier's work. I wish in the first place warmly to thank the Information Departments of the Royal Institute for International Affairs and of the National Book League, and to express admiration as well as gratitude for the ever-ready courtesy and kindness of the almost omniscient Staff of the London Library. In the second place I am deeply indebted to my husband, D. L. R. Lorimer, and my friend A. S. B. Glover, who have both ungrudgingly placed their knowledge and scholarship at my service.

Such errors as may nevertheless have escaped detection are undividedly my own.

E. O. L.

PREFACE

The present work was begotten of a course of lectures. Each chapter is a lesson, whose spoken character I have sought to preserve. The aim of my teaching has been to direct the student's attention to the social problems involved in the expansion of peoples. To this end I initiated the series of *Études de sociologie et d'ethnologie juridiques* in order to awaken the student's spirit of enquiry.

I lived for a long time in the East, and being neither a colonial official nor an armchair lawyer, I am speaking of what I myself have seen and experienced. I offer the results of my observations to those who are keener on facts than on theories, and who desire recorded data on which to base their opinions.

Students of colonial sciences will find in the *Studies* many lines of study to pursue, with carefully-chosen suggestions for their reading, and a general bibliography dealing with the contact of races. Our former students, now scattered in the uplands of North Africa, will find in the *Studies* much to provoke reflexion. They will be able there to recognise, not that hypothetical phantom " the native "—a figure as unreal as " the legislator " —who is represented as reasoning or irrational, but the human, feeling, thinking person, whether from Algiers or Tahiti, whom it is our task to govern

I have sought to be brief ; I have sought to be clear ; I have sought to be outspoken. I record briefly, clearly, unambiguously, what has been and what is, undeterred by the fear of perishing like a heretic at the stake. If this be a sin, I am a hardened sinner. I snap my fingers at those " scandalmongering pedants ", those busy-bodies " who ferret about amongst other men's labours " over whom the old romance-writer of the 16th century, Noël du Fait, so wittily made merry.

Fontvieille-en-Provence.
This 1st of January, 1932.

ix

INTRODUCTION

This book is an itinerary, or a panorama. From a great height, or from afar, it reveals a country all too ill-explored—especially by us French—which stretches to the frontiers of sociology.

Its aim is a study of human relationships between *individuals* or between *groups*. The relationships or the contacts between groups may themselves be superficial or intimate, according as the groups which meet, belong, or not, to one organised and unified society : be it a tribe, a city or a nation.

The relationships even between *foreign groups* vary according as these foreign groups belong, or not, to the same *civilisation* [1] if not to the same society ; according as they have, or have not, the same kind of organisation ; according as they belong, or not, to one and the same cultural sphere, a unified domain where the same manners and customs have spread by borrowing ; according as the same modes of thought and action prevail amongst them, or not ; according as they have, or have not, the same institutions. The contact of groups or of peoples becomes a contact of civilisations, or of cultural spheres, when it occurs between communities which have not the same form, the same constitution, the same laws : which are therefore not on the same rung of the social ladder. If they are obliged to live together, their problem is how best to pass from diversity to uniformity, to reconcile difference and resemblance, to start from isolation and arrive at fusion. Assimilation or adaptation marks the path to unification.

It is in *colonies* more than elsewhere that this social problem crops up. It is the problem of the contact of races or " the clash of peoples ", as the Anglo-Americans call it. Let us be clear that we are dealing with *different* groups, not merely *foreign* groups, who in colonising " new countries " get in touch with one another. So in speaking—as, following the custom, I shall

---

[1] For a fuller discussion of the concept " civilisation ", see M. Mauss (and others), *Civilisation, le mot et l'idée* (*Centre internat. de synthèse*), Paris 1930 : " *un fonds commun, un acquis général* " which different societies possess in common.

speak—of a " contact of races ", I wish in fact to imply a contact of *social types*. The sociological basis of the colonial problem is that colonisation has brought the *nation* or the *empire* into contact with the *tribe* or the *city* and has brought up against each other two radically contrasted forms of life. Territorial group against parental group; national law against local custom; written law against oral; liberty against authority; invention against tradition . . . All these are things which clash, in the relationship between the " rulers " and their " subjects ". Reactions between them are as inevitable, as it is unavoidable that " civilised " and " uncivilised " groups in contact should be affected by this clash. What takes place between them, what comes to birth between them, as a consequence of this contact ? This is a sociological problem which it is our duty to study. There are two colonial problems : the *economic* and the *human* : the exploitation of things, but also the association of persons. The former has received ample attention : the second has scarcely been considered. It is a striking fact that in Puvis's beautiful fresco representing Marseilles in Greek times, not one of the original inhabitants is to be seen.

In order to answer the second of our questions, we should need large-scale detailed monographs methodically and typically setting forth the various ways in which contact took place, and the various results. Up to the present we have as good as none. By collating the records of travellers and observers, we can, at least, trace the outline of questions to be answered, and draw a sketch-map of explorations to be carried out, after the fashion of those maps of Africa of a century ago where almost every entry was *Terra Incognita*. It is this sketch-map which I have tried to draw. I offer the reader therefore a *programme*, not a synthesis : a list of the questions posed by the " contact of races " in the colonies, by which I mean the social contact, the moral contact, the legal contact, between civilisations which are often at the opposite ends of the long line of Man's social achievements.

PART I

AN INTRODUCTION TO
THE STUDY OF RACE CONTACT

Sociologie Coloniale ; Introduction
à L'Étude du Contact des Races

First published in Paris 1932–1942

BOOK I

THE CONCEPTION OF RACE CONTACT

CHAPTER I

DEFINITION OF COLONIES : EMIGRATION

Some people have a conventional conception of colonies [1] which they have in mind when in the newspaper they condemn " the misuse of colonies ". They hold the belief that colonisation is only one form of *conquest*,[2] that is to say the subjection of others by armed force, that the founding and expanding of colonies is only one form of aggression. In this belief they have coined the words " Imperialism " and " Colonialism " and damned these things as infamous.

Are colonisation and conquest then synonymous ? Are these people not allowing themselves to be deceived by imagining a *historic* and *dogmatic* connection between conquest and colonisation, without actually going so far as to assert that colonisation without violent conquest is impossible ? Occupation, but not necessarily fighting, must precede colonisation.

First, the historic connection.[3] In olden days the occupation of new countries and the domination of new peoples was usually achieved by conquest : usually, but yet not always ; colonisation was then a work of violence. We cannot forget how the Spaniards conquered America ; how they extinguished in fire and blood the mighty native Empires of the Aztecs and the Incas. We cannot forget how the exploitation of the New World caused the extension of slavery throughout the globe, and the trade in negro slaves from Africa to America. That is why, even under the Old French Monarchy, the colonisation of America evoked

---

[1] The word *colony* comes through Latin from an Indo-European root. *Colere* meant " to inhabit, to cultivate " ; it was applied to the gods in the sense of " to protect ". *Colonus* meant " a holder of land " and later a " colonist ". The Greeks used to speak of *apoikia*, emigration. See Ernout-Meillet, *Dictionn. étym. de la langue latine*, Paris, 1932, s.v. *Colo* ; Daremberg-Saglio, *Dictionn. des antiq. grecques et romaines*, s.v. *Colonia*.

[2] I. Lameire, *Théorie et pratique de la conquête dans l'ancien droit*, Paris, 1902 ; H. Lévy-Bruhl, *Conquête, Revue de synthèse*, March 1, 1931, pp. 60–3.

[3] The oldest French word for colony, which Littré traced back to the 14th century, *coulogne* (see his Dict., s.v. *Colonie*), was thus explained " quand aucune ville est gaigniée et aquise et l'en trametoit nouvel peuple pour habiter ".

protests against the cruelties of slavery—protests which do honour
to philosophy—the protests of Montesquieu, of Rousseau and,
above all, of Abbé Raynal whose *Histoire des établissements des
Européens dans les Deux-Indes* eloquently, often grandiloquently,
denounced the destructive doings of the colonisers of his day.
It may well be that it is the memory of these protests which in
many minds inseparably associates colonisation with violence.

Secondly, the *dogmatic connection*.   Philosophical theory has
intimately linked conquest and colonisation.   The doctrinaires
of the Old Régime, some Physiocrats in particular, propounded
the theory of annexation in general, without making exception
of colonisation, a form of annexation *sui generis*.   The modern
doctrinaires, in particular some Socialists, have evolved the
theory of the emancipation of all peoples and their right to
" self-determination ", on the ground that conquest is illegitimate
and inhuman.

But this dogmatic association of ideas is not a definition.
Though it is often true that expansion demands conquest, it is
not always true.   Expansion may be arrived at by two other
methods : by *occupation* or by *acquisition*.

Occupation takes place when unoccupied and hitherto uninhabited territory, virgin soil in the true sense of the term, is
occupied without conflict.   Like the Robinson Crusoe of story
who took possession of a desert island, colonisers have sometimes
been able to find a footing in new countries—" new " in the full
sense of the word—unoccupied and uninhabited, where their
only foes have been the climate and the soil.   This was the case
of Reunion Island in 1642 and of the Kerguelen Islands in 1774.

In other cases there has been *Acquisition*.   This is the procedure of the " Social Contract ", where the new arrivals,
coming up against the " earlier occupiers ", make an agreement
or treaty with them, and thus obtain with more or less good will
the right to settle.[1]   There is a solemn, ceremonial, ritual contract, with oaths, embraces, exchange of gifts, the pipe of peace
. . . salvos of cannon : such a ceremony as has been described
by the Jesuit Father Charlevoix in 1701 between the French and
the Algonquins.   This method of acquisition by contract was
used in the 17th century by the Quakers who founded Pennsylvania.   When William Penn wished to plant his colony in the
forests in 1681, on the spot where Philadelphia was later to

---

[1] For various examples, see M. E. Lindley, *The Acquisition and Government of
Backward Territory,* London, 1926, pp. 169 f. and 316 f.

spring up, he earnestly desired that no harm should accrue to the inhabitants ; he established peaceful relations with them ; he was able to conclude a genuine treaty of peace with them whereby the natives willingly agreed to the settlement of the emigrants.

As early as 1636 Roger Williams laid it down that a Royal Charter was not enough to give its holders a right of occupation ; they required also the consent of the first occupiers, the Indians, who alone had the right to dispose of the soil. Manhattan Island, where skyscrapers have since sprouted like mushrooms, was bought from the Indians for 120 francs ! Later, between 1800 and 1820, the " Westward Drive " was carried through by means of sixty conventions with the natives. Even during the course of last century, protectorates were proclaimed without opposition, with the full concurrence of the first occupiers. The most typical of these agreements was surely that concluded in 1839 with " King Denis " for the cession of the estuary of the Gabun River, in what is now French Equatorial Africa, in exchange for a pension, an embroidered coat and the cross of the Legion of Honour. King Denis died decorated by the Pope for his services as protector of missions. The French were even requested to establish other protectorates, such as those of Tahiti and the Marquesas Islands in 1842 and 1843. Acquisition by contract is not the rule ; the fact that it has occurred, however, disposes of the contention that there is an inevitable connection between colonisation and violence.[1]

Let us then set aside this conventional idea and seek to formulate the *historical* and *sociological* conception of colonisation.[2] First, the *historical* : We must determine what colonisation has been in the past and what it is in the present, in order to ascertain its distinctive characteristics. We must define colonisation, as it has been and as it is, and not as we could wish that it had been or might be. Secondly, the *sociological* : We must treat colonisation as a collective fact, a great mass phenomenon, an action which has brought entire peoples into contact ; that is, we must see it as the source of relationships between human groups : as a *social fact*, the study of which falls within the scope of sociology.

Colonisation is a contact of peoples. Apart from cases where

---

[1] For the jurists' doctrines about Contractual Occupation, see H. Bonfils, *Manuel de droit internat. public*, 4th Ed., Paris, 1905, pp. 309–12.

[2] The only systematic attempt to define colonisation, prior to this of my own, is due to G. Hardy : *Colonisation, Revue de synthèse*, I, March 1931, pp. 64–80.

wholly uninhabited territory has been occupied, the colonisers have come up against the earlier occupants, and have necessarily entered into relations with them : colonisation involves inter-communication. A *colony* is called a " new country ", that is to say a country not yet developed in accordance with our industrial methods—a country which, to us at least, appears exotic—where colonisers and colonised enter into relations with each other. As new countries, the colonies form a contrast to our old countries : first, in the economic sense, by our bringing into play the hitherto undeveloped resources of the land ; secondly, in the sociological sense, by bringing into contact human groups hitherto separated. Two social entities are brought into touch, and two differing civilisations, or in other words, two differing traditions, are pitted against each other. In every colony we therefore find the colonisers as the conquerors, the governors, the exploiters, the progeny of old countries, coming from afar, and claiming to bestow on the new countries the benefits of the development of their riches. And we find the earlier occupiers, the dominated, the governed or the colonised, who, by the very fact of their country's being occupied, are reduced to a position of legal or actual tutelage.

From this point of view, colonisation seems to us both a primitive and a general phenomenon. It is both ancient and universal. At all periods of history, and even in prehistoric times, there have been migratory peoples and emigrant peoples ; colonising peoples have swarmed into countries already occupied by others. In the Stone Age, and particularly in Neolithic times, whole peoples have been colonisers, and have crossed the seas to spread their own civilisation among less civilised peoples.[1] With the Ægeans and the Cretans these emigrations led to the founding of maritime Empires—*thalassocracies,* as the Greeks called them—two millennia before Christ. The royal lawgiver Minos from his throne at Knossos dominated a whole empire.[2] In the course of time colonisation took place everywhere and in every continent. The Australians, the Malayo-Polynesians, swarmed by sea into America in very ancient times.[3] This

---

[1] See books on prehistoric archæology, especially Déchelette, *Manuel d'archéologie préhist.*, Paris, 1908, p. 619 f. ; II, 1, p. 393 f. ; G. Dottin, *Les anciens peuples de l'Europe,* Paris, 1916, pp. 240–51.

[2] See especially G. Glotz, *La civilisation égéenne,* Paris, 1923 (Engl trans., *The Aegean Civilization,* London, 1925).

[3] See especially P. Rivet, *L'Anthropologie,* 1925, p. 145 ; *Les Malayo-Polynésiens en Amérique,* Paris, 1927 ; and for the colonies of seafaring Maoris in New Zealand from Neolithic times, see Elsdon Best, *The Mahori,* Wellington, 1924, Vol. I.

great social phenomenon is a fundamental and a universal one. Some even speak of *Animal Colonies*,[1] though the analogy may be challenged. People have even moralised over " slave-owning ants ". The parallel between *colonisation* and *reproduction* has also been noted, in so far as there is a *transmission*, from the mother-country to the colony, of the characteristics of the parent social group : sociological heredity, it is said, is akin to biological heredity. In the Sixth Book of the *Laws*, Plato already said : " Colonies are like children in whom the life of the city or nation is continued." This is the idea expressed in the term " mother-country ".

Let us analyse the constituent elements of a colony to see in what circumstances we may talk of colonisation.

If there is to be a penetration or inter-communication of peoples, there must be, first, an *emigration* of persons, or the occupation of a new country, and secondly, the *government* of the new country or the subjection of its people. Emigration and government, or, in other words, *occupation* and *legislation* : an element of fact and an element of law. When these two factors are present, we have colonisation. Emigration without government is not colonisation, nor is government without emigration. Emigration alone yields only an increase of population, as in the case of Italians in America or Arabs in France. Government alone is annexation or expansion, but not colonisation, which properly consists of occupation, development and administration.

Emigration in itself means only settlement : the fact that a larger or smaller number of persons transfer themselves from one country to another. For a long time this was the only factor taken into account in defining colonisation. Thus in the *Encyclopédie* of 1750, and in the *Dictionnaire de l'Académie*, colonisation was explained as " the conveyance of a people from one country to another ", and colony as " a number of persons of both sexes who are sent from one country to inhabit another ". And dictionaries of synonyms give the word *peuplade* (small tribe or clan) as the equivalent of colony. It is the occupation of a new country by the nationals of an old, often far-distant country : a human tide which seeks to overwhelm and sometimes to absorb the existing inhabitants, which constitutes

---

[1] E. Perrier, *Les colonies animales et la formation des organismes*, Paris, 1881 ; A. Espinas, *Des sociétés animales*, 1877 (new edition 1924), Section I. Swarming is emigration with severance ; separation not colonisation. *Mutualism* and *Commensalism* present a somewhat distant analogy with colonisation. P.-E. Girod, *Les sociétés chez les animaux*, Paris, 1891, Parts 3 and 4 on " Colonial Societies ".

colonisation. Varron compared colonies to swarms of bees. As groups of bees swarm off to form new and distant hives, cities and nations swarm into new countries to form new cities, new nations.

Emigration itself consists of two different factors. To achieve settlement there must be first an *emigration of persons* and secondly an *exportation of goods*, an emigration of capital ; without this latter, the occupation and development of a new country would be an empty sound. Colonists must bring with them products of their own country and tools, or later procure the means of clearing the ground and exploiting its resources. Robinson Crusoe, pattern colonist as he was, took good care to get hold of all the provisions and tools which he could salvage from his ship ; if he had arrived with nothing, his tale would have been soon told. Emigrants are therefore people owning some possessions, or it is at least better that they should be so equipped.

Let us look more closely at these two factors of emigration. First, the *emigration of persons*. You need " new men ", adventurers or the adventurous-minded, who set forth to establish themselves far away : you need the " uprooted " to strike root in the new soil, to occupy, to govern, to exploit it. These are your *emigrants* or your *ex-patriates*.[1] A writer of old defined an " expatriated " person as " one who is absent from and outside his land and country, whether for his country's good, or by order of his prince, or on an approved voyage, or in banishment, or prison, or otherwise ". We must not forget that as late as the 18th century it was a question whether a citizen had the right to emigrate without permission. There are various aspects of the settlement question which we must enumerate.

The peopling of new countries varies in *degree* : it may be greater or less in density according to the conditions of the place and of its setting : according to the inhabitants, the climate and the nature of the country. In this respect we distinguish two types of colony : First, *habitable colonies* whose temperate sky is favourable to a European population : colonies where the settler can live in conditions approximately similar to those to which he is accustomed. Secondly, *colonies for exploitation*, usually situated in the tropics, where the climate does not permit permanent European settlement. These colonies G. Hardy calls

[1] Dutot, *De l'expatriation* . . . Paris, 1840. De Pradt, *La France, l'émigration et les colons*, Paris, 1824.

skeleton colonies. Here the few Europeans are only managing directors or merchants, the tiller of the soil is native or exotic, and the European's life depends on coloured labour. The Belgian Congo is an example, where there are only 10,000 whites. Even in habitable colonies, colonisation has always been the work of a minority, acting like a leaven on the native mass ; the work of thousands, not of millions. Indo-Europeans, Celts, Romans, Europeans governed extensive territories and large populations as much by prestige as by armed force. But there must be some immigration, however slight ; some core of Europeans to organise and direct the development. The peopling of the colony may be " intensive " in habitable colonies, or, as we have seen, " non-intensive " in colonies of exploitation ; but there must always be some immigration. The degree of intensity is not wholly dependent on the climate or the nature of the country ; but also, and very largely, on the qualities and temperament of the colonising nation. Any colonising nation knows, more or less, how to found a colony ; it knows, more or less, how to keep it. Much depends on its own people, on their predispositions, on their ambitions and more particularly on their need of luxury and of society. Volney used to say, speaking in Revolution days of the United States which he had visited, that the English had a greater colonising gift than the French, because they are less dependent on society, more adapted to living alone, and that they are better than the French at producing pioneers, or, as we should say nowadays, " bushrangers ", and at creating " desert-dwellers " (*blédards*) who are able to live divorced from all companionship. That is perhaps the prime qualification for being a colonist in the early days. In borrowing the word " pioneer " [1] from the vocabulary of the military camp, we emphasise the obscure, ungrateful rôle of the first colonists, for under Francis I it denoted the soldier-labourer, the sapper and miner, who was also called *le franc-taupin* because he mined like a mole.

This gift of being able to live alone is therefore one which exists in varying degrees in different nations. It is a product of history ; it depends on national institutions ; and the colonising talent of the English is not an inborn, absolute and mysterious gift, but derives from many British customs which predispose the Englishman to emigrate. One of these is the law of primo-

---

[1] The French Republic of '48 gave the name of " pioneer " to the soldiers of its disciplinary companies !

geniture, which inclines younger sons to seek their fortune abroad and which fills the ranks of the Civil Service.

The settlement of a new country may take various forms : it may be *intermittent* or *permanent*. Frequently, especially at the beginning, it is intermittent, becoming later final or permanent, when a penetration or infiltration takes place which peoples the new country with *colonists*, in the proper sense of the term, settled agricultural colonists wedded to the soil, in the Latin acceptation of the phrase.

Settlement, then, is at first intermittent. You see caravans of merchants making trading expeditions in order to procure from " the savages " the produce of their land, in exchange for toys and worthless knick-knacks, which are acceptable currency among them. The merchants reappear after long absences, but they are already in a certain sense emigrants from their own country. Thus in ancient times, the Ægeans, the Phœnicians, and later the Greeks, founded markets and warehouses where traders took up their quarters for a time and worked out a system of intercourse with the primitive inhabitants, or the " barbarians " as the Greeks used to call them. Later we get travellers' theories recorded by the first tourists, men who themselves set out for discovery and adventure, explorers, observers, who first paved the way for penetration.[1] *Explorations, expeditions* were the first intermittent contacts with distant peoples.

Later comes the *permanent* settlement and we can then speak of colonisation. This is the definite settling down, the penetration, the infiltration of the white men into the home of distant peoples. It was necessary to establish in a new country, occupiers, inhabitants, exploiters. Under the Old Régime, the colonists who took possession of, and worked the soil were in fact styled " habitants ". It was in the same sense that the English—Francis Bacon, for instance, who in the 16th century wrote an essay on colonies—called their colonies " plantations ". But whether they are officials or, it may be, missionaries, whether they are engineers or teachers, they are " colonists " *lato sensu* ; that is to say, permanent settlers. In course of time old-established colonies help to people new colonies which in their turn become centres of expansion. Reunion has been called a *colonising colony* and our Algeria might deserve the same title, for it is already hiving off into Morocco.

In order that human emigration may achieve its purpose,

[1] *Collection des Atlas Plon, Atlas général des grandes explorations,* Paris, 1899.

there must be in the second place the *export of goods* ; the emigration of capital. The colonists must take with them, or procure later, the means of production, the means of exploitation, without which no occupation, whether military or pacific, can reach its completion.[1] The export of capital may vary in form and in degree and may be accomplished by very small means, as we have seen in North Africa. Colonisation has there been the work of very humble colonists, better endowed with industry than wealth. Yet they had their capital : their tools, their animals and later their machines. They took with them processes and instruments which were unknown to the native ; they embodied industrial progress ; it has been capital plus toil which has succeeded in bringing fertility to the soil of new countries. There is no colonisation in the true sense which fails to bring enrichment, a " raising of values " (*mise en valeur*) to new countries by the employment of capital. The history of colonisation is linked with the history of capitalism ; colonisation is in very truth a capitalist achievement.[2] There can be no question of colonisation when tramps and down-and-outs betake themselves to the colonies to lead there a primitive existence, men such as buccaneers and pirates, impotent to lay any foundations, intruders only, not even preparing the way for others. With colonists must come the means of colonising, which can be the case only if people are willing to risk goods as well as men in colonies. Just as much as revolution,[3] colonisation needs " the outlay of money ". It is well known how much capital had to be found by the merchants of London to finance the first Puritan emigration of 1630. During a partnership of seven years they had accumulated a common fund to finance the colonising experiments. Under the old-time French kings, it was the money of the aristocracy, the lawyers, and the merchants, which was risked in the first Colonial Companies. Fundamentally colonisation in its aims is both gamble and adventure.

[1] H. Babled, *Le rôle des capitaux dans les colonies franç. Annales Faculté droit*, Aix, II, 1906 ; P. Chemin-Dupontès, *Le capital engagé dans les colonies françaises, Questions diplomat et colon.*, June 1906 ; P. Restany, *Le prob. des capitaux dans les col. franç.*, Paris, 1924 (Law thesis).

[2] For a comprehensive view of the relation between colonisation and capitalism, see Henri Sée, *Les origines du capitalisme moderne*, Paris, 1926, Chapters III to VI.

[3] See in particular Werner Sombart's great work, *Der moderne Kapitalismus*, of which may be read in French : *Le bourgeois*, Paris, 1926, pp. 86 f. and 366 f. and *Les Juifs et la vie économique*, Paris, 1923. See Waetjen's critique, *Das Judentum und die Anfänge der Kolonisation, Vierteljahrschrift für Sozial- und Wirtschaftsgeschichte*, 1913 (Faculty of Law), which assigns a minor rôle to the Jews, with the sole exception of Brazil.

This is why the greatest colonising nations are the greatest capitalist nations. Trade stimulated the taste for adventure. There people were found prepared to risk in distant countries money lightly gained and lightly lost. Let us recall how the earliest colonial trading companies came into existence : A few " merchant adventurers ", as they called themselves, pooled ample sums to charter a single ship which sailed away for years without a shadow of news reaching its owners. In the event of its fortunate return, they shared the profits. These companies were formed for one voyage only. Colonisation was and remained a speculative adventure. The imperial nations were those which risked not only their men but their money, and for their own aggrandisement grudged neither their riches nor their lives.

CHAPTER II

DEFINITION OF COLONIES : DOMINATION AND GOVERNMENT

We have seen the *factual* aspect of colonisation ; let us glance at the *legal*. Emigration should be accompanied and endorsed by *government*, the actual deed by the legal deed, occupation by administration. The Slavs, the Latins, the Jews, the Germans, who after a generation or two in the United States have vanished into the " melting pot ", have founded no colonies ; they are not rulers but ruled. The Annamites or the Kabyles who have come to live in France, form a colony only in the sense in which we speak of the " French Colony " in Cairo,[1] the " American Colony " in Paris or the " English Colony " in Saint-Raphael. These are only transplantations, not governments, actual but not legal settlements. They have been called " colonies without a flag ",[2] this title signifying that their presence in a foreign country stakes no claim to legal jurisdiction, that they have no legislation or administration of their own : that they recognise their subjection to the laws of the country of their domicile. They are colonies in an old, not a new, country and hence are governed, not governing. Though there are 100,000 Italians in Marseilles, Marseilles is not therefore an Italian colony ! Neither—by your leave !—is Nice ; for there is no legal bond between the ex-patriates and their " mother-country ", or their country of origin. A *colony* presupposes a metropolitan country which directs its destiny. The word " metropolis " is Greek, and denotes that the city, the *polis*, imposes its *metron*, its standards, rule, and law, on the new colony. To be a " colony ", a settlement requires a legal bond attaching it to the country whence the colonists come : that is the meaning of metropolis or mother-country. The Italians living in Marseilles, the Greeks in Alexandria in Egypt, or even the Kabyles who dwell in Paris, have no metropolis, no national flag to shelter under : they are emigrants, not colonists.

---

[1] See N. Carnoy's thesis : *La colonie française du Caire*, Paris, 1928.
[2] R. Gonnard, *L'émigration italienne et les colonies sans drapeau, Questions diplomat. et coloniales*, Jan. 1 and 16, 1906.

The word *domination* conveys this legislative idea.[1] The colonists must preserve their dependence on, their submission to, the mother-country. From this very fact it follows that the metropolis must have dominion over the natives. The fact that the colonists are *bound* to the mother-country, suffices of itself to bind to her the natives also ; they are subjects of the colonising State which exercises over them full powers. A colony is a tentacle of the colonising State. Colonisation is an exercise of power.

This being so, and granted that there must always be a legislative bond to reinforce the colony's actual attachment, we must note that domination has degrees and forms which it behoves us to classify.

When we speak of the power which a State exercises, we may imply an actual domination, what the chancelleries call an " influence ", an " expansion ", a " penetration " ; an actual bond, at least in the beginning, which asserts and paves the way for a legal *imperium*, a domination, or a subjection in the proper sense, which is " protection " or " annexation " : political and legislative power for which " penetration " is only the prelude and the preparation ; this is what the jurists call " allegiance ".

First let us consider domination *de facto*, what diplomats euphemistically term " peaceful penetration ". This is here used in its full sense, not expressing a simple intercommunication of two peoples but pressure and imposition ; it is an attempt to assume command and to impose authority on a new country. Such is the domination which the United States exercise over the countries of South America, and which they will perhaps graciously extend to our divided Europe. It is a *de facto* assumption of power ; these countries keep the name of independent States, they are Republics which owe no legal allegiance to the American Republic. But in fact their loans, their exports, their contracts, give the United States an almost absolute empire over Ecuador, Venezuela and Colombia. Even the export of these countries' fruits is in American hands ; a powerful American company has to its profit revived the *monopoly* of olden days.[2] Such is the power of capital ; production, as well as export, is in their hands. An actual domination can thus be exercised without intensive emigration. In these South American countries, few " American

---

[1] J. Harmand, *Domination et colonisation*, Paris, 1911, emphasises, perhaps over-emphasises, this view. Before him, Lord Brougham had written *An Inquiry into the Colonial Policy of the European Powers*, London, 1803.

[2] See L. Guilaine, *L'Amérique latine et l'impérialisme Américaine*, Paris, 1928.

citizens " are permanent residents : emigration is slight, but domination is very marked indeed ; these Republics are practically annexed.

To achieve infiltration, penetration or expansion, the power exercised is not necessarily *financial* only. There may be empire of a *religious* type, such for instance as missions exercise, who frequently do not confine their work to the conversion of the natives, but amongst the Anglo-Saxons pursue other aims. We have seen it in Oceania and in Madagascar. Missionaries are often unofficial consuls. Or empire may be *intellectual*, such as is exercised by institutions and associations who ply European " propaganda " in a new country, as for instance in the Near East. Heads of schools are in their way political missionaries. Again, empire may be *industrial* : such as is exercised by banking houses and factories. It surely looks harmless enough when foreign capitalists invest their money in a certain country. Yet these undertakings, " financed " by the foreigner, constitute a danger. First there are markets and warehouses, next transport undertakings, especially railways, best of all methods of penetration ; finally industries, whether of extraction or manufacture, by means of which Germans and English especially have penetrated certain new countries without firing a shot. Such undertakings serve political greed at the same time as economic interest. It is no accident that in the East foreign consuls are often merchants or industrialists. It is the proof and the token that exploitation subserves political ambition. The exploitation of a colonised country aims not only, or mainly, at economic profit, but also—and this is often perceived too late—its subjection. The foreigners' General Staff takes over the economic direction of the country. Engineers, directors, merchants, traders, control the destiny of the victim-country, while their home-government makes treaties to ensure the non-interference of rival nations. This state of affairs has already become legalised.[1]

This procedure is utilised more especially in the case of countries which a nation cannot or dare not colonise and legally annex. But it may also be the preliminary to *legal domination* which is frequently the goal towards which it is moving : the status of a " colonial power " or of an imperial power. Rightly regarded, we are here dealing with a form of imperialism, inasmuch as the subjection or attachment of a " new country "

[1] *Encycl. Britann.*, 14th Ed., London, 1929, s.v. *Spheres of Influence.*

has been achieved by another country which has brought the new country within its power.

Looked at from the legal angle, colonisation is *dependence* or *allegiance* in a double sense.

Colonisation spells dependence for the colonists *vis-à-vis* the mother-country. They remain citizens of the country of their birth, preserving rights in it and duties towards it. In olden days this was marked by an eloquent symbol : the Greek colonists carried with them in their ships the sacred fire of their home-land, from which they lighted the altar of the new colony for the first time. Whatever form it may take—feudal homage, fiscal tribute, commercial régime or electoral right—colonists of all periods remain attached and governed. Colonisation spells dependence for the natives too, now fallen under guardianship : whether they be treated as slaves, subjects or " partners ", they have forfeited their autonomy. They can no longer boast a State of their own. And the symbol of their dependence is the arrival of a Governor, whose mere presence, even if he exercise no effective power, proclaims the intention to rule. A Governor who does not govern,[1] even if he . . . has no other duty than to issue invitations to his *garden-parties*, remains a governor, he excludes the State ; his glowing or sparkling uniform speaks to every eye of subordination. Another symbol is the flag : the national or the imperial flag—the flag of the British Empire, for instance, which differs from the Royal Standard [2]—this flag, which supersedes the flag of the local kinglet (henceforward pensioned and dethroned) and flutters above the palace of the Governor ; it also, under whatever sky, proclaims in monotonous European style the intention to reign.

Like the *de facto* domination, this *de jure* domination has its forms and its degrees. Subjection may be more or less emphasised. We must in particular distinguish two types of domination : the one absolute, the other tempered ; the one unlimited, the other limited.

Absolute rule is established in *colonies* in the narrower sense, in what are better called *possessions*, which are in fact annexed. Algeria, for instance, is a colony of this type—unwelcome though

---

[1] H. Couve de Murville, *Le gouverneur dans les dominions britann.*, Paris, 1929 (Law thesis).

[2] [The Royal Standard is the personal flag of the King of Great Britain and Ireland. It is flown only when the King or Queen is personally present and in residence. There is no conceivable reason why anyone should expect to see it flying over the Governor's palace in a Colony. EOL]

this thought may be to many—since its dependence on and allegiance to France is absolute. It has no proper autonomy in the Greek sense of the word ; the colony cannot pass its own laws ; its laws are enacted in France in virtue of the supreme power of the State. This is the very type of colonial attachment. As soon as colonisation by annexation has taken place, as soon as the colony has *received* its law, as soon as, according to French custom (diametrically opposed in this to the custom of the British Empire), all power is exercised by the delegation of French authority, as soon as French law rules and reigns, the colony's dependence is unlimited. Legislative power, executive power are exercised in French colonies by the French of France and by them alone. Legislation, jurisdiction and administration are in French hands. And even if it be native officials who exercise these powers, they do so only in the name of France, as representatives of France. The insignia they wear are granted by the French ; a *képi*, a red or blue *burnous* enriched with embroideries of gold or silver. Their breast is adorned with French decorations ; they bear on their own person the symbols of their dependence ; they take pride in them—which is fortunate —and thus acknowledge their subjection. This procedure is a proclamation of authority and paternity ; beneficent, paternal authority but authority complete and absolute.

Tempered, moderated, limited power, on the other hand, exists in the French *Dependencies*. Of these there are many varying degrees, often a thousand different shades from the semi-independent colonies of dominion-like status, to colonies in the stricter sense, closely attached and bound to metropolitan France, which might be termed *subject colonies*.

The British Empire [1] has of late assumed a new title, " The British Commonwealth of Nations ". It forms a League of Nations. The colonies, henceforth almost completely independent, retain nevertheless a legal tie, almost entirely symbolic, with the English monarchy ; a tie represented by the small Union Jack, woven in the corner of each national flag and by the presence of a Governor. This tie implies a right of veto, or at least a right of intervention, which makes the " Nations " of the Commonwealth still—though ever so slightly !—colonies. They are Nations, but yet not States. They have not absolute and

[1] In preference to more recent heavier books, read : Max O'Rell, *La Maison John Bull & Co.*, Paris, 1894 ; A. Demangeon, *L'Empire britannique*, Paris, 1923 ; and for recent changes, the *Chroniques coloniales* by C. Fidel (*Soc. d'Études et d'information écon.*), Dec. 1926, Jan. and May 1931.

full autonomy but are still linked to Great Britain by a bond strongly felt and obeyed, a bond of loyalty and patriotism, the supreme symbol of which is the British Crown. The celebration of *Empire Day*, which recurs annually on the anniversary of Queen Victoria's birthday, is the recognised rite which re-asserts and re-hallows these feelings. The supreme Head of the Empire, His Majesty *The King* bears the title " . . . of Great Britain, Ireland and of the British Dominions beyond the Seas, King, Emperor of India . . ." Even, therefore, where subordination is limited, and not unlimited, this subordination, though often wholly symbolic and in certain cases sentimental only, constitutes none the less a moral bond.[1]

In the French colonial empire the power governing Protectorates[2] and Mandates[3] is tempered power. In defining *protection* Vattel[4] already spoke of a *reciprocity of obligations* and he contemplated the protector's forfeiture of rights if he failed to fulfil his obligations. Here we see the conception of *Trusteeship* which people have mistakenly thought to be a new idea. These countries are not strictly colonies in the legal sense ; yet in many senses they are, since power in them is divided. A protected country is only a Pseudo-State, or a *Semi-Sovereign State*, which in principle and in theory possesses legislative and executive power or, as the Physiocrats used to say, *potestas legislatrix et executrix*. But though it possesses these powers it has not sole possession of the land. Tunisian decrees, Moroccan *dahirs* are issued in the name of the Bey or the Sultan, but they are formulated and proposed and controlled by France. So there is partnership and collaboration in Protectorates and Mandated Territories between the native power and the French power. And always, in some form or other, there is domination, domination at times but slightly felt, yet never concealed, always open and proclaimed. When the French hold a territory under mandate, their intention is, and ought to be, to withdraw after a certain time. Their domination is therefore only an educative and liberating *guardianship* pledged to be temporary. Even in

---

[1] [The Colonial Conference of 1926 and the Statute of Westminster of 1931 both explicitly re-affirm the long-existing, long-recognised, unquestioned right of any of the " Nations ", at any time, to terminate at will, and without comment, its connection with the British Commonwealth.   EOL]

[2] (Anon.) *Le régime des protectorats*, 2 vols., 1888–99 ; A. Pillet, *Des droits de la puissance protectrice sur l'admin. intér. de l'État protégé*, Revue gén. droit internat. pub., II, 1895, p. 583 f.

[3] H. Rolin, *La pratique des mandats internat.*, Recueil cours Acad. droit internat., IV, 1927, pp. 493–624 ; D. F. Van Rees, *Les mandats internat.*, Paris, 1927–8.

[4] *Le droit des gens*, Neuchatel, 1777, I, Book I, Chap. XVI.

this case domination is exercised ; power is rightly assumed, marked by the army of occupation and also by the presence of that French symbol, the body of officials, who might fairly be styled the army of administration.

Let us now draw up our definition. We may speak of colonisation when there is, and because there is, *occupation with domination* : when there is, and because there is, *emigration with government*. It is not enough for some French people to be in a certain spot, to have settled at a distance, if they remain isolated, unsupported and impotent ; if they have no right to hoist the French flag over their cabin, they are no colonists. But when this right is theirs, or the right of a Governor on their behalf, when they have become the symbol of a metropolitan power, when their country announces its intention of remaining and of governing, then colonisation has taken place.

This is the conception of *Empire* : [1] one rule and one civilisation alone, extending over a divided, organised space ; one law, one administration ruling over a domain which aspires to know no bounds. Did not the Babylonian sovereign Hammurabi give himself the title of " King of the Four Corners of the World " ? *Centralisation* and *unification* are the characteristics of Empire : a conformity of words, of manners, and of laws, which are current along every road to the furthest frontiers, and which by domination and persuasion make for assimilation.

From this point of view it is true that every form of colonisation is *imperialist* and that its aim is to bring new peoples into subjection.

[1] R. Maunier, *La nation et l'empire*, in *Essais sur les groupements sociaux*, Paris, 1929, Chap. VI.

CHAPTER III

CLASSIFICATION OF COLONIES

Having *defined* colonies let us now *classify* them into the forms that they assume according to time and place. To arrive at a classification, let us consider the variations of their two essential elements : emigration and domination. Let us therefore first work out a classification of the *de facto* position and then of the *de jure* position ; or to put it in other words, first the economic classification, and secondly the legal or political classification.

The aspect of *emigration* varies according to duration, to degree and to motive.

As regards duration, we must distinguish *intermittent* and *permanent* colonisation ; the full importance of this distinction lies in its bearing on race contact. According as penetration is intermittent or permanent, colonisation displays less or more activity, intercommunication a lesser or greater degree of intimacy. Markets and fairs set up in a new country are the beginnings of colonisation, from which warehouses and cities may develop. French centres of commerce and industry had their birth from colonies, which in their early days were precarious ; their first white inhabitants came from abroad and were only transitory travellers. Again and again in the French colonies, the temporary laid the basis of the enduring ; offices, missions, cultural and industrial undertakings, are emigrations which began by being temporary, and ended by becoming permanent.

As regards *degree*, we must distinguish *exploitation colonies* and *settlement colonies* which latter are more commonly called residential colonies. Exploitation colonies are those where Europeans live in small numbers, in many cases in very small numbers, mainly because the climate forbids residence. Residential colonies are those where Europeans have made their home and increased in number both by further immigration and by natural reproduction. There are colonies which have been wholly peopled by Europeans,[1] Canada and Australia for instance, which consisted of forests and deserts before the coming of the first

---

[1] For the methods and processes of French settlement, see L. Schöne, *Histoire de la popul. française*, Paris, 1893, p. 155 f.

colonists who have since increased to millions. But in exploitation colonies Europeans are counted merely by thousands, sometimes by hundreds only. In Indo-China the French population totals 20,000.

As regards *motive*. We must distinguish three principal cases which I shall detail in the order in which they occurred, for the logical classification here coincides roughly with the chronological. There is the *political* motive, the *theological* motive and, finally, last but not least, the *economic* motive, which nowadays predominates.

In ancient times colonies were often founded for political reasons. Expansion towards the Mediterranean in particular, was inspired by the craving for authority and security. If the founding of Empires brought greatness with it, it was inspired by ambition : the desire to be more powerful and better equipped for defence against the foreigner. The " will to power " revealed itself already in olden days ; imperialism, in the proper sense of the term, is the desire for greatness. Later, towards the end of the Roman Empire, arose the fear of invasion ; for the Barbarian was already threatening the frontiers, and colonies were the defence outposts of civilisation. The Byzantine Empire was primarily [1] an instrument of self-protection.

So we see that the " spirit of conquest " was frequently responsible for the foundation of Empires often of excessive extent—the Hittite, Assyrian and Roman Empires for instance —the focus of which in course of time might be displaced. Towards the close of the Roman Empire, the capital was transferred to Arles, a town with a population of 100,000, in an ancient colony on the frontier of the Empire. Here Constantine took up his residence, as Julian his at Lutetia (the ancient name of the city that we now call Paris).

Similar transfers of the centre of power have taken place in other Empires. Who knows whether Delhi, or perhaps Canberra, may not one day figure instead of London as the capital of the British Empire ?

The political motive, a motive essentially imperial, the lust of pacific or warlike conquest, is by no means a thing of the past. There are colonies in the French Empire which have, to date, no economic value, but which are of extreme political importance. I have called them " Junction Colonies ", for they serve to link the scattered fragments of the French Empire. The

[1] J. Maspero, *Organisation militaire de l'Égypte byzantine*, Paris, 1912.

Sahara desert, or the river Shari in Equatorial Africa, contribute at the moment nothing to the prosperity of the French Empire, but much to its unity and its security. These territories are liaison colonies which serve to unite colonies otherwise separated.

The *theological* or proselytising motive for emigration is of quite a different order. It was the desire to convert the heathen which first lured the colonisers of modern times to seek to conquer a universal empire. Sometimes this was the chief motive. The explorers who set out by sea to find a North-West passage to Asia —in the course of which America was rediscovered—were, at least in part, inspired by the idea of spreading the Christian faith. This was religious imperialism,[1] the imperialism of the theologian who sought, by persuasion or compulsion, to convert to Christianity all the peoples "without the pale". Spaniards and Portuguese at one time colonised as much for proselytising purposes as for territorial ambition or economic greed. Let us do justice to the "great rôle missions have played in colonial history".[2] It was the preachers, no less than the conquerors and the traders, who pushed penetration forward and opened up communications. In the 17th century they had completed the exploration of New France, or Canada ; they it was who laid the foundation of our knowledge of "the savage".[3] In the 18th century they opened the gates of China ; it was through them that European influence gained a footing at the court of Peking. In

[1] The fundamental document is Alexander VI's *Bull* (1493) of which a French translation is given in *Mémorial portatif de biographie* . . . , Paris, 1822, pp. 351–4. The pope grants the right of conquest on two conditions—the teaching of religion and of morals.
   [As Professor Maunier repeatedly refers to this famous Bull, the reader may be interested to see a few relevant extracts. In 1493 Pope Alexander VI (Rodrigo Borgia, 1431–1503) addressed a Bull relating to the New World to Ferdinand and Elizabeth, King and Queen of Castile . . . " ut fides Catholica et Christiana Religio . . . exaltetur ac ubilibet amplietur et dilatetur . . . ac barbarae nationes deprimantur et ad fidem ipsam reducantur ". He therefore recommends to them " our beloved son Christopher Columbus " in order ". . . aliquas insulas et terras firmas remotas et incognitas, ac per alios hactenus non repertas quaerere et invenire, ut illarum incolas et habitatores ad colendum Redemptorem nostrum reduceretis ". Columbus, however, was at the same time to keep an eye open for gold, perfumes and precious things of every kind and quality, for the glorification and extension of the Christian faith ". . . ut ad terras firmas et insulas praedictas viros probos et Deum timentes, doctos, peritos et expertos ad instruendum incolas et habitatores praefatos in fide Catholica et bonis moribus imbuendum destinare debeatis ".
   This anxiety for the morals of the heathen, and the command to send as teachers learned, God-fearing and upright men, rings oddly on the lips of the most vicious, evil-living and infamous of all mediaeval popes and Borgias. EOL]
[2] C. de la Roncière, *Les missions durant quatre siècles de colonis. franç.*, *Rev. d'histoire des missions*, March 1931.
[3] See Gilbert Chinard's writings on *L'exotisme américain dans la littér. française*. 3 vols.

the 19th century they assisted in the exploration and the penetration of African countries. Roman Catholic or Protestant, they built in forest and desert ; often they were the first to get into touch with the native inhabitants.

These missionary centres led to other establishments. Under the missionaries' wing later comers were able to make peaceful contact ; it was often the missions which made occupation possible. Exploitation, the opening of business and of concessions, sprang up and flourished in the shade of the mission. There were even missions which, on their own initiative, organised plantations in new countries. The colonies of Paraguay and Peru, administered and organised by the Jesuits, were the first attempt of this kind and were extolled by Montesquieu and even by Voltaire. Their founders set out not, like the Spanish pioneers, to seek gold and silver, but to promote the profitable development of new territories.[1]

So we pass directly from the proselytising to the *economic* motive. Political and religious imperialism have both led, sooner or later, to industrial imperialism, which now takes the centre of the stage. Colonies are business, people say ; their aim is profit, not ambition. The desire to get rich has superseded both the desire to become great, and the desire to convert. The economic motive itself, however, is complex ; material interests take many and changing forms.

The Colonies have aimed, and still aim, at the *export*, or alternatively at the *import* of supplies and produce. In the past this was the main interest people had in founding colonies. The motive was predominantly commercial : the export to the colonies of the mother-country's produce ; the import into the mother-country of the produce of the colonies. Colonial possessions were primarily markets, secondarily sources of supply ; outlets for European manufactures, storehouses of raw materials, foodstuffs and exotic produce for European consumption. Even to-day the possession of colonies has in certain cases this overriding use. If Germany passionately coveted colonies, her first desire was to use them, as did the ancient Greeks, to absorb the excessive increase of her population ; also, sometimes primarily, to provide her industry with markets and with supplies of raw materials. But in earlier days the commercial aim was the overriding one. It was in order to secure precious *metals* that the

---

[1] Muratori, *Relations des missions du Paraguai*, French trans., Paris, 1754 ; see G. Atkinson, *Les relations de voyages du xvii*e* siècle* . . . , Paris, undated, pp. 52–62.

Spaniards made such great sacrifice of men and wealth in their colonies. Later it was the quest for spices—as of old in the East the quest for perfumes—that so grievously embittered the struggle between French, English and Dutch for possession of the " Spice Islands ". An adventurous expedition was necessary, as Jean-Baptiste Say has said, to enable that great man of action, " the respectable " Pierre Poivre to secure one clove plant from the Sunda Islands ! That was in 1755.[1]

Nowadays, the cause of battles is neither metal nor spice but *raw materials*. What the producing nations henceforth covet is fodder for their industries, to make them independent of the foreigner. This craving has a special name : it is called " *economic autarky* ",[2] that is to say the need which the great States have discovered of being self-sufficing in peace . . . and in war. They fully understand that they cannot be independent without the aid of their colonies from which they hope to draw food supplies and raw materials of " vital " importance. Here, the political and the economic motives are fused. The mother-country looks to her Empire to guarantee her economic and political autonomy. There is no longer the hope that flourished in the distant days of " mercantile " doctrine, that the Nation, the Little Nation, could live for and by itself ; but a whole Empire, a great universal Empire, constitutes as it were a closed circle : a hitherto unknown type of economic imperialism, manifest in the British Empire with its plans for unity. England, if she were cut off, would have food enough for two or three weeks only. She therefore suffers more than any other nation from colonial or imperial anxiety.

This is where another economic motive is nowadays " on the agenda ". " Interest " in the possession of colonies henceforth centres less on export and import than on *exploitation* or, as we say, profitable development (*la mise en valeur*). Sacrifices of men and money are made in the colonies to promote cultural and industrial undertakings. When we speak of " profitable development "[3] we mean that the colonies are no longer, as they formerly were, simply and solely the means of finding an outlet for our manufactures, or even the sole and obvious means

[1] H. Cordier, *Voyages de Pierre Poivre* . . . , *Mélanges d'hist. et de géogr. orient.*, III, Paris, 1922, pp. 55–137.
[See the series of *Pioneer Histories* edited by Harlow and Williamson (A. & C. Black). EOL]
[2] J. Nowak, *L'idée de l'autarchie économique*, Paris, 1925 (Law thesis).
[3] See A. Sarrault's classic work, *La mise en valeur des colonies françaises*, Paris, 1923.

of supplying our consumer needs, but the means of greatly increasing our resources and our prosperity by the methodical and systematic development of the soil and the subsoil. Profitable agriculture and industrial development are now our major preoccupations.

Such are the various facets of *emigration*. Let us examine the facets of *domination*.

As in the case of emigration, there are three types of domination to be distinguished, according as it is weighty or light : first, *subjection* ; secondly, *partnership* ; thirdly, what I call *separation*, or the emancipation of the colonies. These are in logical order the three methods of colonising which are more or less in fact combined.

Subjection, or colonisation properly so-called in the legal sense, is the most extreme case we have defined. There is subjection—in the passive sense—or domination—in the active sense—when the colony is subject to the authority of the mother-country, when it is ruled and administered by a metropolis, of which it is an appurtenance ; the colony being then merely the " accessory " which " follows the principal ".

Even subjection, however, has its degrees ; it may be unlimited or limited, as in another connection I have said (see p. 16).

We meet *unlimited* subjection in every " possession " properly so called, and more especially in what the English have styled " Crown Colonies ". Such colonies, and the majority of French colonies are of this type, are wholly dependent on the metropolis with no reservation whatever ; legislative, executive and administrative power are exercised in the name of the mother-country. If there exist in such a colony consultative bodies, or—more rarely—representative bodies, they exist solely as a concession granted by the grace of the colonising State. This is the state of affairs which has persisted in the French and almost wholly disappeared in the British Empire, with the exception of some Crown Colonies [1] which are predominantly islands possessing strategic importance. The British Colonies are not subject colonies. They were such in olden days under the system which their historian Seeley has called " *The Old Colonial System* ",[2] the system namely of " Mercantile States " which were wont, if necessary, to sacrifice the colony to the mother-country. This

[1] Mary Kingsley, *West African Studies*, London, 1901, Chaps. XIII to XV ; Sicé, *Les colonies de la couronne*, Paris, 1913 (Law thesis).

[2] Seeley, *The Expansion of England*, 1st Ed. 1883 ; 2nd Ed. 1895 ; G. L. Beer, *The Old Colonial System (1660-1754)*, New York, 1912.

was the system which operated in France under the Ancient Monarchy in virtue of the commercial monopoly known as " The Exclusive ", where trade with the colonies was confined to Privileged Companies or even, as with the Spaniards, to the State itself. This was paradoxically called the " Colonial Pact ", whose aim was to exclude the " interloper ", that is to say the contraband trader.[1]

In other cases subjection is limited, not unlimited. This is particularly the case of Protectorates and even of Mandates. I do not think we can justifiably speak of partnership either for the Protectorate or the Mandate. If we use the term for colonial or pseudo-colonial régimes, it is a fictional not a genuine partnership. Both in law and in fact there is subjection in these cases : tempered subjection in the Protectorate, controlled subjection in the Mandate : but subjection none the less. The dominant State, as principal, exercises the power ; in case of divergence, it carries the day ; and the protected or mandated State is not truly independent.

In the second place, we find at least the germ of *partnership* between colonisers and colonised. In this case the legislation and administration of a new country are not the unilateral work of the metropolitan power, but of two conjoined powers on a basis of equality. In the commercial sphere it is the liberal economic doctrine which has paved the way for such a contractual system.[2] This system, which belongs rather to the future than to the present, but towards which we seem to be making progress, is based on two ideas. On the one hand there is the *equality* of the two countries, the two States ; their full and complete legal assimilation. On the other hand there is their *solidarity*, the *reciprocity* of their interests, weighed and balanced in free discussion.

The A Mandate has more affinity with partnership than with subjection, for under it there exists a certain, if imperfect, equality between the mandatory power and the people under mandate. We may, if we will, conceive an A Mandate as

---

[1] For the *conception*, see Montchrétien, *Traité de l'économie politique*, Paris, 1615, Books II and III (new edition, Funck-Brentano) ; Melon, *Essai polit. sur le commerce* (1734), French trans., Paris, 1742, Chap. IV ; and all the principal " Mercantilists ". For the *application*, see Robertson's *History of America*, 4 vols., 1820, Vol. II, Book VI (Spanish system) ; Bougainville, *Voyage autour du monde*, Paris, 1772, Vol. II, pp. 352 f. (Dutch system) ; Robertson, *ibid.* Book IX (English system) ; Levasseur, *Hist. des classes ouvrières . . . avant 1789*, 1901, Vol. II, p. 275 f. (French system).

[2] Bacon, *Essays*, 1597 (On Colonies) ; Vauban, *Mémoires sur les colonies, Oysivetés*, Ed. 1843, Vol. IV, pp. 1–43 (prior to 1707) ; Adam Smith, *Wealth of Nations*, 1776.

enjoying a status between subjection and partnership, the latter position being still in our day incompletely realised. The Mandatory is a guardian rather than a ruler ; it is his duty to act solely in the interests of the people under mandate, and to be prepared to accord them ultimate liberty.

Lastly there is what we may call *separation* or *emancipation*.[1] This is the legal status which has begun to evolve in the British Empire : separation but not secession, the preservation of at least a moral bond between the colony and the mother-country, for if this tie should chance to be broken, the Dominions or the British overseas Nations would become independent States. In speaking of a separation or, more exactly of a quasi-separation, I mean a separation that remains uncompleted. This is not complete autonomy, in the Greek sense of the word, for it does not prevent certain laws being " suggested " to the colonies by the central power. Such is the position of Australia, Canada and South Africa, which are not absolutely independent States, but pseudo- or quasi-States ; States, much more than half-sovereign States—as are the French Protectorates and perhaps the French Mandates—free, but not separated States. The Greek colonies at a certain period, similarly became quasi-independent of their metropolis, to which they remained linked only by their worship and the payment of tribute ; [2] in the same way, in our day, the " Nations " of the British Empire are quasi-independent. It is chiefly their loyalty to the King, reinforced by a moral and religious bond, which makes the British Empire. This is separation, not domination : a separation which does not exclude free voluntary partnership.

Unquestionably this is the road by which colonies, starting from domination or subjection, will be able to progress towards emancipation. Perhaps it is also the means by which it will be possible to avoid a snapping of the tie between a colony and its distant metropolis, and by which the venerable term " mother-country " may retain its meaning.

---

[1] The abandonment, sometimes complete abandonment, of the colonies was already suggested by a certain Abbé Pradt, *Les trois âges des colonies*, Paris, 1801 ; and Jean-Baptiste Say (*Cours complet d'écon. polit. pratique*, 2nd Ed., Paris, 1840, Vol. I, Chaps. XXII–XXVII) preached their *emancipation* after their early days were over, and in the meantime he wished to see them given such aid as would enable them ultimately to free themselves. Similarly, De Laborde, *De l'esprit d'association . . .* , Paris, 1821, Vol. II, Chap. III.

[2] Raoul-Rochette, *Histoire . . . des colonies grecques*, Paris, 1815 ; P. Roussel, *Délos, colonie athénienne*, Paris, 1916 (*Bibl. Écoles Athènes-Rome*).

BOOK II

DOCTRINES OF RACE CONTACT

CHAPTER IV

DOMINATION

Let us expound the doctrines of race contact and analyse the points of view, or states of mind, which have prevailed in regard to these problems. There are three states of mind which express three different doctrines about the contact of peoples : *domination*, *partnership* and *emancipation*.

The doctrine of domination is what we call Imperialism. It is the state of mind, individual or collective, which desires to rule others ; what the Abbé de Saint Cyran called " The Spirit of Principality ", Benjamin Constant " The Spirit of Conquest " [1] and Nietzsche " The Will to Power ". This is nothing but an exaggerated collective pride. In this sense, imperialism as a national frame of mind is characteristic of every social group. Every human group of any strength desires to expand. The *tribe*, the *sect*, the *party*, even the *school*, has a craving for supremacy, for authority, whence arise condemnations, excommunications, annexations and absorptions.

We are here concerned with Colonial Imperialism [2] as a doctrine. For the imperialist doctrine claims to find a basis and justification of imperialism not only in its practical usefulness but in equity. Oppression seeks legal justification.

In this effort to justify itself, let us separate out two elements : an *authoritarian* and a *utilitarian* ; an idea of combined power and duty on the one hand, and an idea of self-interest on the other ; a legal doctrine and an economic doctrine. On the one side some people assert that certain races have the *right* and the *duty* to dominate others ; this is the authoritarian point of view. On

---

[1] Benjamin Constant, *De l'esprit de conquête*, 3rd Ed., Paris, 1814 (an eloquent indictment of imperialism).

[2] For the history of the *word*, see A. Girard, *Impérialisme*, *Revue de synthèse hist.*, XLI, 1926.

the other side some contend that certain peoples are interested in dominating for the *interest* and advantage of the whole world, that universal civilisation gains from the domination over others of certain peoples ; this is the utilitarian point of view.

From the authoritarian standpoint, it would seem that the imperialist doctrine as professed by the Anglo-Saxons is a judicial system ; it is claimed that the " chosen peoples " have the right and the duty of dominating ; that certain other peoples are necessarily the subjects of the chosen peoples ; that imperial races are bound in duty to exercise their superiority.   In this spirit an apology for slavery was even quite recently formulated : " What a lovely book could be written in praise of slavery ! " an author whom I shall not name published this phrase— in 1896 !

The legal sources of imperialism are to be sought in the old mood of the Anglo-Saxon soul, in the ideal of the *gentleman* [1] who was the standard type of culture and good manners.   The gentleman is not only the polite and polished man ; he is more especially the man who knows how to command ; the imperial man in a certain sense, who, having powers, makes it his duty and his right to use them for the common welfare.   The ideas of authority-as-power and authority-as-duty are the heritage of an aristocratic tradition.

These ideas, however, have other sources too, not political this time, but theological.   Imperialism very early took on a mystic tinge, and allied itself to the idea of *election*, the idea of a mission.   The dominating race is a chosen race,[2] chosen by God, which has received from Him the mission to command, not by any means in its own interest alone, but in the interests of God's work.   The theological idea found, as we shall see, reinforcement from a biological conception, from the idea of *selection* which was soon absorbed into imperialist mysticism.

According to Anglo-Saxon doctrine, the conception of the State is therefore active and expansive.   The function of the State is not only—as Taine would have wished it—the protection of its citizens, nor yet—as Napoleon III would have wished— the liberation of subject peoples ; it is the domination of " inferior " or " backward " peoples.   The aim of the collective organism which we call Empire is to ensure this domination by

---

[1] F. MacEachran, *The Gentleman Ideal, Nineteenth Century*, Dec. 1928.   Daniel Defoe left an uncompleted essay on *The True Gentleman*.

[2] See in general : Th. Simar, *Étude . . . sur . . . la doctrine des races au XVIIIe siècle et son expansion au XIXe siècle*, Brussels, 1922.

the people designed by God, over the peoples destined to submit to its power.

This leads directly to the *utilitarian* point of view. The domination is to the *profit* of the chosen people who are solely in a position to ensure the organisation and development of the world ; the familiar formula : *the Empire pays* must be interpreted in a peculiar sense : the Empire pays, not the English only, but the whole universe. If domination is a duty, it is for the purpose of developing and organising and civilising ; in a word it is to produce wealth to the greatest benefit of the subjugated peoples themselves.

The system, then, is as much economic as political or theological. Nietzsche's phrase no longer applies ; the will to power is a means only, not an end. Not to dominate for the sake of dominating, but to dominate in order to develop ; not to subjugate for the sake of subjugating, but to subjugate in order to enrich ; to guide for the sake of constructing, not in order to destroy. We discover unexpected elements in this imperialism which founds and constructs. As in every aristocracy, there is revealed both asceticism and heroism. Since authority is claimed, not as a right only, but also and overridingly as a duty, we can justly speak of " the white man's task " and " *the white man's burden* " which is to govern in order to fertilise, to promote throughout the world progress which is . . . comfort. With many champions of imperialism it is the heroic and the ascetic aspect which focuses their attention ; the ideas of election and selection lead them to extol the white man's obligation as a sacrifice demanded by God, as a devotion to the divine order of things. They preach the right of *imposing* by force on inferior peoples the civilisation of the superior races.[1] Behind their preaching we can scent Old Testament beliefs.

Imperialism, then, being such, does not imply that it has remained unchanging ; it has itself altered in the course of time. One type of imperialism has succeeded another, according as one motive or another has been emphasised ; according as the idea of right, or of duty, or of interest, has been more strongly stressed ; according as the political or the economic doctrine has held the field. We can in particular distinguish two varieties of imperialism which we may style the *old* and the *new*. The *Old Imperialism* formulated itself, somewhat confusedly, before our day, it is rather the prelude to the imperialist system than the

[1] Bluntschli, *Le droit international codifié*, French trans., Paris, 1881, art. 280.

system itself. It lays stress neither on the idea of advantage, nor on the idea of duty, but rather on the idea of right. Under this aspect the doctrine of a chosen race or of a missionary race is most certainly an ancient one. The Greeks formulated it ; the Jews and Arabs later proclaimed it. The Greeks stigmatised as " barbarians " [1] all the peoples who did not speak Greek ; they were the peoples who by decree of the gods might be enslaved. Isocrates [2] proposed a union of the Greeks against all the barbarians. He was a " colonialist " before the word existed, and he would have liked to conquer Asia Minor from the Persians to plant there a Greek proletariat whose numbers were already excessive. Even Aristotle, most free-minded of men, considered it legitimate to conquer barbarians. The old Imperialism blossomed out under the Jews.[3] With them it was destructive rather than constructive, for it was overwhelmingly a collective egoism. The idea of the Chosen Race triumphs in the Old Testament ; the race of Israel by the rite of circumcision formed an indestructible blood-alliance with Jehovah ; and therefore to it was promised the empire of the world. Genesis already says : " Cursed be Canaan ; a servant of servants shall he be unto his brethren." [4] There, is the idea of domination by the will of God. It was the Arabs who set the seal on this Old Imperialism [5] and the Quran lays down the crudest rules for it. It is the idea of power for the sake of power, what the Arabs called *su'ubiyah*,[6] that is to say, domination in accordance with the will of God by his Chosen People over all the peoples of the Unbelievers. The Unbeliever must always be the servant of the true Musulman, who himself is the servant of Allah. When under the Second French Empire the French and English, aided by the Turks, were fighting the Russians, the Algerians used to say that the Europeans as " subjects and tributaries " of the Sultan, had been summoned by him to fight by his side ! Arab literature includes treatises which enumerate the abusive terms which may be legitimately hurled at the Unbeliever. Arab

---

[1] P. Roussel, *Thucydide et les barbares*, Rev. *études anciennes*, 1923, pp. 281-92.

[2] G. Mathieu, *Les idées politiques d'Isocrate*, Paris, 1925.

[3] Th. Zielinski, *L'empereur Claude et l'idée de la domin. mondiale des Juifs*, *Revue Univ.*, Brussels, Dec. 1926, Jan. 1927.

[4] [Genesis ix. 25.   EOL]

[5] On the Arab idea of the Chosen Race, see Abdel Wahed, *Contrib. à une théorie sociol. de l'esclavage*, Paris, 1930, pp. 140 f. and 161 f. ; A. Jeremias, *Die orientalischen Wurzeln der Idee der Weltherrschaft* . . . ; *Oriens, The Oriental Review*, I, Jan. 1926, p. 1418.

[6] I. Goldziher, *Die Su'ubijja unter den Muhammedanern in Spanien*, *Zeitschrift der deutschen Morgenländ. Gesellschaft*, LIII, 1899, pp. 601-20.

Imperialism has in our day undergone a rebirth as "Pan-Islamism",[1] though now submerged in the Orient by the rising tide of various nationalisms. Pan-Islamism was itself a doctrine of the Chosen, at the same time as a doctrine of oppression.

If the Old Imperialism was not the invention of Europeans, the opposite is true of the *New Imperialism*, the modern imperialism of the 19th and 20th centuries, whose proudest champion is surely Anglo-Saxon Imperialism. Creative, constructive rather than destructive, it is much more a means than an end ; it finds its justification in right, no doubt, but also in duty and lastly in profit. If you wish to rule, it is because you *ought*, because you *must*—to the benefit of the entire world. To bestow on all men the two good gifts, ill-appreciated by inferior peoples : *security* and *prosperity*. To this end the chosen race devotes its efforts. The *" Imperial Task "* laid upon the chosen people is to give *civilisation* to the whole world, civilisation in the Anglo-Saxon meaning of the word, that is in its material sense.

Despite its being so recent a phenomenon, this New Imperialism has already undergone a process of evolution. It is barely a century old [2] and yet its face has already changed. Born in England, it has spread to other countries. Now a thing cannot be transplanted without being also transmuted. In the course of half a century it took root in certain European countries and it has now spread to America and Asia. The imperialism of these new countries is an exotic growth and assumes perhaps a cruder, more warlike aspect than the New Imperialism of Europe. But Anglo-Saxon Imperialism remains the model, though it has two different countenances : Pan-Britainism and Pan-Germanism. Both have sprung from ideas at once mystical and practical.

In speaking therefore of the Anglo-Saxon [3] doctrine of Imperialism I am defining the type itself of the New Imperialism ; that Imperialism whose precursors are found amongst the

---

[1] C.-H. Becker, *Panislamismus, Archiv für Religionswissenschaft VII*, 1904, pp. 169–92 ; O. Depont and T. d'Eckardt, *Le panislamisme et la propag. islam.*, *Revue de Paris*, Nov. 15, 1899, pp. 229–60.

[2] The western imperialist doctrine goes back no further. It had, however, a forerunner in the 13th century, the well-known jurist, Pierre Dubois, who was at once a pacifist and an imperialist and had dreams of organising the world under a French king : B. Hauréau, *Pierre Dubois, Journal des savants*, Jan. 1894.

[3] See in general J. Gazeau, *L'impér. anglais* . . . Carlyle, Seeley, Chamberlain, Paris, 1903 (Law thesis) ; L. Hennebicq, *L'impér. occidental, Genèse de l'impér. anglais*, Paris, 1912 ; Earl of Cromer, *Ancient and Modern Imperialism*, London, 1910. For a vigorous defence of " colonialism " by two women, see Mary H. Kingsley, *West African Studies*, London, 1901, Chaps. XXI–XXII, and Katherine Mayo, *Mother India*, 1927.

English. In the 16th and 17th centuries Hobbes extolled the passion for power which he described as human and natural. Thomas More, whose *Utopia* was published in 1516, was a socialist before that word was coined. He laid down as a right and a duty the organising and development of new countries. Only on these terms is conquest justifiable in his eyes. In the 19th century Carlyle prophesied and Kipling sang. Note that more than a hundred years ago Carlyle firmly and emphatically expounded the guiding principles of Imperialism.

The first of these was the idea of *aristocracy* : in the interest of the whole world, domination should be in the hands of *gentlemen*. It should be the privilege of the strong and the righteous ; this *imperium* being for them as much duty as power. The second was *energy* or, if you will, pragmatism : the idea that the exercise of power is in itself a good thing ; action, struggle, even sport itself, are proposed as ideals ; the vision of the *gentleman* again ! To strive, to play games, to win, that is the destined part for the perfect man to play ; all expansion is sound and good, for it deploys the energy of the strong. The British emblem displayed on the golden sterling coin for all to see is St. George-the-Victor, patron of the *scouts*, winning the victory over the dragon. It is this sporting and active view of imperialism which has been seductive to the French. Gobineau [1]—the aristocratic diplomat—preaches the right and duty of the Aryan, the pure white man, to dominate ; for, he says, the Aryans are strong and handsome and their eyes are blue. This " Gobinism " is not an isolated phenomenon. Nietzsche sets Apollo against Dionysus and sings his Hymn of Action. Another vaunts " The Men of the Tiber ", conquerors of the " Men of the Orontes ". Doctrines of the Beast of Prey : nothing after all but literature !

Thirdly there was *mysticism*.[2] Most pronounced in Carlyle [3] —but as early as Cromwell—this idea of a mission confided by God to England, a mission to enrich the world, becomes an obsession : a divine mission of power and duty. The Puritan spirit is reborn in the imperialist faith, the faith of the strong, but also of the righteous.

Lastly, there was *utilitarianism*. Amongst the scientists, in Darwin above all, the idea of biological utility came to strengthen and reinforce imperialism. *Selection* is for the Englishman

[1] E. Seillière, *Le comte de Gobineau . . .* , Paris, 1903 ; L. Deffoux, *Les origines du gobinisme en Allem, Mercure de France*, July 1, 1925.
[2] K. Völker, *Die religiösen Wurzeln des englischen Imperialismus*, Tübingen, 1924.
[3] L. Cazamian, *Carlyle*, Paris, 1913.

election. The survival of the fittest is a law of peoples and races. In his " *National Life* " (1900) Karl Pearson applies the Darwinian ideas of selection and elimination to collective communities. There is a certain irony in hearing the Bolshevist of to-day invoking imperialist biology, and utilising the law of selection, to proclaim the decadence of the ancient and degenerate West for the benefit of regenerate Eur-Asia !

Gloriously, and sometimes brutally, the poet Kipling struck all these chords, mystic or practical, in his verse. He praised the peace and order which England gave the world by her " men from overseas ", these " Sahibs ", found throughout the world, whose task it was to end the folly and immorality of the native which Kipling harshly denounces. He finds poetry in the fact that imperialism weds the dream to the deed. Herein lies the true greatness of England. Greatly she dreams and greatly she creates ; to what nobler lot can a people be called ?

This European Imperialism [1] has been transposed, and perhaps heightened in American Imperialism. In the 90's Captain Alfred Mahan gave the United States the motto : " Look outside." The United States should beware of the growing menace of the expansion of the yellow races, and should strive to acquire " Sea Power ", should organise the protection of the white races against the " rising tide " of colour. This phrase was characteristic of the time. Mahan's theme was the conquest of the seas in the interests of America and Europe. [2]

In recent times the psychologist McDougall [3] deplored the multiplication of inferior races since, as he says, the previous checks on their excessive increase have been removed : famines, wars, epidemics, which used to keep their numbers down, are no longer in play. The superior races will soon need to defend themselves against the indiscriminate swarming of the inferior races which humanitarian principles tend to encourage.

We are now faced by a new Yellow Imperialism : the imperialism of Japan. [4] Not that the underlying ideals are new ; they are in fact in Japan extremely old. They are *Shinto* and

[1] Pan-Germanism is directed as much against Europe as against Asia albeit there also raged a " colonial Pan-Germanism " ; see *Documents sur le pan-germanisme*, Texts translated from the German, Preface by Ch. Andler, 2 vols., Paris, 1915. There has been of course also a Pan-Latinism, but it has remained in the world of dreams : see *Le panlatinisme, confédération gallo-romaine* . . . , Paris, 1860.

[2] A. T. Mahan, *The Interest of America in Sea Power.*

[3] *Ethics and Some Modern World Problems*, London, 1924.

[4] H. Labroue, *L'impérialisme japonais*, Paris, 1911 ; Inazo Nitobé, *Le bushido* . . . , Paris, 1927.

Bushido. *Shinto* is the ideal of devotion to God ; *bushido* of devotion to the Emperor. These are not merely feudal or imperial ideals, but have become national ideals. The aim of certain Japanese doctrinaires like Okakura [1] is to unify the whole of Asia under the rule of the Japanese Empire and dominate it in the interest of the Yellow Races of whom Japan, in accordance with the divine will, constitutes herself the defender. In parallel fashion, the American Mahan saw the great people of the United States as the defender of the White Races. Japan's ambitions grow daily, to extend over Asia and Oceania. She has annexed Korea ; she casts her eyes on China ; and her covetous glance falls on the Hawaiian Islands and the Netherlands East Indies where she maintains her agitators. Many a Japanese politician cherishes both an Asiatic and an Oceanic dream.

The days of the Imperialist doctrine are not yet done. Whether it is held by Yellow or by White, it affirms that if you are to organise and civilise the world you must dominate it. In this sense, the Old Imperialism lives on.

[1] Okakura, *Les idéaux de l'Orient*, French trans., Paris, 1917.

CHAPTER V

PARTNERSHIP (*ASSOCIATION*)

The doctrine of *Partnership* is born of a conception of long standing. It is based not on the idea of authority, but has sprung in succession from the ideas of *humanity*,[1] *equality* and *fraternity*.

The idea of Humanity comes first in date and in importance. When it comes to building up a society composed of different peoples, it is clear that the first condition of such a society must be to treat foreigners with "*kindness*". If there is to be a society, even in an imperfect form, it follows that the idea of unlimited authority, based on divine right, must first give place to this idea of humanity. There can be common interests and common aims amongst people only if they perceive and realise that they share a common nature, and therefore agree to treat each other " humanely " with that *caritas generis humani* which ought to reign between all members of the human race. For more than a century the relations between conquerors and conquered have been conceived as being governed and tempered by the dictates of humanity ; they have been thought of as protection rather than domination. This legitimate bond which ought to be formed between conquerors and conquered has even been pictured as that binding in a household or in a mutually advantageous contract. Both sides must find a common interest even though this society acknowledges a head or chief.

The doctrine of partnership still presupposes a head : and the " White Man's task " of governing the destinies of the coloured man must still continue. But just as the husband is not head of the house in his own sole interest, and as the owner is not the head of a farm for his own personal profit, so the European, though he still remains the ruler, must also be the protector and guardian, and must act as much in the interest of the coloured man as in his own. Even the relations between master and servant, or between ruler and subject, carry reciprocal duties like the relations between father and son. The idea of a

---

[1] On the duty of *humanity* see James Lorimer, *The Institutes of the Law of Nations, the Jural Relations of Separate Political Communities*, 2 vols., 1883-4 ; *Equality* is supposed to obtain only between *civilised* men.

community or a society composed of colonisers and colonised, under the power of a ruler is thus defined by their common interest. The idea of humanity made itself felt even by men of action, even by the conquerors themselves. Marshal Bugeaud, in his letters, declaimed against the mistake of misbehaving towards the Algerians. Not that he thought it desirable to treat " the Arab and the Colonist " as on the same footing, but he thought that both honour and self-interest were engaged in treating the natives as human beings, in humouring, educating and governing without oppressing them.

This idea leads, however, in the second place to an idea of *Equality* [1] which itself derives from the idea of *society* or partnership and still more from the idea of *friendship*. Partnership demands humanity, but this is not enough ; at best it yields an incomplete, imperfect partnership, as it would in the case of husband and wife under the authority of the head of the household. Perfect partnership requires *equality*, it can exist only between equals. Where equality exists, *solidarity* and *reciprocity* of interests will follow. Granted the hypothesis that a common citizenship should be enjoyed by conquerors and conquered, this theory must be followed to its logical conclusion that equality between them must prevail.

Proudhon was wont to say that the prerequisite of a society was justice, and justice meant each man's feeling himself a free individual amongst others. Starting from aristocracy, you progress towards democracy, and you conceive the relations between colonised and colonisers as the relations between fellow-citizens. You are on the road to this when you create assemblies where the native has the same position as the white man. The Emperor Claudius was wise enough to suspect that Rome's salvation demanded the fusion of the races composing the Empire. He attained fame by a speech in which he placed conquerors and conquered on the same legal footing. After 2,000 years his ideal has been realised. A very recent reform in the Netherlands East Indies gives the Assembly, or *Volksraad*, more native members than Dutch members. For the first time in a colonial assembly the natives are in a majority.

You can, however, go further than the idea of equality, as you have superseded the idea of simple humanity, and reach the idea of *Fraternity*, formulated in the *Rights of Man*. This is the

[1] Anténor Firmin (of Haiti), *De l'égalité des races humaines*, Paris, 1885 ; J. Kollmann, *Das Problem der Gleichheit der Rassen*, Leipzig, 1911.

doctrine of brotherly love.   It asks that by means of education
and interpenetration, natives and white men should attain an
identity of interests and, better still, of feeling ; that a union of
hearts should arise between them such as is the salt of society.
Thus, in elaborating the conception of society, you are led further
and further till you reach the idea of communion.   One heart
and one soul animating the co-partners in the work of progress ;
this is the ideal of those who dream of fusion and assimilation.
Assimilation is unity of spirit derived from education and imitation.   *Fusion* is unity of heart proceeding from unity of body as
in matrimony ; the blending of blood which makes of several
peoples one people.   Thus the dreamer flatters himself that he
recaptures in the relationship of native and white man the ancient
spirit of the city.   The thing which, amongst men of classic times,
created the admirable unity of the human group was this unanimity of feeling, in virtue of which the citizens were of one heart
and mind.   Pushing to its extreme the idea of partnership
between the native and the white man, we arrive at unanimity
and at fraternity : a work of inspiration, a work of love.

Thus we see that the doctrine of partnership wears several
different aspects.   There are two degrees or two stages in particular.   There is *collaboration* on the one hand, where the aim
is purely and simply to harmonise the interests of the two parties.
This may be done from the point of view of humanity or of
equality or of solidarity, but always and absolutely on the plane
of joint advantage.   At the other extreme there is *assimilation*
where the aim is the complete fusing of colonisers and colonised
by preaching to the latter the superiority of our civilisation.   In
this case the emphasis is laid on the idea not of humanity, nor of
equality, but of fraternity and unanimity as an ideal—though
distant—to be attained.

Pure and simple *collaboration* is the first stage.   Here the conception is that the common advantage of white man and native
should be the principle of their common law.   Colonisers and
colonised should co-operate under the white man's authority.
In this form, intermediate, if we may so call it, between the idea
of authority and the idea of community, the doctrine seems an
old one ; we may suitably distinguish the two stages by which
it has been reached.

The ancient world had already begun to perceive that domination ought to moderate, temper and disguise itself by displaying
humanity and bestowing benefit.   The idea of mitigated, *tempered*

domination later led in the modern world to the idea of collaboration between equals or partial equals, to the idea of *equalised
collaboration* which is the very essence of partnership.   The old
idea paved the way for the new.   Centuries had to elapse before
the bull of Alexander VI (1493) divided up the New World, and
proclaimed that conquests must have two aims : to teach religion
and morals.[1]   This document is the first which prescribes
moderation.   Bishop Las Casas [2] came to the court of Charles V,
half a century later, to protest against the conquerors' cruelties.
He remains a champion of slavery, but he wants to see a humanised
slavery, in which the slave and his master would be, as in Rome,
almost relatives.   This notion of modified, tempered domination
is met in the writings and politicians and travellers ; even in the
writings of Captain Cook, whose self-interest leads him to treat
the natives humanely.   It is to the advantage of the conqueror
to secure peace and order for them.   The road towards
humanised, equalised collaboration is here clearly marked out,
It was the French essayist Montaigne [3] who first laid it down as
a real duty : the conqueror's duty is, he tells us, "gently to
reclaim and polish the natives . . ."   Here is in fact the idea of
educating the native, conceived as the duty of the white man, a
duty which can be performed only by collaboration.   A century
later the Jesuit Du Tertre denounced the "unheard-of cruelties"
of the conquerors in the New World.

   That was also the spirit of 18th-century philosophy.   The
obligation of educating and civilising the native is laid on the
white man by Montesquieu [4] and by Abbé Raynal, whose great
work, in which Diderot collaborated, was written to make known
the cruelties of the conquerors.[5]   The fact that as early as 1787
he was able to found a "Society of the Black Man's Friends"
is a sign that a new spirit was abroad breathing the idea of
humanity, and already the idea of equality.   A work that is
to-day forgotten appeared in 1795 which bears witness to this
new spirit ; it was a plea by Joseph Lavallée entitled "The
Negro with whom few White Men can Compare" (*Le Nègre*

---

[1] See footnote, p. 22, n.1.
[2] See : *Œuvres de Las Casas*, French trans., Paris, 1822, especially I, p. 333 f.,
and II, p. 201 f.
[3] *Essais* (1580), Book I, Chap. XXX, *Des Cannibales*, and Book III, Chap. VI,
des Coches.   This latter contains the above quotation.
[4] R. Jameson, *Montesquieu et l'esclavage*, Paris, 1911 (Law thesis).
[5] *Histoire philos. et polit. des établissements* . . . *dans les Deux-Indes*, 1770 (Ed. 1775,
7 vols. and Supplement, Paris).   The student need turn only a few pages of this
farrago to get an idea of the indignant note it strikes throughout.

comme il y a peu de blancs). The author's avowed intention is
" to make the Negroes loved ", to teach the white man that love
as well as self-interest should reign between conquerors and
conquered.[1] Here there appears not only the humanity already
shown by Alexander VI, not only the idea of equality which we
have seen in Montesquieu, but the idea of fraternity. This did
not remain a mere doctrine. It was a great man of action who
gave perhaps the best definition of present-day colonial policy.
As he sailed towards Egypt on board the *Orient*, Bonaparte [2]
issued a proclamation commanding his officers and men to respect
and to show consideration towards the Egyptians. On his
arrival in Cairo, a proclamation issued in Messidor of the Year
VI (viz. 1798) formulates the doctrine of partnership. This
proclamation was addressed to the Egyptians, not this time to
the French, and it announces that the French have come to the
East to bring justice to all the inhabitants, to put an end to the
oppression exercised by the Beys, to the exactions of the Mamelukes, and to establish the guarantee of just rights in the valley
of the Nile. Here was the conception of equality and even
already of fraternity. Realisation speedily followed ; Bonaparte
established in Cairo a large Deliberative Assembly, a *Mixed
Diwan* in which French and Egyptians sat side by side. Bonaparte remained the " ideologist ", the unrepentant reader of
Jean-Jacques Rousseau.

It is, however, amongst the reformers of the last century, the
Utopians and the Prophets—men like Fourier [3] and Saint-Simon
—that the idea of fraternity becomes a declared ideal. Their
disciples certainly proclaimed and partly realised the partnership
of conqueror and conquered.[4] Natives are men ; we must
behave as men towards them ; we must teach them our justice
and pave the way for fusion between us and them. It was thus
that the " Fourierists " of Algeria used to talk. " Let us march
resolutely forward ", said one of them, " on the road to partnership " ; therewith the order of the day was given. Saint-Simon's
successor, Enfantin, who was nicknamed " The Father ", went
to Egypt and to Algeria, and formulated a colonial doctrine

---

[1] See also the works of Abbé Grégoire : *De la littérature des nègres, ou recherches
sur . . . leurs qualités morales . . .* , Paris, 1808 ; and *De la noblesse de la peau, ou
du préjugé des blancs contre la couleur des Africains . . .* , Paris, 1826.

[2] C. Cherfils, *Bonaparte et l'Islam . . .* , Paris, 1914.

[3] J. Zynski, *Colonis. de l'Algérie d'après . . . Charles Fourier*, Paris, 1839 ; Bugeaud,
who had lived through " Fourierism ", did not forget it.

[4] Enfantin, *Colonisation de l'Algérie*, Paris, 1843 ; *Correspondance politique*, Paris,
1849.

which may be compressed into one word : " Affamiliation " : family union, kinship, intermarriage between the European and the native. In Algeria many disciples of Saint-Simon, acting in this spirit, became Musulmans ; a certain Ismail Urbain for example voluntarily embraced Islam in order to become a friend of the Algerians.[1] It is from this period that we date the sentiment known as " Arabophilia ". Arabophilia became the fashion, and was encouraged by Napoleon III, faithful to Bonaparte's Messidor proclamation . . . This proves, at least, that a feeling of kinship and brotherhood had arisen and found expression.

At this point we have passed beyond *collaboration* pure and simple, and have reached a new phase in the doctrine of partnership : the *assimilation* of the native by the white man.[2] The " Arabophil " reformers had already begun to seek in this the road to fraternity. Assimilation involves in fact familiation ; and it renders collaboration perfect and complete. For how can there be co-operation without moral and mental rapprochement ? Partnership demands that the white man should educate and civilise the native. The motive for, and the justification of, colonial enterprises is deduced from this " elevation " and " Frenchification " of the native by the European.

There is in this nothing absolutely new. There have been imperial peoples who have tried to secure the assimilation of conqueror and conquered ; but they have always done so by the exercise of authority. The Romans were assimilators, so were the Incas of Peru, who carried off the conquered chiefs to Cuzco, to instruct them in their language and in the worship of the Empire of the Sun. These empires succeeded by military force in transporting and transplanting entire peoples, to mingle and assimilate them by imposing the same manners and customs on them all. This, however, is not the idea of partnership . . . It was the French who, in the last century, at the time of their conquest of Algeria, first expressed the idea of assimilation, properly so called, by means of education, the idea of *propagating* civilisation. The theorist and man of action, Émile de Girardin, revealed this attitude of mind by publishing in 1860, in collaboration with another theorist, Clément Duvernois, a pamphlet entitled : *Civilisation de l'Algérie*. In this he formulates the

---

[1] (I. Urbain) *Indigènes et émigrants*, Paris, 1863.
[2] For the vicissitudes of this idea in Algeria, see Ch. Tailliart, *L'Algérie dans la littérature française*, Paris, 1925, pp. 125–60 and 619–33.

idea of peaceful assimilation by means of education which he lays down as the conqueror's duty. We must note the contrast between civilising and colonising. It is not enough to colonise, to organise, to develop ; the primary task is to civilise and to educate ; by liberal and humane methods to make the natives French, to lead them to accept and to like the French. To *civilise* and not only to *colonise* ; and in order to achieve this not, as in olden times, to subordinate the native, but to make him a partner ; to accept and invite his co-operation ; to give him rights as well as duties, liberty at the same time as responsibility. To bring therefore to the native the ideas of private property and of monogamy ; to destroy the ancient errors of Arab law which gave women and wealth to the powerful. To call property and monogamy into being, but not by force ; to strive by wise and considered action to reduce abuses, and particularly by industrial progress to prevent a man's having more than one wife. In one sense this entailed prophecy, for it was precisely the penetration of European industry into Africa which in practice put an end to polygamy. Similarly, they tell us, the French must know how to offer the native one impartial law for all, as Napoleon pictured it ; there must be an end of all tyranny. This is the mission that the French have to carry out in Algeria ; only justice can make conquest just. In this pamphlet the spirit of Napoleon's Messidor proclamation lives again.

The ideas of partnership and assimilation are so strong in this pamphlet that the authors wished to see public functions in the colonies entrusted to natives : collaboration, therefore, not subordination. This is French policy at the present day, the policy foreshadowed by Girardin and Duvernois ; the policy which inspired Paul Bert when, as Governor of Indo-China, he had posted on the walls of Hanoi the Declaration of the Rights of Man ; the policy which has justly been called " The Colonial Policy of the Republic " ; [1] the policy which Albert Sarraut has defined better than anyone ; the policy which in the colonies sets up the Republic for all men, and whose spirit permeated the two treaties of Saint-Germain and Versailles, which proclaimed the " sacred duty " of civilising.

[1] A. Demangeon, *La polit. coloniale* in *La polit. répub.*, Paris, pp. 417–84 ; A. Sarraut, *Grandeur et servitude coloniales*, Paris, 1931 ; E. Cimbali, *L'assenza della democratia nella questione di politica coloniale*, in *Scritti . . . Angelo Majorana*, Vol. I, pp. 183–99 (Legal Faculty).

CHAPTER VI

EMANCIPATION

Lastly there is a doctrine of *Emancipation* or *Liberation,* according to which conquered peoples should regain their autonomy. This liberation has been prophesied for many a long day. In 1748, for instance, Turgot said that colonies were like ripening fruits, which sooner or later were bound to fall from the parent tree. In speaking thus, however, he had in mind colonies inhabited by white men, the plantations of exiled republicans.[1] In our day, this emancipation is wanted *for* the natives and *by* the natives, and at the same time there are *pro-native* agitations in the mother-countries and *native* agitations in the colonies. Amongst the French, there have been people pleading for the freedom of the native, long before the said native has dreamt of demanding freedom. According to this doctrine expansion is to be condemned. The colonisers, say those, who hold it, ought if not to abandon their colonies, to abandon at least the claim to dominate them and leave the subject races free to govern themselves as they like.

This condemnation of colonial enterprises was first enunciated from considerations of *utility* ; and economists of the liberal school, like Jean-Baptiste Say, believed that the possession of colonies was damaging to the mother-country. People advanced from this standpoint to blame colonial policy from considerations of *equity.* Two further stages followed. First, over half a century ago, *anti-slavery* arose,[2] criticising the abuses of which in the colonies the enslaved worker was the victim. Next, especially in our own day, came *anti-colonialism,*[3] condemning in the name of liberty and justice all colonial enterprises as such. This time, not only the means, but the ends themselves are condemned ; colonisation is *in itself* henceforth declared to be unjust. Anti-colonialism draws its inspiration sometimes from *pacificism* [4]

[1] See above, p. 27, n. 1, the schemes for abandoning the colonies, preached about 1800. Auguste Comte speaking of the downfall of the colonies, considered the British Empire as " an exception, probably ephemeral ".

[2] Relevant literature abounds, but lies outside our subject. See P. Allard, *La philo. antique et l'esclav.* in *Études d'hist. et d'arch.,* Paris, 1899 ; L. Deschamps, *Histoire de la question coloniale en France,* Paris, 1891, pp. 318 f. and 358 f.

[3] P. Louis, *Le colonialisme,* Paris ; see J. Lénine, *Pages Choisies,* Paris, 1929, III, p. 100 f.

[4] J. Dumas, *La colonisation, essai de doctrine pacifiste,* Paris, 1904.

which represents expansion as a cause of armed conflict ; sometimes from *socialism* which represents expansion as a crime against the equality of nations. Bolshevik propaganda, directed by an Institute of Colonial Propaganda with its headquarters in Moscow, is active throughout all colonies.[1] Nevertheless anticolonialism has long been at home in France. People vie with each other in branding " colonial crimes " and stigmatising as infamous " the glory of the sabre ".[2] As early as the 18th century we may find in one or another the anti-colonial attitude of mind. Diderot was prepared to condemn the domination of the white man as illicit, and to preach the native's right of self-determination, as we should now call it.

Let us try to give an indication, rather than a definition of these ideas ; for we are dealing with aspirations, desires, claims, which remain indeterminate, being in their very nature unlimited. At the starting point we note two main ideas which draw the eyes of the subject races : *nationality* [3] and *sovereignty*.

The idea of *Nationality* amongst coloured peoples springs primarily from their contact with the white man. There is a fatal, inevitable contradiction in colonial history. The first effect of colonisation is to lift the natives from tribe to town, from town to nation ; to engender amongst them common interests and common feelings, to awaken in them a national spirit : token and consequence of the revolution in their social status. For the white man's rule brings to them either territorial or national law. These men, who have heretofore recognised only tribal or local law, are by us ourselves subjected to a general law. It is the Frenchman who has taught the Algerian to think of himself as an Algerian, the Tunisian and the Moroccan to think of Tunisians and Moroccans. Previously each felt himself, primarily at least, as a Kabyle or a Chaouia, a Fasi or a Tounsi.[4] The conception of a wider community was introduced by the French ; it was contact with them which gave the native that " feeling of a common destiny " which is the spirit of nationality. Albert Sarraut has aptly called it *le retour de flamme*. There is no use in

[1] E. Bonin, *L'institut de propag. orient de Moscou, Acad. Sciences coloniales*, 1929, X, p. 555 f. ; G. Gautherot, *Le bolchevisme aux colonies*, Paris, 1930 ; J.–P. Blumberger, *Le communisme aux Indes néerland.*, Paris, 1929.
[2] See the violent pamphlet by P. Vigne d'Octon, *La gloire du sabre*, Paris, 1900 ; and A. Vollard, *La politique coloniale du père Ubu*, Paris, 1919.
[3] See in general, Hans Kohn, *Geschichte der national. Bewegung im Orient*, Berlin, 1928, with maps ; criticised by P. Wittek in *Archiv für Sozialwissensch.*, LXII, 1929, pp. 139–52 ; Upton Close (J. W. Hall), *The Revolt of Asia*, New York, 1927.
[4] [I retain the French spelling of place and tribal names except in cases where the word has a well-established English form familiar to the general reader. EOL]

blaming French propaganda, as people tend at times to do . . .
It is true that the French have a fancy for preaching their philosophy on all occasions, and for teaching nationalism or socialism
to their subject peoples. The " assimilating Frenchman " was
a subject of mockery in France as early as the middle of the 18th
century.[1] But under the English and under the Dutch we see a
native patriotism arising, which owes nothing to propaganda.
The fact is well established : the idea of nationality is born of
contact with an alien race.

Secondly, the idea of *Sovereignty*, which from a collective
point of view is only one aspect of the idea of nationality. A
nation exists and endures only in virtue of freedom ; autonomy
is the first essential of a mother-country. A country can boast
of no dignity if she has not the right to lay down her own laws.
Subject peoples seize on this idea of sovereignty more than on
any other : they want to rule, to be masters in their own house ;
to pass laws rather than to have laws passed for them ; they
demand their *Constitution* like the Tunisian *dasturians* [2] (destour-
iens). That is the gulf which, in their eyes, yawns between
colonial and national status. Similarly amongst peoples who
until yesterday were semi-subject. The idea of a constitution
is in the forefront of every theorist's programme : in Turkey,
in Egypt, in China, as in Sun Yat-sen's. It is the idea of *freedom*,
if not personal, at least collective, freedom which springs from
the idea of the *equality* of nations. In some cases it is even the idea
of *superiority*. Many Musulmans, whether Egyptian or Tunisian,
believe that they are the " truly civilised " ; morally, socially,
mystically—if not economically—superior to the European, not
inferior, not equal, but of a truth superior. The ambition which
is spreading amongst " coloured peoples " is to achieve *sovereignty*
and *freedom*. Some people were surprised when in 1921 the
Nigerians presented to the League of Nations a request for
independence in virtue of a people's natural right to liberty,
self-government and dignity . . . as this right had been defined
in the Treaty of Versailles. Since then the ideas of nationality
and of sovereignty both exist in the Nigerian's mind ; this is an
important intellectual and social phenomenon which marks a
new era in history.

Where diversities of peoples and races are found, we find

---

[1] De Boissy, *Le Français à Londres*, Paris, 1750.
[2] From the Arabic word *dastur*, custom, constitution. See *La presse destourienne
en Tunisie, Afrique franç.*, Sept. 1930, pp. 506–8.

that native desires for freedom take diverse forms. Without wishing to play on words, we may say that the idea of emancipation has a different colour and a different flavour amongst Black, Brown, Yellow [1] and White races. In particular we must distinguish two manifestations of the craving for independence amongst exotic peoples : one amongst the Negroes, the other mainly amongst the Brown and Yellow races but also amongst the Whites of Northern Africa.

The former is based—strange though this may seem !—on the idea of progress ; it is a yearning for material and spiritual advancement. It is " advanced ideas " which prevail among the Negroes of the United States. Amongst the Brown and Yellow races, on the other hand, and even amongst the Whites of North Africa, amongst Arabs and Berbers, it is " retrogression " that is desired—not progress. Their eyes are on the past ; they long to turn back, to restore and reconstitute what is gone. Their ideas are " backward ", as is strikingly the case with Gandhi.

Let us therefore separate the Black Movement from the Brown and Yellow.

Danger to the white domination may seem greater in the case of the *Blacks*. The change from Negrophilia to Negrocracy was rapid. The exaltation of the Negro in contrast to the white man, or at the very least his " rehabilitation," [2] has been known as negrophilia, or negromania or even, not infrequently, as negrolatry. It was the white man, not the Negro, who invented negrophilia and it is he who for a century or more has vaunted the Negro's pre-eminence. In 1813 Schopenhauer asserted the original superiority of the Negro race. He contended that the earliest civilisations were tropical ; that the first man was black ; the progress later passed from tropical to temperate climates ; that if, after a great lapse of time, white men appeared on the scene, they represented primitive Negroes who had lost their coloration owing to the effect of cold . . . If earliest man was created in the image of God, are we not entitled to assume that God was black ? . . . Has not the Frenchman Gobineau assured us that while the white man may be the stronger, the Negro is

---

[1] [Here and in several later passages Professor Maunier appears to include the brown races, Indian and others, amongst the " Yellow " races. In English the " Yellow " races are the Chinese, Japanese, etc. I have therefore ventured to insert a " Brown " category. EOL]

[2] See the works of Grégoire previously quoted, p. 41 n. 1, and M. Delafosse, *Les nègres*, Paris, 1927.

the more subtle ? Long before it became the fashion in America, Gobineau extolled the artistic and musical superiority of the Negro . . . Negrophilia, negromania, negrolatry ended in due course by infecting the Negroes themselves. They became convinced of the superiority which white men vied with each other in proclaiming. . . . Thus there arose in the United States the phenomenon known as " The Negro Awakening ",[1] the emergence of a new Negro feeling of independence demanding for the black man the same freedom and authority as for the white ; this is the Negrocracy which at the moment stirs public opinion in the United States.

The causes of this phenomenon are obvious. First the *emigration* of the Negroes. Until the other day, they were hemmed in in the Southern States, kept in the background, despised, some-times lynched ; [2] but to-day they abound in Northern cities where there exist no separate trams, schools or churches for Negroes. This new contact with the white man has led, in the second place, to their *civilisation*. Leaving the plantation they have invaded the big towns ; for some years now they have been town-dwellers. Thirdly they have thus been *urbanised*, a development unprecedented in their long history, and one which has profoundly affected their attitude of mind. In the Harlem quarter of New York they may be counted by the hundred thousand and they live exactly as white men live. It is said that when you pass from the white to the black quarter, there is no change to be seen in the appearance of the houses or shops ; nothing—but the colour of the face at the window ! The urbanisation and civilisation of the blacks has brought about, in the fourth place, their *enrichment*. These sometime slaves obtain paid jobs : they become traders, lawyers, doctors. In a word, schooling, life and contact made them into *bourgeois . . .* From Black Slave to Black middle-class Citizen : that is the Negro's evolution. Hence there arises a great *assimilation* between white man and black. The white has let himself be contaminated by the manners and arts of the black—by their music and dancing, as we know but too well. The Negro has received great intellectual stimulus ; he has learnt to read and write ; he publishes his newspapers ; he has now a Negro Press which spreads the white man's discussions and aspirations among

---

[1] See the book by the American Negro, Alain Locke, *The New Negro*, New York, 1927 ; and Frank L. Schoell, *U.S.A.* . . . , Paris, 1930.
[2] J. E. Cutler, *Lynch-law . . . History of Lynching in the United States*, New York, 1905.

the blacks. Here and there, there are mixed trade unions with black and white membership. The Press promotes an ever closer and closer assimilation. More than half a century ago the Negro ex-slave Booker Washington (1859–1915) founded in 1881 the University of Tuskegee for his " coloured brethren ".[1] Here lawyers, doctors, priests and pastors are educated who lead the black Americans along the paths of progress. All these things have changed the very soul of the Negro, from them he has drawn the yearning for a freedom and an authority to which he henceforth more and more " consciously " lays a claim. Even in the French colonies this assimilation is taking place : in church, in school, in politics. It is said that in the Gabon colony the President of the League of the Rights of Man is himself the Great Medicine Man or Witch Doctor ! This blending of past and present is assuredly a sign that a new day has dawned.

Let us read a book by a Negro writer [2] who caused a great stir in the United States. It supports the idea of Negro Emancipation by two arguments : the theological and the democratic, both of which contributed to Dr. Du Bois's success with the American public. The *theological* argument was based on the biblical and puritan conception of the unity of mankind : black and white are alike the created works of God ; they are kinsmen . . . albeit distant kinsmen ; they should be equals. Dr. Du Bois shows that he can also make play with the *democratic* argument : majority in numbers confers authority ; now, he points out, in certain States of the United States, and still more in Bantu Africa, the Negroes form the majority. Admitting that the majority should form the government, authority in these countries should revert to the Negro. Not at all a bad retort ! This reasoning constantly recurs in the Negro newspapers.[3] A well-known negro, Marcus Garvey, has founded a society already possessing considerable power : the " Universal Association for Negro Emancipation ". It preaches the ideas of Du Bois which Garvey reduces to the slogan : " Africa for the African ! " What the black men of America want, is to return to their lost home, to spacious Africa ; there, as in happier days, to dream and procreate free from toil and care but . . . with all American

---

[1] Booker Washington, *The Future of the American Negro*, 1899.
[2] Du Bois (W. E. Burghardt), *Dark Water*, New York, 1920 ; *The Souls of Black Folk* . . . , Chicago, 1903. Since 1895 Du Bois has published a number of Negro studies.
[3] Bi-monthly accounts of the Negro Press in *La journée planétaire du Comité national d'études sociales*, 45 Rue d'Ulm.

comforts. This is called " Pan-Melanism " ; and the idea is preached in *Pan-African Congresses* held in the United States, the last of which took place in New York in 1927.[1] These congresses carry on propaganda in America and in Africa. They sent Negro missionaries and Negro reporters into French West Africa who denounced in the Negro Press the " abuses " of French power ; these articles were speedily reprinted in the big American newspapers. Negroes were found in French West Africa who were converted to the faith, and became in their turn propagandists for Pan-Melanism. One of these was a Bantu Negro, Pastor Molema, who preached the black man's right to emancipation.[2]

While amongst American and African Blacks the desire for emancipation takes the form of a desire for progress and the future, the reverse is the case amongst the Browns and Yellows and also amongst the Whites of the Maghrib (Algeria). Their yearnings are for the past, a longing for regression, not progress. For what Musulmans and Hindus want, and no doubt the Indo-Chinese too, is liberty and authority : in order to live again according to their ancient traditions. There was, however, a doctrine of an *Economic Pan-islamism* which preached the adoption of European progress in order to oust the French. And there is a Tunisian *Modernism*, deriving from the Egyptian, which finds expression in a student movement, the *Khalduniyah*, but this is by no means generally popular. The Musulmans are, it seems to me, in the first instance pre-occupied not with the idea of nationality, looking towards the future, but rather with the idea of superiority based on the past, an idea vigorously alive in every good Muslim ; the law of the Quran is the perfect law ; liberty could mean nothing but return to the law of the Quran.[3]

Such is also the predominating frame of mind amongst the prophets of Indian liberty, especially in the case of Gandhi.[4] Not that Gandhi's doctrines are self-inspired ; it is European influence which has aroused the conscience of Brown and Yellow. If Gandhi is anyone's disciple, his masters are Rousseau and

[1] The first International Congress of Negro Workers was announced for June 1930 at Soviet instigation.

[2] See a curious anticipation of this in a book by a Belgian colonial, P. Salkin, *Le problème de l'évolution noire*, Paris, 1926 ; cf. de Warnaffe, *Le mouvement pannègre* . . . , Congo, May, 1922.

[3] Lothrop Stoddard, *The New World of Islam*, 1921.

[4] R. Rolland, *Mahatma Gandhi*, Paris, 1923 ; C. Freer Andrews, *Mahatma Gandhi's Ideas* . . . , New York, 1930 (with selected extracts) ; M. Markovitch, *Tolstoï et Gandhi*, Paris, 1928.

Tolstoi. . . . There is a Christian-Gandhi, a Rousseau-Gandhi and a Tolstoi-Gandhi. The ruling vision of this great agitator is the return to the primitive—an idea which the European has brought, with many other evils, to the Browns and Yellows ; regret for a lost " state of nature ", nostalgia for past barbarisms, longing to recapture the purity and austerity of olden days. According to Gandhi the Hindus must become once more simple and good, must work unaided by machines—invented of demons—by hand alone. Hence derive the tactics or politics of his co-called *swaraj*, passive resistance to the unjust domination of the English.

What the anxious-minded European sees as the foreshadowing of a great upheaval is the fact that this doctrine has infiltrated even into Western thought. Spengler and Keyserling, prophets of Western decadence, are obsessed by the greater purity and holiness, in short by the superiority of primitive as compared with civilised man. East and West are in their eyes contrasted, as moral progress is contrasted with material progress. According to Spengler [1] in particular, ancient history shows that we have now passed into the " autumn season of the West " and that decadence is therefore at hand. Its symptoms are manifest : first urbanism, the crowding together of the peoples in towns ; cosmopolitanism and humanitarianism too, where the feeling of nationality is superseded by a feeling of humanity ; then socialism, the product of these last ; finally, and above all, rationalism, the power of reason and the power of reckoning, whose foundations have been laid, in our Western countries, by the despotic power of the machine. Sins and sicknesses all of them, by which the East is untainted. Let us therefore take refuge in Eastern thought ; let us there seek renunciation and find deliverance, and let us peacefully and passively await Asia's conquest of Europe . . .

If such sentiments exist in Eastern thought, they testify to the aspiration of exotic peoples for liberty, and to its reaction felt also by the white man himself. To find contented people we must go to the Pygmies who have remained unconquered . . . The more the exotic peoples become " civilised ", the more they become " assimilated ", the more they clamour to be emancipated.

The Yellow people of French Indo-China nowadays display a patriotic feeling that is often passionate.[2] With some, the

---

[1] A. Fauconnet, *Oswald Spengler*, Paris, 1925.
[2] Nguyen-al-Quoc, *Le procès de la colonis. française*, 1st Series, Paris, 1926. Cf. Semaoen, *L'Indonésie à la parole*, Paris, undated (1927). See *Cahier des vœux annamites, prés. à M. A. Varenne* . . . , Saigon, 1926.

impulse is destructive, as with the worshippers of the God Caodaï who is represented by an open eye surrounded by massed clouds. With others, like the Republican Partisans, it is a reforming impulse. The " Constitutional Party " would like to see the liberation of Indo-China, not perhaps going so far as complete secession from France, but extending to partnership on a footing of equality. This party has addressed moving appeals to the France of the Rights of Man. . . . And the Chinese Republicans, steeped in Rousseau's [1] ideas, are close at hand to turn against the French their own teachings.

It is a law of all colonisation that civilised man should bring to the stranger the ideas of nationality and of liberty. To tribe and town he has offered the ideas of autonomy and of a mother-land, ideas which grow steadily stronger. He has set the process of unification in motion to enlarge the human grouping. If contact between races connotes the *civilisation* of inferior peoples, it inevitably carries with it their *nationalisation*. The chief result of colonisation is to give the subjugated peoples the consciousness of their identity and unity.

---

[1] On Rousseau in China, see Avesnes, *En face du soleil levant* . . . , Paris, 1909, especially pp. 11–19. The Young Turks were also obsessed by Rousseau.

BOOK III

FORMS OF RACE CONTACT

CHAPTER VII

THE FIRST STAGES OF RACE CONTACT

Let us first examine the forms which race contact may take, and in order to do so let us describe its early stages. Let us observe the contacts that arise at the very beginning, between two peoples previously separated. These earliest contacts have frequently been forbidden by custom or by law. The ancient Egyptians forbade emigration to foreign parts ; and in the Greek cities, especially in Sparta, there was a law of *xenelasia* which forbade any stranger to live in the town.

The first contact of all is frequently indirect ; it is, or was, made by intermediate agents, whose task was to forge a link which could not otherwise have been made. In African and Asiatic trading all these intermediate agents have played their part under various names, " *ambakists* " [1] in the Portuguese colonies, " *hannists* " in China, and " *compradors* " in Eastern Asia. In North Africa, especially in Morocco, it was the Jews who served as go-betweens in the first contacts of the French with Arab and Berber.

Not infrequently, however, the first contact is direct. A single European, at first quite alone, makes his way into a strange country and gets into touch with the inhabitants. The part played by the first immigrant is a decisive one ; he is the real " pioneer ". This man is often himself a semi-savage, or soon becomes one. Such was the " trapper " and the " buccaneer ", the hunter of the 17th century, like Nicolas Perrot [2] the Canadian trader-adventurer. From his account, we see how these immigrants, penetrating the forest for the first time, entering for the first time into friendly relations with the Red Indians, used to live and dress like natives, to speak the native language, and

---

[1] On these go-betweens, see M. Buchner, *Zeitschrift für Ethnologie*, XLVII, 1915, pp. 394–403. Their name is derived from the place-name Ambaca in Angola, Portuguese West Africa.

[2] *Mémoire sur les . `. . sauvages de l'Amérique septentrionale* (about 1700), Leipzig-Paris, 1864, especially pp. 130–1 and 297–99. For the buccaneers, see below.

paddle down the rivers Indian fashion in bark canoes. Even as late as the beginning of last century the pioneers of the Far West followed the Indian tracks or glided with the current in flat-bottomed boats, which they dismantled on landing, to furnish building material for their shack. In those days the men tilled and the women wove, and all lived a savage life.

These pioneers were explorers and discoverers, but ambassadors too. By their daring and love of danger they made the first race contacts secure. Sometimes they were *conquerors*, sometimes *traders*, sometimes *exploiters*.

It was the *conquerors* who first penetrated new countries and under arms initiated intercourse with the inhabitants. As a general rule, only very small bodies of men are in question, but even the warriors played the part of go-betweens. They were soon followed by the *traders* [1] whom the French used to call *traitants*. The bas-reliefs of Dair al Bahri show Egyptian vessels arriving in Somaliland and the sailors palavering and bartering with the natives. These traders or " merchant adventurers " were not merchants in the modern sense. They were adventurous dare-devils who set out into the blue, on chance, almost penniless, with but a modest pedlar's pack—often in the wake of an army, as we recently saw in Morocco—to arouse the greed of the natives. This is how the fur-trade [2] started in Canada, New France. Lastly, after conqueror and trader, came the *exploiters*. They are the pioneers properly so called, men who set out to develop the soil and build their house on it. It is they who make lasting contact with the original occupiers ; these " habitants ", [3] (settlers), cultivators or miners, have borne most diverse names, and their literary works have set the tone from Cooper to Louis Hémon. The unforgettable figure of Leather-Stocking, the authentic pioneer, who wins his way through the forest, neither to fight nor to trade, but to clear the ground, the man who, at the risk of his life, makes a home and starts development. With their own hands these people built their own wooden houses, aided by their neighbours,

---

[1] Their relations with the Pacific Islanders have been described by R. L. Stevenson, *In the South Seas*, 1900.

[2] See S. Marion, *Relations des voyageurs français en Nouvelle France au XVII* siècle*, Paris, 1923.

[3] On the life of the " habitants " see, for instance, De Préfontaine, *Maison rustique à l'usage des habitants de Cayenne*, Paris, 1763 ; Duccœurjoly, *Manuel des habitants de Saint-Domingue . . .*, 1802 ; for the life of the Algerian " colonists ", S. Chaseray (Father Robin), *Gens et bêtes de l'Oued-Melhouf*, Constantine, 1918 ; a series of extremely veracious sketches.

pioneers like themselves, who might live at a distance of 5 to 60 miles away. Sheer necessity compelled them to come to terms with the natives. They were the first to gain real insight into native manners and customs. By them the foundations of the first joint society were laid.

Let us consider what this first contact of all was like ; what were the *first impressions* formed by native and European when they came into touch ; what were their *first relations*, how was it possible for inter-communication to have been established between them, and what was its nature.

What are the first impressions of peoples who meet for the first time ? What more especially are the native's impressions at first sight of the foreigner ? [1] We may take one axiom for granted : the foreigner never fails to arouse interest, his coming is never meaningless. Sometimes the native is disturbed and annoyed ; sometimes he is pleased and gratified. He may admire or despise the foreigner ; he will never, or almost never, be indifferent to his arrival. This is a point which colonisers, and even colonists, have all too often ignored. They have lived on what has been called the " myth " of their own superiority. The white man is all too ready to believe that the native must be overwhelmed by admiration at the sight of him, and that by merely putting in an appearance he has acquired immense prestige. But, as travellers' records have noted, the native not infrequently feels contempt for the intruder, sometimes repulsion, which the pioneer has to overcome. The native's frame of mind is always mystical ; the foreigner is for him either angel or devil ; more often a blend of both. These are the obscure and complex reactions, sometimes disquieting, sometimes thrilling, which the stranger's arrival rouses in his soul.

Let us take some examples and note how the conqueror's coming was a sign, now of *benediction*, now of *malediction*. At one moment the foreigner was worshipped, at another accursed, at yet another simultaneously accursed and blessed.

Benediction. The ancients already had the idea that a new-comer, because he was new and because he was unknown, brought blessing ; the gods had willed his coming ; his friendship was a " blessing from the gods ". Thenceforward he himself was treated as a god. The welcome which primitive peoples offer to the foreigner is not always hostile and warlike, as we

---

[1] See in general, E. Westermarck, *Origin and Development of the Moral Ideas*, London, 1906, Vol. I, p. 581 f.

read in novels ; it is often friendly.   The stranger is met with
the consideration due to a divine messenger.   For primitive
peoples often invest with divine attributes the new, the original,
the unknown.   This is why, amongst many peoples, and in
earlier days in North Africa too, the stranger arriving for the
first time was hospitably entreated by his tribal hosts ;   the
goods, and even the women of the tribe, were placed at his
disposal.   There was a time when on his arrival in a Kabyle
village a stranger was always " lent " a woman of the tribe ;
this was a time-honoured inviolable rite.

The stranger then may be a sign of benediction ; he himself is sacred, or he is even a god.   The first conqueror, the
first trader, thus finds himself the object of a " superstitious
ovation " as an old traveller expresses it, for it seems to the
native that this apparition, clad in brilliant raiment, decked
with golden braid, brought from afar on ships whose cannons
thunder, can of a truth be nothing less than a god.   In the
course of his last voyage which was to end in tragedy, Captain
Cook was thus deified in the Hawaiian Islands.   The bright
red uniform of an English officer gave the Hawaiians the idea
that he was the reincarnation of an ancient local god called
Rono come to revisit the faithful, and so James Cook became
Rono II.   With incense, with offerings, with sacrifices, the
worshippers celebrated his return.   In much more recent times,
in Haiti, the American Protectorate, it happened some ten years
ago that a young lieutenant, the governor of a tiny island, a
certain Faustin Wirkus, in virtue of his Christian name was
taken to be the reincarnation of the god-emperor Faustin I,
Soulouque, the Black Emperor of savage ways who had reigned
about 1850.   So Faustin Wirkus became Faustin II [1] under
which title he enjoyed superb prestige !   In such cases the first
impression made may be favourable and highly advantageous
to the conqueror, and this makes his first relations with the
natives amazingly easy.

Malediction.   There are, however, other cases where the new-
comer seems to bring a curse rather than a blessing, and where
he becomes the object of execration.   The foreigner is impure,
the foreigner is accursed, simply because he is something new.
There are primitive peoples for whom the new is beneficent,
but others who see in it evil only.   Pure and impure are closely
allied ; this explains the different lines of conduct which natives

[1] See William Seabrook, *The Magic Island.*

display towards strangers. Sometimes, to his own surprise, the foreigner is subjected to precautions and fumigations, in short to purification, to avert the Evil Eye. It is not only among primitive peoples that the foreigner is thought to be impure and dangerous ; we read in Herodotus (II, 41) that the Greek himself was impure to the Egyptian. Even in our own old Europe the same may be the case. In Naples cabbies and shopkeepers on seeing a foreigner hastily touch the little coral charm which hangs on their waistcoat to keep off the evil eye, the *malocchio* of the stranger. Thus the stranger is often feared, and it follows that the native must by certain rites be purified from contact with him. This impurity inevitably hampers and sometimes estops all social relations. The foreigner is kept at arm's length, as it were in quarantine. He is subjected to rigorous taboos and a vacuum is created round him.[1]

Thus benediction or malediction is the lot of the foreigner in a new country. He is never impartially ignored ; the impression he makes on the native mind is never " the golden mean " which would be no doubt more convenient for him and would ease his efforts to penetrate or to develop the country. In either case he is embarrassed ; blessed or cursed, in either case he is " taboo " ; pure or impure, he is fraught with menace, not to be approached without precaution. Relations between colonists and natives are thus prevented or at best constrained. In a fine book of Robert Louis Stevenson's we see how a merchant was tabooed by a native superstition which made him both pure and at the same time impure, and how this brought about his irretrievable ruin.

Next, let us see what form the *first relations* take, which are more or less the consequence of the first impressions. This is one of the big problems of psychology and sociology. What can the first relations be, between people who are strangers to each other ? How can an interchange of goodwill and interest be set up between them ? How does a sociable feeling arise between people previously unknown to each other ? Here we touch on the problem of the origin of Society itself.

The amazement which seizes the native at his first sight of the foreigner is often the measure of his ignorance. Those who first saw horses disembarked, and then saw horsemen mount them, sometimes took man-and-horse to be one composite, divisible animal ! We know too how stupefied the Tahitians

[1] See, for instance, Sonnerat, *Voyage aux Indes Orientales*, Paris, 1782, Vol. I, p. 101 f.

were when the English sailor Wallis casually doffed his wig ; they thought the ship's surgeon could scalp himself at will.

We must therefore expect the first relations, or the first opening of relations between conquerors and conquered, to wear a double aspect. As the first impressions may be happy or unfortunate, as the strangers may bring with them a blessing or a curse, so the first relations may reveal confidence or mistrust, may awaken friendship or hostility.

Mistrust may arise from errors committed or from misunderstandings based on mutual ignorance. Even if the native is welcoming and the European well-intentioned, the good intentions may be misinterpreted and sometimes taken wholly amiss. A certain form of greeting may be thought to be an insult. We can imagine the indignant surprise of the sailors when a chief of the Solomon Islands in token of friendship offered them —a quarter of a baby ! It was to him the right and natural way of associating himself and them in holy communion.

Such misunderstandings are not confined to primitive countries. In Islamic countries we stumble against obstacles which sometimes greatly impair our first relations, and produce mutual contempt between Europeans and Muslims. The Musulman still retains some contempt for us because he thinks us irreligious or insufficiently religious. And indeed our Christian faith does not hold so obvious a place in our life as his, where religious observances are in the forefront of his day. The religious tolerance on which we pride ourselves, seems to him neither humane nor right, but simply impious and impure. This misunderstanding cleaves a deep gulf between us.

Contempt born of misunderstanding has all too often given rise to hostility between races.

At times, war begins at once and relations are forthwith the relations of enemies. There are peoples who have never allowed a stranger to enter except in battle. In his voyage of 1765 in Oceania, Commodore Byron gave the name of " Disappointment Island " to an island where to his chagrin the tribesmen greeted him with assegais. There was also a " Thieves' Island " ! The Ivory Coast in Africa, also called " Tooth Coast ", was also long known as " The Coast of Evil Peoples " (*Côte des males Gens*). The warrior people of New Zealand also greeted the first sailors with weapons ; it took a long time to make peace with them. The first travellers into Islamic countries could penetrate them only by guile or in disguise. This was the experience of Caillié in Timbuctoo and of Vambéry in Bukhara ; of Burckhardt, Léon Roches and Snouck Hurgronje in Arabia ; and no less of Segonzac, Mouliéras and de Foucauld in Morocco.   This was the period of *secret journeys* when the traveller's every gesture might imperil his life.

In other cases hostile reactions are secondary ; they are preceded by friendship, and it is often the European's fault if this early friendship turns to hostility.   Soldiers were particularly to blame where having been welcomed with signs of peace [1] they proceeded to pillage and murder the tribes who had hospitably received them.   This occurred with Bougainville in Tahiti in 1768.   He and his soldiers had been welcomed with open arms by men . . . and women, and he gave the archipelago the auspicious title of "Society Islands" to emphasise the peace that had been established.   A few days later he found native troops assembling, against whom he was forced to fight, for his soldiers had come and plundered and slain.

Let us change the scene and turn with better heart to the *confidence* which sometimes arose—more often than people realise —between conqueror and conquered.   Captain Cook gave the name of "The Friendly Islands" to the Tonga Archipelago to preserve the memory of the happy relations which followed the first contact.   His record is almost idyllic : there are nothing but gifts and courtesies ; and the idyll proved lasting.   In other cases friendly relations succeeded hostile ones, just as we have seen the reverse take place.   It is often the case—fortunately for the white man—that lasting peaceful relations are established after initial war and conquest ; lasting, if not finally permanent, and perhaps not entirely whole-hearted, they at least make it possible for conqueror and conquered to live in peace side by side.   Even in South America after the devastations and massacres organised by Cortes and Pizarro, treaties of alliance were concluded between Spaniard and American.   The American native was given place and rank in the conqueror's army.   The happiest example after the conquest of Peru was that of the Inca, Garcilaso de la Vega, who became a Spanish nobleman.

In the course of time confidence and alliance marked the relations of the French with the Musulmans and Berbers of North Africa.   It is hardly necessary to recall that friendship

---

[1] Peter Martyr already observed this, and showed how the conquerors earned the natives' hate : *De orbe novo* (1500), Gaffarel's trans., Paris, 1907, *passim*, especially pp. 210, 241 and 599–604.

even with the Berbers was successfully concluded only after hostilities ; fighting was the necessary preliminary to peace. Peace in the full sense of the word has to be won or achieved by conquest. It seems that only gunpowder (*barud*) could open their hearts. The Frenchman's hold on the Berbers and the Kabyles is all the stronger because the French have twice defeated them ; perhaps they have thereby won also a moral victory.

This relationship of confidence and alliance was the background against which the European mind formed its picture of the noble primitive man, or the " noble savage ",[1] which was at one time current amongst us. The very first explorers and the very first missionaries invented an ideal savage. In him they found the perfect natural man who lived stark naked, as the gods were wont to live ; the virtuous man and the happy man. They saw the " savages peaceable and friendly to one another ", as Brunetto Latini said of the Seres of Asia in his day. If the first impact had always been hostile, the origin of the noble-savage theory would be unintelligible. The ancient philosophers believed in it ; we find it in Montaigne and Rousseau ; Rousseau got it from the writings of the Jesuits. It was in fact in the Jesuit missionary reports from Canada that Rousseau found important passages glorifying the savage. His conception of natural man, enjoying happiness in simplicity, far from the corruption of cities, is the fruit of the earliest contact of the European with the Red Indian in the forests of the New World. So the history of man's thought suffered the ricochet of this first experience.

How did this relationship of alliance come into being, which inspired the Old World with its idea of the noble savage ? It was by means of many strange gestures and rites ; symbolic acts whereby the natives offered peace and the foreigners expressed acceptance ; rites of *communion*, of association, out of which a treaty grew.

First came the *exchange of names*. To the savage the name is the very person himself.[2] To take the name and work on it is to take and act on the person himself. To give your name,

---

[1] A whole literature exists on this point. See especially G. Chinard, *L'Exotisme américain . . .* , 3 vols., Paris, 1911 ; H. Fairchild, *The Noble Savage, A Study in Romantic-Naturalism*, New York, 1928. The school of Elliot Smith and Perry, of which I have spoken elsewhere, clings to the theory of the noble savage ; and G. Landtman in 1927, describing the Kiwais of Papua, imagines that amongst them he has discovered " Rousseau's ideal community ".

[2] L. Levy-Brühl, *Les fonctions mentales dans les sociétés inférieures*, Paris, 1910, p. 45 f.

is to give yourself to the stranger ; to exchange names is to exchange souls. When Mendana came to the Marquesas Islands in 1598, he and a local chief performed a ceremonial rite and exchanged names ; and when Captain Cook in the island of Oahu in 1769 exchanged his name of James for that of an Hawaiian chief it was believed that they were thus brought into spiritual communion.

Next comes the *exchange of gifts*. To the primitive mind a possession is an emanation of the possessor. This thing is mine ; it is therefore a part of me ; it contains a portion of me and of my power. If I exchange it, I give away a part of my very substance and of my strength in return for someone else's. To exchange goods is the equivalent of exchanging names.[1] When the Tahitians gave a present of pigs to Bougainville it was certainly a token of friendship and good-will. All such gifts are the small change of *hospitality*.[2]

It is the same with the *gift of women*. When the natives offered their wives, their sisters, their daughters to the Europeans, these first explorers were shocked at the debauchery which seemed to be customary amongst the islanders. Bougainville or Cook arriving in Tahiti, and seeing bronze sirens swimming round their ships and offering themselves, concluded that the peoples of Oceania were all corrupt, and that Rousseau had made a grave mistake in thinking them more " moral " than we. Diderot did not lose the chance of expatiating on the subject. The native sees the matter in a wholly different light, as the best means of securing communion. Sexual communion, or the communion of blood, is for him the essence of all communion. This is *sexual hospitality* or *ceremonial prostitution*, a ritual held in honour by many peoples.[3]

Further, there are *communal meals*. The banquet is the type of food communion ; to eat together, to drink together and to smoke together is to bind yourselves together. The " pipe of peace " is on a small scale the brotherly " Communion Service ". It is a rite customary in North Africa in which the European cannot refuse to take part without giving grave offence. To refuse a dinner offered by a *qaïd*, an *agha* or a *bashagha* is a sign of contempt ; for the meal is in a certain sense a communion

[1] M. Mauss, *Essai sur le don* . . . *Année Sociolog.*, New Series, I, 1925, pp. 30–186 ; R. Maunier, *Recherches sur les échanges rituels* . . . , idem, II, 1927, pp. 11–97.
[2] On primitive hospitality, see Westermarck, *The Origin and Development of the Moral Ideas*, London, 1906, I, p. 574 f.
[3] A. Van Gennep, *Les rites de passage*, Paris, 1909, p. 40 f.

service.   To share the same food is to seal an alliance.   When therefore the host plunges his arm into the sheep's inside and offers the kidneys to his European guest, it is good manners for the guest to take this choice and honourable titbit in the hollow of his hand and devour it with all speed, accepting it as an offer of peace.   Later, when the dinner is over, it is likewise good manners noisily to belch, to indicate that the dinner has been good.   There are methods, sometimes shocking, sometimes touching, of celebrating the rites of friendship between conqueror and conquered.   Methods less subtle, no doubt, than the solemn treaties of peace, decorated with seal and signature, by which our great civilised States think to end their wars.   Progress was made towards drawing up *treaties* [1] with primitive races. William Penn concluded one of these, the text of which has been preserved, with the natives of Pennsylvania.   In it he stipulated for joint arbitration in disputes between natives and Europeans, to be carried into effect by a Commission composed of an equal number of delegates from each side.   This was an *alliance* [2] in the European sense of the word.   Whether according to ancient rites, or according to new-fangled treaties, we still find signs and tokens of friendship.

There is, however, yet another means of marking fraternisation : by *imitation* or by *borrowing*.   When the native begins to borrow manners and customs from the European conqueror ; when we find him aping European fashions, it means that he has accepted the European.   In 1767 when Wallis cast anchor at the island of Tahiti, distrust appeared to reign ; the natives severely kept their distance.   Suddenly one, more courageous than the rest—a fore-runner, an innovator !—rushed up in front of the officer, snatched his hat and donned it.   A little while afterwards seeing the English officers on the ship eating with fork and spoon he seized on these two implements and was the first among all the Oceanic islanders to employ them.   When matters take this turn and borrowing begins, it is a sure sign that communion will arise.   The first imitation is the first step towards fusion.

[1] See, for example, the text of a treaty confirmed by oath which was made in 1782 with the " six nations " of the Iroquois, quoted in the *Encyclop. Méthodique, Économie politique,* 1788, Vol. IV, p. 168 f.

[2] R. Ricard, *Sur la politique des alliances dans la conquête du Mexique par Cortez, Journal Société Américanistes,* XVII, Paris, 1925, pp. 245–60.

CHAPTER VIII

ASPECTS OF RACE CONTACT

Exploration, from which the first fleeting contact comes, is the precursor of emigration and penetration, from which the first real contact springs. We must now trace the forms and distinguish the types of contact. To classify these it is well to consider the *place*, the *time*, the *method* and the *purpose* of the relations established.

First, the *Place*. The relations between conquerors and conquered are sometimes sea or coastal contacts, sometimes land contacts. Sooner or later the immigrant colonisers penetrate the *hinterland*. In the case of the Romans, and even more in the earlier case of the Greeks, we can speak chiefly of maritime or coastal relations ; and with Greeks and Romans the custom was to use guile rather than force in dealing with the natives.[1] It was not until the Roman Empire extended, and the legions pushed south into the gorges of the Aures Mountains in Algeria, that serious and lasting contact took place.

Secondly, *Time*. As I have already said, contact may be either intermittent or permanent. It often is, and remains, intermittent. We then get only snatches of contact with no future ; temporary liaison, not enduring partnership. Our business is with durable and lasting contact, such as results from the occupation of the country or its settlement by European colonists.

Thirdly, *Method*. We must distinguish collective from personal contacts, and relations of a public from those of a private nature. Sometimes the intercommunication of races is a collective or mass phenomenon, resulting from large-scale expeditions or immigrations, where perhaps a whole collection of different races comes to lose identity in one great melting-pot. Sometimes it is a single act, the work of individuals, of pioneers, who first penetrate a primitive country alone. Inversely this individual contact operates to-day in the opposite direction ; outsiders from afar penetrate into our countries, making direct and personal contact with European civilisation ;

[1] B. J. Bonner, *Greek Colonies and the Hinterland*, *Classical Journal*, XX, 1925, p. 359 f.

they have in their turn become pioneers and the ambassadors of their subject-peoples.

Lastly, the *Purpose.* It is primarily an *economic* or a *theological* purpose. These are, very roughly, the chief aims pursued when the older races make contact with the new : to do a deal or to make a convert. Business offices and missions are the main organs of our relations with colonial peoples.

Let us analyse into their main elements the facts we have just recorded, distinguishing three forms, or degrees of relationship. First, *juxtaposition* : the penetration of a people's country by occupying or by settling it. Secondly *collaboration* with the people, by domination of or partnership with them. Thirdly the *fusion* of races by blending them. Such are the steps, the one leading to the next ; they are the successive stages along one road. Juxtaposition leads to domination, and this in turn to partnership, since ties of propinquity create ties of law, and since, as we shall see, legal domination is inevitably bound to lend security and support to actual penetration. Domination sometimes results in fusion, for if it is a stable condition and if it lasts, it foreshadows a mingling of the races.

Let us briefly examine these three aspects.

Penetration or *juxtaposition* : we have here the simple, material fact that Europeans have established themselves in a primitive country. They are immigrants, they are occupiers, in a word they are settlers, and not merely birds of passage like the sailors and explorers of whom we were talking. We have a genuine juxtaposition of different races in one and the same place.

This juxtaposition of two social groups, the first stage of their contact, itself appears under two aspects; it may be warlike or peaceful. From the legal point of view it is either *occupation* or *penetration.*

In legal language *occupation* means *warlike penetration.* The new occupants are then conquerors, and the soldiers are colonists while remaining soldiers. This was the state of affairs in North Africa under the Roman Empire. This is what Bugeaud dreamed that French domination might be.[1] In such circumstances, as is well known, fairly close contact is made between European and native. The soldier-colonists get into touch with the natives, they borrow native words and native manners. In the supplement to Littré's Dictionary we find a long list of

[1] P. Jaillet, *Essai histor. et critique sur la colonie militaire*, Paris, 1903 (Law thesis) ; V. Demontès, *Bugeaud et la colonie militaire en Algérie*, Paris, 1918.

Arabic words which have passed into French mainly from the soldier's vocabulary. Even the rank and file are agents in establishing relations. " Close relations ", says Joubert in his *Pensées*, " always spring up between peoples who are long at war. War is a form of commerce which binds together even those it disunites." Warlike occupation produces communication and imitation between conquerors and conquered. Even piracy entails contact.[1] Contact arises in many other ways : especially through the influence of prisoners. European prisoners who have lived in native towns or amongst the tribes [2] bring back habits and words which penetrate into their home country. Arab prisoners of the French, returning to their tribes, take back from prison—which they remember with regret—ways and words which penetrate to their people. The influence of such ex-prisoners has frequently in Algeria led to the " Frenchification " of the natives.

Finally, war-like occupation has given rise to the exchange of populations carried out under authority ; the transfer of entire peoples to pacify and to assimilate them. The Romans did this ; so did the Byzantines, the Chinese and the Incas ; [3] other nations too have tried thus to hasten the assimilation of their subjects. Some French proposed the " displacement " (*dépaysement*) of young Algerians to colleges in France to speed up their Frenchification. Mohammed Ali had acted on these lines. And the English have their " Oxford Cycle ", reinforced by the oath of loyalty (*le serment de loyalisme*).[4]

In legal language, *penetration* on the other hand is pacific. It is unpremeditated and accidental in its beginnings, the work of the pioneers we have spoken of. The work also of those other pioneers, the ambassadors, like those who under Louis XIV gave knowledge of Siam and Morocco to the world. The work also of doctors, who by practising in a new country were the first to get into touch with the inhabitants ; such a doctor was François Bernier,[5] philosopher and traveller, who for twenty

[1] W. J. MacGee, *Piratical Acculturation, Amer. Anthropologist*, 1898, p. 243 f.

[2] See *L'heureux esclave, ou relat. des avent. du Sieur de la Martinière en Barbarie*, Paris, 1674. The best-known case is that of Regnard, a prisoner in Algeria, J. S. Quesne, *Histoire de l'esclavage en Afrique . . . de P. J. Dumont . . .*, Paris, 1819.

[3] Prescott, *History of the Conquest of Peru*, 1847, Montezuma, Ed. 1904. H. Beuchat, *Manuel d'archéol. améric.*, Paris, 1912, p. 591 f.

[4] [The implied suggestion that colonial or Indian students have been induced, persuaded or compelled to come to Oxford to be " Anglified " will naturally stagger the English reader. It is of course a pure myth. See my note at the end of this chapter, p. 73. EOL]

[5] *Voyages de François Bernier . . .*, 2 vols., Amsterdam, 1711.

years was physician to the Moghul, and peacefully acted as an intermediary between far-distant peoples.   The work of magicians and musicians too, who in Roman times successfully found means of penetrating the Mediterranean countries ; just as to-day Negro civilisation is infiltrating into Europe through singers, musicians and dancers : similar phenomena belong to all ages.   Finally, the work of traders also, such men as Marco Polo [1] who for a quarter of a century lived at the Emperor's court in China, or Tavernier who travelled about Hindustan, and many others after them, especially in Africa.   Traders and merchants were able to forge an economic link between native and European, though they were not infrequently the victims of persecution on the part of those whose countries they penetrated.   Herein lies the reason why such initial penetration or juxtaposition, however pacific in itself, almost always led to premeditated or unpremeditated domination.   We know how the Inca Empire grew.   Traders were first sent out, who embarked on traffic with distant tribes.   They were in due course killed or robbed, and therein was a pretext for conquest.   It has usually proved to be the case that penetration has had to be upheld by domination.

Next came permanent and lasting penetration ; no longer the trader as a fleeting bird of passage, but presently the real merchant, who took up his permanent residence in the new country.   In the Middle Ages in Europe such *mercatores*, foreigners always,[2] became the founders of cities.   They began as nomadic traders and finally settled down under the walls of some castle and became the creators of commercial and industrial towns.   Western merchants later did the same in the ports of the Levant ;[3] they took up their quarters in certain well-defined districts and followed their own laws subject to *avania* extorted by the Turks.   In the colonies such merchants are known as *traitants* or *factors*, they were founders of business firms and also, in new countries, of towns.   They have been also the creators of what have been called " colonies without a flag " ; Italians, Greeks, Syrians, Basques, Corsicans or people of the Lower Alps [4] have peopled these settlements of a private, not public,

---

[1] P. Vidal de la Blache, *Marco Polo*, Paris, 1880.

[2] In this connection we may justly speak of " merchant colonies ".   See H. Pirenne, *Les villes du Moyen-Age*, Brussels, 1927.

[3] W. Heyd, *Hist. du commerce du Levant*, French trans., Paris, 1885, I, pp. 129 f. and 410 f.

[4] [We might add Chinese in Malaya and the Far East, Indians in South and East Africa, and Armenians everywhere.   EOL]

nature, which have been nevertheless a medium of contact. All these merchants are representatives of their home country, in whose name they willingly or unwillingly advance, acting as consuls and sometimes concluding treaties with the natives ; [1] their business premises are already chrysalis colonies.

Thus penetration leads to domination. For, anyone who wants to secure peaceful conditions for trade, must establish a lawful régime. Some legal obligations must be recognised, whence there invariably results *collaboration* between European and native, the second stage in their relationship. Colonisation and the reign of law produces collaboration between conquerors and conquered. It is not possible to maintain a reign of law without practical co-operation between European and native. It arises in domestic life, in political life also, and finally in economic life. In these three spheres the two parties are led to act in unison in the organisation and development of the new country. There arises between conqueror and conquered domestic, political and economic co-operation ; willingly or un-willingly—unwillingly rather than willingly—they are linked together by their work and their interests. It is inevitable that Europeans should support the native chiefs ; sooner or later the natives must become soldiers, agents and employees. All colonised countries since ancient times have had to go through this phase, and they have all been subject in their domination to the law of collaboration between conqueror and conquered. In their Asiatic possessions the ancient Egyptians used to keep barbarian chiefs—long before our " policy of the great chief " —on whom they conferred the dignities of a Pharaoh.[2] The Romans [3] acted in the same way ; so too Byzantines, Arabs, Chinese [4] and Incas. The natives have always been obliged, however reluctantly, to promote the domination of their con-querors. Long before our time the Byzantines were wont to bestow robes of honour on the chiefs. And for a long time the Arabs used to keep Christian employees. In our day the natives collaborate in another way, by taking their seat in various assemblies.[5] In the French colonies consultative and even

---

[1] For West Africa, see the Memoirs of one of them, A. Verdier, *Trente-cinq années de luttes aux colonies*, Paris, 1897. Rimbaud's life in Abyssinia is of the same type.

[2] On these pseudo-protectorates of the Egyptians, see J. de Morgan, *Les premières civilisations*, Paris, 1909, p. 277 f.

[3] V. Chapot, *Le monde romain*, Paris, 1927.

[4] Wells Williams, *The Middle Kingdom*, London, 1851, I, p. 151 f.

[5] A good picture of penetration and collaboration is given by Charles Diehl in his *L'Afrique byzantine*, Paris, 1896, pp. 533–709.

deliberative assemblies are set up ; mixed assemblies in which the natives have their delegates. There are the Councils of Algeria, Tunisia and Madagascar, and more particularly those of Indo-China, to which natives can be elected. Napoleon had already organised the Mixed Diwan of Cairo, a council on which French and Egyptians sat in equal numbers ; and he sought to secure the support of the Muslim " clergy ".

Before his day, in the Latin Orient, the Crusaders had set up mixed Courts of Arbitration, composed both of French and Syrians—Courts of the *Rais*—which were in effect a form of collaboration procedure, before ever that word or doctrine had been heard of.[1] Another form of collaboration between rulers and ruled is seen at work in those classic colonial institutions the *shikayah (chekaia)* [2] and the *palaver* [3] in which French administrators regularly meet their subjects, to hear their desires, complaints and hopes, to offer those good counsels that the French are so fond of, and so ready promptly to forget. This, also, is collaboration between rulers and ruled.

Collaboration appears in another, more surprising guise, not only in political and administrative, but in religious matters too. You need native chiefs and native officials, you also need native priests. As you convert the people you must organise a coloured priesthood to supplement the efforts of the white priesthood. In Israel the ancient Egyptians retained the Jewish priests in order to learn their secrets.[4] Modern conquerors have often retained the magicians and sorcerers of the conquered country to bolster up their own rule. The Churches, too, have created a native clergy. There are to-day Chinese bishops and we shall probably see black bishops to-morrow, as we already have black curates and black pastors who serve as the means of converting, and often also of civilising, their fellow-countrymen, though they sometimes, as we have seen, sow the seeds of agitation.

In the development, as well as in the administration of a country, there arises practical collaboration between European and native ; and economic co-operation is added to political co-operation. Whether rendered with a good grace or a bad,

---

[1] V. H. Lammens, *La Syrie*, Beyrut, 1921, Vol. I, pp. 235–71.

[2] M. Le Glay, *La chekaia* in *Récits marocains*, Paris, 1921.

[3] G. Joseph, *Manuel des Palabres*, Paris, undated. The French word *la palabre* (Eng. palaver) comes from the Portuguese *palavra*. It means a *meeting* and sometimes also the *presents* which traders exchange at such a meeting.

[4] On this self-interested " liberalism ", see J. G. Frazer, *Folklore in the Old Testament*, London, 1918, III, p. 84 f.

whether freely or under compulsion, co-operation there is, always and everywhere. Slavery even, or domestic service, contribute to it, for we know that, especially in ancient times, servants and slaves tended to become part of the family, and that intimate relations sprang up between master and servant. The masters were sometimes influenced by the manners and customs of their slaves ; who has not read *Paul et Virginie* ? [1] Sometimes the slaves were inspired by the manners and customs of their masters. Even slavery itself, and at a later date domestic life, promoted and still promotes a social exchange. It is well known to what abuses the régime of " the boys " can lead, who insinuate themselves between the white men and their subjects.[2] Nowadays economic co-operation takes other forms, neither the natives' enslavement nor his domestic service, but free and voluntary partnership. As partners and equals, the natives join in European enterprises. We already find in North Africa, especially in Morocco, cultural and industrial societies for native and European. Companies, syndicates and even sports clubs exist which are equally divided ; they are meeting places of reciprocal penetration.

If penetration thus leads to domination and then to partnership, partnership in its turn frequently—but not always—leads to *fusion* between the peoples. In time this involves a blending of the races : what is known as cross-breeding. Legitimate marriages, and in still greater number irregular matings, take place, which bring new human types into existence. Without travelling any great distance, merely crossing the Mediterranean from Marseilles to Algiers—little as people realise it, Algiers is nearer to Marseilles than Paris !—it is easy to see that a new race has grown up in Algeria. The intermingling of strains, the blend of European and Arab, more especially of Frenchman and Spaniard, has created an ethnic type different to the eye from the old French type : an " Algerian people " which has its own spirit [3] and its own aspirations and already clashes with the French. A century then has been enough to show in an adjacent country the beginnings at least of a racial blend, such as has long since been achieved elsewhere. A very ancient

---

[1] [A highly artificial and sentimental idyll by Bernardin de Saint-Pierre (1787) about two " children of nature ", which in its day enjoyed immense popularity. It is still read in France. EOL]

[2] A. H. Smith's remarks about Chinese servants apply equally to the Indo-Chinese : *Chinese Characteristics*, 1890 ; *Village Life in China*, 1900.

[3] M. and A. Leblond, *L'esprit algérien, Revue bleue*, 1903, pp. 507-12.

writer had already noted that the principal agent of the fusion of races was woman, and he asserted that durable and permanent race contact is brought about solely by women. It is in fact—let us corroborate him !—sexual union between peoples or, if you will, *exogamy*, in a very comprehensive sense of the term, which is the major and most complete form of race contact. This is the reason why reformers have preached the desirability of such matings to pave the way to communion.[1] Even while violent warlike conquest was in progress, this factor was by no means absent. While the first contacts were still hostile, native women came to the conquerors ; they it was who often formed the first links between the two races. Cortes had a native mistress, Marina by name, who on occasion betrayed the Mexicans, and directed the Spaniards' strategy. This is no exceptional case ; Chateaubriand used the subject for a romantic novel ; native women have often been the first agents of contact. This provides the classic literary motif of the tragic romance between the European man and the native woman. Such things occur still more easily where contact is pacific. When the race barrier is down, interbreeding, whether in legitimate marriage or irregular liaison, very soon takes place between the conquerors and conquered. Thus the number of what are called mulattos, mestizos, half-breeds or half-castes increase. In the French kingdoms of the Latin Orient, the offspring of Crusaders and Syrian women were known as *poulains*. Such half-breeds are nothing exceptional ; there are more than 40 million of them in South America, where the bulk of the electorate are mestizos of mixed Spanish and Red Indian stock, whose very features betray that they spring from the race of the " Topanimbous ".[2]

Cross-breeding can thus give rise to new races. There are other half-breeds besides the Spanish-Indian variety ; there are some who have kept themselves apart and sometimes form separate groups in South America : the Paulistas of Brazil, the Gauchos, half-breed horse-herds, of the Argentine ; the Mulattos of the Antilles, a blend of Negro and creole ; the Bastards of South Africa, sprung from Boer and Hottentot. Such half-castes have features partly of European, partly of native type. If it is true, according to Mendel's Law of Hybrid-

---

[1] C. Pecqueur, *Des intérêts du commerce* . . . , Paris, 1839, II, p. 328 f. F. de Soliers proposed systematic cross-breeding in Algeria, but between Europeans only. See Demontès, *Le peuple algérien* . . . , Algiers, 1906, p. 218 f.

[2] [An Indian tribe of Brazil and Argentina. EOL]

isation, that there occurs a reversion to the more primitive type, that the native element will tend ultimately to preponderate, yet there still remains some white ingredient. In this sense there are races, who never before existed, that have been created by the fusion of peoples.

We must distinguish two forms of cross-breeding : what I call the *masculine* and the *feminine*. The masculine form—by far the more common—is where the European man mates with the native woman. Race contact here follows the usual line of class contact : the superior male mating normally, as in marriage, with the inferior female : the nobleman's son may marry the trader's heiress, the nobleman's daughter will not marry the merchant's heir.[1] In the same way, in the colonies the white man mates with the native woman, but not the white woman with the coloured man. This is the romantic motif of Chateaubriand's *René*, his predecessors and his successors.[2] Crossbreeding is, however, sometimes feminine : the European woman in that case making an exotic marriage ;[3] as in our time a middle-class youth occasionally marries an aristocratic wife—not without provoking much ill-natured comment—as occurs in a novel by Georges Ohnet. Since the War, there have been marriages between French women and Kabyles ; but these men, as we know, are counted white. Such a case, however, is exceptional, and may be reckoned as an aberration. This is where the half-breed's problem comes in. The son of a white man, he demands the rights of a white man ; he claims the paternal inheritance ; the novel laments his cruel lot.[4]

Such is the nature of the relations between conqueror and conquered in the colonies. But to-day we are witnessing a reverse phenomenon which seems to us—quite wrongly—to be something new. Exotic foreigners immigrate into our countries and settle in Europe ; race contact then takes place in both directions. As the European occupation of new countries may be either individual or collective, the penetration of coloured people into our countries may be so too. Personal or individual contact of this type began long since ; " savages " have for a

---

[1] In the drama, from Molière to Marivaux, to Dallainval, to Voltaire, to Émile Augier, the *mésalliance* is always the man's.

[2] See in particular the works discussed by Tailliart, *op. cit.*, I, p. 572 f., and by Roland Lebel, *Hist. de la littér. coloniale*, Paris, 1931, pp. 141–2, 152, 159, 169, 170.

[3] This theme occurs more recently in novels and more frequently on the stage and on the screen.

[4] Especially for Indo-China ; Mme C. Chivas-Baron, *Confidences de métisse*, 1926 ; J. Cendrieux, *François Phuoc, métis*, 1929 ; Herbert Wild, *L'autre race*, 1930.

long time been coming to France. Apart from the visits of exotic royalties, primitive men have been living the romantic theme of Voltaire's *Ingénu*. The list of such " savage " ambassadors of the natural man would be a long one : the Brazilian Essomeric (1505) ; the Caribbeans (1550) ; the Natchez (1731) ; the Indians (1785) ; the Osages (1827) ; the Arabs (1844) [1] and thousands since then. I have specially in mind the Tahitian Aotourou [2] whom Bougainville brought with him, and who lived two years in France, only to die in Mauritius on his way home ; and that other Tahitian, Omahi,[3] whom Cook took to England and who, it seems, made difficulties about kneeling before the King for fear of being eaten ; and the Chinese [4] whose patron was Turgot,[5] and who came to Paris and saw Versailles. The Physiocrats, who had a passion for China, were able to study these Chinese at leisure and Turgot plied them with an ethnographic questionnaire about China, which was the first of our recorded " questionnaires ". I think too of Mokrani, the Kabyle chief who came to Paris " to initiate himself into French civilisation " ; in which faith he later stirred up the Berber Insurrection. Lastly, I think of Tarqui Ouksem, whom Charles de Foucauld brought to France before the War and placed with a noble family in a château in Limousin. It is said that this Tarqui used to eat everything except fish and pork, and that they taught him to knit—a degrading occupation for a man of the desert. History does not record what afterwards became of him. Whatever his fate may have been, he at least provides us with a new specimen of *l'Ingénu*.

To-day's contacts are quite different ; collective contacts or mass contacts. Workers [6] and students have immigrated into France by the thousand, and the hundred thousand. More than a hundred thousand yellow workers are installed on the Hawaiian Islands ; in Paris there are perhaps a hundred thousand Kabyles.[7] This represents a new wave of migration the danger of which may be grave. The ancient Egyptians knew the same danger ; they had had a large number of black workers in the

---

[1] L. Roches, *Trente-deux ans à travers l'Islam*, Paris, 1884, II, p. 430 f.
[2] Bougainville, *Voyage autour du monde* . . . , Paris, 1772, II, p. 93 f.
[3] *Narrations d'Omaï, insulaire de la mer du Sud*, Rouen-Paris, 1790.
[4] H. Hauser, *Revue de la littér. comparée*, IX, 1929, pp. 714–27.
[5] Turgot, *Œuvres*, Schelle's edition, II, Paris, 1913, pp. 523–33.
[6] B. Nogaro and L. Weill, *La main-d'œuvre étrang. et colon. pendant la guerre,* Paris, 1926.
[7] L. Massignon, *Cartes de répartition des Kabyles dans la région paris.* . . ., *Revue Études islamiques*, 1930, p. 161 f.

Delta, and in the time of Rameses under the 19th Dynasty these workers revolted and kept the Delta in their power for over ten years.

Are we face to face with the same danger again ? Must we wonder, with Kipling,[1] whether the Indians have taken home with them a spirit of rebellion or a spirit of allegiance ? This penetration of exotic races into our old countries : is it a good thing—or a bad ? It may be both. It must fill us with a great fear—and a great hope.

Note on Professor Maunier's " Oxford Cycle "

Being mystified by the author's suggestion of an " Oxford Cycle ", which was in some way more or less forcibly to bring coloured students from the Empire to Oxford in order to " Anglify " them, imposing on them at the same time an " oath of loyalty ", I enquired of him what exactly he had in mind. He replied :

" It was the custom in English India to choose out exceptionally gifted boys (*tout jeunes gens . . . esprits d'élite*) from superior native families, who were called (*appelés*) to complete their studies at the University of Oxford. This practice was continued to my knowledge (*à ma connaissance*) for some 50 years or so. These young people, who were recruited from princely families and from the Parsees, were thus the object of a design (*travail*) of 'intellectual assimilation'. This is why I have alluded thereto in this passage, so as to emphasise that the English themselves, little addicted to assimilation tho' they be (*si peu assimilateurs*) have on occasion been tempted to adopt this policy. As I have implied, this type of 'student bursary' (*bourse d'études*)—as one may perhaps call it—entailed an 'oath of loyalty' (*serment de loyalisme*). I do not know whether this practice still prevails."

(*Signed*) RENÉ MAUNIER
11 X 1946

This amazing statement challenged further enquiry. An official answer from the India Office informed me that " nothing corresponding to the ' Cycle of Oxford ' to which M. René Maunier refers, has ever, so far as this Office is aware, existed ".

I next enquired of the authorities of Oxford University, and Sir Richard Livingstone, the present Vice-Chancellor, replied : " There never has been any ' Cycle d'Oxford ' or anything like it. It is surprising if such a statement appears in the work of a Professor of the University of Paris."

Thinking that perhaps Professor Maunier had in some way heard misrepresentations of the Rhodes Scholarships, whose much-coveted

---

[1] R. Kipling, French trans., *Les yeux de l'Asie*, Paris, 1921. [A collection of short tales, which does not correspond to any single English collection that is easily traceable. EOL]

privileges were open not only to British Empire graduates but also to German and American students (from whom oaths of loyalty could hardly be exacted !), I wrote to the Rhodes Trust, and received from Lord Elton, the Secretary of the Trust, the following reply : " I have no idea what ' le cycle d'Oxford ' can mean. . . . I should be interested to hear what Professor Maunier's explanation is."

These authoritative answers dispose of the Professor's myth. We can only surmise that he has been the victim of some mischievous German or Indian-Congress anti-British propaganda. EOL.

BOOK IV

RESULTS OF RACE CONTACT

CHAPTER IX

OPPOSITION

Let us now come to the *effects* of race contact. Three relations may arise. Relations of hostility and enmity, which arouse opposition. Relations of familiarity and intimacy, which give rise to imitation. Relations of kinship and consanguinity, which produce fusion. These therefore are the three effects which may result from two peoples coming into contact in the colonies : *opposition, imitation, fusion.*

First, *Opposition.*[1] This is the collision or impact of the two civilisations which the English call " *the clash* ". When we speak of the *Clash of Cultures* we mean the way in which the cultures of two different peoples suffer from the impact of their meeting, and we emphasise the fact that the repercussion creates a gulf between them.

The resulting opposition has two aspects. The first arrival of conquerors in a conquered country used in olden days to have as its chief result the *elimination* of the original inhabitants : whether this was caused by warlike destruction, or by spontaneous depopulation without intentional destruction.

Even where elimination did not take place, where fortunately the native inhabitants were able to continue living under the power of the newcomers, opposition took another form : a contradiction between the feelings and interests of conquerors and conquered. This is the *clash* proper, the irritation and friction which are almost always present in the beginning.

First, however, *Elimination.* This took place, and still takes place, either by destruction or by depopulation.

Destruction or extermination in war was sometimes organised and deliberate, and was pursued until the natives were almost completely extinct. Spanish scholars of to-day defend the action of their nation in having wished, in former times, to accomplish

[1] See in general : L. Gumplowicz, *La lutte des races* . . . , French trans., Paris, 1893 ; G. Simmel, *The Sociology of Conflict, Amer. Journal of Sociology,* IX, 1904, Nos. 4–6 ; and *Soziologie* . . . , Leipzig, 1908.

75

the destruction and obliteration of the natives.   The destruction of the American natives was at least tolerated, if not always premeditated.   There were laws for the protection of the poor Red Indians, but these laws were not heeded.[1]   The fact remains : in less than half a century there had been hecatombs in Mexico and Peru.   Wherever the European settled, he was again and again compelled to conquer by force of arms, even when he tried peaceably to find a footing.   For, as I have said, traders and settlers become the object of persecutions and impositions which they are bound to resist.   The Inca merchants who sought to pursue their trade in distant parts were molested and sometimes massacred, after which the Inca Empire embarked on conquest.   Similarly we have seen European countries in West Africa first attempt a peaceful occupation of the bush, only to find themselves, almost always, driven to military conquest.   Did not the French in Algeria, at one time think of driving the Arabs southwards " to eliminate the Arab race from our colony " ?   That was the doctrine of *extrusion*.[2]   Warlike occupation has thus often been a necessity ; the European has been forced to fight, even when he has not had the least wish to do so.   Do not let us be for ever suspecting the sinister working of a " militarist party " and blaming it for every conquest.   Cortes himself exhorted his soldiers to behave gently : but we know how desperately the Aztecs resisted.   At other times it has been the perpetual inroads of the natives which have compelled the Europeans to fight.   In the 18th century, in the English colonies in America, and even among the Quakers of Pennsylvania, a reward was offered to anyone who could bring in an Indian scalp ; at one point the reward was 130 dollars. Cooper's celebrated story, *The Last of the Mohicans*, published in 1826, tells the tale of the deliberate extermination of the natives.   The colonist has had to fight in self-protection ; he has had to fight to put an end to a million atrocities of black sultans and try to civilise their peoples ; he has had to fight in order to organise, and organisation involved the taxation of the native races.   For Europeans have brought taxes, like other evils, to their subjects.   You must raise revenue, if you want to administer ; the tax is the very symbol of all civilisation, and one to which natives have the most obstinate objection.   So

[1] Peter Martyr, *De Orbe Novo*, Gaffarel's French trans., Paris, 1907, p. 599 f. See Ern. Nys, *Les publicistes espagnols du XVᵉ siècle et les droits des Indiens*, Brussels, 1890.
[2] E. Bodichon, *Considér. sur l'Algérie*, Paris, 1845.

there arose " tax wars ", fought solely for the purpose of collecting the revenue. The petty kinglets and sultans of North Africa were already waging tax wars before the arrival of the French : even in Morocco, even in Tunis, as had been the case in many an ancient empire, an armed expeditionary force was needed to bring in tribute. It has thus often been necessary to conquer in order to " subdue " in the full legal and fiscal sense.

Such have been the motives which have led to the armed destruction of natives. The amazing thing is that it has been carried out with very meagre resources. The colonial conqueror has had no need of legions or armies : a handful of men, a few guns, a few rifles, have sufficed to achieve the occupation and complete the destruction. We have exact information— Hernando Cortes committed it to writing in his despatches [1] to Charles V—of the number of men and of the minute force which conquered the vast Empire of Mexico : 40 cavalry, 550 infantry and 8 guns ; and he was soon able to put in the field a large army of renegade Mexicans.

Even where conquest is not in itself destructive, it may result, as a side issue, in the elimination of the natives. Almost always it brought slavery in its train.[2] If war did not exterminate the natives, slavery did, with its excesses and its theory of cruelty. It was slavery which brought about the extermination of vast numbers of Mexicans and Peruvians ; wherever slavery reigned there followed numerous native suicides. Slavery taught the native to commit suicide—a crime almost unknown to primitive man—and it was the European who taught him ! [3]

Nowadays elimination is, happily, not the result of deliberate extermination ; it arises, however, from spontaneous *depopulation*.[4]

---

[1] *Lettres de Fernand Cortès à Charles Quint*, pub. L. Vallée, Paris, 1879.
[2] For the deaths due to slavery, see Harriet Beecher Stowe, *A Key to Uncle Tom's Cabin*, 1852.
[3] S. R. Steinmetz, *Suicide among Primitive Peoples*, Amer. Anthropologist, VII, 1894, p. 53 f.
[The suggestion that primitive peoples first learnt suicide from the White Man is certainly not correct. Primitive man is exceptionally sensitive to the blame or ridicule of his neighbours and will commit suicide to escape it, or to escape the dread consequence of having, even inadvertently, broken a taboo. See Malinowski's studies of the Trobriand Islanders and Raymond Firth's reports on Tikopia. Even amongst the eminently sane, well-balanced and unsuperstitious Burusho of Hunza in the Karakoram suicide, though rare, is not unknown. In these—and doubtless countless other cases—there can be no question of European influence. EOL]
[4] See in general J. L. Ward, *Colonisation in its Bearing on the Extinction of the Aboriginal Races*, London, 1874 ; W. H. R. Rivers, *Essays on the Depopulation of Melanesia*, Cambridge, 1922 ; G. Pitt-Rivers, *The Clash of Cultures and the Contact of Races*, London, 1927 ; K. Sapper, *Das Aussterben der Naturvölker*, Zeitsch. für Geopolitik, VI, 1929, pp. 490–508 ; L. Jalabert, La " grande pitié " de l'Afrique noire, Études, Jan. 5, 1931.

In Africa, in Asia and amongst the happy-go-lucky peoples scattered in the fortunate islands of the Oceanic Archipelago, depopulation follows from the fact, the mere fact, of white men's establishing themselves there. The birth-rate falls ; the death-rate rises ; the two phenomena together have meant the complete, or almost complete, disappearance of certain Oceanic races : the aboriginal Tasmanians and Australians, for instance. The Tasmanians have vanished completely ; not one of them remains to cherish their traditions. Only a handful survive of the superlatively primitive Australians and these few are domesticated on the farmsteads of the desert " squatters ". The newspapers recently announced that they had gone on strike, exactly like civilised workers—an unexpected result of what we call progress !

Why this tragic disappearance ? The subject has been carefully studied for the Oceanic Archipelago by the English anthropologist, Pitt-Rivers, whose loss is sorely to be regretted. Owing to the fact, and solely to the fact, that Europeans have come and settled : that is the answer. But why, if the European neither oppresses nor persecutes the native, why does the birthrate fall, and the death-rate rise ? Why have whole islands become depopulated in less than a hundred years ? Why are there, even in the United States, despite the policy of " reservations ", only 250,000 Red Indians ?[1] There are two sets of causes : the one physical, the other spiritual.[2]

First, *the physical causes*. The European brings with him to the native the great evil of *alcoholism*. Alcohol is certainly not, as some have asserted, the chief cause of the depopulation of Oceania, but it is the basic cause. It is the native's headlong rush for alcohol which first introduces him to the European. Buccaneers and bushrangers, pioneers and colonists, taught the native to drink. That Nicolas Perrot of whom I have already spoken, one of the first bushrangers, who lived in the 17th century, denounced with justified indignation the " fire-water " barter which the Europeans carried on with the Indians who came to sell their furs. They exchanged bottles of alcohol for skins of marten, ermine and beaver. Already under the Old French régime, the king forbade the bartering of alcohol ; though laws were passed to combat the practice and to prevent the ruin of the native by alcohol, nevertheless, always and every-

[1] *Dept. of Commerce* . . . *Indian Population in the U.S. and Alaska*, Washington, 1915.
[2] See Ravalonahina's monograph, *Des causes de dépopulation à Madagascar* . . . , 1902 (Medical thesis, Montpellier).

where we find, and still find, the trader teaching the native a taste for drink. Ossendowski has with bold strokes painted a picture of the Siberians intoxicated by the brandy of the Russian traders which, he says, they pour out lavishly, the better to further their fraudulent traffic.

Above all there are *the spiritual causes*. These we must conjure up, if we are to grasp the nature of what has been called this " mortal contact " between the European and the native. The mere presence of the European causes the disappearance of the native. We have seen this throughout the whole Oceanic world and in particular in Tahiti. Within a few years the natives are, without apparent reason, overcome by a lassitude, seized by a despair for which there seems to be no cure. You see them die off, gradually, one by one, without the Europeans' having done anything at all. Race contact may sometimes be tragic ; it may be fatal, however friendly ! Max Anély (Victor Segalen) described this in his great book " *Immémoriaux* " in 1907 : the inevitable disappearance of the Maori race,[1] attacked by the lassitude which was already endemic among them, a disease known by various names in the world of Oceania. In Tahiti they call it *erimatua*, in the Bismarck Archipelago, *tatareri* : a boredom, a despair, for which there is no remedy, which marks the death of a race.

What then is it which makes the European a messenger of death to the native ? Has the native been right in believing that the presence of Europeans brought a curse with it, and in seeing the new colonists as the personification or reincarnation of evil spirits ? Without his wishing it, without his always being able to prevent it, the settlement of the white man in a primitive country has the effect of disintegrating the tribe, destroying the customary political and traditional order, abolishing established power. The very presence of the European undermines the chiefs' authority and violates the time-honoured taboos, those traditional commandments which protected man and his goods. How beneficent the part they played, we can see from the mere fact that their abolition has spelt anarchy. The truth is that, without in the least desiring it, the white

---

[1] [The Maoris of New Zealand have happily not died out. They are to-day a flourishing, contented and progressive community, supplying their country with professional men and even Cabinet Ministers. The tide turned about 1901 (see Pitt-Rivers, *op. cit.*) and the Census figures for 1926-36 show a rise from 52,000 to 67,300, plus a rise in Maori half-castes from 11,600 to 15,000. The estimate for April 1947 (including half-castes) is 105,700. EOL]

man brings with him an anarchy which grows in proportion as primitive life necessarily adjusts itself to civilised life. Old authorities are shaken ; old taboos effaced ; and nothing is provided to replace the ancient rules and laws which the European has been obliged to break down by the mere fact that he is trying to colonise.

As Robert Louis Stevenson [1] noted for the Marquesas Islands, the white men have done worse, they have brought in their train not only nor chiefly disintegration and dissolution, but boredom, overwhelming boredom, without hope and without end, by putting an end to wars . . . and pleasure. They establish peace, which is for the native both an evil and a good. For the warrior, who is fitted only to be a warrior, life has henceforward neither meaning nor purpose. " Savages ", as Cabanis used to say, " repudiate the peaceful and more productive occupations of civilised nations, in order to go on living in the midst of danger and hardship." Thus it is that, at least in the transition phase, peace is the source of most depressing boredom. In the same way, as has been said—not without a touch of malice—religious missions cultivate boredom by suppressing pleasures. They forbid dances and festivals ; they frown on nakedness ; they seek to bend the native to asceticism. There are certain cases—which have, however, surely been exaggerated —where this has aggravated the boredom which saps the native's strength and will. The Code of Pomaré II of Tahiti which was enforced in 1819 under pressure of the missionaries was, like those which followed, a Puritan Code. The Maoris produced no Paul-Louis Courier [2] to write on their behalf a " Pétition des villageois qu'on empêche de danser " (Plea of the villagefolk who are prevented from dancing). Dancing was for the native a religious ceremony, not a profane amusement. Perhaps it was wrong to deprive him of it. [3]

Another thing contributes in other countries to the native's disappearance. Europeans bring with them not only *taxes* and *peace*, but also *towns*. They are founders and builders of towns ;

---

[1] *In the South Seas*, 1888.

[2] [Paul Louis Courier (1773-1825), French scholar, Hellenist and political writer. He championed so vigorously the cause of his humbler country neighbours that he became one of the most redoubtable opponents of the Government of the Bourbon Restoration. The eloquence, irony and brilliance of his pamphlets have won him a permanent and honoured place in French literature. EOL]

[3] For the two opinions on this point, see : M. Delafosse, *Broussard ou les états d'âme d'un colonial*, 1923, p. 159 f., and L. Germond, *Laissez l'Africain chanter et danser*, *Journal des missions évang.*, June, 1930 (in criticism of this formula).

this is part of their mission of organising and civilising new countries. It is yet another factor in the native's demoralisation. He sets out for the town ; soon we see amongst the coloured townsfolk all the uprooted people who too often are also people in despair. Having emigrated to the town, and having in consequence lost touch with his tribe, he has lost touch also with his faith and with his moral code. This problem had arisen before our time. It is over a century since the Duchess of Duras described in her novel *Ourika* the mental and spiritual conflicts of an uprooted Negress who had left the territory of her tribe and exiled herself in the white man's cities [1]—a transposition, often all too true, of Rousseau's diatribe.

Even where destruction does not take place, there often arises *contradiction* or *opposition* between conquerors and conquered, a clash of traditions, aspirations, feelings and judgments ; [2] an opportunity for the native to save his soul.

Enmity or hostility between European and native is then confirmed, whether open or concealed. More than this, opposition may exist even where relations appear friendly. When intermittent or permanent trade is carried on between white and coloured, it is often tinged with hostility ; it is a distrustful exchange, not one of confidence. When white and coloured people first begin to barter goods, the exchange often takes the well-known form of *mute* or *silent trading*.[3] This intertribal or international procedure is frequently employed even between Europeans. The parties do not speak ; often they do not even see each other. The sellers deposit in a given spot the goods they want to sell ; they then withdraw and the buyers approach in their turn. This *impersonal bartering* may prove to be the basis of hostile exchange, but not of friendly exchange. In which fact we find proof that self-interest alone is not enough to establish a friendly relation between two parties.

Even when amicable social intercourse has been begun, we may find the native growing restive under the propaganda of the European. He strives to retain his traditions and institutions

---

[1] This is also the subject of the novel, *Le Zézère*, by M. and A. Leblond.

[2] We should here collate all that has been written about the "mentality of primitive peoples", which remains a subject of controversy. See especially the four works of L. Lévy-Bruhl (1910–30), in particular, *La mentalité primitive*, Paris, 1910 ; and the different interpretation of F. Boas, *The Mind of Primitive Man*, New York, 1911. L. Marillier presents a brief and fair picture in his article *Religion*, *Grande Encyclop.*, Paris, Vol. 28, p. 346 f.

[3] P. J. Hamilton Grierson, *The Silent Trade* . . . , London, 1903 ; A. H. Post, *Grundriss der ethnolog. Jurisprudenz*, Oldenburg, 1895, II, p. 628 f. See Herodotus, IV, 196.

unimpaired ; he does his best to avoid becoming infected by the conqueror's customs and manners.   In this case we are entitled to speak of " the refusal to imitate ", or resemble : a phenomenon we are familiar with as arising also between different social classes.   Race-consciousness, class-consciousness thus assert themselves.   This refusal to borrow indicates opposition, the forms of which we must now outline.   There is first of all an opposition of perception, of *appreciation*.   In spite of having already entered into close relationship, native and European nevertheless misjudge and despise each other, because they misapprehend each other.—There is also an opposition of tradition and of legislation. Though they have come closely into contact, each side nevertheless jealously guards its faith and its law ; each wishes to remain a stranger to the other, to preserve the difference.   Each in his own place, each himself, if not each for himself.

Far from being smitten by admiration at the sight of the European, the native, on the contrary, more often despises and misunderstands him.   The white man despises and misunderstands no less the native's civilisation.   From Greek times onwards he has considered, and considers, it " primitive " and " barbarous ".   The Greeks in their turn were despised by the Romans [1] as Orientals.   The European classifies everything exotic as " uncivilised ".   Misunderstanding is the normal thing between the white man and the coloured.   Each devotes much ingenuity to discovering the faults and vices of the other.[2]   Let us note in what way the white man has misunderstood the coloured man, and the coloured man the white.

The white, in the first place, reproaches the coloured man with his *familiarity* and his equality.[3]   In the tribe all men are equal ; there, a man is always a man ; each is of the same blood and of the same rank ; in the black man's mind, a black man is as good as a white ; the white man believes he has stumbled

[1] G. Boissier, *Jugement de Juvénal sur les Grecs et les Orientaux, Revue cours conférences*, VIII, 1900, pp. 444-54.
[2] The best survey of these states of mind is in W. T. Willoughby, *Race Problems in the New Africa*, London, 1923.
[3] For the European's opinion of the Egyptians, see E. W. Lane, *An Account . . . of the Modern Egyptians*, London, 1836, Chap. XIII.   A good collection of European opinion of the Moroccans is to be found in G. Hardy, *L'âme marocaine d'après la littér. française*, Paris, 1926.   It would be necessary to examine all " colonial literature " to arrive at an agreed opinion about each coloured race from the various judgments of individuals.   This task has by no means been done ; and the difficulty is that many various attitudes of mind prevail amongst European men and women towards our French coloured subjects.   There are at least three : the *degenerate*-native ; the *refractory*-native ; the *misunderstood*-native ; see J. Liorel's analysis, *Kabylie du Jurjura*, Paris, 1892, p. 526 f.

against an obstacle . . . a failure to appreciate his superiority. He also reproaches the coloured man with his *instability*, his *emotionalism*, his *impulsiveness* [1] which make relations with him extremely insecure. In the same way—to continue our comparison—the French upper and middle classes were long wont to reproach their humbler compatriots with a tendency to be over-emotional. [2] The primitive man is quick to change his mind. He is different to-day from yesterday, you can never count on him. His *unreliability* is also cast in his teeth ; his disregard for a promise or a contract. He frequently disregards both, for the simple reason—and herein lies a real social misunderstanding—that he is often enough unaware of any contract in our sense of the term. In his tribe, rights are collective and traditional ; the individual can, as a rule, do nothing to alter them. When a native therefore makes a contract with a European, this act has for him by no means the same meaning as it has for us ; he does not consider himself bound by it, or he feels bound in quite a different way. He does not possess, what we normally possess—at least we say we do—respect for a contract. Lastly, the white man accuses the coloured man of *incompetence* ; this is the recurring complaint of every white colonial ; the native can do nothing right, nothing as we do it. It is true that the yellow, brown or black man often makes the same accusation against us. The Chinese heartily despise the white man [3] who cannot do what every Chinese can : if it were only eating rice soup with chopsticks. Our man's dress is ridiculous, our woman's dress indecent. Our manners are far too crude and far too rude ; the art of greeting, like the art of eating, is a sealed book to us. Our inventions are of the Devil ; and finally all Chinese with one accord agree—that we smell unpleasant ! Misunderstandings, fed on ignorance, fasten on trifling details of daily life, ill-understood and misinterpreted.

Let us give ear to another voice. Let us ask whether the coloured man has no grievances against the white. He has plenty. In his *Natchez*, Chateaubriand, lending his eloquence to the dark-skinned American, drew up the brief for the prosecu-

---

[1] See an attempted analysis, by C. Arrii, *De l'impulsivité criminelle chez l'indigène algér.*, Algiers, 1926 (Medical thesis).

[2] See Pierre Charron, *De la sagesse* (1588), Book I, Chap. 48.

[3] Arthur Hamilton Smith, *Chinese Characteristics*, 1890 ; *Village Life in China*, 1900 ; Upton Close (J. W. Hall), *Some Asian Views of White Culture. Atlantic Monthly* (N.Y.), March 1924, p. 353 f.—Montesquieu was fully alive to these contrasts : *Esprit des lois* (1748), Book XIX, 12, 17, 18 ; and he concludes that we must not judge Chinese ideas by our own.

tion—years before to-day's Pan-Negro Congresses. The author of the *Lettres iroquoises* [1] has admirably presented this state of mind : the Iroquois Igli, travelling in France, writes us down as insane ; he is surprised but not attracted ; shocked by our ways, alarmed by our progress, he remains a stranger to us.

Coloured men reproach Europeans with their exercise of *authority* ; their mania for regimenting and regulating, especially in matters where more primitive men are governed by customs which they take for granted. The regulations weigh heavily on the native.—They also reproach the European with his *simplicity* —this accusation comes as a surprise !—the absence of ostentation which the French indulge in their colonies and which to them seems weakness. The native measures greatness and importance by expensive display ; and liberality bestows prestige. The stingy European who does not spend lavishly incurs contempt.—More frequently still, the natives reproach the French with *punctuality*, which to them appears monotonous and tyrannical. In many cases this last item is the major cause of friction between conqueror and conquered. This passion for punctuality which the European brings with him, spells boredom and disgust to his subjects. The native is no longer free to live in his own way at his own pace. He has got to be mindful of days and hours ; he has got to remember when taxes fall due ; he must not forget laws and contracts. All this is sheer slavery.—Let us confess that above everything else, the coloured man accuses us of being *irreligious.* Even if the European is genuinely religious —and many in the colonies are—religion does not take that prominent place in the very forefront of his daily life that it does in the native's. Be he pagan or Musulman, religion dominates everything, while with us it takes a secondary place, and we give the impression of having none. This is a moral conflict. The pride of the true believer rises in revolt against

[1] (Maubert de Gouvest) *Lettres iroq.*, 1755, " at Irocopolis " (?).—Analyses are almost wholly lacking. Only imaginative literature provides us with the view of the " sly savage " on " the civilised ", such as we find in the forerunners and the imitators of Montesquieu's *Lettres persanes* up to and including the 19th century, from Malebranche to Eugène Simon. Addison makes some shrewd criticisms in the *Spectator* when recording the visit of the Indian Kings, No. 50, April 27, 1711. —A few coloured tourists have already passed judgment on us, Muhib Effendi and Rifaat Bey ; Lutfullah (Indian Musulman), *Mémoires de Lutfullah*, Lanoye's edition, Paris, 1858. But these are all from the pen of " assimilated " natives. The attitude of the native masses towards us must be sought in their *proverbs* about " Christians " and " Franks ", in such collections as Ben Cheneb has made for Algeria and J. Hanki for Egypt, where translations of modern proverbs are to be found.—For the tempered judgment of a nomad about the French, see E. Daumas, *Le Chambi à Paris* in *Mœurs et coutumes de l'Algérie*, Paris, 1855, p. 103 f.

our half-heartedness. We have neither the same forms of worship, nor the same aversions. Our mania for keeping dogs fills the Muslim with disgust. Is it not written in his scriptures that you must wash seven times, and once at least with sand as well as water, any dish from which a dog has drunk ?— Further, they accuse us of *indecency*.[1] Our close-fitting clothes lack modesty ; our social intercourse with women, our dances and games, even our " aimless walks " shock their sense of propriety. We talk too loud ; we talk while eating ; we make water standing, instead of crouching : every one of these things is a mark of *ill-breeding* ! Even our inventions, on which we count to secure our prestige, are reckoned by them as the work of black magic. They believe that we have allied ourselves with evil spirits ; this is why our very presence is frequently considered a misfortune in itself. The progress that we bring, that we often even impose, is nothing but corruption and impiety ! This is the reason why Musulmans who find themselves under Christian rule are exhorted to fly as a duty into a Muhammedan country. It has not seldom needed some diplomacy to prevent their doing so.

Great as may be, however, the opposition of appreciation, it is the opposition of *legislation* or tradition which must be stressed. For the greatest shock comes from French laws and native customs which must be harmonised, if Europeans and natives are to live together. This is the problem of " the clash of laws " in the French colonies.[2] In every point, there is, it would seem, a radical difference between European law and native custom. Administrators are naturally tempted to abolish barbarous customs, and to set up in a new country the reign of French law, either by *persuasion* or by *compulsion*. But our subjects are far from being convinced of the excellence of French laws.[3] Yet some form of " public order ", of law and order, must be established in the colonies, with the native's goodwill or more often without it.

The problem is a very old one. Herodotus (II, 35–6) is conscious of a strong contrast between Egyptian and Greek ;

---

[1] E. Daumas, *La vie arabe et la société musulmane*, Paris, 1869, pp. 99 f. and 355 f., gives a brief and lively sketch of the Algerian opinion of the French.

[2] Details will be found in my *Loi française et coutume indigène en Algérie*, Paris, 1932 ; I therefore only mention the subject here.

[3] V. J. Desparmet, *L'œuvre de la France en Algérie, jugée par les indigènes*, Bull. Soc. Géogr. Algér., 1910, pp. 167 f. and 417 f.

and he has a low opinion of the strange manners and customs of the Egyptians. Old Plutarch in his *Roman Questions* asks, in Question 83, whether it is seemly in the colonies to countenance the practice of human sacrifice. As a good Roman, he comes to the conclusion that the governor must intervene to put an end to the barbarous custom.

The conflict therefore is age-old. If social ties and legal order are to be established between European and native, we must in our legislation achieve a *conversion*. Whether by education or by compulsion, we must bring the native within the orbit of our law.

CHAPTER X

IMITATION BY THE INFERIOR

Imitation or adaptation takes place, first and foremost, *de haut en bas* [1] as Tarde expresses it, namely imitation by the native of the European. The subject imitates the ruler ; the conquered adapts himself to the conqueror. This is a law of life that operates in every society, and has long been recognised. In the 14th century of our era, the Arab philosopher, Ibn Khaldun, commented on this tendency of the subject to imitate the ruler, and dwelt on the attraction which " the leaders " exercised on " the led ". The responsibility of kings is heavy, as the Preacher reminds us, for their subjects take them as models. The governed think to ennoble themselves by adopting the ways of their governors. [2] This instinct comes into play from the first moment of contact. I have already mentioned Wallis's visit to Tahiti, when a native, more daring than his fellows, asked the captain for his hat and donned it forthwith ; and seeing the ship's officers eating with knives and forks the same man seized on these implements and tried to use them, however awkwardly. Unconsciously this innovator was enacting the scene of the native's seduction by the white man.

Let us first consider the *means* or the methods by which this imitation of the superior by the inferior may be carried out, and then note the aspects, the *effects* of this imitation and the limits that must be placed on it.

The means and the methods of the imitation [3] of the white by the coloured man may be classified under two heads : the imitation or adaptation may be either *spontaneous* or *induced*.

It may arise without pressure or suggestion from the side of the dominant European, simply from the fact of contact and penetration. This is what takes place among the immigrants to the United States. To the American mind the problem of

---

[1] [" Downwards from above " to the English mind seems exactly upside down, if it is intended to express imitation by " those below." EOL]

[2] Slane's trans., *Prolegomènes*, 1861, I, p. 306 f. Ibn Khaldun is thus the first to remark on the social phenomenon of imitation.

[3] See in general my Bibliography on Race Contact at the end of this volume, and for the present position : H. Dubois, *Assimil. ou adaptation, Africa*, II, Jan. 1929, pp. 1–21 ; for a comprehensive view of the whole question, H. de Saussure, *Psychologie de la colonisation française* . . . , Paris, 1899, is to be preferred.

the new arrival's *adjustment* [1] is distressing. His *Americanisation* happens of itself, with difficulty or with ease, as the case may be ; similarly the *Frenchification* of the Spaniard in Algeria. Very soon the assimilated Spaniard despises the newcomer, the *pataouète*, and makes mock of his rusticity.[2]

Imitation may also take place on the suggestion or at the instigation of the colonisers, they either proposing or imposing it. When we speak of " Assimilation " we have in mind this imitation dictated by the conqueror. The word was already in general use in French in the 18th century in the sense of " creating a resemblance ". Enfantin used to denote this process as *affamiliation*. Later the terms *accommodation, acculturation* were used, or, more frequently, *adaptation*.

When imitation is *spontaneous* it takes place without any prompting by the conqueror, simply from voluntarily copying his example. Here, race contact by itself, by the mere fact that it occurs in a " new country ", becomes a means of diffusing and unifying manners and customs. In this case one could speak of the native as " rallying " to our ideas. It may even happen—as we see in North Africa—that the native apes the ways of Europeans who are not the conquerors. The effect of the conquerors' immigration in that case, is, not that the native learns to copy their manners and customs, but that he adopts the ways of other Europeans who have entered the country by the grace and favour of the dominating conqueror. In North Africa the natives are fond of playing cards—despite the Quran—but they play with Spanish, not with French cards. After a hundred years of French occupation in Algeria, they are still playing *ronda* ! The reason is that the devices on the Spanish packs are derived from Arab iconography ; they are the heraldic symbols of the old Moorish sultans—swords, bowls and coins—which are still national symbols for the Algerian Arab. This is one of the cases where assimilation bears no relation to conquest. Imitation is governed by laws ; there is an *attraction* of like to like or at least to the less unlike. In this way, the Arab takes kindly to the French shirt, which is not unlike his own *gandura*, but less willingly to French trousers.[3]

It may happen that the native borrows the European's ways

---

[1] See W. J. Thomas and E. Zanicki's great investigation into Polish adaptation, *The Polish Peasant in Europe and in America*, 5 vols., Boston, 1918–20, especially Vol. V.

[2] See the life-like portraits in Louis Bertrand's novels.

[3] P. Lapie, *Les civilisations tunisiennes*, Paris, 1898, p. 60 f. This is almost the only attempt that has been made to formulate the laws that govern assimilation.

even when the latter is most unwilling to lend them for this purpose.[1] In this case the native becomes " assimilated " in a way which to us seems undesirable, and takes from us something which we do not consider suitable for export. He has learnt, for instance, to found professional trade unions and to go on strike. He has taken a great leap : from the Tribe to the Trade Union ! So we have seen the native modernise himself in most unexpected ways, by no means always welcome to the European. The native's ambition to imitate the European is by no means regulated by our wishes. The French law which accords the Algerian the right of option between French and Muslim law, is a recognition of the fact that he is apt to learn of his own accord the lessons of his conqueror. He uses this right too seldom for our taste, for reasons which I shall presently discuss. Yet we can quote cases where the native has voluntarily opted for French law. If he applies for and obtains naturalisation, thereby becoming a French citizen, he is compelled to renounce the personal law which has hitherto regulated his life : he is therefore forced to prove that he feels an urge spontaneously and easily to imitate the French conqueror ; he is bound to show that he can " Frenchify " himself without being invited or urged to do so.

What motives prompt this voluntary and sometimes daring imitation, even in cases where there is no great sympathy between rulers and ruled ? I recognise three main motives : an impulse of *admiration*, a craving for *distinction*, a movement towards *emancipation*.

It is—occasionally !—to testify the *admiration* he feels for the victor, which impels the defeated, especially if he is himself a fighting man, to abandon his own manners and customs, and which converts the ruled into the assimilated subject. Amongst certain races, you must, if you want to win their hearts, first conquer them by force of arms : imitation then expresses admiration.

More often, however, spontaneous imitation springs from a desire for *distinction*. This is the same social phenomenon which we note in the relations of towns, provinces, classes and nations. The coloured man distinguishes himself, and rises in the social scale, when he imitates the white, in proportion as he thus cuts himself off from his fellows and separates himself from his like. Assimilating himself to the white man, means dis-similating him-

[1] A similar problem arises in Japan : H. Yokoyama, *L'assimilation des idées étrangères par l'esprit japonais, Le Monde nouveau*, Oct. 1927 ; Basil H. Chamberlain, *Things Japanese.*

self from his brothers of yesterday, and taking leave of the herd. This social-climbing-by-mimicry is the method by which the *élite*, or the pseudo-*élite*, try to increase their own importance. Those who have acquired wealth freely make use of it and the enrichment, often unforeseen enrichment, of the native [1] has paved the way to assimilation. It was this craving for personal distinction which led to the Oriental imitation of our European orders of knighthood : Turkey led the way in imitating them by founding the Order of the Crescent in 1799. . . .[2] All this is in order to gain, as it were, a diploma bearing witness to your being an assimilated or a civilised person. To dress yourself as a European is equivalent to wearing a decoration. In the same way, the working man used to imitate the middle class, or in olden days the bourgeois the aristocrat. In this craving for distinction, for a higher position on the social, if not on the moral ladder, we find a powerful incentive to imitation.

Finally, we find imitation appearing, more recently, as a means of achieving *emancipation*. By copying the conquerors, the imitator is methodically and systematically endeavouring to shake himself free of them. You draw inspiration from them to use it for your own deliverance ; this is deliberate, calculated imitation. You go to school to the European, to seek out the secret of his victory in order to overthrow the victor. We see this motive at work in Islamic countries : their " modernism " has often no other aim, though they choose to call it " Economic Pan-Islamism ". The purpose is to introduce into Islam all the economic " progress " of Europe which, it is thought, is the key to her power.[3] You repurchase the colonists' land, often on a large scale, to rewin from the Infidel the territory of the Believer, *dar al Islam*. In other cases you found banks, the Muslim theologians obligingly acquiescing—despite the Quran—in the exaction of interest on capital ; banks which are intended to compete with European banks. Such is the *Misr* Bank, the " patriotic bank " designed to rival the National Bank (that is, the British bank) which is trying to create industries managed by Egyptians not by foreigners. This is the idea underlying *imitation for the sake of emancipation*. This is particularly to be seen in Turkey. The *Ghazi* Mustafa Kemal's policy had no other aim

---

[1] M. de Mercier, *L'étonnante fortune des Indiens Osages, Revue mondiale,* June 1, 1929, pp. 291–99 (oil-wells). On Bedouin enriched by the War, and the *camel-boom* in Arabia, see Austin Kennett, *Bedouin Justice* . . . , Cambridge, 1925, Chap. VIII.
[2] [The Order of the Garter was founded by Edward III of England between 1346 and 1351 ; the Order of the Bath by Henry IV in 1399. EOL]
[3] See above, p. 50.

than to "modernise" the Turks, to establish a new Tanzimat,[1] as we should formerly have called it, and to stultify European enterprise.[2]

Imitation is also often *induced*. Rightly or wrongly, the coloniser has then stimulated it by appropriate methods. It is frequently the traveller or the professor coming from outside who, often unwittingly, sets a new fashion. A new outlook was thus introduced even into the seclusion of the harem by governesses from the West, who were largely responsible for the growth of Muslim feminism.[3] The most important agents in promoting assimilation or conversion have been people inspired by the rationalism or the absolutism of the Latins, people who believe that Man is everywhere the same and that there are certain, human, "civilised" manners and customs which it is a duty to impose on primitive peoples. If necessary, we must, in short, make the native happy in spite of himself. Induced, compulsory assimilation is an ancient, obsolete form of colonisation. The American ethnologist, Clark Wissler, goes so far as to assert that colonisation is nothing but "organised diffusion". It is indeed true that legislators and, following them, administrators, have normally—perhaps disastrously—been possessed by the desire to assimilate and civilise those whom they governed, whether with or against the natives' will. The Romans in their day attempted it.[4]

This prescribed or induced imitation shows two degrees. It may be merely *suggested* or prompted, where the colonisers proceed by persuasion or by education ; when they try to reason and indoctrinate, hoping to assimilate with the goodwill of the people. Or it may be *compulsory* or commanded, where they exercise practical or legal pressure and strive to compel the adoption of their laws.

Imitation at least *suggested*. It has been said that colonisation is always a Crusade ; let us, rather, simply say that it is always a form of propaganda. The idea is an old one ; it emerges clearly in the famous Bull of Alexander VI[5] which states that men should colonise not merely to enrich themselves or magnify

---

[1] [A reforming Edict of Abdul Mejid, 1839. EOL]

[2] P. Gentizon, *Mustapha Kemal ou l'Orient en marche*, Paris, 1930, gives the details of the reforms.

[3] This phenomenon as seen in Egypt is described by Niya Salima (Mme H. Rouchdy Pacha) in her book, *Les répudiées*, Paris, 1908 ; see also my *Bibliographie . . . de l'Égypte*, Cairo, 1918, Nos. 6071 and 6078.

[4] F. Charvériat, *De l'assimilation des indigènes dans l'Afrique romaine*, *Revue algérienne de législation . . .* , 1886, pp. 45–60 ; and S. Gsell, *Histoire ancienne de l'Afrique du Nord*, Paris, 1913.   [5] See footnote above, p. 22, n.1.

themselves, but to preach morals and to teach. Amongst the conditions, under which the Pope gave to the conquerors the grant of the New World, was the stipulation that they must make it their duty to manifest to the new countries the splendour of the Christian faith. The conception of assimilation and conversion which this famous document reveals, was later to assume more childish forms. It had its exaggerations and aberrations, at the hands both of missionaries and officials. A singular book, *The Confessions of a Conjuror*,[1] published in 1858 by the famous Robert Houdin, is worth reading in this connection. The Emperor sent him to Algeria to expose the trickery of the native witch-doctors or *marabuts* and to convince the Algerians by his skilful conjuring tricks that the " powers " of their living saints were natural, not supernatural. Robert Houdin did not succeed. He has quaintly told the story of his disappointment.

Propaganda was thus not confined to the economic sphere, but invaded the mystic and liturgical sphere as well. Imitation, recommended, advised, suggested, but not imposed, may be achieved by two methods : most often by advice, but also by gifts or presents.

By *Advice*. The part which the official or the colonist is in general expected to play is to be the social instructor of the native, and gently to induce him spontaneously to adopt our civilisation. There is no lack of passages in their speeches painting the beneficent rôle of the colonisers. The French administrators fulfil their task nobly, but assuredly not with ease. It is their job, amongst other things, to persuade or educate the natives ; to convince them that it is to their advantage to adopt French ways and to accept French laws. This is the important part which the official plays in French colonial countries, where in his sessions he preaches in his own way, and exhorts the people over whom he rules, in his *shikayahs* in North Africa, in his palavers in West Africa. You can see him at work in the book I have already quoted by the " Aofien " Gaston Joseph, the *Manuel des Palabres*, which skilfully indicates the difficulty of educating the Negro. It takes a very long time to persuade the black man that it is not a good idea to keep a corpse in the house ; that it is bad to divorce a wife without cause ; that it is ugly to over-indulge in alcohol in the competitive drinking bouts which the Africans consider honourable and praiseworthy. You have to coax them into paying the tax, their name for which indicates their attitude

[1] *Les confidences d'un prestidigitateur.*

of mind ; they call it " the fine " : considering it a judgment of Heaven inflicted through the agency of the European. You have to induce them to allow themselves to be counted for census purposes. They have a great horror of anything in the nature of a census. They believe that counting them foreshadows proscription or persecution or taxation. They also believe that counting them offends their gods ; they have in fact a census-taboo. So it was in Old Testament times where a counting of heads was reckoned a grievous sin ; [1] and is there not a French proverb which says : " The wolf devours the counted sheep " ? [2] Or if you set about trying to vaccinate them, they think you are working black magic on them ! You have got somehow to convince the native that these unexpected manifestations of our civilisation are meant to bring him good and not ill. You have to convince him—and this is if possible yet more difficult—not to offer a French official gifts of wine, and that the official who refuses such presents is an honourable man, not an object of contempt. This is a misunderstanding which constantly arises : to refuse a gift seems to the native an unpardonable insult !

Yet it may happen that imitation is suggested, not by advice but by the giving of a *gift*. So it is sometimes the colonisers themselves who have encouraged the natives' love of presents. This was the case of missionaries, especially Anglo-Saxon ones, who in Egypt, in Algeria and in West Africa obtained conversions by the distribution of gifts. I know a certain mission among the Copts in Upper Egypt where each conversion has its price ; it costs the mission only a guinea to breathe the Holy Spirit into a new Christian : this is : . . . the culminating triumph of St. George. Let us admit that these bogus conversions sometimes smooth the path to genuine conversion ; progress is from without to within, and the gesture leads to the idea. It is a simpler and easier business to pay the native to cover his nakedness and teach him to appreciate all the advantages of clothes . . . nordic and modest as they are. And this, at the very moment when " nudism " is being boosted at home.

The conqueror then sets about compelling the native to be assimilated. When Nicolas de Villegagnon had native women in Brazil thrashed to make them wear clothes, he brutally initiated the policy of compulsory assimilation.[3] In our own day too

---

[1] [II Samuel, 24, and I Chronicles, 21. EOL]
[2] J. G. Frazer, *Folklore in the Old Testament*, London, 1918, Vol. II, p. 555 f.
[3] Bayle, *Dictionnaire* . . . , s.v. *Villegaignon*, 2nd Ed. 1702, Vol. III, p. 2963 f.

similar action has been taken by means of legislation, even indeed by persecution. The French have asserted the principle that native traditions must be respected, thinking thus to solve the problem by denying its existence. The text of French laws lays down that the native is permitted to retain his customs and must not be compelled to give them up. But this solution has not proved final. It has been found necessary in certain cases—which grow ever more numerous—to constrain the natives to observe French law ; the principle of respect for native custom is subject to an increasing number of exceptions. To arrive at this point, the idea of law and order has been invoked. In France there exists a national public order, so too there ought to prevail in the colonies a colonial public order, or an imperial public order. There are laws which ought to apply to all ; and there ought to be in the colonies, as in France, *territorial* laws, absolute laws, no longer merely personal laws such as govern the tribe. From this standpoint many native customs have been abolished or at least reformed. It did not seem possible to reconcile some indigenous practices with colonial law and order. How was it possible to acquiesce in the parents arranging a forced marriage between tiny children, the right of *jabr* which is sanctioned by Islam ?[1]   Was it possible to condone the sacrifice of the widow on her husband's death, the rite of *suttee* which was current in India, China, Japan and Java ?[2]   This custom the English thought to have abolished as early as 1829, leaving the widow the option of voluntarily immolating herself on her husband's pyre, but forbidding her being compelled to do so, as Hindu law enjoined. Must we acquiesce in slavery ?—slavery, which the Africans invented and practised long before we did, and which, even to-day, has not completely disappeared, and persists especially in Negro countries. Finally, how can we accept cannibalism [3] and infanticide, even if they masquerade as religious rites ?[4]   In all these questions, and many others, is it not our duty to interfere—if necessary with authority—to abolish barbarous customs ?   The ancient indigenous rulers were driven to doing so ; the sultans of Morocco tried to impose more advanced

---

[1] On this point see R. Maunier, *Loi française et coutume indigène en Algérie*, Paris, 1932.

[2] Montaigne, *Essais*, Book II, Chap. 29 ; Dubois, *Mœurs . . . des peuples de l'Inde*, Paris, 1825, II, p. 18 f. ; Ebert, *Reallexikon der Vorgeschichte*, XIII, 1929, s.v. *Witwentötung* by Wilke.

[3] [Interesting light on religious cannibalism is thrown by Tom Harrisson in his *Savage Civilisation*. EOL]

[4] Westermarck, . . . *Moral Ideas*, II, London, 1908, p. 553 f.

manners and customs on the Berber tribes; and even the Negro empires pursued a policy of assimilation.

This is not by any means to imply that native customs should always and everywhere be abolished. Far from it. There are many native laws and customs far too deep-rooted and too highly respected to be touched. There are laws of theirs too which we could not dream of applying to French subjects. We could not justly forbid the natives to marry under eighteen, without taking account of the tropical climate. Nor could we forbid poly-gamy [1]—though simple bigamy is with us punished as a crime. " The best man", says Al Bukhari, "is he who has had most wives " ! [2] We cannot forbid the natives to go about naked, which is frequently their natural right, and which many ancient authors have held to be a sign of virtue ; there has been praise in plenty for " the naked ". Can we forbid them to hold the head of the family or tribe responsible for a crime as well as the actual culprit ? The culprit himself would not understand this point of view. All such questions are the very stuff of conflicts which will persist and which cannot always be solved by authority.

Spontaneous diffusion, induced diffusion, suggested diffusion or, it may be, compulsory diffusion ; whichever form it takes, diffusion it remains, whereby the conqueror is bound, *nolens volens*, to civilise. Even if he is a destroyer, as he too often was in olden times, he is nevertheless a civiliser,[3] whether he will or no. For he brings the natives not only *prosperity*, not only *security*, but also, and always, be it sooner or later, he brings them *unity*. Unity of manners and customs, unity of laws by the spread of the conqueror's own ways and his own laws. The personal régime gives place to a realist régime, the parental code to the territorial code. In earlier days every tribe had its own code, but the diffusion of the new law provides a law common to all, which henceforth governs all. This is the public order, or the common law and order, which the European comes to bring to the native. Just as the Romans long ago gave a common law to the Gauls, and put an end to their tribal divisions, so, in our time, our colonisers bring to native populations the great boon of unified law, the hall-mark of progress.

[1] Father W. Schmidt, *Die Behandlung der Polygamie in unseren Kolonien, Verhandlung der deutschen Kolonialkongress*, Berlin, 1902, pp. 467–79.

[2] [Al Bukhari (810–72) is the compiler of the most generally accepted collection of the Traditions (*hadith*) from the days of the Prophet. His *Sahih* forms a complete system of jurisprudence, the earliest of its kind. It enjoys among Muslims a sanctity second only to that of the Quran. EOL]

[3] The word *civilisateur* is used for the first time, as far as I know, by Lamartine, *Le civilisateur, journal historique*, Paris, 1852.

CHAPTER XI

RESULTS OF IMITATION BY THE INFERIOR

In its effects, as in its methods, imitation of the colonisers by the colonised takes various forms according as it is *technical, linguistic, juridical, political* or *theological*.

Technical. Technical imitation, or diffusion of an industrial nature, at first takes place separately, in isolation, without concurrent imitation in other spheres. Tools and manufactured goods are the things which the native most readily accepts. He can normally take them over without any apparent infringement of his traditions. When a well-to-do citizen of Cairo plants a glass-fronted cabinet in French suburban style in the very centre of his " drawing-room ", he has no feeling that he thereby ceases to be a good Egyptian and a good Musulman. In the same way, when the King of Wagadugu in Haute-Volta [1] claims to be the only person entitled to look at himself in the mirror of his wardrobe, this does not make him an " assimilated " person. The wheelbarrow has penetrated in this way into French West Africa —a great step forward for the negroes ; and the plough, a typ specially designed for shallow work, has been gladly adopted by the Bambaras and the Peuls of Senegal. In other colonies the motor-car has become a commonplace. There are wealthy negroes in the Sudan, black *nouveaux riches,* who drive about in their Rolls-Royces. In 1915 there was not a single motor-car in the Republic of Haiti, for the simple reason that there was not a single road, but in 1927—only twelve years later—there were twelve thousand ; which shows that in a new country technical penetration may be very pronounced and very rapid.

But there is a tool—if we may dignify it by that name—whose diffusion repays careful examination ; for it seems to me the symbol of the eagerness with which the natives adopt and adapt our inventions. I mean the petrol tin which spreads everywhere throughout all the Mediterranean countries, [2] and is put to the most unexpected uses. Amongst villagers and nomads, in the hut or in the tent, everywhere that a traveller

---

[1] [Wagadugu is the chief town of Haute-Volta, one of the eight provinces of French West Africa. EOL]

[2] [Throughout the Near and Middle East, no less in India and in the Himalayas —everywhere. EOL]

has been able to go, you will find in some obscure corner or another : the petrol tin. It serves as a container ; women drawing water on the banks of the Nile carry it on their heads in place of the graceful pottery jars of yester-year. In Egypt it is also used as a scoop or bucket for the *noria* or the *sakiah*, the water-wheel turned by the blinded oxen to raise the water for the fields. In Algeria, a pair of petrol tins—the *shuari*—have superseded the ancient panniers on donkey-back. The petrol tin serves as cooking-stove, replacing the *qanun* of baked clay for the open-air kitchen. It is even used to build walls ! They used to build light walls of pots in Egypt ; they build them now with petrol tins. At no great distance from Algiers you may see native huts built of adapted petrol tins : a testimony to the practical advantages of European products. The age-old *shaduf*, the primitive machine based on the lever principle, that is common in Mediterranean areas, for raising irrigation water, now uses a petrol tin as counter-weight. I have even seen in Arab cafés a petrol tin irregularly pierced with holes, doing duty as a lantern. In the Greek islands the petrol tin is cut up and turned into a fan for blowing the fire. Here and there it is even used as a shower-bath. From this especially-choice example we can see that the spread of inventions may involve their reproduction, their transformation or their conversion to new purposes ; they are adopted but also adapted. The same applies also to *clothing* : shoes may be adopted but not hats—a partial and eclectic imitation.[1] We notice the same thing in *housing*. The architecture in Algerian towns, and even in Kabyle villages, is growing more French to the eye—despite the regrets of those who love the past,[2]—but much more from motives of vanity than from considerations of practical utility !

Linguistic and Æsthetic. Linguistic—and also æsthetic—imitation is one variety which is evident from the very first. The adoption of words runs parallel to the adoption of things. It is well recognised to-day that Semitic words occur in the Negro languages. It is conjectured that the Phœnicians introduced their language into North Africa and that caravans carried Phœnician terms as far south as the Sudan.[3] I have already alluded to the theory, recently propounded, that certain West

---

[1] G. Marcais, *Le costume musulman à Alger*, Paris, 1930 (study in transformations).

[2] Ern. Feydeau, *Alger*, Paris, 1862, has protested against the vandalism of the rebuilders. Native financial delegates have recently appealed to the Administration for a plan to improve Algerian architecture.

[3] M. Delafosse, *Les noirs de l'Afrique*, Paris, 1922, p. 32 f.

African languages may have sprung from Egyptian. In more recent times the founding of the great Inca Empire resulted in an assimilation of languages ; [1] the speech of the conquerors spread simultaneously with the conquest itself. It is hardly necessary to-day to recall how the colonisation of North Africa promoted an exchange of words between the colonisers and the inhabitants. In every colonised country, colonisation gives birth to these *sabirs* or mixed languages, a blend of European and native words : *pidgin-English* in the Far East ; *bêche de mer* in Oceania ; the *Chinook jargon* in the United States. These bastard languages are a kind of slang or jargon produced from the rough and ready collaboration of immigrant traders and the natives, and are the earliest medium of communication between them. Nowadays reciprocal contamination is more effectively produced by the *newspaper* : Arabs, Negroes and American Indians have nowadays their own papers, published in their own dialects, but European words inevitably creep into them.[2] And attempts have been planned and even tried to substitute the Latin alphabet for the Arabic script.[3]

Juridical and Political Imitation. It is, however, imitation in the legal and political spheres which it is more especially our business to examine. When we talk of assimilation in our speeches or discussions, it is this we have chiefly in mind. We are thinking of the transference to the native of European institutions, whether of a private or more especially of a public nature. Like every form of transference this may arise by *spontaneous* imitation, *induced* imitation or *compulsory* imitation. This is the end desired by those people—who tend more and more to gain the upper hand—who seek to assimilate the natives on the legal plane, and to make Europeans or Frenchmen of them, if not in mind—which is of course not in our power—at least in the matter of rights and duties. Our French subjects seem, for the most part, keener to welcome our manufactures than to accept our manners and customs or to obey our laws. Nevertheless, they frequently acquiesce with a good grace in the propagation—or

[1] And also the exchange of literary subject-matter. See Elsie Parsons, *Der spanische Einfluss auf die Märchen der Pueblo Indianer, Zeitsch. für Ethnol.*, 1926, Nos. 1–2 (Spanish elements in the tales of the Pueblo, in the south-west of the United States). I have here space only to draw attention to the subject, which deserves to be studied in its entirety.

[2] B. Chatterjee, *Origin and Growth of Journalism among Indians, Annals of the American Academy of Political . . . Science*, Sept. 1929, pp. 161–8. For the Negro and Arab Press, see above, pp. 46 and 49.

[3] M. Wood, *Latinising the Turkish Alphabet, American Journal of Sociology*, Sept. 1929, pp. 194–203.

in the " propaganda " as it is called—of our legal and political institutions. Great Eastern countries, long since exposed to European influence, have spontaneously adopted our laws. In Egypt and in Turkey, in Japan and Siam, and more recently in Afghanistan, we have seen Oriental States asking of their own accord for our French codes, and appealing to our French experts to give their laws " a European flavour ". The reforms of Mustafa Kemal in Turkey are the culmination of a century and a half of modernising effort ; this is too easily forgotten when people express themselves as amazed at his success. In this type of phenomenon there are fashions and enthusiasms as in other phenomena. In the most primitive countries, and even among actual barbarians, we have long since been able to observe a gradual infiltration of Western law ; which may well appear more surprising still. It is easy to imagine that the Egyptian,[1] the Turk, the Japanese, the Annamite [2] or the Persian —who has changed not a little since the days of Montesquieu— may feel disposed to accept our French laws and to welcome our professors of law ; and even that he should be inclined to *combine*, as in fact he does, the codes of various European countries to distil therefrom to his own benefit the quintessence of perfection. I have myself collaborated in this work. Such a code will be elaborated by taking one article from our French codes, another from a German, yet another from a Swiss code ; so that, without a trace of paradox, it is in an Oriental country that we find the most advanced codes of law. It is quite another thing when we are dealing with primitive or pseudo-primitive races, where colonisation is in progress. How can an African negro appropriate to himself our French institutions ? Can they then be imposed on him, or even proposed to him ? Yet history, none the less, demonstrates that he accepts them, that he even desires them, that he often appeals for them. From the mere fact that he has had contact with the immigrant colonist, the savage has been known to abandon the tradition of his tribe and voluntarily take his place under national law.

As early as the 18th century, after the French had been occupying and penetrating Canada for more than a hundred years, certain Red Indian peoples thus requested and obtained from our legislators a Constitution on the French model. It was

[1] To estimate the degree of imitation here, see J. Aziz, *Concordance des Codes égyptiens . . . avec le Code Napoléon . . .* , Alexandria, 1886–9.
[2] See J. Leclerc, *De l'évolution . . . des institutions annamites . . . sous l'influence française,* Rennes, 1923 (Law thesis).

in the days when Pasquale was begging Rousseau to give Corsica a constitution that, round about 1760, the Oneidas,[1] an Indian tribe, neighbours of the Iroquois, asked Count de Moustier, the French Minister in Canada, for a Constitution. He drew it up for them, and the text has fortunately been preserved. It was a Rousseau-inspired constitution designed for Universal Man and not expressly for Primitive Man. It started from the conception of the Sovereignty of the People with direct government in the hands of the Annual Assembly of the savages, in which the majority enjoyed absolute power. According to the Oneida Constitution the legislative power lay in the hands of the Assembly ; while the executive power—on Montesquieu's principles : not Rousseau's—lay with a Grand Council, appointed for three years with an elected Head. The Council's powers were to be exercised by Representative Agents who were to bear the curious titles of a Grand Bailiff, a Censor General and a Director of Education. That was how the French hoped to transplant—without success in this particular case—the ideas of their philosophers into primitive American soil. If nothing else, this abortive experiment teaches us that both Europeans and Indians spontaneously conceived it possible to convert the Law of the Tribe into the Law of the Nation ! It is, moreover, the proof of the belief, long held, that imitation may arise without pressure of any kind. We have at least been able to see how, at a later date, the natives throughout the Oceanic world of Indonesia allowed the laws devised by the missionaries for them,[2] to be imposed on them without their striking a blow. So too, formerly, in Paraguay the missionaries played the part of legislators and were able without arms to enforce their laws.

We can see the same thesis upheld from different motives by the American Negro of to-day. When the Negro, Dr. Du Bois, of whom I have already spoken, who is himself a reader of Rousseau, applies the postulates of democracy to the black man's claims, and ventures to base the justice of their case on the majority principle, he is only borrowing from the white Americans, and turning against them, the weapon of their sacred

---

[1] See de Montbas, *Avec Lafayette chez les Iroquois*, Paris, 1929, pp. 107 f. and 118 f. (texts). For the Constitution of Orlie I in Araucania (1860) see M. de Villiers du Terrage : *Rois sans couronne* . . . , Paris, 1906, p. 339 f.

[2] Texts in : P. Lesson, *Voyage autour du monde* . . . , Paris, 1839, I, p. 437 f., and in W. Ellis, *Polynesian Researches*, London, 1831, III, p. 175 f. For Madagascar : G. Borrel, *Le Code des 305 articles* . . . , Paris, 1931. As early as the 16th century in India the Roman Church was anxious to interfere with the caste system : J. Castets, *L'Église et le problème de la caste*, Revue d'histoire des missions, Dec. 1930,

dogma. He extends to the Black Man the Declaration of the Rights of Man drawn up by the White Man for himself. The fact that the French have, themselves, been able here and there strongly to modify native custom, and that they have recently been able by a decree of the Commissary of the Republic to touch the question of " fetish marriage " in the Cameroons, is proof that French ideas had already penetrated the native mind.

Theological Imitation. There is, lastly, imitation of a liturgic nature or imitation on the theological plane. The diffusion of religious cults, otherwise called *conversion*,[1] seems to me to be contemporaneous with colonisation itself. It seems clear that in prehistoric times objects of worship circulated in just the same way as industrial products, not only from country to country, but probably also from continent to continent. We are particularly well informed about what happened towards the end of the Roman Empire when *Syncretism* arose—as it was then wrongly thought, for the first time—namely a blend of different faiths, parallel to a blend of different legal systems. The blending took place in both directions, for the religious rites and gods of the Romans were bestowed on the Africans, while later the rites and the gods of the Africans were taken over by the Latins. Wherever they went, the Romans carried with them their gods and their *sacra*. The first monument they erected in their cities beyond the seas was the Capitol, the dwelling-place of the gods. Soon, alongside their national gods and their indigenous Latin gods, they were worshipping the gods of their new subjects.[2] Thus it came about that in the last days of the Roman Empire a Pantheon had been created, where Roman and Oriental gods sat side by side, in wary, wondering intimacy. Here was conversion in both directions, brought about in certain cases by voluntary adherence, in others, by suggestion or under pressure. The Romans carried on religious propaganda concurrently with military conquest.

I have also reminded you how, at the very end of the 15th century, the idea of conversion was intimately linked with the very thought of conquest. In those days colonisation without conversion was not even dreamed of ; it seemed that the propagation of the faith lent sanctity to conquest. When the last

---

[1] The fundamental authority is the large work of Raoul Alliers, *La psychologie de la conversion chez les non-civilisés*, Paris, 1925. For the discussions and controversies reference must be made to the history of missions.—Roman Catholic : A. Kannengiesser, *Les missions catholiques françaises*, Paris, 1900 ; and the *Revue d'histoire des missions*, since June 1924.—Protestant : P. Pisani, *Les missions protestantes à la fin du XIXᵉ siècle*, Paris, 1903, and the monthly *Journal des missions évangéliques*.

[2] See below, p. 114.

Crusade was being organised, the worthy Joinville, chronicler to King Louis IX, used to speak of " attracting to our faith " the native Africans. This is how colonisation was thought of in olden days : as a work of evangelisation as well as of organisation. The Europeans were, however, not the first so to conceive it ; they had their forerunners. Before the Christianisation of Africa or Asia could be spoken of, there was the Islamisation of the Middle Ages to consider. Islam carried on religious as well as warlike conquest ; to-day it embraces three-quarters of the universe. Believers in the ancient Quran are to be found scattered from the western coasts of Africa as far as the islands of Japan. It is the first example of a religion spreading across immense stretches of territory. Let us note that the Musulman apostles—as, after them, we must admit, the Christian apostles also—not infrequently carried out their conversions by armed force. These are aspects of French history too easily overlooked. You have but a poor grasp of African history if you forget that in the course of these last centuries it has been dominated by the struggle between Islam and Christianity : [1] a clash of two religious imperialisms, rather than of two national imperialisms.

As for this Christianisation, which we must not omit to discuss, this is now the place to consider its conditions and note its results. What then is this conversion ? What factors are necessary to produce it ? By what means is it achieved ? Are not Europeans under some illusion about it ? Is conversion a genuine conversion ; is it a real adoption, a true allegiance, or is it not rather an adaptation, a distortion ? Does it not bear two entirely different meanings in the Christian mind and in the mind of the fetish-worshipper, or the idolater, as we call him—or used to call him ? When we think of converting a pagan, and when he thinks of himself being converted, he and we have two totally different, irreconcilable views of the process, for the simple reason that our two states of mind are foreign to each other, and that the primitive's logic and his moral code are quite other than ours. I confine myself here to raising the question, calling attention only to the fact that it is one problem for the Musulman and quite another for the " idolater ". Having at one point hoped to Christianise the Muslims,[2] people have almost completely abandoned all hope of succeeding ; and in some countries, notably the Sunda Islands, the authorities have themselves for-

---

[1] G. Bonet-Maury, *L'islamisme et le christianisme en Afrique*, Paris, 1906 ; C. H. Becker, *Islamstudien*, Leipzig, 1924, Vol. I.
[2] (Anon.) *De la conversion des musulmanes au christianisme*, Paris, 1846.

bidden the attempt. In practice, it is only among fetish-worshippers that conversions have been made. And in their case, the conversion is frequently more apparent than real. When the native solemnly confesses his acceptance of the Faith of Christ, the dogma to which he offers his allegiance is one transformed and distorted to his taste.

Yet, let us admit that in certain cases it is perfectly true that conversion is possible, and that the great religions of the West have been able to win adherents in new countries ; faithful believers who nobly deserve the title and who have sometimes suffered martyrdom for confessing their faith. It would be futile to deny the genuineness of such converts ! Furthermore, there have been some amongst the idolaters, and even amongst the Musulmans, who have shown no trace of fear in publicly renouncing their religion. There was one at least who published a book in which he attacked the religion he had abandoned. He was a Muslim who had become a Christian, one Jean-Marie Arifi, whose book is a damning indictment of Islam.[1]

Such cases, it seems to me, are extreme cases. When we think of primitive pagans whose mental processes are so remote from ours, we are compelled to wonder whether they are suitable subjects for any conversion worthy of the name.

This brings us to consider the *limits* of imitation. Though there is always imitation of the conquering people by the con-quered, this imitation has its frontiers and its confines. These borrowings by one people from another, which are hailed as an explanation of progress, these borrowings which by no means explain everything, themselves require an explanation. Imita-tion comes up against *distortion* and against *opposition*.

First, imitation is limited by *Distortion*,[2] or adulteration, whereby the borrowed customs are more or less transformed. In this connection the Germans make use of two terms for which French offers no exact equivalent : " Wanderung ", they tell us, entails " Wandlung " : to transfer is to transform. Circulation and distortion are synonymous. We can observe this in all four spheres of borrowing : technical, linguistic, juridical and theo-logical. In passing from the one language into the other, words change either in form or meaning. It is the same with laws,

---

[1] *L'Anti-Coran, ou le Mahomét. condamné par lui-même* . . . , 2nd Ed., Paris, 1926.

[2] See some just comments in : de Gobineau, *Les religions et les philosophies de l'Asie centrale*, Paris, 1865, Chap. V, and *Trois Ans en Asie* (1859), New Ed., Paris, Vol. II, Chap. VI : " les Asiatiques restent ce qu'ils sont, avec quelques vices de plus." (Asiatics remain what they are, plus a few new vices.)

with tools or products, and with beliefs. I shall quote two examples only, but they are striking ones : the first technical, the second political.

A *technical* example. When French administrators introduced the wheelbarrow into the French Sudan, this marked a great step forward ; they thought it would serve to abolish the fatigue of carrying burdens. The wheelbarrow instead of a load on the head, why, that would be the ideal way to get rid of that disguised form of slavery, the employment of porters. But what happened ? In a very short time the natives took the wheelbarrow to pieces . . . to carry it on their head. The same thing happened in the Chinese Empire. That is how tradition, or routine—as the impatient European exasperated by Negro inertia prefers to call it—results in the misuse of our tools when they pass into primitive hands.

Secondly a *political* example, quoted without over-emphasis. If the conception of the uses of a wheelbarrow inevitably changed when the native took it over, what happened to the conception of an elector ? [1] Even if we can muster sufficient faith to believe that the French elector at home is divinely enlightened by some magic power—one of those " charisms " Max Weber talks of— can we believe this of the Negro voter too ? Not that I should wish to deny them the right of enjoying themselves by taking part in political contests, and finding therein a new entertainment to compensate for the many we have deprived them of. Just watch the proceedings : an election in the colonies is parody and mummery. I have seen voting in Upper Egypt—for they have a Parliament in the Valley of the Nile ; I know full well just what you must do, and what you must not do, if you want to be elected by a constituency of completely illiterate voters.

Imitation is limited also by that opposition which hampers the progress of our ways ; an instinctive, often unconscious resistance on the part of " savages " ; but also, on the part of the more civilised, a methodic, often systematic resistance. This is the *refusal to borrow* : a means of self-defence against the conqueror by breaking a lance for the cause of tradition. This was active in the French provinces of France, long after their absorption into a unified French kingdom. And it is now active in the French colonies. In technics, linguistics, law and theology a prolonged and obstinate defence is often maintained.

[1] See A. Corre, *Nos créoles*, Paris, 1902, Chap. V, and the novel, *La sarabande*, by M. and A. Leblond.

Even in matters of a technical nature—privileged domain of diffusion though it be—we find a reluctance to imitate the tools and products which have found their way into colonial countries. Take the plough, for instance. In North Africa you can see in a corner of the fields the wrecked remains of model ploughs. So too with the windmill : I have already mentioned Napoleon's windmills, long since in ruins. The same story may be told of clothing and food ; food is the very stronghold of local prejudice and local colour.

Similarly in matters of a *legal* nature, whether domestic or political, there is resistance to French innovations. The Algerian native has been granted the opportunity of placing himself under French law, by simple convention or by simple declaration ; he has even the opportunity of becoming a French citizen if he is willing to renounce his own code. Yet he never, or scarcely ever, avails himself of either of these privileges. He clings faithfully to his Quran ; for the true Muslim believer, to change his law is to change his faith. He has no wish to become a French citizen unless he can at the same time retain his personal law.[1] Even in non-Islamic countries the conflict between French law and native custom is overt; the power of the chief over the tribe, of the father over the family, has so far resisted all attempts to shake it.

It is, finally, in matters of a liturgical, or *theological* nature, that diffusion is most completely halted. Since the primitive man's logic and morals are in such complete contrast to civilised man's, since the two have two such different minds and souls, how could the white man's beliefs be acceptable ? Conversion best demonstrates to us the vigour with which religious borrowing is repelled. It has been possible to speak, without inaccuracy, of " crises of conversion " ; and it would be possible to speak in general of " crises of assimilation ".[2] Simply by suffering our infections, the native is shaken ; he enters a mentally critical phase, for he must break with his past, quit the company of his fellows and abandon his tradition. It has been proved that one result of conversion is a mental revolution ; another, if mass conversion occurs, is a social revolution. A personal and a collective crisis supervenes which has sometimes driven the convert to suicide. Even where resistance has broken down and mass conversions have been effected ; even where, in certain cases,

---

[1] See the enquiry into this question begun in French West Africa, by Delafosse : *Enquête sur . . . la famille indigène*, Paris, 1930.

[2] The assimilation crisis has been well mirrored in a novel, *Mansour*, the story of a young Egyptian, by F. Bonjean and Ahmed Deif.

following their King's example, whole peoples have come to find the " True God ", there has always arisen another obstacle to diffusion : the distortion of which I have already spoken. Conversion is not complete and pure conversion. What the native grasps is not what the missionary teaches ; the Christian dogma is curiously refracted in passing through the native mind. In accepting the doctrine of the *Trinity* the black man has believed something quite different from what the missionary intended ; he himself possesses traditions not dissimilar to the doctrine of the Trinity ; he has felt able to preserve his own traditions and avoid becoming an apostate. This has often been due to a misunderstanding. Who will make a study of misunderstanding or formulate the theory of the give-and-take in the colonies ? When you speak to the natives of the *Duality* of soul and body, this is not, as you imagine, a new doctrine for them ; in their religions, even the most barbarous of their religions, duality is already present. This is why some people have maintained— and far be it from me to judge the question—that amongst the Pygmies, the most primitive of all primitives, there already existed a belief in the " True God ".[1] This shows, to my mind, how easy it is to deceive oneself about native thought. In preaching religious doctrines to them, you must bear in mind that there are other ideas which they take—or which they keep.

Though there are these grave limits to imitation, we must not underestimate its great social influence. It is to imitation that we owe that unification of the human race which increases with time, and which has introduced the native mind to our ideas of equity, equality and humanity which will ultimately—as philosophers have dreamt—become universal. We bring as a gift to the savage of the idea of personality, of individuality, the conception of the dignity of Man as such, which the savage in the grip of his tribe could never have even suspected. That ought, I think, to be credited to our account. When in our own day Mahatma Gandhi, the deified Hindu prophet, struggles against the English in India, his doctrine has come to him from us. He preaches the rights of the individual after us and according to us. This is a European, not an Asiatic idea. His theories of asceticism are Christian and Tolstoian as much as Indian. In indicting the European, Gandhi is pitting Europe against Europe. It is in the light of Western teaching that he denounces the sin and the crime of the West !

[1] Father W. Schmidt, *Origine de l'idée de Dieu*, French trans., Paris, 1930.

CHAPTER XII

IMITATION BY THE SUPERIOR OF THE INFERIOR

Imitation by the inferior by no means precludes—though Tarde forgot this—imitation by the superior. It is the return-shock which occurs in colonies : reciprocal transmission or cross-transmission : imitation in two directions, distortion in two directions. Already in classic times the East penetrated the West ; Greeks [1] and Romans [2] were contaminated by the gods and the manners of Asia ; and old Herodotus thought he had discovered in the countries of the Levant the source of all wisdom. There has long been denunciation in France of the " degradation " of the civilised by the primitives. Montesquieu pointed to it. Sermons and adjurations have long been addressed to French colonists urging them to protect themselves against evil example " from below ", which they are never able to avoid. " Face to Face with Islam " [3] is the title of a book which caused some little stir, and whose text was that the Latins should with all their might resist the seduction and the prestige of Islam.

Writers have dwelt on this contamination of the conqueror by the conquered. For more than half a century they have been satirising colonists and colonial society, never failing to emphasise those elements in the colonists' life which they have very obviously taken over from the native. From Daudet to Robert Randau, they have all painted a highly-coloured picture of the French or Spanish immigrant as he appears to us, falling a victim especially in Algeria to the contagious manners of local life.

In this, we note once more the analogy between race-relations and class-relations. Just as the so-called " higher " classes have been unable to avoid some imitation of popular manners and customs, the conquering peoples have been equally unable to avoid some imitation of exotic manners and customs. No inventory has yet been compiled of the middle-class ways and aristocratic customs whose origin has been all too willingly

[1] Herodotus, II, 43–5, etc. W. Ramsay, *Asianic Elements in Greek Civilisation*, London, 1927. See below, p. 114.
[2] Juvenal, Satire III, verses 30–4, and F. Cumont's classic work : *Les religions orientales dans le paganisme romain*, 3rd Ed., Paris, 1928.
[3] *Devant l'Islam.*

forgotten, but which have in fact been derived from the humbler classes. Innovations and readjustments have frequently been going on, working upwards from below. It has become the fashion to " approach the people " and to borrow their ways ; in the hope of thus finding refreshment and renewed youth. Under the Old Régime in France the rustic gavotte became a favourite dance at Court, and the lackey's game of *lansquenet* was adopted by " respectable " card-players. We are always confronted by the same sociological problem.

From this point onwards, imitation by the superior [1] follows the same lines as imitation by the inferior. It is possible to observe these two varieties of imitation running parallel, in their forms, their causes and their effects. We meet the same phenomena again.

The *Forms* of imitation. The spread of the white man's manners and customs amongst coloured people takes place, as we have said, now as a personal, now as a collective phenomenon ; in exactly the same way, the penetration of native manners and customs into European circles is either personal or collective.

At the very beginning such imitation is *personal*. It is isolated colonists who in the first instance catch the infection. It was the individual traveller, the pioneer, the " bushranger ", whom I spoke of earlier, who used to live wholly in native style, and whom missionaries and officials were wont to mistake for a " native " ! They became men of the forest and they developed both the appearance and the mentality of natives. Of such were the buccaneers of the Antilles, hunters who dried by fire the pelts of their quarry ; they returned, without knowing it, to a primitive life, without imagining that they would later pass for a romantic if not heroic type. When warlike conquest took place, other carriers of infection played a part : prisoners, renegades, deserters, carried off by the natives into tribe or camp, men who often spent long years in native circles before being released or ransomed. There was the convict Regnard, a galley-slave in Algiers for instance, and before him Cervantes ; [2]

---

[1] For a general view of the problem, see J. G. Frazer, *The Golden Bough*, 3rd Ed., Part II, *Taboo and the Perils of the Soul*, Chap. VII, *Our Debt to the Savage* ; and A. J. Chamberlain, *The Contribution of the American Indian to Civilisation*, *Proceedings of the American Antiquarian Society*, New York, 1903. See also W. B. Newell (an Indian Mohawk), *Indian Contributions to Modern Civilisation*, *36th Annual Archæological Report*, *Ministry of Education* (*Ontario, Canada*), 1928, pp. 18–26 (*The Iroquois League*, an anticipation of the League of Nations).

[2] [The author of *Don Quixote* was in his young days captured by Barbary corsairs off the coast of Marseilles and taken as prisoner to Algiers, where he spent five years (1575–80) before his family succeeded in ransoming him. EOL]

they brought back words and ideas into their own country. Lastly, the *habitants* or European residents, that is to say the colonists properly so called, in daily and hourly contact with the natives, were, and are, led to adopt some native customs in their daily life. In Algeria we find the colonist wearing the burnous. We also find him making contracts in native style, lending on security by adopting the practice of *rahniyah*, or creating a mortmain by founding a *waqf* :[1] all these procedures are unknown to French law, but they proved convenient to the colonist. In certain cases the law even compels the European to accommodate himself to local customs. In Egypt the law makes it compulsory for a European State-employee to wear the tarbush or fez—the same rule held in Turkey up to the time of Kemal Ataturk.—I have myself worn the fez, and like a good Musulman taken my weekly rest on Friday, instead of Sunday ! Even in a colony or a protectorate, certain local laws may regulate the life of a European.

At a later stage imitation is *collective* also. There is a mass-diffusion, where whole groups, communally, not as individuals, take over native ways. This is seen in colonial societies [2] in which native habits and customs have always been current, without anyone's knowing who was the first to introduce them. Even those colonials in new countries who attempt to keep themselves to themselves, safely entrenched behind invisible walls, those " men from overseas " as Kipling calls them, who seek in their associations and their clubs to live apart from coloured people, even they, despite their efforts and intentions, cannot avoid becoming more or less " gravely " contaminated. At first sight it would appear that colonial " society " is not continental " society " ; that the colonist is no longer the *régnicole* [3] that the French used to call him. The climate affects him, his surroundings affect him, and after a certain time he has become, both physically and morally, a completely different man ; [4] he has

---

[1] F. Laloë, *Un Européen peut-il constituer un wakf en Égypte* ; *Égypte contemporaine,* I, 1910, pp. 585–629.

[2] See in general : Aspe-Fleurimont, *Le colonial, Revue internat. de sociologie,* XVIII, 1910, p. 116 f. ; J. Maigret, *Le colon,* Paris, 1930. In particular : C. M. Andrews, *Colonial Folkways,* New York, 1910 ; P. de Vaissière, *Saint-Domingue, Société et vie créoles* . . . , Paris, 1909 ; E. Bonnefont, *La vie coloniale,* Hanoi (Tong-King), 1907 ; F. Duchêne, *Mouna, Cachir et Couscouss,* Paris (Algeria), 1930.

[3] [*Régnicole,* " One who inhabits the country of his birth, and of which he is a citizen."—Larousse. EOL]

[4] Jauréguiberry, *Les blancs en pays chauds. Déchéance physique et morale,* Paris, 1924. Of many passages in this book one might say to the author : " The people you have killed off are feeling pretty fit ! "

acquired collective habits which set him apart.   When we begin
to observe colonial groups in any new country, we find certain
characteristics reappearing in every case.   Thus, at least in the
beginning, a tendency to *communism*, one aspect of the return
to primitive living which we have noted in the pioneers ;   unlimited mutual help between neighbours in jungle or forest ;
disregard of private property ;   the formation of communities
organised in the style of old-time French Agrarian groups,—
so it was even with the first Virginia Company (1607) and still
more so with the Pilgrim Fathers (1620)—who preserve in
distant lands laws already abolished in their old home-country.[1]
All these things are, at least to a great extent, a reflection of
tribal life, and are due to the identity of place and surroundings.
—There appears also a tendency to *despotism*, often denounced.
It would seem that the colonist has recaptured the taste for
commanding.   He is a chief and he wants to be a chief.   Though
slavery may have disappeared, though the colonist is no longer
in a feudal atmosphere, as he used to be, he wants to remain
a potentate ;   and the native, even when drawing a salary,
remains a servant in his eyes.   This attitude is encouraged by
the colonists' vision of the tyrannies to which the native was
accustomed passively to submit.

Finally, we note a tendency to *sensualism* and to *cynicism*,
shown in the vices which colonials frequently develop from
contact with the natives.[2]   Hashish and opium are certainly
no French inventions ;   nor the vendetta, regular murder of
daily occurrence as in the Far West of early days.   These things
are to a large extent the native's gift to the colonist.   Ossendowski has drawn a terrifying picture of the Russian colonists
in Eastern Asia.   He describes the happenings of the " Tiger
Club " at Novokievsk, where after lights were extinguished
orgiastic scenes were enacted worthy of the most savage savages.
We have heard talk of " coloniality ", the corruption and degradation of the colonist ;   though the phenomenon is by no means
so common as people say, it does nevertheless occur, induced
partly by the climate, partly by the surroundings.

[1] For this " social retrogression " in the colonies, see Tarde, *Les transformations
du droit*, Paris, 1893, Chap. IV ;   A. Loria, *L'importance sociologique des . . . colonies.
Annales Institut international Sociologie*, IV (1897), 1898, pp. 137–66 ;   and various
monographs in the *Johns Hopkins University Studies* of Baltimore (Cape Ann. Salem,
New Amsterdam).—On Socialist Colonies, see Ch. Gide, *Les colonies communistes . . .*,
Paris, 1928.

[2] Desbiefs, *Le vice en Algérie*, Paris, 1899 ;   (Dr. Jacobus X) *L'amour aux colonies,
isngularités . . . observées durant trente années*, Paris, 1893.

For these are the *causes* of the European's imitation of the native : the natural atmosphere and the social atmosphere.

The Natural Atmosphere. We cannot assuredly afford to overlook the influence exercised on the colonist by the climate and the country ; principally in the tropics where the colonists, few in number, are exhausted and decimated by the climate ; where the European temperament, product of the physical as much as of the mental atmosphere of the home-country, tends slowly to dissolve. When French newspapers condemn French colonists for their failings . . . and their excesses, they too easily forget that the colonist is exposed to the effect of a depressing, desiccating climate, "under an arid, hostile, scorching sun" as Émile Verhaeren puts it.

The Social Atmosphere. If in the colonies Europeans are inclined to renounce the law which governs their opposite numbers at home, this is to be accounted for by the composition of their society. Groups of white people in a new country are composed in a peculiar way which explains their vulnerability. The colonial atmosphere is a singular one, singular from three points of view : age, sex, and family.

First, *Age.* Colonists are usually young. They are therefore more susceptible to outside influences ; they are more malleable than maturer, older men. We can still see, in the United States, how easily young immigrants are melted in the American melting-pot.

Then *Sex.* Colonial society is composed of many more men than women. While, in our older countries, the numbers of the two sexes are approximately equal, it is far otherwise in distant lands. Men are in a great majority. For this reason alone, the surrounding atmosphere can exercise a stronger influence. The men are much more at the mercy of external influences than are their sisters. Among civilised people, just as among primitive people, women are the guardians of tradition.

Finally, the *Family.* Groups of white men in the colonies being composed for the most part of young men, their members are, much more than at home, doomed to celibacy. They are thus less protected against sex relations with the natives. They have no home of their own ; they must live at the Club or in quarters outside it. They are therefore often driven to seek a temporary woman-companion amongst the coloured women. This is the path along which, as I shall presently show, reciprocal contagion travels, contagion in all senses of the word. These three circumstances, the last especially, account for the fact that groups of white men in the colonies are more plastic than in our old societies at home.   We can see how grave was the frequent error of legislators who—especially in former times—forbade the colonist to marry, and who, in the days of the Old Régime in France, forbade a merchant to take his wife with him even to the ports of the Levant.   This simply meant driving them into the arms of " little wives ", who were often welcoming enough, and who thus unsuspectingly became propagandists of exotic manners and customs.   Progress is now being made under our very eyes which will profoundly modify the colonists' ways, by the increasing flow of white women to the colonies.   The population will thus be increased—with advantage—by white marriages.[1]

Let us now pass to the *effects* of native influences on the European.   We shall look for them in the various spheres of life : economic, ethical, juridical, linguistic, æsthetic and theological. [2]

First, *Economic Imitation*.   We very rarely borrow from the native his methods of *production*.   Yet we have seen people develop a passion for exotic technique, *batik*,[3] for instance, and more particularly the new sculpture, drawing its inspiration from the so-called primitive arts.   We are more inclined to adopt primitive people's " consumer goods ".   Native foods and spices, native clothes and ornaments, and even—at least in the colonies themselves—native buildings, are adopted or adapted by us.   White women will wear the Javanese *sarong*.   No one has yet drawn up a complete list of the foods and other exotic products which have been taken into European use : [4] cocoa, coffee, cinchona, rubber, tobacco, the cigar ; even the pipe, which is said to have come to us from the Iroquois ; the turkey and the hammock, sugar, maize, ipecacuanha, quinine, manioc, cloves ; from China, the mulberry, opium, painted paper, porcelain, silk and tea ; from Arabia, muslin, damask, morocco

---

[1] J. Chailley-Bert, *L'émigration des femmes aux colonies*, Paris, 1897 ; P. Duret, *La femme dans les colonies françaises*, Paris, 1898 ; (Mme) C. Chivas-Baron, *La femme française aux colonies*, Paris, 1929.

[2] The wide subject of the influence of colonisation on *ideas* is outside my terms of reference.   See Sir Henry Maine : *The Effects of Observation of India on European Thought*, Rede Lecture, 1875, reprinted in *Village Communities in the East and West*, 3rd Ed. 1876.   French trans. in *Études sur l'histoire du droit*, Paris, 1889 ; G. Atkinson, *Les relations des voyages du XVII*e *siècle et l'évolution des idées*, Paris, undated ; Muriel Dodds, *Les récits de voyages, source de L'Esprit des Lois* . . . , Paris, 1929.

[3] [*Batik*, a beautiful method of wax-painting on textiles, learnt by Europe from Java, but probably of ultimate Indian origin.   EOL]

[4] See especially : A. Franklin, *Le café, le thé et le chocolat*, Paris, 1893.

leather : all of them products now essential to European life. European luxury is, to a very large extent, of exotic invention. King René in the 15th century used to collect " Turkish works " ; and the theory has been propounded that the tambourine of Provence came to us from the negroes through the Arabs, through the Crusaders ! Exotic fashions are, at any rate, not of yesterday.[1]

Ethical and Juridical Imitation. Ethical and juridical imitation present a more disturbing problem. It is easy to imagine Europeans acquiring from the Peruvians a taste for *maté*, or for tea from the Chinese. It is a very different thing to have to admit that they allow themselves to be won over by the manners, customs and laws of indigenous peoples. Is not this a case where we may fairly use the word " retrogression " ? For people designate as " faults ", habits which the colonists have picked up from their intercourse with the natives. The " old hand " who has, in the course of time, cast aside his European inhibitions, tends in his ways to lean towards indigenous lines of conduct—he grows fond of *ostentation* and inclines to take extravagance for a sign of greatness ; this is the most obvious failing which even the casual observer can detect in certain colonists. He grows addicted to *gambling* ; like the Arab he is obsessed by a love of gaming and often dreams of no other way of growing rich. And he is said to be a prey to *inactivity*, again, just like a native. He is no longer the man he was when he first landed : he has " gone native " with the lapse of time. I have known Europeans who affected such a degree of inertia, which they thought lent them distinction, that they used to get their black servants to put on their shoes for them. Don't let us moralise about it, or exaggerate, but let us look facts in the face.

Is there not even—it has certainly been asserted—a demoralisation of the white man ?[2] Europeans have great vices of their own, which, all too often, they have communicated to their subjects, but natives have their vices too : these " natural men ", who before the Frenchman's arrival ran about stark naked, have vices which they communicated to the French. Just as European and native have exchanged diseases—a subject I have purposely avoided—they have made an exchange of

---

[1] M. Besson, *Les précurseurs de l'expansion française et les modes du jour, Afrique française,* March, 1931, pp. 190-3 ; *Les colonies françaises et la mode* (*Animateur des temps nouveaux*), Paris, 1931.

[2] A. Corre, *L'ethnographie criminelle,* Paris, 1895 ; *Nos créoles,* Paris, 1890.

sins. Europeans in the colonies have often acquired a taste for opium [1] . . . and many another taste which leads them along the downward path of the " decivilised ", whose portrait our writers have drawn.

Let us turn to a pleasanter subject and talk of *linguistic* and *æsthetic* imitation. From the most ancient times the passage of words and arts from colonies to the mother-countries has been a well-recognised phenomenon. Hellenic art was influenced by Asia ; and in France since the conquest of the East and West Indies we have seen exotic artistic fashions succeed each other. Words and arts current amongst the conquered peoples find entry into France ; plastic arts, literary arts, musical arts. It has recently been shown that there was in ancient Greece a time when the Negro was all the fashion ; the Greeks went through a phase of " melano-mania " [2]—if the word may be allowed—just as the French much later went through the phases of " Ottomano-mania " and " Sino-mania ". Explorations and expeditions [3] have been behind a considerable interchange of vocabulary. Arabic words [4] have filtered in very large numbers into French speech ; so have Asiatic and African words and also American-Indian ones. When a Frenchman says *ouragan*, *savane* or *manitou* [5] (Great Panjandrum, big boss) he is speaking like an Iroquois. The French have found pleasure not only in Turkish and Chinese arts, but in the Negro arts of Africa and the Melanesian arts of Oceania ; their figures have acquired citizen rights in our French drawing-rooms and museums. French decorative art has reflected exotic methods. [6]   *Tales* [7] and *songs, dances* and *games* [8] have reached France from untraced sources : canary glass, the chacona dance, the moresque ornament ; the games of chess, ombre and *manille* ; and uncounted " tales of wonder " which are still popular, are part of France's debt towards the races she has conquered.

[1] Jules Boissière, *Fumeurs d'opium*, 1896, and *Propos d'un intoxiqué*, published posthumously, 1909.

[2] Grace H. Beardley, *The Negro in Greek and Roman Civilisation*, Baltimore, 1929.

[3] See Pasquier's *Recherches de la France*, 1633, Vol. VIII, Chap. 20. *Mots empruntés des Voyages d'Outre-mer.*

[4] M. Devic, *Dictionnaire étymol. des mots français d'origine orientale* . . . , Paris, Supplement to Littré's Dictionary.

[5] [*Hurricane* and *savannah* have reached English through the Spanish ; *manitou* (Red Indian name for a great nature spirit), though familiar to anthropologists, is not naturalised in ordinary English speech. EOL]

[6] R. Brun, *Les thèmes coloniaux dans l'art décoratif* . . . *Revue de l'Art* . . . , May, 1931.

[7] E. Cosquin, *Recherches sur les migrations des contes populaires*, Paris, 1922.

[8] Leber, *Coll. des meilleures dissertations*, X, p. 212 f.

Finally, what of *Theological Diffusion*? How does it happen that Europeans, who go to a pagan country expressly to convert the heathen, are sometimes themselves converted to native cults? Yet this has been known to happen, and is by no means a phenomenon of only yesterday. The *Syncretism* of ancient times was, as we have seen, a reciprocal hybridisation of various cults. There were even little statues or images, known as *pantheons*,[1] figures of several deities in one body, where Egyptian was blent with Roman symbolism : fit image of the confusion reigning in men's minds ! A Mithraic column has been found at Arles, a shaft with a serpent entwined ; the god Mithra had travelled as far as that.[2] Last century saw a fair number of European converts to Islam, all following the example of Bonneval[3] who was made a Two-Tail Pasha. Amongst these converts were General Menou,[4] Napoleon's successor, who took the Muslim name of Abdullah (servant of Allah), and Suliman Pasha, a French colonel who was instructor to Mahomet Ali's troops ; many French residents in Algeria also became Muslims, men such as Léon Roches, Ismaïl Urbain and Étienne Dinet. There are European contemporaries of our own who have become Musulmans. The Muslim sect of the Bab, or Babi-ism, and its offshoot Bahaism have followers in Germany, England and the United States.[5] It is the religion of Muhammad, not any form of fetishism—except in art—which has to some slight extent been able to infiltrate into the West.

There exist also, among the native subjects of France, what can only be called " superstitions ", which are nowadays exercising extraordinary seductive power in Europe. There is talk of a " drift towards the East " ; and it is the great colonial powers who are most affected by it. The English owe the fact that they are so superstitious, in part at least to contagion ; and English

---

[1] [The Greek *To Pantheon*, Latin *pantheon*, originally meant a *place* where " all the gods " were worshipped, the most famous being the Pantheon in Rome, built under Augustus. In later Latin the word was used to mean " all the gods ", the divine community. Still later it was applied to such little composite god-images as the author alludes to. EOL]

[2] And even as far as England : W. Williams, *The Cult of Mithra in Britain*, *Archæological Journal*, 1928, pp. 1–24.

[3] [Bonneval (1675–1747), a French adventurer who, having served in the French and Austrian armies, entered the service of Turkey and reorganised the Turkish artillery. He took the Muslim name of Ahmad, and became famous as Ahmad Pasha. EOL]

[4] [General J. F. (Baron de) Menou (1750–1810). When Napoleon quitted Egypt in 1799, the command of the French forces there devolved first on Kleber and after Kleber's assassination on Menou. EOL]

[5] See Carra de Vaux, *Les penseurs de l'Islam*, Paris, 1926, Vol. V, p. 397 f. and *passim*.

superstition is the price they have had to pay for English expansion.[1] The various forms of Theosophy are these semi-religions or semi-superstitions, dished up to suit European taste; they have their churches in all our French countries. In quite recent times the entire collection of Oriental cults have found an entrance into Western countries. Beyond the Rhine there is a strong current—which deserves fuller treatment—strengthening the " drift towards the East ". German philosophers have exalted the primacy of the Orient and maintain—following Schopenhauer, who expounded the theory a full century ago—that light must come from the East. Keyserling and Spengler, prophets of the Decline of the West, have been the importers of the religions and the superstitions of the Oriental peoples. A forerunner of theirs was a certain Fabre d'Olivet, an Oriental zealot and fanatic.[2] Amongst us in France there is quite a wave of admiration for Hindu thought ; we are reminded that, according to Gobineau, we owe everything to Asia.[3] People are endeavouring to blend East and West in a Pan-Humanism. The days when the Acropolis was a sacred spot are gone. Another fashion ! Always a new fashion ! Shall we be taught one of these days to look on Europeans as *déséduqués* and " decivilised " ?

At the extreme, we already find, in certain exceptional and abnormal cases, a " decivilised " white man in the colonies; a man such as the novels depict [4] who has returned to the primitive. He is, however, not only a fictional type ; he is and was a real type ;[5] Gauguin in Oceania, Rimbaud in Abyssinia, men like these, are in their way " decivilised ". It began with several of the followers of Cortes ; Guerrero, for instance, who had become an Indian chief and refused to leave his tribe. And in the early days you might have found in the Canadian forests men who had reverted to savage life. There was Jourdain of Longpré-les-Corps-Saints for one, the man from Picardy who had become one of the Oneida, and had forgotten his mother tongue ; he had become a savage.

Without seeking these abnormal and decivilised men in

---

[1] [Are we as a nation superstitious ? EOL]

[2] *De l'état social de l'homme*, Paris, 1822.

[3] Sylvain Lévi, *L'Inde et le monde*, Paris, 1926.

[4] From the *Florello* of Loaisel de Tréogate (1776) down to Somerset Maugham's *Edward Barnard* (*The Trembling of a Leaf*, 1921). See especially Ch. Renel, *Le decivilisé*, Paris, 1923.

[5] See Tylor, *Primitive Culture*, London, 1871 ; cf. *Un évadé de la civilisation* (in *Bourgeois et gens de peu*), Paris, 1909, pp. 179–236 (John Nelson who became a Sioux).

forests, let us look in our towns at home, in Europe and in America, and see primitive influences at work. Let us look especially at the United States ; think of Tammany Hall, which bears an Indian name ; think of the Ku-Klux-Klan ; think of societies for scouting [1] and sport. Think even of these professional unions with their rites and ceremonies, their emblems and totems, their pass-words and their ritual initiations ; with their parades in Red Indian dress, each carrying a Red Indian pipe ; with their titles of " sachems " (chiefs) and " warriors ", all these trinkets, toys and junk borrowed from savages, which the primitive American has bequeathed to civilised America, which is indeed not the most self-disciplined country in the world, but at least the most forward-thrusting. It is in America that people are advocating " tribal training ", apprenticeship to the tribe, return to the energy of natural man. It would seem that the civilised, perhaps over-civilised, American feels the need to live again " the epic of primitive man " if he is to recapture strength and virtue.[2]

[1] On the " Indian inspiration " in American Scouting, see J. Sevin, *Le Scoutisme*, Paris, 1928, p. 135 f.

[2] [A most illuminating discussion of reciprocal imitation by " the dominant minority " and " the internal proletariat " will be found in Toynbee's *Study of History*, Vol. V. No serious student should fail to read Toynbee, either in the 6-volume edition or at least in the 1-volume abridgment of D. C. Somervell. EOL]

CHAPTER XIII

FUSION

After *opposition*, after *imitation*, the *fusion* of races is the crowning result of their contact : the *racial* and *social* blend is the ultimate product of colonisation.

I have indicated the paths by which peoples arrive at this fusion, the phases through which they pass, from opposition to aggregation or fusion. Imitation is the first step ; to imitate each other, to adapt each to other, to receive and to give ; this points the way towards unification. Imitation then leads to *partnership* and collaboration, by the very fact—and that fact alone—that the conqueror dominates the conquered. Both in the political and in the economic sphere there inevitably arises a *de jure* and *de facto* concurrence of ruler and ruled. As a sequel to collaboration we see fusion ultimately coming into play, a blending of races from which a new race may emerge.

Imitation, partnership, fusion ; these are the three stages, not always completed, on the road which two races travel who set out to meet each other. Fusion remains the exception. Yet it is of far-reaching consequence, by its antiquity and by its present-day significance.

By its Antiquity. The story of the fusion of races is in all probability as old as the story of the human race itself. It is well known that *exogamy* is a primitive practice. In the most barbarous of all human societies, among the aboriginal Australians for example, marriages are arranged not inside the one group but rather between one group and another, without and not within the community ; exogamy not endogamy is practised. As soon as we use the word *exogamy* [1]—borrowing it from MacLennan, its creator—we are speaking of a blend of human groups ; a blend of families ; later, a blend of tribes or clans ; a blend also of classes and finally of nations and peoples. The Bantu Negroes who founded the great Sudanese Empires inter-married with the Negrillos who are known as Pygmies, and

---

[1] See, in general, A. Lang, *Exogamy, Revue études ethnographiques et sociologiques,* I, 1908, pp. 65–75.

already no doubt with the whites. The term Sarakolle [1] means " white man ".

As soon as the Greeks and Romans penetrated into the Mediterranean countries—which now are old, but in those days were new countries—the fusion of races began. At Susa in Persia, under the Empire of Alexander, it was reckoned that there lived ten thousand men of mixed race ! The Greeks and Romans married the daughters of the land ; and the legend of Gyptis, [2] associated with the Phocæan [3] colony of Marseilles, remains a witness thereto. In the Provençal country you may frequently see preserved even to-day, especially amongst the women, a definitely Græco-Latin type, Roman and Hellenic, which has survived the lapse of two millennia and which well attests the antiquity of racial fusions. [4]

The great fact of the aggregation or fusion of peoples has, however, a living significance in the present. It is the great problem of to-day. We meet it, not only in the colonial empires but also in the great new countries, which will be perhaps the Empires of To-morrow ; especially we meet it in the United States, where the major problem which disturbs and distresses public opinion is : the blending of races. I have already spoken of that vast crucible, that Melting-Pot, which is the American Republic, this huge population of cross-breeds, whose unforeseen, almost miraculous progress in the last century is the achievement of the hybrid. The fusion of peoples is therefore a dominating fact in all history. Always and everywhere, races have blended ; anthropology recognises to-day that there are no pure races, no " races " [5] in the full sense of the word, which remain for ever immutable ; no population groups which have persisted for a great length of time without admixtures of blood.

We must now consider this blending in its *forms* and its *effects*. We shall then find that this fusion has not at all times

---

[1] [The Sarakolle are an endogamous, long-haired, dark-skinned people in Senegal, Mauritania and the French Sudan. They lay claim to white ancestry. EOL]

[2] [Gyptis was the daughter of a Ligurian chief, Nannus, to whom the Greeks applied for permission to found a city in his territory. Nannus gave a feast to which he invited the Greeks, thus giving the Ligurian princess the opportunity to choose a husband from the assembled suitors. She chose Protis, one of the two founders of the proposed colony. The earliest authority for the story is Aristotle, but it is accepted as essentially true. EOL]

[3] [Marseilles was founded about 600 B.C. by Greeks from Phocæa in western Asia Minor. EOL]

[4] See E. Weiss, *Endogamie und Exogamie im römischen Kaiserreich*, *Zeitschrift der Savigny Stiftung, Roman. Abteilung*, XXIX, 1908, pp. 340–69.

[5] See J. Deniker, *Les races et les peuples de la terre*, 2nd Ed., Paris, 1926, or A. C. Haddon, *The Races of Man and their Distribution* ; and for the history of ideas, Th. Simar's book quoted above, p. 30, n.2.

and in all places the same quality or the same beneficial results. If it has taken place at all times and in all places, it has taken place in very various ways. It shows diversity and complexity as well as inevitability and universality.

The *forms* or methods of fusion are subject to one great distinction whose effects are decisive. If the blend results from a temporary mating, an illegitimate, irregular union which is recognised neither by the laws of the ruler not even by those of the ruled, that is one thing. If it is the product of a legitimate marriage, a regular conjugal union, declared and proclaimed in conformity with the laws of conqueror and conquered, that is quite another thing : an enduring marriage, with all its legal rights, which may form the foundation of a new race.

In most cases, especially at the beginning of race contact, we are dealing with the illegitimate and temporary mating. These unrecognised matings of rulers and ruled almost always take the form of what I have called *masculine unions* : that is, cases where white men for a time—according to local custom— live with coloured women ; this is what, in law, we call concubinage. We almost never find such irregular matings taking place between white *women* and coloured men : the theme of Pierre Mille and André Demaison's *La femme et l'homme nu* (" The Woman and the Naked Man ") remains aberrant . . . at least in times of peace. This, as we shall see, is not always the case in legal marriage.

In mediæval times, our French sea-dogs, sailing between the islands of the Archipelago or the ports of the Levant, behaved in like manner. They contracted *temporary marriages*, known as *kabine*, with Greek or Turkish girls. So too our French pioneers or colonists after the occupation of the East and West Indies. This was the foundation of the story—based on many real-life occurrences—of the union, quickly formed and quickly broken, between the white man and the female savage, a motif generously exploited by the novelist. Abbé Raynal's book, *Histoire des Établissements des Européens dans les deux Indes* (" History of the European Settlements in the Two Indies ") contains an engraving of Eisen's, portraying a Negress deserted by an Englishman. From this situation there sprang a literature not yet extinct in our own day.[1] The play which caused perhaps more tears to flow than any other in the era of the " tearful comedy " was

---

[1] G. Chinard, *L'Amérique et le rêve exotique* . . . , Paris, 1913, pp. 26 f., 400 f. and *passim*.

Chamfort's *La jeune Indienne* ("The Young Red Indian Girl ")
of 1764. The young Indian is a girl-savage deserted by a
European adventurer, to whom she had " given her heart " ;
but the play ends, as is fitting, by the couple's getting married.

Even where *concubinage* did not prevail, *slavery* often brought
about sexual intercourse between rulers and ruled. Concubinage
and slavery were for centuries the two main causes of sex relations
between conquerors and conquered. These " little wives " were
often, against their will, or it might be without their knowledge,
the intermediaries of relations of a moral nature between the
savage and the civilised. Through them European fashions
penetrated savage circles, and through them the Europeans
became familiar with the customs of their subjects. The
Moresques of Algiers, the *Moussous* of the Sudan, the *Congayes*
of Indo-China, the *Ramatous* of the great " Red Island " (New-
foundland ?) formed the corps of " exotic " or " savage " diplo-
matic envoys accredited to the " civilised " conquerors.

These temporary and irregular unions, which are at the
same time what I have called masculine unions, represent cross
breedings of a double nature. They create a bond between two
different *races*, and a bond also between two different *classes*.
The black or brown or yellow people whom the pioneer or the
colonist must necessarily live amongst, are of inferior rank, or
almost always so. It is never usual—except in story-books—
for the foreigner like Captain Corcoran to marry the King's
daughter. It is low-caste girls who offer themselves to the
stranger. This has its good and also its evil side. On the one
hand, it is partly good, since the European thus becomes
acquainted with all strata of the native population ; on the other,
it is partly bad, since the European thus forfeits his prestige
and his pride. What sort of a fellow is this, in a mandarin's
eyes, who lives with the daughter of a low-born man ?

These illegitimate unions have thus been one of the means
of bringing about a fusion of peoples, but we have also seen—
though exceptionally—other unions between colonisers and
natives : *legitimate unions*, regular conjugal marriages in the full
sense of the term—not only in the native sense, which is often
laxer in these matters than the white man's code—in the full
meaning, as understood in French law. These true marriages
used formerly to be known in the Latin Orient as " marriages
in Frankish style ", since at one time—a time now, alas, for ever
gone—all Europeans were " Franks " to the Levantine. Such

legitimate marriages were nearly always also "masculine";
but they were sometimes, though much more rarely, "feminine".
The European woman, who almost never stoops to an irregular
association with a native, can sometimes be induced to acquiesce
in a regular marriage with one, as we may observe in North
Africa. We have therefore to distinguish two types of mixed
marriage : the *masculine*, where the white man marries the
coloured woman ; and the *feminine*, where the white woman
marries the coloured man.

The *masculine* marriage is by far the more frequent. Marriages
in the forest or the bush, for which it might well be risky to
seek the permission of the French authorities, were not un-
commonly contracted according to native custom. Even in
towns of the Latin or Islamic East, "Coptic marriages", or
at least marriages in native style, might occur. Gérard de
Nerval in the first volume of his *Voyage en Orient* has described
these Coptic marriages where he relates his attempts to achieve
a legitimate union . . . at least in native style.

Very soon, however, we find legitimate marriages—in the
full French sense of marriage—taking place. As soon as the
European has found his footing, and the permanent resident,
the "habitant", has arrived, it is possible in the French colonies
for a white man to conclude a French-style marriage with a
native woman. Similar marriages, though they were long forbidden, were nevertheless already tolerated in ancient times.
In his colony of Brazil (1557) Villegagnon permitted legitimate
marriage with native women on condition only that the wife
was baptised ; and he punished one of his companions, an
interpreter, for having lain with a native woman without being
married to her. It was, none the less, the rule under the Old
French Monarchy that marriage with coloured women was
forbidden. In the early days of Rome the *connubium* of her
citizens with pilgrims was frowned upon, just as the Greeks
discountenanced *epigamy* of Hellene and Barbarian. Despite
the Quran—which allowed the True Believer to take in legitimate marriage the daughter of a Christian or of a Jew—the
Muslim Arabs, from the time of Malik to the present day,
forbid the mating of a Believer with an Infidel.[1] The main
reason of this is that even a *kitabiyah* [2] drinks wine, and her

---

[1] E. Zeys, *Traité élémentaire de droit musulman algérien*, Algiers, 1885, I, p. 75 f.
[2] [Viz. "A Woman of the Book". In virtue of their possessing written Scriptures
the Quran calls Jews and Christians "People of the Book" (*ahl al kitab*) and the
Muslim considers them less unenlightened than other "Unbelievers". EOL]

baby might absorb it in the mother's womb ! The Hindus also consider invalid the marriage of Hindu and Christian.[1] At the outset of their conquests, the Spaniards also forbade legal marriages of white man with Indian woman ; in the course of time they authorised it ; and the Portuguese Albuquerque even looked on it with favour. The French " Black Code " of 1685, Article IX, forbids concubinage, but permits marriage, between white and coloured. A French decree of 1724, however, prohibits the marriage of white man and black woman, and a later decree of 1778 prohibited it between the white man and the half-caste woman. The Frenchman had to wait for the Civil Code [2] for the right to marry a native woman, and even then Article 12 of the Code granted the right by implication only. It spoke, without making distinction, of " the foreign woman " who was the wife of a Frenchman. Thus, by preterition the Code legalised the " motley marriage " (le mariage bigarré).[3] Up to yesterday the Germans were placing restrictions on mixed marriages in their colonies.[4]

Such mixed marriages have in general been *masculine* unions, but occasionally, though much more rarely, *feminine*. Nowadays it is a shade less uncommon to see a European woman marry a coloured man : a white exotic in North Africa, a yellow exotic in French Indo-China ; almost never a black. For a long time past the French theatre has enjoyed raising the problem of the European woman imprisoned in the harem ; white women carried off as slaves by the corsairs, and later, others who, of their own free will or not, have married Muslim pashas ; at a still later stage white women have been known to marry middle-class or even lower-class natives. There are well-known examples ; there is the French woman known as Niya Salima who became an Egyptian and who described the manners and customs of Egyptian harems ; there is Aurélie Tedjani, consort of a big chief in the south of Algeria, who was called " The Princess of the Sands ".[5] Such cases remain exceptional, and public opinion is strongly against them. European conquerors have sometimes

[1] L. de Gruyter, *Mixed Marriages*, *Journal Comparative Legislation*, XI, Feb. 1929, pp. 34–41.
[2] [The *Code Civil des Français* was promulgated on March 21, 1804 ; on Sept. 3, 1907, it was renamed the *Code Napoléon*. EOL]
[3] A vigorous criticism of *mariages bigarrés* is to be found in Count du Buat's *Éléments de la politique* . . . , London, 1773, IV, p. 32 f.
[4] Th. Grentrup, *Die Rassenmischehen in den deutschen Kolonien* (Görresgesellschaft, No. 25), Paderborn, 1914 (Faculty of Law).
[5] Niya Salima (Mme H. Ruchdi pacha), *Harems et musulmanes d'Égypte*, Paris, 1908 ; Marthe Bassenne, *Aurélie Tedjani* . . . , Paris, 1925.

been reproached for this feeling, but it is not peculiar to them. All colonising peoples, even if themselves coloured, share this hostility to the feminine mixed marriage. Obsessed by their own greatness, they feel it an outrage that their daughters should become the wives of the conquered. In Malabar, men of the conquering races used to form misalliances with women of the conquered races, but not their women with the men. In the Sahara the Tuareg are willing enough to marry slave women, but a Tuareg woman will marry only one of her own kind. Misalliance—and the mixed marriage is generally felt to be a misalliance—is tolerated in one direction, and one only, between races as between classes.

Let us now consider the *effects* of the fusion of races in the colonies : what Anglo-Saxon writers call *miscegenation*. We note particularly that this fusion is both a racial and a social blending ; it is both a biological and a sociological phenomenon. Contact of races, but also contact of strata ; contact of *groups* which are not of the same social status ; cross-breeding or hybridisation in the biological and at the same time in the sociological sense.

This is scarcely the place to speak of the *racial mixture*,[1] even were I qualified, as I am not, to deal with it. What may be the effects of the mixture ? Is it physically desirable to cross colonisers and natives, or is it not ? We know how great are the differences of opinion on this point : one set of thinkers maintain that cross-breeding, at least in the course of time, leads to biological deterioration ; others maintain the exact opposite and contend that it leads to biological betterment.[2] They vie with each other in adducing analogies from the cross-breeding of horses and dogs. They call in Mendel's Laws[3] and they quote the sayings of Gobineau. What has taken place in the colonies is for the most part too recent for a satisfactory judgment to be formed on it.[4] My concern is to

---

[1] See in general : R. Martial, *Traité de l'immigration et de la greme interraciale*, Paris-Mons, 1930.

[2] *Favourable* : F. H. Hankins, *The Racial Basis of Civilisation*, New York, 1926 ; R. E. Park, *Mentality of Racial Hybrids*, American *Journal of Sociology*, Jan. 1931, pp. 534–51. *Unfavourable*, more frequent, especially in the United States. W. Gregory, *Race as a Political Factor*, London, 1931 ; P. Nolf, *Le problème des Races*, *Flambeau*, Brussels, XIII, Dec. 1930, pp. 289–314. He proposes the prohibition of mixed marriages in the Belgian Congo.

[3] See the summary by Y. Delage and M. Goldsmith, *Le mendélisme . . . Revue scientif.* (*Revue Rose*), Feb. 15–March 8, 1919.

[4] Mixed marriages between Europeans present a different problem in certain colonies, notably Algeria. These are warmly advocated by F. de Soliers, a champion of " crossed marriages " ; see Demontès, *Le peuple algérien . . .*, Algiers, 1906, p. 218 f.

emphasise that this racial blending already shows social effects ; that, in itself and by itself it is a social blending ; from the fact alone that a mixture and a continuing mixture has taken place between different peoples, it follows that categories of a social nature arise amongst these peoples.

This blending is no simple matter. It is not only the mating of one white man with one black woman ; in the course of time it gives rise to the mating of a white man with a mulatto woman ; and later still the mating of a white man with an octoroon and so on. The play of prolonged miscegenation thus goes on producing divisions of a social nature, and sometimes, as we shall see, of a legal nature ; always and in all cases, divisions of a moral nature. The confusion of groups is not the only result of racial mixing ; conversely and, as it were, in compensation, the mixing causes the division and separation of existing groups. We see this at work amongst the early American half-castes. There are more than forty million of them and gradations of rank have spontaneously sprung up amongst them.

Distinctions were made, especially in the early days, between true half-castes of the first generation, then hybrids with a third, a quarter, an eighth, a fifteenth of coloured blood ; there were also the *guassos* of Chile, the *peons* of La Plata, the *zambis* and the *paulistas* of Brazil, the *kastices* of Java. These last drew subtle distinctions of colour, and split hairs over their varying shades of skin ! . . .[1] Between these people who are distinguished only by varying gradation of fairness . . . strata and sub-strata have developed degrees of social rank ; hierarchies and cascades of graduated contempt. In the Mediterranean area there used to be the *muladis*, a cross of Muslim Arab and Spanish Christian, and the *coulouglis* in Tunis and Algeria, a cross of Turkish warrior and woman slave.[2] Racial blending creates in the human family both unity and diversity. Whether the word *mulatto* comes from the Spanish *mulo*, a mule (as Littré believes) or from the Arabic *mu'allad* (which denoted the child of an Arab and an Unbeliever) it certainly defines a category of society.

Where there is a racial mixture, there inevitably arises a *social* mixture. From the mere fact that unions have taken place between two different peoples, even if no issue result

[1] See in J.-J. Virey, *Histoire naturelle du genre humain*, Year IX, Paris, Vol. I, the " genealogical tree " of these mixtures with the names given to their issue.

[2] The fact that cross-breeding has *not* taken place, may provide another ground for contempt ; many despised *castes* are separate *races*. See Fr. Michel, *Histoire des races maudites* , . . . , Paris, 1847.

therefrom, a fabric of social intercourse is woven between them. Marriage is the very prototype of society itself. We have seen that amongst primitive peoples sexual union is considered the best means of achieving communion and alliance. Between peoples, as between clans, intermarriage is the symbol of alliance. The natives themselves have often perceived this ; they have themselves demanded that marriages between white and coloured couples should be recognised so as to emphasise and strengthen the bond between the two races. A touching petition was presented by the Oneidas, begging the Government of Canada to authorise white men to marry their daughters, for only so, said they, could peace be guaranteed. These " savages " then held the belief that exogamy creates a social bond.

From the very fact that the fusion of peoples is a social mixing at the same time as a racial mixing, legal and often political problems ensue. The multiplication of mixed matings gives birth to a body of half-breeds or hybrids whose status must be defined. This brings the colonists face to face with one of the old, old problems of sociology which confronted the primitive clans who first practised exogamy. When exogamous marriage takes place between two clans or two tribes, and later between two cities or two nations, what is the position of the offspring of these matings? Shall they belong to the father's group or to the mother's ? The question arises from the fact that these unions have been in accord with the law of exogamy—marriage outside the group—and not in accordance with the law of endogamy—marriage within the group. Two solutions have been found : the validity of maternal descent or the validity of paternal descent.

In the most primitive grades of society the child who is born of two separate clans or tribes, if not of two different races or peoples, is considered as belonging to his mother's and not to his father's group. *Maternal* descent precedes paternal descent.[1] Without knowing it, we were obeying this age-old law when under the Old French monarchy we decreed in our French law that the half-caste child belonged to his mother's and not to his father's people. In the same way, in mediæval Europe serfdom was inherited through the mother and not through the father. In Champagne in olden days the mother and not the father conferred nobility on the child, for, as the

[1] After discussions which lasted for half a century, people are now agreed on this point : see E. Sidney Hartland, *Primitive Paternity*, London, 1909.

old saw had it, " the sow ennobles the piglet ". It was the same in the French colonies, the half-caste child belonged to his mother and to his mother's people. Legally, he was therefore a native, a slave or a servant. Under the Old French Monarchy the law forbade a Frenchman to make a bequest to a native. Progress has, for the half-caste, meant that he is now granted paternal descent. Quite exceptionally, in Ancient Sparta the *mothrakes*, the half-caste offspring of Spartan fathers and helot mothers, were treated as and brought up with pure Spartans.[1] This was probably a device to increase the population. The tendency among the French of to-day in recent decrees is to grant the half-caste the right of being a Frenchman,[2] if his French paternity is proved ; thus applying to him the Roman rule of paternal and not of maternal descent. In Indo-China the French go so far as to *presume* a half-caste to be French if his parents are unknown. A decree of September 5, 1930, extends this presumption to French West Africa. It is therefore nothing new for the half-caste to claim the right of being French, to claim, in other words, to be his father's son. Henceforward in the French colonies, half-castes may be French citizens and this will be a long-awaited recognition of their paternity.

There continues nevertheless to persist a general feeling, which will assuredly linger for a long time to come, which depreciates and excludes the half-caste. Though the half-caste may be recognised as French, public opinion does not consider him a real Frenchman. This is wrong, but this is how things are.[3] In " The Islands " under the Old French Monarchy there was a special mess for the mulattos apart from the white man's mess. In France, and in the chief French colonies, society creates a barrier between the white and the half-caste. When the French speak of " coloured people "—too often in a tone tinged with contempt—they mean just as much, and more often, the half-castes or mulattos as the Negroes. Contempt for the half-caste is just as much a phenomenon of to-day as it was in days of old. Herodotus called Cyrus " a mule ".

[1] [But did not enjoy full citizen rights. *Encycl. Britann.*, 14th Ed., s.v. *Helot*. EOL]

[2] See in general : A. Girault, *Rapport sur un projet de décret concernant les métis . . .* , Paris, 1926 ; and the same writer's *La condition juridique des métis dans les colonies françaises, Revue polit, et parlem.*, April 10, 1929, pp. 124–31 ; H. Sambuc, *. . . Des enfants nés en Afrique occidentale française de parents légalement inconnus, Recueil de législation . . . et de jurisprudence coloniales*, XXXIV, Jan.–March 1931.

[3] A whole literature on this subject exists, especially about the mental and spiritual conflicts of the Indo-Chinese half-caste. See, finally, Herbert Wild, *L'autre race*, Paris, 1930.

One of Martial's epigrams (II, 12) tells us that amongst the Romans the word " half-caste " was an insult. The passage of laws does not kill prejudice amongst us Frenchmen either ; and if in law we are progressing towards a solution of the miscegenation problem, the moral problem remains. The sentimental barrier remains ; we have still to establish real equality between the white man and the half-caste. There is a long road ahead ; the same road which older societies have travelled in their advance.

CONCLUSION

We have considered in their diversity the phases of race-contact. We have classified its aspects and its effects. We have seen the development of opposition, imitation, fusion. We have emphasised that these problems are problems of all places and of all times. We have noted the similarity and also the dissimilarity of the solutions attempted at various times and in various places. We have thus tried to sketch the outlines of a comprehensive picture of this social phenomenon in the colonies.

Yet it is more a problem of the future than of the present, and we must at least mention the future before closing, for it is bound up with the history of *ideas* concerning race contact. It is the problem of one *Universal Civilisation*. Is it then possible—or will it, perchance in the future, perhaps the far-distant future, become possible—to found, by contact and by fusion, one civil order for all human beings throughout the world of Man ? This has been the dream of philosophers ; the dream of a *Pan-Mixia* or a universal blending.

The Ancients had dreamt of it ; the mystic system of philosophy known as Orphism was already cosmopolitan and humanitarian.[1] The thinkers of the Age of Enlightenment spontaneously reverted to the idea.[2] Bernardin de Saint-Pierre, in his *Vues d'un solitaire*, wished that a moment might come when " lovers of all the nations " might gather together, to give Humanity the single civilisation for which it waits. Before him and after him, many another has dreamt of a United Humanity : from the philosophers of antiquity with their vision of the *genus humanum* or of the *Civitas Jovis* down to the reformers of recent times : a Saint-Simon, a Comte, a Fourier, a Pecqueur [3] who hoped for and foretold a *Universal Unity*. Let us hope that one day, far off though it be, there may appear the " City of God " so long awaited, more all-embracing than the Christianity of old ; a city for all, founded on the unity of the human race, in which the old word of the Greeks, *philanthropy*, will have at last attained a universal application.

[1] M. Mühl, *Die antike Menschheitsidee*, Leipzig, 1928.
[2] P. Hazard, *Cosmopolite*, in *Mélanges Baldensperger*, Paris, 1929, Vol. I.
[3] This last reformer in particular : *Des intérêts du commerce*, Paris, 1839, II, pp. 328 f. and 507 f. ; he suggests a methodical miscegenation, to create a " cosmopolitan society ". See also G. Ferrero, *L'unité du monde*, Paris, 1925 ; and D. Draghicesco, *La nouvelle cité de Dieu* (Vol. I), Paris, 1929.

PART II
PSYCHOLOGY OF EXPANSION

Psychologie des Expansions

First Published in Paris 1936

PREFACE

Part II of this book is written in the same style and in the same spirit as Part I. I have tried to utilise, and yet to keep command of, a very large mass of material. I should have found it easier—as the reader will readily believe—to write a thousand pages than three hundred! Had I made the book thicker and heavier, it might have been more welcome—to some people at least. But I have consulted my own taste and made it brief and clear. Let us not over-tax our gifts, nor change our manner! I think in French; I have written French . . . or have at least tried to. The reader must judge.

If I have studied books, I have also studied life. Here therefore, as before, I offer not only what I have read but what I have seen. My aim has been : to seek, behind the gesture, the feelings and the opinions of " the colonial " ; to find the *social facts* which are always *states of mind* ; to trace relations, to record mutations ; always to depict, never to judge. There is no " message " in this work of mine! I was gratified when an American friend, commenting on the preceding volume, complained : " One can never tell what you think! Are you for, or are you against ? " I do not know. That is as it should be. I hold, quite simply, that it is our duty to look at facts, humbly to ponder them, not to condemn. This is the " positive spirit ". In our day—when nonsensical and fantastic theorisings are two a penny—let us more resolutely than ever cling to fact.

Fontvieille-en-Provence,
   this month of April, 1936

CHAPTER XIV

THREE OBJECTS : PSYCHOLOGY, SOCIOLOGY, ETHOLOGY

I propose to examine the action of "mental forces" (*idées-forces*) in the evolution of colonies. In other words to emphasise that the founding and the extension of colonies, while directed no doubt by interest and ambition, are also always strongly influenced by feelings and illusions, by agitations and enthusiasms ; by visions and by myths.

As far as colonies are concerned, this will therefore be a contribution to what we might call *ideology*, taking this word in its philosophical sense, as it is used by Destutt de Tracy ; [1] a positive and descriptive analysis of those "ideas" which are the driving force of our expansions.

This word has, however, as we know, taken on a new meaning, and when people nowadays talk of "ideology" they are thinking of the tenets of sects and of parties. So it will be better for us to speak of a *psychology* of the colonies, for we want to paint the intellectual or sentimental impulses and revulsions which have led the master-peoples to acquire colonies, to extend their colonies, to abolish their colonies, and which have led the subject-peoples to sigh for liberty.

Let us first take as it were a bird's-eye glance at the action of these mental forces in the colonies.

One controversial question must be raised. When we use the words "mental forces", may we not be reproached with postulating a *colonial idealism*, with imagining that ideas rule the colonial world, with setting ourselves up against that materialism to which the modern destroyer pins his faith, according to which the evolution of all societies is the result or the reflection of the action of self-interest ? Comtist or Marxist ? Is there here a dilemma ? Must we choose ? Surely it is possible for those who like ambitious systems, to contrast colonial idealism and

---

[1] [Antoine Louis Claude Destutt, Comte de Tracy (1754–1836) was a disciple of Condillac. His first great philosophical work was the *Elements of Ideology*, 1801. EOL]

colonial materialism, according to whether they prefer to seek the great driving forces of change in ideas or in deeds. It might be thought that our phrase, mental forces, was an indication that we were casting a vote in this dispute. There is no need so to interpret it, and this is not the place to solve the problem. Colonisation : capitalism and mechanisation, that's all ; exploitation and oppression, that's all it is ! Not at all. That is too rough and ready. Societies, and empires too, are moral beings ; " organisations of ideas ", worlds of feelings, wherein exist states of soul and states of mind which inspire the founding and the transformation of colonial empires. Little need it concern us if these states of mind be themselves derivative, if they be but results of other things, mere products like sugar, or it may be vitriol ; that they may be indissolubly linked up with changes in the material world ; that the evolution of ideas may be the reflex of another evolution, which someone will prove to have been predestined. We are none the less entirely justified in examining these states of mind as they themselves exist, in following their transformations, and noting how by these same transformations they had produced transformations in colonial empires.

In so doing, we are in no wise taking sides for or against either idealism or materialism. We are observing in a nation the collective mental attitudes which have furthered or hampered its expansion ; those states of mind, reacting on the body, not intellectually or rationally only, but emotionally and passionately too. The philosopher Alfred Fouillée who first coined this phrase " mental forces " (idées-forces) included under it both opinions of a rational nature and feelings of a passionate nature : ideas and emotions ; opinions and impulses.

It is the same with colonial phenomena. These are social phenomena inasmuch as they occur within societies, inasmuch as expansions are generally the work of collective bodies, in particular of *nations*. It is States, Nations, Peoples which have founded colonies and kept them. The colonial phenomenon is a collective phenomenon, though it be at the same time a material one. A material phenomenon since it is always translated into visible and tangible realities, since it is characterised by monuments, by buildings, by a whole gallery of external manifestations—were it only by a flag !—expressing the intention and the claim to rule.

These colonial phenomena, which are collective and material, are spiritual too. Like all social phenomena they are of a dual nature : composed of *practice* and of *faith*. Colonial phenomena are *the practices and the faiths of Empires* ; they are what men feel they ought to do and what they believe they are doing ; they are results or it may be the plans ; they are confidence or hope ; they are what men do and what men wish ; they are therefore— like all social phenomena—at once things *lived* and things *dreamed*.

Let us classify colonial phenomena on these lines.

Practice. In the first place, practice or material deeds : acts producing a visible result ; these are of two kinds having two separate aims. First, the advantageous use of distant lands, otherwise called the *exploitation of things.* Secondly, the creation of contact between the home people and the distant people, who are almost always the prior occupants of the distant lands, other-wise called the *association of peoples.* The exploitation of things or, if you prefer it, *profitable development* ; the association of peoples, or, if you prefer it, the establishment of *race contact* ; these are the two aspects of the colonial phenomenon in so far as it is practically expressed in action. There are therefore two branches of, or two sides to what C. de Lannoy calls *Colonistics,* namely colonial studies ; first the study of advantageous development, that is, Colonial Economics ; Secondly the study of race contact, that is, Colonial Sociology. These are the two facets of colonial science as far as it deals with practical matters or results.

Faith. Faith comes in the second place since the motive underlies the action and the result. The motives of colonisation comprise all the opinions, all the feelings which urge a State to expand ; an obscure world of impulse and desire ; of plan and project ; of wishes, not of actions. This is another subject to ponder over : the study of beliefs, not of deeds : the psychology of colonies.

There are thus three elements in Colonistics or colonial study : Colonial *Economics*, Colonial *Sociology* and Colonial *Psychology*. The two first aim at studying practice and results, or, in a word, *actions* in colonial Empires : advantageous developments and human contacts. The last aims at studying not deeds but thoughts, not results but motives, not practice but beliefs, not actions but *ideas*.

I intend to devote this second volume to the Psychology of Colonies, an aspect of colonial study hitherto unduly neglected. We shall therefore give our attention to what Fustel de Coulanges calls the history of beliefs, for faith has played a large part in the expansion and extension of the great colonial empires both of the past and of the present.

It will be our task to sketch colonial psychology in outline and as usual first to note what its *objects* are, and what its *methods*.

Objects. The study of beliefs implies the examination of the opinions and feelings of the collective groups concerned. We must not pursue the method favoured in the " Age of Enlightenment ", and theorise about the psychology of Man in general, of Man as man, of the human being as such ; we must rather examine the states of soul and the states of mind of men as they have been and as they are ; of *men* not of *Man*, of *men* possessing traditions and conceptions which change greatly according to time and place.

Colonial psychology, thus understood, involves also colonial sociology ; for these states of mind are collective rather than individual. We are dealing with the psychology of peoples or of nations. With the nations of our day, as with the tribes and cities of the past, it is collective impulses and collective revulsions which play their part in promoting or preventing expansion. At all times there has been a great conflict between forward impulses—hopes and passions inducing conquest—and on the other hand, backward revulsions—fears and distastes inducing renunciation.

Our psycho-sociology presents us with the spectacle of a drama, where hostile forces meet in combat : actions and reactions *for* and *against* colonisation and domination. Our study of colonial psychic states will thus aim at painting those impulses which sociology calls " currents of opinion ". We shall first describe the *aspirations* which create great colonial empires : the dreams and the hopes, the desires and the designs, all the passionate enthusiasms which at times, as in the days of the Crusaders, have been the immensely powerful driving force behind the expansions of the conquering peoples who under the inspiration of their faith carry all before them. There has been, I shall maintain, such a thing as *colonial fanaticism*, and a great thing it was.—We shall also describe the stirrings of opposition which have sometimes brought everything to a standstill : the fears, the remorse which have compelled men to renounce the power to rule. Nations have their attacks of humility ! It has always been the victory of the one side or the other which has solved the moral problem of the right of conquest, the right of exploitation.

Colonial psychology is on the one hand sociology, since it deals with the collective states of soul which nations display ; on the other hand it is finally *ethology*. I am using this word in the sense in which it was used by its inventor, John Stuart Mill. When he used to speak of the " psychology of peoples " he was referring especially to the state of mind of human communities organised in States, in so far as this state of mind is " realised " and experienced by other human communities. He thus presented a whole new aspect of sociology : the study of the picture formed by one community of another. Peoples, and nations in particular, form for themselves conceptions of other communities, distant or near ; and the manner in which each society has developed its opinions and feelings about the character of other societies forms the subject-matter of ethology.[1]

Now this is exactly what occurs in every case of colonisation ; since colonisation is a contact and a struggle between groups which differ in their degree of advancement, which are not at the same stage of evolution or civilisation, and, thus defined, colonisation implies the forming of an opinion, a feeling, between groups foreign to each other. Rulers and ruled are busy sitting in judgment on each other.

In colonies ethology has three aspects.

There is, first, the ethology of the *rulers* : the views and feelings they develop about the ruled. Almost invariably, the ruler suffers from a " superiority complex ". We shall call this *Cultural Imperialism*, inasmuch as the colonisers' domination of the local culture is inevitable. At times too, and in all ages, but more especially in our own day, the dominating peoples are conscious of a feeling of inferiority ; there always exist among them groups or parties ready to deny the value of their own civilisation, to believe in the virtue of the primitive, to rate the value of the ruled above that of the ruler, and to endorse the " theory of the Noble Savage ". Here we recognise the influence of Rousseau, whose state of mind was typical of theirs.

Secondly, there is the ethology of the *ruled*. They also have their state of mind and their own psychic reactions ; so they either love us or they do not ! How do the subjects judge their masters, how do they feel about them ? All too often we must seek an answer in the novel. We must distinguish two tendencies.

---

[1] [The English reader will be well advised to bear in mind this definition of *ethology*, as used by Mill and Maunier. Its form suggests a misleading connection with *ethics*. EOL]

The dominated peoples are irrational and passionate, their opinions and feelings are stronger and more definite than you would think. Sometimes they feel fear and hatred, which beget *opposition* to the rulers. Sometimes they feel themselves drawn towards the rulers by a liking, an attraction so strong that they quite spontaneously imitate them, and feel no embarrassment at adopting their manners and customs ; this begets *imitation* of the ruler by the ruled. Finally, they sometimes—but not often —feel neither fear nor mere attraction but actual affection. Occasionally the ruled feel a glow of enthusiasm for the rulers which tends to promote fusion between the two. A new grouping thus comes to birth when through sexual intercourse two separate groups merge to produce a third. This is what I call *fusion* (agrégation) which begins in partnership.

There is, lastly, the ethology of the *outsiders*. For colonial empires have at no time been completely isolated groups. There are always outside groups whether distant or adjacent—tribes, cities, nations, States, according to time and place—who also have feelings and opinions about colonisations. This is particularly obvious in our own day when all the great colonial empires are compelled, willingly or unwillingly, to take account of the opinion of outside strangers. The problem is no longer one between rulers and ruled alone. There is a tribunal of outside opinion, which through the newspapers interferes more and more with every activity of the great colonial domains to favour or prevent certain decisions. Henceforward there are people everywhere sitting in judgment on us ; our " gallery " is the world which barracks the players ; and our " pit " hisses the actors !

Colonial ethology thus divides into three parts : the ethology of the ruler, of the ruled, and of the outsider.

These are the three objects of our study ; what are the *methods* by which we can pursue it ? Through what instruments, by what procedures, can we both positively and objectively ascertain this psychology which is also sociology, which is even more ethology ? We must now enumerate the " sources " on which our study must be based.

Since we are dealing with the psychology of human groups, we must first and mainly direct our attention to peoples and nations to understand their various states of mind. They have their traditions, which are documents of a spiritual nature ; they have their monuments which are documents of a material nature.

First, *Traditions*. Traditions are beliefs, or, it may be, legends, or, it may be, customs ; written and preserved in their literature, and notably in their maxims. As regards the peoples of antiquity, traditions of migration and expansion are preserved in their popular literature. These give us the clue to their opinions. In these we see the figure of the colonial *hero*, the conqueror and founder who overcomes and governs. This is particularly illuminating as suggesting how naturally the subjects of colonial empires have been liable to pass in the course of time through many phases of feeling, how they have been able simultaneously to experience and simultaneously to express opposing beliefs : fear or hate on the one hand, attraction or affection on the other. If we want to know how the Algerians have for a long time judged and regarded the French, if we want to assess French prestige in Algeria, it is in tales and proverbs that we must look. I shall frequently refer to these sources.

Secondly, *Monuments*. Monuments are documents of a material, not spiritual nature : palaces, towns, industrial creations. We can easily get light on the mental attitude of the subject peoples towards the French by observing the decoration of the most modest mosque : it bears witness to a dream of the past and not of the future, a religious archaism, a collective cult of " bygones " which the Musulmans use as a defence against the inventions and innovations of the dominant power.

Industrial monuments are therefore in a certain sense elements of information. But much more they are intellectual monuments which may serve for our instruction. Statutes and codes of customary or written law are often our sole source of information about states of mind. In these we can detect the opinions and feelings of the ruled towards their rulers. In the clauses of these statutes relating to the Unbelieving Foreigner we can see that the Muslims continued for a long time to express their repulsion, we see how they were consequently able to resist the penetration of French laws and ideas, and how their opposition formed an obstacle to imitation, partnership and fusion. Read Al Bukhari : you will get an idea of the length of the road to be travelled !

Traditions and monuments are thus elements of information which we can find amongst human societies. When we approach recent times we must give attention to the deliberate expression of their states of mind which may be found in " authors ". It is the authors whose writings will give us documents on the " mentality " of rulers, ruled and outsiders.

These authors, however, are for us nothing more than sources, than witnesses. I am not writing the history of " doctrines " ; nor am I seeking to discover how such and such a " thinker " may have judged colonial affairs. That is no business of mine. Authors are for me only evidence, open to criticism, evidence on behalf of the various groups : rulers, ruled and outsiders. They are just interpreters more or less consistent. They are, but always only more or less, in tune and in harmony with their time ; often they are *in advance* of their time, not less often they are *behind* it ; they may therefore be taken as indicating collective states of mind not necessarily of to-day, but perhaps of yesterday or of to-morrow. They are therefore sometimes heralds of the future, sometimes exponents of the present, sometimes reconstructors of the past. At the same moment or in the same place, there are always several thinkers who bear witness to different states of mind of the past, of the present, of the future.

These authors, however, . . . who are merely interpreters and as such have need of explanation, give us nevertheless the key to opinions and feelings of peoples or nations. By the spoken and by the written word, all these authors, whether authors of vast tomes or of tiny booklets, who have brought into consciousness what was lurking in the unconscious of their contemporaries, who have thus made known and codified the law governing men's minds, who have given clear expression to what had been obscure, all these authors will for us be interpreters of collective states of mind—whether orthodox or unorthodox—relating to colonial phenomena.

It is therefore not such and such a thinker's individual thought which concerns me ; he is for me an echo only. In his thought I shall seek the uncertain trace of another thought, that of all these groups, rulers, ruled, and outsiders for whom he is acting as the mouthpiece. We are describing the impulses and revulsions of societies ; the aspirations and the protests which are at strife in great empires ; we are in fact in search of the collective.

CHAPTER XV

THREE VISIONS : RULERS, RULED, OUTSIDERS

Above all, I want to describe the ethology of the *rulers*, for it is the one with which we are expressly most familiar, we know it from our own observation.

Introspection. The state of mind of the ruler is our own state of mind ; to throw light on it, we need only question ourselves.

Observation. The state of mind of societies ruling over distant peoples may be discerned in their traditions, in their monuments and in the doctrines of their writers.

Let us then sketch a large picture of the states of mind of the ruling peoples in relation to the ruled. Let us stress three conceptions of our rôle which prevail in our spirit as dominators.

The three visions which all governing peoples entertain in their relations with the governed may be summed up in three words : domination, partnership, emancipation.[1]

First, *domination* which implies the superiority and the responsibility of the governing people. In its full and total sense, domination is the affirmation of authority and of paternity ; for this power is thought of as a power similar to the old *patria potestas*, the power of the father over his child. The colonies are children, placed under a power equal to the paternal power as understood in Roman Law. Paternity and authority are both implicit in the word domination.

Secondly, *partnership (association)*, or the equality of the ruled and ruling peoples, tends at least to represent the two groups as equals possessing the same powers and the same duties ; partnership ultimately, in the course of time, bringing about equality. A bond between two peoples on an equal footing, reached by mutual agreement, is an expression of fraternity. The original conception of kinship as expressing the relation between human groups which used to be thought of as a paternal relationship has gradually assumed the form of a *fraternal* relationship. Brother stands to brother as equal to equal, and in this second phase such is to be the relation between rulers and ruled. Brotherhood or affection are both implicit in the word association.

---

[1] Some remarks on this subject in *Doctrines coloniales*, by A. Garrigou-Lagrange.

Thirdly, *emancipation*. Emancipation in the eyes of civil law means the liberation of the governed. The desire is that the governed people shall not only be equal or tend to become equal in partnership with the governing, but that they shall be free and independent, that they shall be legally, if not actually, free to separate ; that they shall be in control of their present and of their future ; at liberty to live their own life ; that they shall consequently be—a Nation ; a State. That, of their subjection to the governing people who formerly ruled them, there shall in very truth remain nothing but a subtle, secret bond of faith and loyalty. Pushed to the extreme limit this situation would present a strange novelty from the point of view of former times. By the emancipation of the ruled the two peoples would become *strangers* to one another. There would be no more subjection, no more partnership ; nothing but a moral, sometimes a secret tie which would not impair the complete autonomy of either of the two nations. This estrangement might even go so far—as we have seen with the Romans—as to pass into unfriendliness and hostility. The emancipated nation, having resumed its liberty, might, in indulging its own ambitions, and seeking its own interests, turn against the overlords of yesterday, oppose their designs and hamper their policies by counter-policies ! As I shall point out, some would go so far as that. Looking through the other end of the telescope, putting ourselves in the place of the ruled instead of the rulers, we should see the same three phases in reverse : *subjection, conjunction, disjunction*. Subjection the reverse of domination ; conjunction the reverse of partnership ; disjunction the reverse of emancipation.

These three phases of the relations between colonisers and colonised recur elsewhere in all human groupings. We pass into the domain of sociology, for the concepts which characterise the relations of rulers and ruled characterise also all human groupings. Between husband and wife, between the sexes, between classes and ranks, as well as between the People and the State, we always find these three pairs of concepts : domination or subjection ; partnership or conjunction ; emancipation or disjunction. It is impossible to see how human groupings could have other phases of relationship than these three and the infinite gradations between them.

This being so, it is our business to enquire exactly how these three ideas are presented in the minds of peoples and authors. Describing these three ideas, distinguishing their varieties, and enumerating their manifold aspects we shall briefly accomplish our task.

Domination and subjection are products of a very old idea, the idea of paternity, the original form of authority. Partnership and emancipation originate in another, also very ancient conception, an idea not of paternity but of equality and brotherhood. You have either paternity or else equality ; legal relations, in all their complexity and diversity, proceed always from these two notions.

Paternity. Paternity : since colonisation, in the case of all the peoples we know of, notably in ancient times, has been conceived of as a filiation or even as reproduction. Colonies, said Plato, are children. Colonies, said Varro, are swarms. Various authors have described colonies as children born of the metropolis, the mother-country, children who ought therefore to remain under her governance.

In the course of time, however, paternity developed two meanings. There was, as we know, an evolution of the *patria potestas* in private life ; an evolution characterised by the important fact that the father's power became more and more a guardian's authority, no longer totalitarian authority, but authority implying more duties than powers.

The same evolution occurred in public law. The old idea of domination was superseded by the idea of guardianship. Thus two forms of paternal authority regulated the relations of the mother-countries with the colonies : *paternal-authority* or, alternatively, *paternal-guardianship*.

Paternal-authority, which we shall first consider, meant unqualified, unlimited domination : the ancient idea of the *patria potestas* which in public law as in private life connoted absolute power and right. When we speak of Imperialism in general, it is in this sense that we affirm paternity in so far as it implies a right and a power.

It would, however, be sound to emphasise two aspects of paternity which co-existed, though the second tended more and more to prevail. Paternity is conceived, or was conceived, now as power, now as *profit*.[1]

As *Power.* This is paternity for the sake of paternity and power for the sake of power. This is Imperialism in its first meaning, in its narrow meaning : the desire for *dominium*. In

---

[1] Cf. W. Sulzbach's analysis in A. Vierkandt's *Handwörterbuch der Soziologie*, s.v. *Imperialismus*, 1931, p. 253 f.

this case, the element of authority stands in the foreground ; the conquering peoples then imagined that they were exercising authority because it was right and seemly that they should do so, because power was of itself a thing of so much value that it was worth attainment by conquest.

This power, this first aspect of paternal authority, was conceived of as a *mission* or a *right*.

It was conceived of as a *mission* ; for power was among the ancients frequently taken to be a manifestation of God or a duty imposed by God.   It was held to be the will of the Eternal which desired and decreed this paternal domination.   The dominating peoples believed themselves the objects of a divine election ; of a spiritual destiny.   And when power and authority are the Gift of God, they are all the more untempered.   This earliest form of Imperialism is therefore *spiritual imperialism*.   Its basis is the sense of mission, its argument is the sense of destiny.   The *divine will* confers the *divine right*.   Kings being gods or viceregents of the gods, their reign was the reign of gods.

In the course of time, however, power became secularised. It was no longer conceived as a mission, but as a *right*, and thereafter power is sought, simply for the sake of power.   It is a good thing in itself to dominate, it is right and proper to dominate for the sake of dominating ; and it is good for the subject-people to be subjected to domination.   There is no longer a question of the Will of God ; the idea now is that power creates the right to power, and that great and strong peoples ought to rule ; that the subject-peoples are in duty bound to be ruled ; and that there is no need to appeal to the permission of the gods.   Power is a right, not a mission ; a secular, not a divine power. Imperialism at this stage has become power-imperialism ; *imperium* for the sake of *imperium* ; the " will to power ", the goal of ambition, the craving for greatness, the instrument of pride.

Conceived of as power, paternal authority is therefore either a mission of spiritual nature, or a right of material nature ; either *spiritual imperialism* or *power-imperialism*.

As *Profit*.   This idea of paternal power has developed into the idea of *Paternal Profit* ; the authoritarian element has receded from the foreground, giving way to a utilitarian element.   The desire now is to impose authority, not for the sake of power, but for the sake of advantage.   Material interest has carried the day.   This has now been the case with the great colonising nations for the last three hundred years.   Paternal authority seeking interest of one kind has tended towards exploitation and passed over into *Material Imperialism*, since the chief stress is now laid on the quest for gain.

Paternity thus seeks either power—mission or right—or profit, and is in consequence either spiritual imperialism or power imperialism or, finally, material imperialism. But always it retains authority, always superiority.   The judge of the ruler remains always the ruler himself.   Such is the *potestas* of Roman Law.

Already in very ancient times, however, with the Romans as well as with the Greeks, paternity had developed from paternal power into *paternal guardianship*. Public law amongst the Romans experienced the same evolution of paternal authority as was seen in private life and nowhere more than in the colonial sphere. The colonies are still considered as inferior and therefore subject, owing obedience to the metropolis or mother-country ; but the mother-country's authority has assumed a new attitude ; it has become guardianship, not merely authority ; duty, not merely power.   The accent is now on the burdens of paternity ; not on its benefits or its advantages.

Paternal guardianship implies the duty of *protection*, the duty of *education* : the education by the father of the son, by the ruler of the ruled.   The idea of protection, of education, conceived as a moral duty, was already latent in the old idea of paternity. That it should emerge from the background and take its place in the foreground : that duty should win the day over both power and profit, sufficed to allow the idea of paternal guardian-ship to develop, by a simple and natural process of evolution, out of the idea of paternal authority.

This idea of guardianship to-day tends to prevail amongst all colonising peoples. It is true that the authority of the ruling people still remains, that the superiority of the rulers, and the inequality between rulers and ruled, still remain ; but the con-viction has taken root that authority carries more duties than rights, that government is a burden in itself and a task, and that the rulers' first aim must be the protection and the education of the subject peoples.

The duty of the colonisers to protect and to educate, to improve and to *civilise*, results in *Cultural Imperialism*. *Imperialism* still, since we are still dealing with Government, since guardian-ship implies undisputed authority. *Cultural* Imperialism, or civilising imperialism, since the aim and the reason of this power is to civilise and " cultivate " the ruled by the efforts of the rulers ;

since the maxim is that colonisation should mean civilisation ; and that imperialism is now based on the diffusion and extension of " culture " in the overseas countries.

Paternity being thus guardianship not authority, duty not power, has suffered a re-direction ; it is no longer unlimited and untempered ; its effects are dictated by the intention that guides them. Regulated by its own aim, limited by its own purpose, it is exercised, above all and before all, in the interest of the ruled. Its re-direction implies moderation and limitation.

There is limitation of authority in regard both to its effect and to its duration. Limitation in its *effect* : since its aim is to work in the interest of the ruled, it is circumscribed by this interest. Limitation in its *duration* : since the idea of guardianship implies an earlier or later emancipation ; since the minors must one day come of age ; since the virtue of a guardian is worthily to fit his ward for liberty. This idea of authority-as-duty has in our day crystallised in the doctrine of the *Mandate*, pledged to work, not only in the chief but in the exclusive interest of the mandated country. Thus the idea of paternity, power first, then guardianship, has gradually evolved more and more from *authority* to *humanity*. In olden times it was authority only, for *potestas* was wholly unregulated, and prevailed in the interest of the master and not of the subject. In our times it has become *humanity*, since it is conceived more and more as a duty, and tends more and more to prevail in the interest of the governed. If inequality remains, this inequality gives birth to duties in both directions. Following step by step the evolution of paternal authority, colonial power has progressed from power to guardianship, from authority to humanity.

Pursuing this same path for a further stage we find that it leads to an idea of *equality*, another idea which was latent in paternity. We arrive at conceiving mother-country and colonies forming a perfect, a total society, which as the ancients—Plato foremost among them—had already perceived implied equality. True society, as Plato says, is friendship, valid only between equals. Thus, in the course of time the idea of humanity, evolving from paternity, has led us to an idea of equality, where we conceive the relations of rulers and ruled to be relations between equals.

This idea of *equality*, however, the second aspect of the relation between the governing and the governed, has itself two distinct aspects : it may be either friendship or liberty. Equality between tribes, cities, nations and States may be looked on from two points of view.

Either the two groups will establish between them relations of intimacy and friendship, in which case a *social* bond will be formed between them, resembling *fraternity* rather than paternity. This will be a relationship such as exists between brothers, not the relationship of parent to child. This fraternal relationship will henceforth be the model and the reflection of the relationship between the colonisers and the colonised. There will be equality in friendship or in society. Alternatively, the two groups will establish relations of freedom between them. The peoples or States which were formerly bound together will free themselves from each other, will separate or secede. In the first alternative we have *association*, in the second *dissociation*. These are the two alternative courses to which equality may lead : equality in friendship, equality in freedom.

First *Equality in Friendship*. This arises when " partnership " develops so successfully as to form a firm bond between colonisers and colonised, so that separation from each other becomes inconceivable. There will be community of interests and feelings, social ties both material and spiritual, solidarity, co-operation and if possible unanimity. A social link will have been forged and preserved by free will, and guaranteed by an agreement perpetually, though tacitly renewed.

Solidarity and reciprocity are needed. For what creates partnership and equality is the possession by both parties of bilateral rights and duties : not rights existing on one side only, not rights of a superior over an inferior, as in the case of domination of master over subject, or even of a father over his children, but bilateral powers, bilateral rights on both sides, exercised reciprocally in both directions.

At this point it has ceased to be Imperialism ; there is no longer domination, there is association ; there is no longer authority, there is *reciprocity*. So it has become *Mutualism* or Associationism. There is no authority, not even authority tempered by humanity, but instead community and fraternity. The evolution seen in our time is from authority to humanity and from humanity to fraternity. Fraternity and reciprocity, and in consequence—let us note also—we have familiarity and intimacy. Meeting together forms a moral bond ; to meet each other, to seek each other out and sometimes to marry each other ; here we see association opening the way to fusion.

Secondly, *Equality in Freedom.* Following the path we have chosen, we come to associate equality with other virtues. There is a desire—and in our days a desire felt most strongly by formerly subject peoples—that equality should result in liberty. There is a feeling that this desired equality cannot realise itself except in freedom and through freedom. There is in fact no actual equality in the partnership status ; created, regulated, by the old-time rulers, it remains in a certain sense and to a certain extent a partnership of un-equals. Equality is Liberty . . . since 1789. Equality must realise itself by secession. True partnership exists . . . when there is freedom to separate ; true friendship . . . when it can be broken off ! From criticism of the *abuse* as seen from the point of view of humanity or of fraternity, we should pass on to examine the question of *right* in itself. Thus both camps—not only the camp of the propagandised subjects but also the camp of the repentant masters—profess the belief that to have equality you must have liberty and that the subject peoples have the right to provoke their emancipation.

Two motives underlie the preaching of this idea : utility and equity. First there came, a good hundred years ago, the idea of utility. Liberal economists pleaded for the freedom of the colonies, not as a matter of justice, but on grounds of interest ; the advantage of the rulers, the advantage of the ruled, demanded, as they thought, separation ; and the common advantage of colonisers and colonised ought to lead to liberation. Nowadays, however, the idea of separation is based on *equity* or on *morality*, no longer on advantage but on sentiment. The education that we give to subject peoples arouses in them a feeling for right. This sentiment inspires the French colonies with nationalism and with collectivism, since these are both hostile to French authority, and since both insist that equity requires that the colonies should be set free, and that anything short of secession is a betrayal of humanity. Equality is thus made synonymous with *estrangement*. The contention is that the two peoples, so long linked together, have become foreign to each other, that they are perfectly well able to live separately ; and that each has the right to plan and promote its foreign relations in its own way and according to its own taste. The contention is, in fact, that the subject people have the right to become not only a foreign people but if they wish, or at need, an enemy to the rulers of yesterday ! This has been said, this has been written. Not only estrangement is suggested, but if necessary hostility, enmity. These are other ideas which are acts of faith and we must not shrink from facing them. We should then have neither imperialism nor reciprocity, but *autonomism* or separatism.

Having traced these main lines of thought and noted these different phases, we have delimited our field of action. Let us traverse it ; let us follow these mental forces and observe them at work constructing, destroying, the great imperial edifices.

BOOK V

DOMINATION

The idea of domination in the relations between conqueror and conquered arose from the transplanting of the ancient statute of the *patria potestas*. Paternal Domination must be considered on two different planes : of *motive* and *effect*. Its motives and aims are, in other words, the degrees to which the idea of domination was developed in one or another of the conquering peoples. We shall thus understand how the idea of paternal power begot the idea of paternal duty.

However great the change may have been both as regards motive and effect, the idea of domination has always had, at every time and in every place, certain abiding characteristics : two in particular, amongst many others : the claim to *immensity* and the claim to *eternity*.

The claim to *immensity* took account of *space*. The sovereigns of antiquity who founded great colonial empires claimed and intended to extend their authority over the whole known world. Hammurabi, King of Babylon,[1] author of the famous Code (now in the Louvre), proclaimed himself " King of the Four Zones ".

The claim to *eternity* took account of *time*. The great colonial empires, whether of ancient or modern times, have been imagined and proclaimed as being destined to endure for ever ; to build and to reign in the present and the future. This claim to eternal duration, carrying over into the future the idea of paternal authority, is the most striking characteristic of the desire of domination.

[1] [Reigned from 2067 to 2025 B.C. EOL]

CHAPTER XVI

SPIRITUAL IMPERIALISM : MOTIVES

Though the distinctive characteristics of this state of mind are always permanent, motives change with time and place. As we have already seen, domination was founded on a *spiritual* imperialism, or a *power* imperialism, or a *cultural* imperialism or a *material* imperialism.

Spiritual Imperialism. Spiritual imperialism is domination of a religious nature. Spiritual or religious imperialism is the first phase of all colonial imperialism. This surely provides us with an opportunity of unveiling the primitive driving force and the original urge to expansion. We must seek in religion the spirit of the first conquerors. Colonial illuminism led them to act ; it was dreams or visions, myths or legends, annunciations or revelations which guided their steps and placed weapons in their hands. Religion inspired them for one of two reasons : *fear* or *hope*. Religion is fear, in so far as its aim is to protect its votary from harm and save from sin, in so far as it is a procedure for the expulsion of evil. It is hope, in so far as it is a procedure for obtaining good, in so far as its aim is to achieve purity and attain virtue. It combines fear of evil and hope of good.

In the famous phrase of the Latin poet, " in the beginning fear creates the Gods ", *primo facit timor Deos* : amongst many peoples, peoples archaic and primitive, fear of evil was the father of colonisation. Many episodes of migration and of deportation were methods of expelling evil and of purifying the human group to avert the vengeance of the Spirits.

First, *Migrations.* The emigration of the whole group, of the entire tribe or city, later of an entire people, was an emigration ordered by the gods. The oracle or the augur, consulted by the elders, commanded the emigration of an entire people. Or it might be, as we have seen amongst Polynesians or Melanesians, that an oracle by promises favoured emigration without exactly commanding it. Whether by actual command or by strong suggestion, it was the Gods or the Spirits who brought about the transplanting of an entire group. We read in Herodotus (Book IV) how the Libyan city of Cyrene came to be founded. There was a king who, on consulting the oracle, received from the gods the command to transfer his kingdom with all his subjects to the country of Libya. At first he resisted and protested against the oracle delivered by the Pythian prophetess. It was then suggested to him that he should go to Delphi and consult the superior oracle. This also gave him the command to transplant his entire kingdom to Libya to put an end, so he was told, to the quarrellings that were going on between his subjects ; to give peace which is virtue ; to purify all his subjects from this sin of dissension ! [1] Amongst the populations of Oceania, notably the New Zealanders, entire peoples have thus set forth at the command of a God, whose pronouncement—so said the oracles—was that there was one way alone of purifying the " social body " (the word is literally rendered) from its sins, and this way was to quit the old land defiled by human sins, and depart to a new land. The people of the Marquesas Islands were also acquainted with similar marching orders ; to which the oracle attached the promise of God. It was their duty to go ; they desired to go. Fear and hope thus joined hands and this from the beginning. [2]

Deportations. We meet with deportations also, not always only transplantations : the emigration of a section of a people, or of one tribe, but not of the group in its entirety. Thus it sometimes happened amongst the peoples of antiquity when a calamity had occurred, that the priests decided that a purification was called for to appease the anger of the Spirits. It was then decided that a section of the tribe, or in the case of the Romans, a section of the citizens, should be expelled, so that these victims laden with the sin should carry it away with them. We do not need to seek examples among " savage " races, we find a well-known custom prevailing amongst the Romans, the institution of the *Ver sacrum* or the *Sacred Springtime*. [3] When a calamity had occurred, a drought, a famine or an epidemic, amongst the early Romans, all the children born the following year were dedicated to the gods by a procedure known as *devotio* ; and when these

---

[1] [The English reader is recommended to refer to Herodotus, IV, 150–9. The " king " in question was not the settled ruler of a settled population tilling the lands of their forefathers, but an adventurer king-errant (as one might say) whose " subjects " were wandering adventurers like himself. I can find in the text no suggestion that on either occasion the oracle at Delphi ordered the foundation of a colony in Libya as an expiation for sin or for dissension. EOL]

[2] For the American Indians, see J. W. Fewkes, *Tusayan Migration Traditions, Bureau of American Ethnology*, Report XIX, 1897–8, pp. 577–633.

[3] Daremberg-Saglio, *Dictionnaire des antiquités grecques et romaines*, s.vv. *Colonia* and *Devotio* : Strabo, V, 4–12 ; VI, 1, 6.

children reached maturity, they were deported to a distant country and there became the founders of a city. To a Roman mind this was a method of expelling the sin and exporting the evil. The babies who had been born after the calamity were made scapegoats to bear the burden of the sin, and twenty years later as young people they were obliged to betake themselves sin-laden to a distant place and there to found a city.

All the early European explorers were convinced that they were following God's call ; Christopher Columbus, Vasco da Gama and Fernando Cortes had each his astrologer with him. If they were leading, they were also led !

Colonisation of this type was a form of penance, and if we were seeking suitable words we might call it *Penitential Imperialism.* It was an expansion which would never have taken place if the Romans had not believed that it was necessary from time to time to put an end to evil by purifying the entire city, not, as formerly, by transplanting the whole body of citizens, but rather by deporting those citizens whose birth after a calamity indicated the wish of the gods to lay on them the sin. The *devotio* of the *Ver sacrum* was the occasion of the founding of many Roman colonies. There were thus sacred deportees, before occasion arose to deport ordinary folk. Deportees of one kind or another, men expelled for various reasons, have thus from earliest times played a leading part in the drama of colonisation. We know details of the cere-mony of the *Ver sacrum.* The young men born in the fatal year were led to the City Gates and a bull was driven in front of them. The spot where the bull ultimately halted was the site of the new city. Their deportation was the purging of the city's sin. Faith and fear are both evidently represented here.

Hope is also a motive force in religion. It embraces four different motives : hope of *salvation*, hope of *happiness*, hope of *advantage*, hope of *adventure*. Religion is always Hope : hope of a moral, spiritual or mystic good : communication with God, communion with God to obtain from Him all his benefits.

These benefits vary with the nature of the hope.—The hope of *salvation* by purity and holiness is sometimes to be fulfilled only by emigration to distant lands.—The hope of *adventure* : when a man has ambition to distinguish himself and earn the title of hero. The heroism of the conqueror is a religious heroism. The hero is a god, the hero is a saint.—The hope of *happiness* is a utopian or idyllic dream, in pursuit of which men up to our own day have sought to create in distant places a world of justice, where social sin shall be unknown and social evil ended, by founding Icarias [1] where a human ideal is to be realised in a far distant place, rather than a far distant future.—Hope of *advantage*. The lure of gain, the driving force behind many an expansion, was coloured by religion. It was a mythical, mystical idea ; for gain is also a benefit, a virtue, a way of salvation, and to many minds gain is itself good. So the greed of gain is exalted and magnified by divine support. Prosperity and Blessing are one and the same to a Musulman, one and the same to a Protestant. The lucky and the fortunate is the man blessed and chosen of God. Thus each religion has its Promised Land, its Eldorado to which God will guide . . . those whom He loves. All such hopes are myths and visions ; illusions sometimes realised, but " ever pursued ". The *saint*, the *hero*, the *righteous* and the *prosperous* : of such are the conquerors.

Hope of *Salvation*. First, we consider the hope of salvation. Many colonisations have had as their primary aim the attainment of salvation : salvation for the rulers *themselves* or mayhap salvation for *others*, namely the ruled ; or, more often, salvation for both at once. For many a day, and down to our own time, colonisation was undertaken for self-salvation and the salvation of others. First, it was the conquerors who were to be saved ; they were *Pilgrims* or *Crusaders*. The founding of colonies was the translation into practice of that " Crusading Spirit " which inspired the great colonising peoples of East and West. Pilgrims and crusaders alike set out to seek their own salvation and incidentally also the salvation of others.

They sought self-salvation in seeking *penance* and *indulgence*, in the time-honoured and canonical sense of these words. Expansion was thus both an expulsion of evil and an attainment of good. The Crusaders had been cleansed of their sins by undertaking a Crusade, by enlisting under the Sign of the Cross, which betokened their vocation to go forth and conquer, to go forth and govern the Unbeliever. In 888, long before the First Crusade, we find the Western Church advocating crusades into pagan countries and promising the Crusaders, even those who survived to return, the reward of salvation. This religious expansion as a means to salvation was the master thought of the Middle Ages in Europe.

---

[1] [Icaria is a small Greek island, one of the Southern Sporades, off the south-west coast of Asia Minor. The French Socialist Étienne Gabet, an admirer of Thomas More's *Utopia*, published in 1840 his *Voyage en Icarie* and eight years later led a party of idealists off to the United States to found a communistically-run colony on the Red River in Texas. EOL]

Already the idea of self-salvation was not enough ; more and more the salvation of others, the salvation of the conquered, became the inspiration which underlay colonisation. Expansion was carried out in order to *convert*. Belatedly, but very often in good faith, the conquerors armed themselves with anxiety for the salvation of others. None of them, not even the conquerors of the New World of the Americas, considered himself merely as a conqueror. All believed that they were actuated by a religious motive ; they felt themselves to be pledged in bounden duty to convert the heathen beyond the seas. We shall see this fully manifest in the novels and poems of Spain and Portugal. All the works of imagination which in these countries served as colonial propaganda, especially in the 16th century, are mystical quite as much as political literature. Lope de Vega wrote a poetical drama, *The New World Discovered*, which represents idolatry as Columbus saw it ; Columbus was, he thinks, compelled to cross the seas to put an end to idolatry, to convert the inhabitants of the West Indies and establish in these new countries that unity of faith which Roman Catholicism offered : religious universality. This was one of the favouring breezes which swelled the square sails of the great explorer's three caravels which bore on them the sign of the Cross.

We shall return and deal more fully with the hope of salvation. Meantime there was also the hope of *adventure*, the hero's craving to distinguish himself by famous exploits ; in a word, the ideal of *chivalry*. Herodotus tells us (II, 32) that he heard from men of Cyrene, of some young Nasamonians, " certain sons of chief men who were of unruly disposition ",[1] who when they reached maturity felt an urge to ennoble their manhood by some distinguished feat : they chose by lot five of their number to explore the deserts of Libya. The purpose of this exploit was to sanctify their initiation into manhood ; such was the mystical virtue of a brilliant deed. Similarly, religious inspiration was the father of early chivalry ; beneath the surface of chivalry lay the idea of some great exploit, or, as the phrase ran, some deed of high *emprise* : some adventure without utilitarian aim, some heroic action, some unprofitable exploit. Chivalrous emprise was sought for the adventure itself, for its own sake, for the honour it conferred. The Holy War offered risk and danger.[2] The

---

[1] [I quote G. C. Macaulay's English translation, but find in the passage no trace of a religious or mystical motive behind this " extravagant " adventure. EOL]

[2] Anouar Hatem, *Les poèmes épiques des Croisades*, 1932, pp. 34 f. and 45 f. (thesis).

knights of old were suitors of fortune and adventurers pursuing a religious ideal. Nobility and prestige rewarded the exploit : but the unprofitable exploit was itself virtue. Glory was of God and those who won it were of the elect. This held true both in the East and West.

Such was the earliest conception of adventure : heroism, asceticism ; toil and privation ; maximum effort, but for the sake of others ; and, for this reason, fraught with benediction. Let us revert to Herodotus. He tells how five young men of the Nasamonian tribe were chosen by lot to set off to explore far-distant Libya. These were, we may well believe, heroes marked out by the gods, for amongst the Ancients the result of a drawing of lots was held to indicate the divine will. So it was the gods who wished for heroes, it was the gods who chose out the heroes. The hero's exploit was therefore the work of the gods ; it satisfied and served them, and thus came to be a method of purification and sanctification. If the exploit involved action, such action was beneficent. Divine inspiration *creates* heroes and it is in the name of the gods that they conquer in their combats. We find therefore that we have not only the religious deportee but also the religious adventurer.

This explains the vast rôle played in all Spanish and Portuguese expansions by the mass of novels and narratives which are the epics of chivalry and which were fervently read by the conquerors of the New World. One Portuguese novel in particular, the *Amadis of Gaul* by Vasco de Lubeira, was the inspiration of many adventurers. Cervantes' *Don Quixote* was, as we know, a satire on *Amadis*.[1] For this novel of mystic and heroic ingredients was the bedside book of the great explorers. Fernando Cortes was fond of reading it, and took it with him on his American voyage. Thanks to it he was haunted by a " heroic and brutal dream " and imagined himself chosen of God to abolish the barbarism of the Mexicans.[2] Other conquistadors too were steeped in the same literature, dwelling especially on the episode where the knight who was known as the Chevalier of the Lion had crossed the sea to conquer and organise an island. The Chevalier of the Lion, Amadis himself, became the inspiration of adventure-seekers in his romantic character, not only of explorer and navigator, but also of ruler and legislator. So

---

[1] E. Baret, *De l'Amadis de Gaule et de son influence sur les mœurs et la littérature au XVI⁰ et au XVII⁰ siècles*, 1873 (thesis) ; H. de Tourville, *Histoire de la formation particulariste*, 1903, pp. 431–2 (Chivalry and Portuguese Discovery).

[2] J. Babelon, *Fernand Cortes*, 1928, pp. 38–9, 90, 97, 170, 191–2.

strong was this influence, that in 1543 Charles V issued a decree directed against the over-indulgence in all these novels of chivalry, in particular against the *Amadis of Gaul*! In his opinion too many adventurers were contaminated by this novel. I am therefore not drawing on my own imagination when I emphasise the very great effect produced by this novel of religious heroism. We are told that at the very moment when the Emperor was forbidding his subjects to read the *Amadis* he himself was surreptitiously enjoying it in private! The book had been translated by a Spaniard, possibly Montalvo, who had added in 1521 a lengthy sequel, *The Exploits of Esplandion*, assuredly enough to turn any Spaniard's head!

All these mystical and heroic novels were the literary ancestors of a prolific family of secular romances and adventure stories of filibusters and pioneers, novels like those of Le Sage, André des Vosges, Fenimore Cooper, de la Landelle, Duplessis, Gabriel Ferry, which we have all read, and the contemporary novels of Melville and Conrad. All these have tended to strengthen the forces of expansion.[1] These epics coloured many a dream. The spell of these adventure-yarns lured many off to try their fortune in distant lands. Speaking of his own childhood in *Une Saison en Enfer*, Arthur Rimbaud tells us : "I dreamt Crusades, voyages of discovery whose tale was as yet untold, . . . migrations of races, displacements of continents." As we know, he realised his dream. The quest for salvation, the quest for adventure . . . these were religious dreams, later secularised. In his *Decades*, which he began to publish in 1552, the Portuguese historian João de Barros,[2] stands at the cross-roads : his history is an epic . . . of propaganda, the tale of feats of arms deliberately intended to encourage further feats of arms. Its great success was then . . . publicity! Barros was, in fact, already in those days an imperial poet![3]

There is, however, the hope of *Happiness* also, a dream of bliss, religious dream and hope : an idyllic or idealist dream no longer heroic. Then, as now, people hoped to find in distant

---

[1] G. C. Bosset, *Fenimore Cooper et le roman d'aventure en France vers 1830*, 1929. Prévost's *Cleveland* tells the fictitious story of a colony in Negro Africa of people from La Rochelle.

[2] [The able and disinterested administrator of John III of Portugal wrote a *History of the Portuguese in India* in four volumes called *Decades*, the last of which was published in 1570, the year of his death. EOL]

[3] In the Preface to his *Sauvages* (1603) Samuel Champlain wrote :

> Shame on the coward who stays in one place,
> His life to my thinking's degrading and base.

> (Fi des lâches poltrons qui ne bougent d'un lieu,
> Leur vie, sans mentir, me parait trop mesquine !)

countries the happiness that was not possible in ancient lands. They dreamt a dream of *Utopia*, distant not in time but in space. When we long to quit the saddening spectacle of a corrupt world, two ways are open to us : we can escape in time, we can escape in place.

We can transport ourselves into another day, take refuge in the past or in the future, still pursuing our dream ; indulge in retrospective or futurist visions, which is nothing more than to satisfy a Platonic yearning. We can transplant ourselves in space : create afar what we cannot create at home : establish justice by organising virgin lands according to a " straight plan ". We can act and not dream. Instead of indulging regrets and enduring disgust, we can make plans, we can try experiments, we can desire and foresee, we can build and reign. We can sail into the distance, as men on manifold occasions in the past have done, and seek the Fortunate Isles where we can dispense equality and justice to the pure and happy. The Utopia of place leads men to action. As Talleyrand said in Year V of the French Revolution " the colonies reopen the gates of Hope and consign to oblivion hatreds and regrets ". Stendhal sometimes thought of retiring to the colonies to seek a simple, natural life.

We see therefore that there was a type of adventurer who set out to seek at a distance not salvation, not adventure, but happiness, who believed that he could find liberty, equality or fraternity beyond the seas. Under Louis XIV it was the recalcitrant and the adventurer, filibuster or buccaneer, who quitted France in search of gain, but in search also of liberty and equity. The adventurer feels a kind of home-sickness for a free life and a just one. Le Sage has incarnated this state of mind in Chevalier Beauchêne (1732). Once having " crossed the Line " they considered themselves free from the King's jurisdiction ; they dictated their own laws, they created a new order and their conventions of " seamanship " were unanimously respected.[1] Among them were ignorant men who acted without reflection, but there were planners also who reduced their dreams and hopes to writing, by drawing up all the statutes of the many new kingdoms which they hoped to found, and which in some cases they did in fact succeed in founding.[2] As early as 1689, under

---

[1] Details will be found in Œxmelin (Œxquemelin) : *Histoire des aventuriers et filibustiers* . . . , French trans. 1786. On " Beauchêne ", see G. Chinard, *Revue du XVIII*[e] *siècle*, I, 1913, pp. 279-93.

[2] Bishop Las Casas and after him the Jesuits had already formed similar plans. For details, see Prévot's *Histoire générale des voyages*, 1754, XII, p. 198 f., and XIV, pp. 81-2.

Louis XIV, a son of Admiral Duquesne's drew up a draft constitution for a "True Republic" which he hoped to found in
the Île de Bourbon.[1] Though this project resulted in nothing,
it was a signal, and many other plans followed.[2] Many of the
reformers were to see their Utopias realised. Colonies of
Socialists or Communists [3] were founded in America or Africa,
and survived sometimes for a few years, sometimes for a few
decades. There were the Icarian [4] and the Brook Farm experiments (the latter known as "the Phalanx") in the United States ;
the Anarchist colonies of Algeria, notably that of the brothers
Reclus ; all of these testified and witnessed to the fact that overseas adventures may be inspired by a dream of happiness. The
great mind of Talleyrand was well aware of this. Amongst the
various aims of colonisation there has always been this : to offer
a haven of hope to the "refractory", the rebel, the dissatisfied,
to all in short who hunger and thirst after an ideal. In his
Questions contemporaines Renan reproached the French Revolution
with having checked the colonial movement, and thus closed
the sole outlet which might have calmed "socialism" down !

Lastly there is the dream of *Advantage,* or the hope of gain, in
so far as this carries a mythical religious tinge. It is from this
point of view that we discuss it, for greedy of gain as the adventurers were, their greed long took the form of an inspired hope ;
illusion has been a driving force to which the world owes some
very great achievements. The gain they sought in distant lands
was far from being an assured, guaranteed gain, for they knew
nothing of the fabulous countries where they went to seek it !
But they imagined that these countries were a Land of Gold,
in short an Eldorado. The Greek legend of the Argonauts—
probably the first of all colonial romances—combines the dream
of *adventure* and the dream of *booty*: you perform exploits, you
carry off women, you amass gold on sheepskins. You display
your strength, you exercise your guile, you seek your gain.

[1] G. Atkinson, *Les relations de voyages* . . . , undated, p. 52 f.
[2] Restif de la Bretonne had formulated a circumstantial scheme for "transplanting
beggars to Africa" : *Le Thesmographe,* 1789, p. 329 f. A similar idea in Goldsmith's
Deserted Village imitated by Delille in *L'homme des champs.* Rustic happiness—
especially at a distance !
[The English reader may query this interpretation of *The Deserted Village* (1770).
Professor Maunier is quoting Rutlidge's French translation which appeared in 1772
under the title of *Le retour du philosophe, ou le village abandonné.* EOL]
[3] G. Atkinson, *Les relations de voyages* . . . , undated ; C. Gide, *Les colonies communistes* . . . , 1928 and C. Nordhoff's earlier *Communist Societies,* 1876 ; F. Lepel-
letier, *Réforme sociale,* April 1906 ; B. Fay, *L'esprit révolutionnaire aux États-Unis,* 1925,
pp. 156–79 (thesis).
[4] See footnote p. 157.

Moses led the Hebrews out of Egypt hoping to find the Promised Land within sight of which he was destined to die. Such was the fate of many such adventurers. Hope infinite, hope inspired, hope : and loot ; these were the things which lured many colonisers towards distant shores. Not Jews alone, but later Christians too ; for our Middle Ages—though Eldorado had not yet been dreamt of—had the vision of the Land of Cockaygne, the country so often told of in the mediæval *Fabliaux*, a country where the only law was idleness and plenty ; [1] a country of which the very earliest explorers were in search, as they set out on their treasure hunting. We know that the crusading adventurers had all been reared on the *Fabliaux*. They went forth to deliver Jerusalem from the Infidel—and to annex the treasures of Mecca, all the treasures of Araby whose fame, as reported by the pilgrims, had fired every mediæval heart. The most adventurous of them all—adventurous in every sense of the word—the famous and notorious plunderer, Renaud de Châtillon, Lord of Trans-Jordan, sought for vast booty in Arabia : which was no small act of faith ! Westwards too they sailed, looking for the Paradise of St. Brendan and the Fountain of Youth. When, at the beginning of his third voyage (1498), Columbus reached Terra Firma he thought he had found St. Brendan's Isle. On discovering Florida in 1512 Ponce de Leon also imagined that he had there found Paradise ! [2] Later people were to search for Prester John, lord of fabulous treasures, king of a horned, one-eyed race of men, who lived in luxury and whose coins were discs of gold ! Popes and kings alike were firm believers in Prester John. [3] He did exist ; but not as seen by the eye of childish faith ! The distant successors of Prester John, the Kings of Ethiopia, reaped benefit from his fame.

Treasure-Seeking : this was the idea which finally crystallised into the dream of *Eldorado*, [4] a dream which inspired many

---

[1] *Li Fabliaux Coquaigne* in Vol. IV of the Barbazan Collection. Cockaygne is a country where roasting spits turn of themselves in the streets which are watered by rivers of wine. Rabelais remembered it well !

[2] D'Avezac, *Les îles fantastiques de l'Océan* . . . , 1845 ; W. H. Babcock, *Legendary Islands* . . . , 1922.

[3] Ch. V. Langlois, *Le connaissance de la nature et du monde au Moyen Age*, new Ed. 1908. P. Gruyer, *L'Atlantide du " Prêtre Jean", Le Correspondant*, March 25, 1920, pp. 1123-34. Consult Moréri, *Prêtre-Jean* (New Ed. 1759, VIII, 558).—On St. Brendan's Island, see H. Beuchat, *Manuel d'archéologie américaine*, 1912, p. 37 f. Cf. C. de la Roncière, *Jacques Cartier*, 1931, p. 11 f.

[4] On Eldorado : La Dixmerie, *Voyage en Espagne*, 17 . . . , I, pp. 24-31 ; E. Fournier, *Le Vieux-Neuf* . . . , 2nd Ed. 1890, I, pp. 400-5 ; A. F. Bandelier, *El Dorado, the Gilded Man*, 1893 ; and a Spanish book which I have not seen, by Professor Manuel Ferrandis Torres of Valladolid.

explorations. El Dorado is the " gilded one ", the " gilded king ", a being who was supposed to exist in the New World and whose skin, each morning, was anointed anew with gold. It was in this guise that the Red Indian Chibchas of Bogota used to enthrone their new chief. After a fast, he took his place on a raft, stark naked and smeared all over with sticky clay which was then sprinkled with gold-dust. Balal-Cazar, conqueror of Ecuador, has left us a record of it all. It was only later that the word Eldorado came to mean no longer the gilded king but the country, that country of " Manoa " which Orellana professed to have discovered in the neighbourhood of the Orinoco. For over two centuries men searched for it, and numerous explorers, many of whom never reappeared, travelled, especially through South America, in this quest. The great early voyages in the direction of Guiana—where Eldorado was mistakenly believed to lie—made it their chief purpose to discover this famous country, which Baltasar Gracian, author of *El Discreto* (the typical courtier) imagined that he had described ! Queen Elizabeth's favourite, Sir Walter Raleigh, was, he tells us, seeking for Eldorado in his expedition of 1595 and right skilfully he exploited this illusion by publishing a book full of fables to promote the English occupation of Guiana.[1] People also believed in a town called *Cebola*, whose houses were covered in gold. When people saw the *pueblo* of Zuñi, a poor Red Indian village in New Mexico, they took it also to be an Eldorado. That was about 1540.

Later it was the *Terra Australis* which was believed to be the home of treasure and the first exploration of Australia in 1595—then known as New Holland—by Pedro Fernando de Quiros, was undertaken in the hope of acquiring this loot.[2] Vairasse and Sadeur, both of them authors, located their utopias in the " Southern Seas ". In times less remote from our own, within the last hundred years, the foremost purpose of the colonisers of California was the discovery of gold. The " thirst for gold ", as it has been called, was, at least in the beginning, stimulated by an illusion which remained for ever an illusion for the majority of the gold-seekers. Columbus himself was on the look-out for gold. In his Letter of 1503 to the King he wrote thus : " Gold is an excellent thing : . . . it is by gold that everything in the world is done . . ." And at Veragua, where the " lords " are

---

[1] L. Lemonnier, *Sir W. Raleigh*, 1931, p. 81 f.
[2] A. Reinaud, *Le continent australien. Hypothèses et découvertes*, Paris, 1893 (Literature thesis) ; G. A. Wood, *The Discovery of Australia*, 1922.

buried with their gold, he thought he had discovered the strata worked by the Jews under King Solomon ! The Spaniards thought the mines were enchanted ; they feared them at the same time as they sought them. These treasure-hunters were seeking gain, but theirs was a search inspired and lighted by illusion, and often born of deliriously intoxicating myth. It offered an escape from the miseries of our old countries. The Californian prospectuses of 1850—the memory of which is preserved by Cham's drawings [1] hoping to attract new immigrants, spoke of an " Earthly Paradise, a new Canaan ". If we were bent on coining words—but we should need too many—we might talk of *Starveling Imperialism* ! Throughout the whole oceanic world the " Treasure Islands " [2] have kept their secret.

Hopes and dreams, faith and illusion ; they outstripped reality and in the world of far-away they sought the beyond-the-possible. But Man was not daunted by failure. Imagination works wonders ! He went on hoping, he went on seeking ! Colonisation has in the past been built on . . . vanished dreams and hopes unrealised.

[1] [Amadée de Noé, known as Cham, a famous French caricaturist (1819–1879). EOL]
[2] *Treasure Island* is the title of a well-known story by Robert Louis Stevenson. See Hazel Ballance Eadie's *Lagooned in the Virgin Islands*, 1932 (Routledge).

CHAPTER XVII

SPIRITUAL IMPERIALISM : EFFECTS

Spiritual Imperialism, so diverse in its *motives*, remains, as we shall see, constant in its *effects*.

Let us first note how old the idea is and how immortal ; how societies in every age have felt the stirrings of spiritual imperialism. It is an ancient and at the same time a universal phenomenon. Every human group which possesses a God and worships him, seeks to spread the worship of its God. Whether among the Ancients or the Primitives, every human group, tribe, clan or city, has its own peculiar god, as it has its own peculiar blood ; in the early stages of human development, the human group is defined by its blood and by its god. Possessing his body —literally—and his spirit, the human group acquires the consciousness of its own identity and the feeling of its own superiority ; its god is its own god and therein lies the greatness of the group.[1] Hence it despises the foreigner : for the foreigner adores another god and is therefore an unbeliever, a being of different blood and of a different deity. The notion of " unbeliever " goes back to the beginning of time. If you are not of the clan, of the tribe, of the city, if you are of other blood and of another god, you are a stranger and therefore an enemy. These are relations founded on contempt. For the tribe, or for the city—so it was amongst the ancient Romans—there are only two courses to follow with regard to the stranger, who is at once despised and feared : he must be either exterminated or assimilated. If you are to assimilate him you must impose on him the god you have of your own, you must spread and extend the worship of your god : you must convert the unbelieving stranger.

The ambition to convert by conquering is the attitude of mind which in France Monsieur de Voltaire has represented in his tragedy of *Mahomet*. Zopire, a confidant, addressing Mahomet, and raising the whole grave question of spiritual imperialism, expresses himself thus :

> And yours is this project ? Your arrogant scheme
> Claims the right to remodel the earth to your whim.

---

[1] On this primitive *organicism* see R. Maunier, *Essai sur les groupements sociaux,* 1929, Chap. III.

Bringing bloodshed and terror, you fain would compel
To think as you do, other humans as well.
You ravage the world, to teach men what's right,
And darken their heaven to give them more light.
What right has been granted you . . .

To which Mahomet replies with the famous couplet :

The right which a mind, vast and sure of its plan,
Has to lift up the spirit of low-minded Man.[1]

Contempt for the stranger, that is obvious enough ; yet a contempt which presently becomes tinged with affection : benevolent not malevolent contempt. First of all, contempt : for you begin by despising those you intend to convert, you teach them and indoctrinate them in order to raise and uplift them. It happens, however, that contempt becomes affection, and you arrive at feeling that it is a moral duty to convert these foreigners who are backward and degraded folk, whose impurity you *ought* to change into sanctity by their conversion.

To understand it better, we must thoroughly investigate the idea which people formed of the Unbeliever. Two attitudes to the Infidel were possible.

Amongst the Ancients—and this attitude long persisted— every Unbeliever was just an animal. Foreigners were animal, not human, since for the Ancients [2]—and for the Primitives [3]— the essence of Humanity, the thing which distinguished man from animal, was : religion. To be a man you must have a god. Better still : to be a man you must have *my* god, or rather *our* god. He who has not our god is not a man like us, he is not an equal. Talking of the natives of the Southern Sea, the philosopher Maupertuis spoke of them as " a species intermediate between us and monkeys ". In *Mein Kampf* Hitler writes of the Negro that he is a "half-ape " capable of training but not of culture ! This conception has prevailed amongst many peoples ; not only amongst the primitives and the ancients, but in the Middle Ages among ourselves in the West. Many texts

[1] Voilà donc tes desseins, c'est donc toi dont l'audace,
De la terre à ton gré prétends changer la face,
Tu veux, en apportant le carnage et l'effroi
Commander aux humains de penser comme toi,
Tu ravages le monde et tu prétends l'instruire.
Quel droit as tu recu...
Du droit qu'un esprit vaste et ferme en ses desseins
A sur l'esprit grossier des vulgaires humains.
[2] Aulus Gellius, the whole of Book IX (Ed. Panckouke, II, pp. 91-7) ; Solinus, *Polyhistor*, Chap. LIII (same ed., pp. 315-23).
[3] Granet has clearly shown that for the Chinese also distant barbarians were criminal monsters against whom war was therefore legitimate.

exist in which Unbelievers are called animals, and under the French king Saint Louis, the law treated intimacy with Infidel women as " buggery ", in other words as bestiality committed with " beasts devoid of reason ". The Sea Code known as the *Rôles d'Oléron* granted the right to seize the goods of " enemies of our faith " as if they were " dogs " ! [1] This sounds like the Malays of the Cape speaking to the English Burchew in 1910, and voicing their contempt for the Hottentots by calling them offspring of orang-utangs. For the ancient Aryans the free man was one whose second birth had been celebrated ; and their black slaves for whom this rite had not been performed, were therefore also animals !

Another conception of the Unbeliever later became current among the Ancients, but it also expressed contempt. He was no longer an animal but a *savage* in the fullest sense. The savage was just a person who did not share the religion of the human group who were estimating him, the religion of the conquering or dominant group. The conception of the barbarian or the savage was thus for a long time a religious idea, before it became what it is nowadays, a political, economic or sociological idea. An Animal or a Savage, a being without a god : such was the foreigner.

We thus perceive how spiritual imperialism, under whatever sky, displayed two constant features : *duty* and *domination*. Whatever the motive or the aim may be, whether salvation, adventure, happiness or gain is sought—but particularly if salvation is the object—imperialism is a duty for the dominant party and is imposed on the dominated.

First the *Duty*. Duty is the quality in which spiritual imperialism differs profoundly from every form of temporal imperialism. For salvation is a duty. There is no religion in which salvation is optional. The fundamental characteristic of every religion is that a man is in duty bound to save his soul ; salvation is the end, the cult is his means to that end. Collective or personal salvation, public or private blessing, it matters not. It is for salvation that duty is decreed ! [2] You must preach your religion, you must spread it among the Gentile peoples, for this is your

---

[1] J. Loiseleur, *Crimes et peines*, 1863, p. 139 f.   On the Red Indians as " animals devoid of reason ", see Robert Ricard, *La conquête spirituelle du Mexique*, 1933, p. 111 f. (thesis).

[2] For what follows see L. Capéran, *Le problème du salut des infidèles*, I, *Essai historique*, 1934 ; Th. Simar, *Étude sur . . . la doctrine des races*, 1922, p. 36 f. ; B. Landry, *L'idée de chrétienté . . .* , 1929.

duty to and for yourself. Salvation and blessing are obligatory for every human being ; for the believer this is what distinguishes man from beast. The aim of man's life is to attain salvation and to bring salvation. An unknown sculptor has expressed this biblical idea in the famous tympanum at Vézelay where we see the Apostles teaching distant savages. His carving is but the paraphrase of the famous command : " Go ye therefore and teach all nations " (Matthew xxviii, 19). Every religious imperialism therefore includes the universal : the duty of humanity towards humanity. This is the idea which for centuries held sway in the West, for the Old World and for the New.

For the Old World there was in the Middle Ages the idea of the Crusade ; the Crusaders believed that they had both a right and a duty to propagate in battle the Faith of Christ.[1] For two centuries or thereabouts—from 1096 to 1291—the good Christian accomplished on the battlefield the work of achieving his own salvation. Emigration was a purificatory sacrifice, since the adventure and " emprise " of the Crusader was in effect a warrior's pilgrimage. His adventure was at the same time an act of penitence, a bid for pardon. Pilgrim and Penitent were one. The man who had gone forth, bearing the Cross— even when he returned in safety—had won pardon for all his sins, and reaped the benefit of all the indulgences offered. There are texts to prove this : the Crusade was a duty, or at least a proof of zeal ; war for the Faith brought blessing. You must, like the apostles and martyrs, suffer to win salvation, so says Rutebeuf[2] in his *Dispute du Croisé*.

Let us realise that other motives also underlay the Crusades, and we are here dealing with the Crusade in itself. It was capable of unleashing every type of greed and covetousness. The Crusade gave vent also to a delight in vengeance on the Musulman who had defeated the peoples of Christendom. The poet Rutebeuf, in his *Complainte d'Outre-Mer*, seeks to stir up the king Saint Louis not to abandon the Country of Christ to " all these Bedouins ". Ambition, self-interest and vanity all found an outlet in the Crusades. For the Crusaders were not recruited only from the ranks of the humble ; princes, nobles and

---

[1] A. Luchaire, *Innocent III. La question d'Orient*, 1907 ; L. Bréhier, *L'Église et L'Orient au Moyen Age*, 1907 ; R. Grousset, *Histoire des Croisades et du Royaume Franc de Jérusalem*, 1934–5. We lack the magnificent book on psychology which Alphandéry might have written. E. Bridrey, *La condition juridique des Croisés*, 1900 (thesis).

[2] [Rutebeuf (*circa* 1245–85), famous French *trouvère*, satirist and narrative poet. EOL]

wealthy merchants played their part. The Crusades were always compounded of spiritual imperialism, power imperialism and material imperialism. Crusaders made conquests : and hunted for relics. Greed and hope were alike almost infinite. In the background and at the beginning, however, there lingered always the idea of the Christian's obligation to seek his own salvation by conquering, in order to extend the Faith of Christ. In 1452 Philippe le Bon, Duke of Burgundy, gave a banquet to encourage his household and retainers to enlist under the banner of the Cross. To stimulate them he provided as an intermediate " course ", a tableau of Religion held captive by a Saracen. Much later, the conquerors of the New World wore on their breast a Cross, and deemed themselves Crusaders of a new era and a new world : Columbus, Albuquerque and Vasco da Gama all wore the Cross and planted the Cross on reaching distant shores.

The idea of the duty of a " spiritual conquest " of the Old World already found expression in the doctrine and especially in the theology of the Middle Ages in the West. In the bailiwick of Coutances there was a certain lawyer, Pierre Dubois by name, who published in 1306 a large treatise entitled *De recuperatione terræ sanctæ*.[1] This was a scheme for the conquest of the Holy Land, but also and chiefly for the administration and organisation of the lands of the Levant. His plan would have seen the great European countries form a sort of international alliance, a kind of League of Nations—long before the phrase or the idea was conceived—to govern and develop the countries of the Latin Orient. And this lawyer, Pierre Dubois, considered it a duty to achieve this conquest, at once a spiritual and material conquest, of the Near East. He dreamt of encouraging not only legislation and development but education too ; and he outlined a scheme of instruction to proselytise and to convert the inhabitants.

This first characteristic of " spiritual conquest ", the idea of duty or obligation, was here confined to the Old World. Later, from the 15th century onwards, it was reformulated for the New and we have seen the Papacy impose on Christians the obligation to conquer in order to convert. " Fishing for souls " is then a legal duty. It was the Borgia Pope Alexander VI who first initiated this universal religious imperialism. His Bull of 1493 extended to the New World and thence to the entire universe, the duty of propagating the Faith of Christ as the sole justification

[1] B. Hauréau, *Pierre Dubois, Journal des Savants*, Jan. 1894.

of every occupation.[1] The natives of America were held to be neither animals, nor savages, nor barbarians, but simply " naked men living peaceably together "—so says the text—happy, virtuous folk, already believing in a Creator God, men who lacked nothing of perfection save that they were not Christians. Little as we should expect it, the text suggests the " theory of the Noble Savage ", the naked, uncorrupted man, living in happiness and honour, far removed from the evils of our countries, a man whom the Faith of Christ could ripen into a perfect human being. In dividing up the New World between Spaniards and Portuguese, the Pope formally laid down the condition that taking possession of any part of the country must imply *teaching* religion and morals to all the inhabitants of the new land and sending to them good men, learned, expert and god-fearing !

The popes were not alone in preaching spiritual imperialism ; after them the humanists, and later still the economists, preached it too ! Half a century later, the same universal religious imperialism flourished in Erasmus : the duty of Christians to conquer in order to convert. Another half-century after Erasmus, the economist Montchrestien dedicated in 1615 to the Queen Mother a *Treatise of Political Economy*—he was the inventor of the word, if not also of the science itself—in which he also proclaimed the conqueror's obligation to evangelise. Theorists and ordinary people were in this at one : the propagation of the Faith was obligatory. Lawyer, traveller and adventurer, Marc Lescarbot went to the New World and wrote in 1612 an account of La Nouvelle France. His preface elaborates the same opinion : the aim of expansion is conversion. The Kings of France recognised the duty and proclaimed it. The commissions given in 1540 and 1541 by François I to Jacques Cartier and to Roberval for Canada, commanded them to " instruct " the savages " in the love and fear of God and of His Holy Law ". The Charter granted in 1600 by Queen Elizabeth of England to a colonising Company spoke of " duties higher than those of commerce ". If merchants must buy and sell, they must also convert.

Such is the ancient source of the idea of universal duty on which all Christian missions are based. The idea of the missionaries, or the " missionary idea ", is, that there exists a duty to spread the Faith for the salvation of all men. When the greatest

---

[1] The French translation will be found in G. Gourd, *Chartes coloniales*, 1885, I, p. 199 f. See also Martin V's indult awarding certain lands to the Portuguese on condition that they should take chaplains with them to " carry Christ's message ". See footnote, p. 22, n.1.

missions were founded in the course of, and especially towards the end of the 18th century, notably the great Protestant missions, the idea of salvation by conversion stood out in high relief. It was the Protestants who most firmly asserted the idea of obligation. First of all the Methodists, and a little later the Baptists, two sects which in our day are still actively alive, made the duty of preaching their guiding principle. These are sects of zealous Christians whose aim is to spread the Scriptures throughout the world by preaching and singing for the glory of God.[1] The Baptist minister William Carey [2]—William, not Henry—published in 1792 a book entitled *The Christian's Obligation to Spread the Faith*.[3] Shortly after the appearance of Carey's book, three great Missions were founded : the Mission to Tahiti in 1795 ; in 1799 the African Missionary Society ; in 1822 the Society of Evangelical Missions.

The hundred and five exiles who embarked in the *Mayflower* in 1620 had announced in their famous *Compact* that the primary aim of their voyage was the Glory of God and the advancement of Christ's faith.

We see therefore that the *Duty* or *Obligation* was recognised, but on the other hand the means to salvation was *Domination*. Obligation imposed on all the rulers ; domination imposed on all the ruled. When you desire your own salvation, you ought also to desire the salvation of your neighbour. From this angle it was easy to conclude, as in particular Methodists and Baptists did, that saving the souls of others is a condition of your own salvation ; that you can yourself attain salvation only by saving your neighbour. It is therefore obvious that we must establish a domination over distant peoples and for the sake of *our* salvation impose on them *their* salvation. The idea of domination, implicit in all forms of imperialism, was therefore to germinate in this spiritual imperialism. In other words, when we are dealing with the propagation of the Faith, *empire* is at the same time a *church* ; colonial empire is an empire-church or *church-empire* and this name was necessarily early applied to it. In the Middle Ages in the West the Church was regarded as the Body of Christ ;

---

[1] *Encyclopædia Britannica*, 14th Ed. 1930, s.vv. *Methodism* and *William Carey*.

[2] [The great pioneer of organised systematic Mission work, famous as a great Oriental scholar, responsible for the translation of the Bible into forty Indian languages and dialects. EOL]

[3] [The full title of this book is " An Enquiry into the Obligations of Christians to use Means for the Conversion of the Heathens, in which the Religious State of the Different Nations of the World, the Success of Former Undertakings and the Practicability of Further Undertakings are considered by William Carey ". EOL]

it was felt to be an immense living organism which by its divine vocation was destined to gain the whole world and bring about the reign of a *sacrum imperium*.[1]

This idea of domination acquires, however, in the course of time, two aspects : untempered or tempered, unlimited or limited domination, domination by force or by speech, in other words by *imposition* or *persuasion*. There are only two ways of propagating your faith ; you can impose it or propose it. You can propagate belief in your gods by violent conquest ; and then later, much later, by preaching and education.

Imposition : This form of domination is, in the Believer's sense, *Holy War* against the Infidel. The prophet Micah reported Jehovah as threatening " I will execute vengeance and fury upon the nations which hearkened not " (v. 15, R.V.). It is the Musulmans whose doctrine of the *jihad* gives the most forcible expression to this idea of warfare for the faith.[2] According to the text of the Quran, still theoretically valid to-day, one of the five duties of every Muslim Believer is to wage Holy War in every territory of the Infidel. This is the " territory of war "— *dar al harb*—as opposed to the " territory of peace"—*dar al Islam*— and on such territory every holy war is justified. From very early days, however, the Musulmans maintained that the propagation of the Quran by violence could only be made after conversion by other means had been tried ; that, in fact, persuasion should precede imposition. Only if the Infidels resisted, if the Christians, Jews, or more especially the Idolaters, refused to be converted, only then did the Quran proclaim it a right and a duty to compel them to accept Islam. It is a duty, at least for those who are warriors, and who, if they are slain in a *Jihad*, will be saved and will go forthwith to Paradise the moment after death.

The conception of a Holy War was, however, not the property of the Musulman alone. The Romans were not without it, and it remained for a long time alive among Christians ; it is celebrated in the famous French poem, the *Chanson de Roland*.[3]

Amongst the early Christians, the Christians of the propaga-

---

[1] Gierke, *Political Theories of the Middle Ages*, Eng. trans., 1900, p. 22 f. See St. Augustine, *The City of God*, XXII, Chap. 18.

[2] Al Bukhari, *Sahih* (Collection of the *Genuine* Traditions of Islam), French trans., *Traditions islamiques*, Vols. 2 and 3 ; C. Solvet, *Institutions du droit musulman relatives à la guerre sainte*, 1837 (translated from Reland, 1708). For the ancient Jews, F. Schwally, *Der heilige Krieg im alten Israel*, 1901.

[3] H. Pissard, *La guerre sainte en pays chrétien*, 1912 ; E. Nys, *Les origines du droit international*, 1894, p. 140 f.

tion, there had arisen a sect of Zealots, full of zeal not to live the life of apostles, but to conquer the Kingdom of God by the sword. Many mediæval theologies championed this idea. Henry of Susa, known as Hostiensis, worked out the idea of a Holy War at great length in his writings. He maintained that the Infidel should be won for the Faith by armed force if necessary, so that the City of God, of which St. Augustine had dreamed, might be extended to include the entire universe. The Faith should be victorious through the sword. He called his holy war *bellum romanum* so as to awaken the memory and the prestige of the Roman conquerors. In the days of Charles V the *Songe du Vergier* [1] spoke of " fighting down the miscreants ". We might say that the Infidels being devoid of grace and of salvation were therefore devoid of right and of power.

As late as the 16th century we still find a number of theologians, prominent among them the Spaniard Sepulveda—the great opponent of Bishop Las Casas, defender of the American native—preaching the Holy War and contending, in opposition to Las Casas, that it was a duty to convert the American Indians by battle, and to treat them as the Spanish had, not long before, treated the Muslims in Spain itself : and that with cruelty ! The native Americans who were conquered in the name of this creed had themselves conducted bloody warfare on the same theory ! For the Incas of Peru—so the Inca Garcilaso de la Vega has testified—held the belief that the aim of conquest was to compel the conquered to accept the faith of the great Peruvian God, Pashacamac, whose realm had been extended . . . by persevering massacre !

Amongst all these peoples minds were found which lifted this dogma on to the universal plane. Various theorists upheld the view that arms should be employed to spread the Faith, achieve universal conversion and establish a universal theocracy. The 12th-century Arab philosopher, Al Farabi, preached a Jihad to impose the reign of Allah on the entire world. A hundred years later in France, a humble priest dreamed of a universal *dominium* of a Religious Order : an entirely Christian world conquered by all the Religious Orders ! Three centuries later, a French mystic, Guillaume Postel—whom even his contemporaries of the 16th century considered mad—also conceived a religious imperi-

---

[1] [A curious anonymous work, possibly inspired by the king himself, rehearses in allegorical form the claims and counter-claims of the Papacy and the French Monarchy (1376). EOL]

alism maintained by one conquering dominant nation. He believed himself called by the voice of God to compel all men to shelter under the mantle of the Christian dogma [1] and submit to the power of the Kings of France as descendants of Noah. As late as the 19th century an Italian philosopher, Rosmini, published *The Philosophy of Right* (1841–5) in which he supported a universal *imperium* for the Roman Church, to assure security and equality for the benefit of all men, this *imperium* to be established by armed force so far as force was necessary ! These theorists believed in the domination of the wise in association with the great to found peace in liberty, but by overmastering the infant-peoples of the earth.

Persuasion is the second method. Spiritual imperialism, which is far from dead, aims nowadays at propagating the Faith, not by violence but by persuasion ; by preaching or by education to bring about the willing conversion of the inhabitants of the " new countries ", to win victory by the word, not by the sword. The Revelation of the truth might of itself suffice. Missions are to-day inspired by faith in this conversion by persuasion. This was a vision cherished by many a theologian in the European Middle Ages in defiance of the conquering imperialism of men like Hostiensis and Sepulveda. St. Thomas Aquinas wished to see the Faith propagated by the word and never by the sword. The same vision sometimes visited the conquerors themselves. We possess the letters of Cortes,[2] who wrote that he wished people would send to the Americans not " dissolute bishops "—as was the custom—who made the Indian despise the Spaniard, but " pious monks " who would reveal Christ to the heathen. In the time of Bishop Las Casas, Montesinos, another humble priest, put up a fight against forcible conversion. He based his protests on the mandate which, he said, the Popes had given to the Spaniards, and to them only, to propagate the Faith by preaching ; the Spaniards were thus, so he contended, *guardians* of the natives. Here we have the inventor of our " mandate ".[3] Long before his time, a similar spirit inspired two of the great religious Orders, the Dominicans and the Franciscans, who went forth to preach in Tunisia and in Africa. The same spirit immortalises the name of the great theologian Raymond Lull of

---

[1] *De orbis terrarum concordia*, Book IV, Bâle, 1544. Lope de Vega's verse drama, *El nuevo mondo discubierto*, is a vision of a world won by conquest to the Faith of Christ.

[2] *Lettres de Fernand Cortez*, edited by Vallée in a French translation, 1879, p. 264.

[3] M. Brion, *Las Casas*, 1927, pp. 51 f., 157 f., 223 f.

Majorca ;[1] he desired, and in this he was almost the first, to see the conversion of the Africans accomplished by the virtue of preaching. He devoted his whole life to this cause ; his chief work, his *Arte major*—on which theologians still write commentaries—was published as a Christian catechism for Africa. He was stoned to death in Tunis in 1315 when preaching to the Gentiles.

In our day this preaching form of imperialism has moved on to another plane ; it has been secularised and socialised. Missionaries of a wholly new type betake themselves abroad to teach their doctrines to the " infidel ". The champions of democracy make it their business to propagate their faith ; the " rights of man " are preached to the colonies. Always there is the idea of duty, however, and always there is domination. The idea exists that those who possess what Albert Bayet called " a great treasure of ideas ", are under an obligation to share their treasure by spreading far and wide "the Knowledge " which is theirs and which ought to enlighten all mankind.[2]   Let us keep the colonies . . . to secularise them. This is an " idealist " disinterested task, an effort to diffuse Reason, to preach the " Rights of Man " for the benefit of peoples who, when they are ultimately free, will be the champions of our ideal. There is always conversion and preaching. Revelation is to come through our teaching ; our propaganda, as it is called, is the final testimony to our need to share our spiritual blessings. Are our blessings welcome to more primitive peoples ? That is the problem. It is not for us to decide.

[1] A. Cabaton, *La croisade spirituelle chez les Musulmans* in *La conquête du monde musulman*, *Revue monde musulman*, 1912, p. 196 f. ; A. Condamin, *Raymond Lulle et les Musulmans*, *En Terre d'Islam*, Nov. and Dec. 1935.

[2] A. Bayet, *Cahiers des droits de l'homme*, March 10, 1931, pp. 154–5. But there remain people for whom *conversion* is the sole aim of *expansion*. Thus A. Prou-Gaillard, *La France extérieure, colonisation politique et morale*, 1890, for whom all expansion ought to be " catholic and missionary ".

CHAPTER XVIII

CULTURAL IMPERIALISM

Spiritual imperialism already includes *cultural* imperialism ; the spirit is the highest point of culture ; propaganda for religion may be an element of civilisation and of assimilation.

Cultural imperialism, or civilising imperialism, is a lay version of spiritual imperialism. Its claim to domination is based on a superiority of civilisation. Domination thus rests on a foundation of contempt ; the superior human type assumes the rôle of instructor towards the inferior ; his contempt, however, is benevolent and beneficent—or at least may be so. From now on civilisation takes the stage.

Cultural imperialism is universal and of ancient date. Every human group, large or small, State or Tribe, has its pride, just as it has its god. One of the moral components of the human group is its pride, or what is called its scale of values ; the feeling in some way of its own superiority.[1] There is a tendency therefore to what the folklorists term " blazon " ; [2] a habit of vaunting themselves, of making fun of the foreigner, of decrying his qualities in their sayings, and of making him the target of their mockery. We possess large stores of " blazon " in this sense, collective mockery—the satire by one city of another, of one country by another—very artlessly displayed.[3]

Cultural imperialism in its antiquity and its universality is woven of two threads : feeling and judgment.

The emotional *feeling* is contempt of one group for the other. The contempt of the superior—or the group which imagines itself superior—for the group supposed to be inferior : contempt sometimes kindly, sometimes malicious, sometimes a blend of both. When the chronicler Joinville writes of the " Tartars ", or the Orientals, in his account of King Louis's Crusade, he speaks of them as inferior peoples who must be taught ; but he describes them good-humouredly and without grievance ; he calls them " gentlemen " and thinks them peaceable and deserving of happiness. When you despise the foreigner you

[1] Seligmann, *Encyclopædia of the Social Sciences*, Vol. V, s.v. *Ethnocentrism.*
[2] See, for instance, Gaidoz and Sébillot's *Blason populaire de la France*, 1880.
[3] [This tendency is still very marked between one Persian tribe and another, one Arab tribe and another—as well as in our own country. EOL]

are led to wish to remould him. Whether your contempt be kindly or malevolent, it is an active reforming feeling, which leads to the idea that this inferior can be, and ought to be, civilised.

The *judgment* is, on the other hand, rational ; the dominant group's philosophy analyses its own superiority. Spiritual imperialism was based on an idea of holiness, of purity ; the chosen people conceived themselves to possess the right and the duty of converting the unrighteous and impure. Cultural imperialism rests on the non-religious conception of superior civilisation. The " thinkers " of the various empires set themselves to analyse the idea of civilisation to find therein what they sought. Among the Ancients the contrast between savage societies and civilised societies encouraged the latter to assume—in good faith, or bad faith, or both—that they had the right to rule and the right to educate the inferior peoples.

We shall trace this feeling and this judgment amongst Romans and Greeks, amongst Chinese and Hindus . . . in olden times ! Everywhere the conception of the universe is that it is ordered round a nucleus of a superior people, feeling itself and adjudging itself more advanced and more cultivated than the backward and retarded peoples by whom they think themselves surrounded. For the Hindus of ancient times, the earth was flat ; it was a world on one plane formed of seven concentric continents, India lying at the centre, India, a civilised land surrounded by barbarian countries. Such is the idea, more or less clearly defined, of all cultural imperialism.

Taking this view of cultural imperialism let us examine two fundamental questions : its *attitude* and its *conclusion*.

Its *attitude* to its basis, the principle on which it is founded, is the fact that expansion is the contact of the more civilised with the non-civilised or semi-civilised. Thus colonisation means bringing into touch two (or more) human groups who are not at the same stage of civilisation ; and since the purpose of domination is to educate, it pertains of right to the more civilised in relation to the less civilised. Their conception of savagery or barbarism reinforces the colonisers' cultural domination.

The Ancients considered *savagery* [1] to be the first condition,

---

[1] The history of this word and of the idea underlying it still need to be worked out. I here briefly compress a mass of fragmentary material : hinted at in the works of Chinard quoted below.

the first degree of human development ; and the token of savagery was idolatry.   Later, it came to be assumed that every distant people was a savage people who knew no civilisation ; and that peoples existed who were in the fullest sense of the term *non-civilised* ; and that while it might be true that savages were men, not animals, while they possessed an embryonic humanity, they were people lacking the particular human characteristic : civilisation.   It was the fashion when reviewing either their psychology or their sociology, to consider them devoid of all progress ;   they were considered to be *primitives*, or, as Maupertuis phrased it, peoples midway between animal and human. From Herodotus (IV, 104–7) onwards, it was customary to picture them living in isolation, composed of individuals recognising no laws, in a state of complete anarchy, enduring unlimited and unregulated solitude ;   " savages " therefore in the literal sense of the word.[1]   For anyone holding these views, domination was justified, without restriction or restraint : for a bottomless gulf yawned between these savage peoples and those who gave—or sold—them civilisation.

It was, however, *barbarism*, or semi-savagery, which more often gave the pretext for colonial imperialism.   The Greeks were the first to formulate the conception of barbarism, for the word comes to us from them.[2]   For all the Greek peoples, foreigners were *barbaroi*.   Whether they lived far away, or were near neighbours, so long as they did not worship the Greek *gods* and live according to the Greek *laws*, and did not share the Greek traditions, they were " barbarians ".

For the Greeks, colonisation meant contact with the semi-civilised.   In the West the word barbarian has meant a group which is not absolutely savage, which has already an elementary civilisation of its own, but which is only half civilised, which is on the path of true progress but is only at the beginning of the road and which is therefore far behind.   *It's a long way to go* . . . : that is what we say to them, and say again !

This idea of barbarism has two aspects : appreciation and observation :   the emotional and the rational aspect.

Observation is the more important.   In so far as one people is qualified to pass judgment on another people, barbarism sorely needs definition !   Nothing has undergone greater changes

---

[1] [This is far from the interpretation I should put on the passage of Herodotus in question.   EOL]

[2] P. Roussel, *Thucydides et les Barbares, Revue Études anciennes*, 1923, pp. 281–92.

than the conception of barbarism.   It has been defined in turn
as a *mental* condition, a *moral* condition and a *social* condition.
Mental barbarism, moral barbarism, social barbarism : three
different aspects of " barbarism ".

When considered as a *mental* condition, barbarism was an
intellectual inferiority ;   inferior peoples were thought to be
devoid of reason, that is to say of our type of reason.   Everything we know, or think we know, about the "mentality" of
primitive peoples has encouraged this view.   And we take
pleasure in insisting, not without some degree of complacency,
that the primitive's state of mind is *magical,* or *animistic,* or
prelogical, and not logical.[1]

The mind of primitive man is a-logical or pre-logical.   He
does not reason as we do ;   he is led, not by deductions of thought
or association of words, but rather by mystical and symbolic
" participations ".   In the great works of Lucien Lévy-Bruhl [2]
we see how different the " primitive " mind is from the " progressive ".   The primitives do not use Reason, or else their
reason is different from ours.   Not only by the Ancients, but
also by various writers of our own day, barbarism is defined
as a form of arrested intelligence.   Psychoanalysis, when in
fashion, saw a close correlation between the mental attitudes
of the primitive and of the neurotic.   One of Freud's theories
is that the neurotic is in fact a primitive [3] and that the mentally
abnormal amongst us are the survivors of early men who have
strayed out of their own day into ours.   Paranoiacs, according
to this theory, are animists ;   and their phobias are taboos.

Barbarism was also pictured as a *moral* phase.   " Barbarism "
was a moral inferiority.   Thus, in the tirades of the early theatre,
a cruel father was stigmatised as a " barbarian ".   Barbarism
stood for cruelty and grossness, and these qualities were implicit
in the Greeks' use of the word " barbarian ".   In our Renaissance philosophy—born of Greece—one point was singled out
for tireless denunciation, as the criterion of barbarism :   an-
thropophagy or cannibalism.   Cannibals were the barbarians !
None but the sceptic Montaigne could be found . . . to excuse

---

[1] J. Dewey, *Interpretation of the Savage Mind. Psychological Review*, May, 1902 ;
J. Sageret, *De l'esprit magique à l'esprit scientifique, Revue philosophique*, 1907, I, 289 f. ;
F. Boas, *The Mind of Primitive Man*, 1911.

[2] L. Lévy-Bruhl, *Les fonctions mentales dans les sociétés inférieures*, 1908 ;   *La mentalité
primitive*, 1922 ;   *Le surnaturel et la nature dans la mentalité primitive*, 1931.

[3] In *Imago*, I, 1912.   Cp. *Revue philosophique*, 1912, II, 428 f. ;   1913, I, 110 f. ;
1914, I, 108 f.

them ! Leibniz shared the current opinion about barbarians when he was speaking about the savage habits of the American Indians. In one of his *Nouveaux Essais* he writes, " one would need to be as brutalised as an American savage to approve their custom of cruelty which surpasses even the cruelty of beasts ! " Bayle too did not hesitate to describe the American natives as being more nearly akin to animals than to men. In the 16th century, Peter Martyr called them " cruel Cannibals " ; and his contemporary Jean Fonteneau, another explorer, reports in his *Cosmographie* that he has seen some who are " evil and dangerous ". The same opinion was held by many 18th-century philosophers, who were very far from believing in the " noble savage " ; and was held most firmly by the traveller Volney who had seen American Indians in the United States and said that these " primitives " were thieves and cruel barbarians without a trace of morality.[1] In opposing Rousseau, who vaunted the natural virtue of primitive man, Helvétius, basing his views on the observations of actual explorers, spoke not—like Rousseau—of the " natural goodness of Man ", but of the " natural cruelty of Man " ![2] Jean Baptiste Say was presently to speak of the " inborn perversity " of human beings.

Lastly, we find barbarism figuring as a *social* phenomenon. In the social sense, barbarism implies inferiority in manners, in the life of a society, a coarseness and a lack of refinement in the forms of intercourse. It is in this sense that philosophy makes a distinction between uncivil and civil men.[3] The economist Montchrestien used to call those peoples barbarian who were " devoid of all civility ". The uncivil man is one who does not fit in with our accepted forms of social behaviour. The unsociable or imperfectly social person is a barbarian. Oresme defined barbarians as " all those who talk a foreign tongue ". La Bruyère considered barbarian the antithesis of polished. Thus there are degrees of social barbarism. According to

---

[1] E. Seillière, *La doctrine de la bonté naturelle de l'homme, de Montaigne à Delisle de Sales*, *Séances Acad. Sciences Morales*, May–June, 1925. A list of the devotees of both theories will be found in G. Chinard's *L'exotisme américain dans la littérature française aux XVIIᵉ et XVIIIᵉ siècles*, 1913, II.

In Voltaire's copy of *Discours sur l'inégalité* there is a marginal note in Voltaire's own hand strongly criticising the idea of the compassionate savage, *Revue hist. litt. France*, July–Aug. 1933.

[2] G. Chinard, *Volney et l'Amérique*, 1923, pp. 156–8 ; F. Baldensperger, *Le mouvement des idées dans l'émigration française*, 1924, I, p. 105 f. ; Helvétius, *De l'Esprit*, V, Chaps. 2–4.

[3] L. C. E. Marin, *Lettre de l'homme civil à l'homme sauvage*, 1763, Amsterdam (Paris).

some, to Rousseau in particular, it was a state of individual isolation, the dispersion, the liberty of persons each living *sui juris*, who forewent their individual rights in entering into the *Social Contract*.

Already amongst the Ancients, social barbarism was no longer individual isolation, but collective isolation ; the autonomy of the family to the exclusion of the related groups.   The same view was held by Plato and Aristotle—by Locke too, and in our own day by Spencer and Sir Henry Maine.   Their vision of savage peoples is of parental groups, small, closed, restricted groups, which they think of as isolated, having no permanent contact with each other, living on their own resources and their own products, and knowing no way of escaping from their narrow prison.

Barbarism as involving individual or family isolation, is a conception that has long persisted.   Even when, more recently, distant and backward peoples have been more carefully studied and it has been realised that they display many various types of human groupings, that they have often formed Cities and States —or pseudo-States—we have still tended to think that they always lacked civilisation and that the groups they formed were inorganic rather than organic.   Sociologists and ethnologists alike have imagined that in a backward people society was composed of groupings which possessed neither solidity nor stability, and that if such a people was to be civilised it must first be organised . . . by domination and by legislation.

Such were the conclusions about barbarism which resulted from observation.   As for *appreciation* ; this consisted of a feeling of superiority which was informative but also emotional.   It is impossible that observation—genuine or imaginary—should be free from an element of contempt : active, scornful contempt, whether kindly or malicious, which is never absent from the relations between human groupings.   Feeling is not, in reality, wholly divorced from opinion.   You *think* yourself superior, you *feel* superior.   In contact with barbarians, you know and wish your relation to them to be one of patronage, based on an irremediable or remediable difference, according as you believe the natives to be *degenerate* or *backward* or *inveterate*.   On your side there is a " superiority complex " ; on theirs, an " inferiority complex ".

Primitive peoples have often been thought to be *degenerate* ; this was Joseph de Maistre's theory.   He considered all savages to be, not men in their original state, not primitives who had always been primitive, but degraded and degenerate men [1] ; in other words men who had formerly possessed a civilisation and had lost it. This writer believed them to be degenerates who having known the Fall—to which his philosophy attached great importance—might, he hoped, some day be regenerated by contact with the chosen conquerors !

Primitive peoples have also been considered *backward* or retarded peoples ; human groups who have proved unequal to pursuing the path of progress, and have therefore halted at a stage which progressive peoples have left behind ; who have been heavy-footed in " the march of progress "—as Auguste Comte phrased it ; slow people whose pace might be quickened and of whom there was no reason to despair. In the second volume of his *Social System* d'Holbach has spoken of the errant hordes of primitive times who made progress by contact with the more advanced foreigner who gave them gods and laws. They are on the right road ; in contact with more fortunate peoples they will assuredly be able to advance along it. This is to-day the popular view.

Lastly, primitive peoples have been held to be *inveterate,* so to speak. According to Buffon, they have always been primitive ; we must not imagine that they are no longer such ; they are smitten with impotence and cannot make progress ; there are natural laws governing their condition which make advance impossible for them. Despair lurks in this widespread belief ; it is the bitter confession : *non possumus.* For if primitive peoples are only backward or retarded, we may hope to regenerate them. If they are inveterate, and impossible to civilise, if God has laid them under a curse, we can only leave them in their abasement : the Scripture can be made to furnish arguments ! Far from being good, they are bad. In a Greek comedy of Crates called *The Savages* the dramatist denounces the error of considering them happy. Pierre Bayle in his *Dictionary* under the word *Leon* declares them corrupt and brutal : their pleasures, according to him, are prostitution and sodomy. We have here the tradition of the *Bad Savage* in opposition to the much vaunted *Noble Savage.*

Whether degenerate, inveterate, or retarded, the primitive

---

[1] J. de Maistre, *Soirées de Saint-Pétersbourg,* 2nd conversation ; J. C. Anglade-Delcros, *Nouvelle étude de l'homme ou de l'état sauvage considéré comme dégénération,* 1820 ; C. Renouvier, *Psychologie de l'homme primitif* (*Critique philosophique,* 1875).

was represented to us as living in a state of *anarchy* or in a state of *tyranny*.

Some people who leaned to the anarchy theory, believed that barbarians were unsociable people living without rules and without laws [1] and thus incapable of social progress. The early explorers in the New World, Vespucci and Magellan for instance, represented the American Indians as isolated individuals without laws, without priests, without chiefs, living thus in a state of anarchy. " No king, no law, no god," wrote Lahontan in 1709 in his *Nouveaux Voyages*. " Neither rules, nor masters," Buffon said later. For Diderot there might be a herd, but not a society among them. Volney shared this view in his *Tableau des États-Unis* and depicted the natives as ignorant of authority and security, and subjected to family vendettas and intertribal wars.[2] To be civilised you must have government, law and order.

Other people dwell more on the idea of *tyranny* amongst barbarians. According to these observers, primitive peoples are subjected to the law of tyrants ; their chiefs and kings are all-powerful, possessing powers of life and death. The sight of Mexican and Peruvian sacrifices, and later those of Ashanti and Benin, brought to the mind a vivid picture of murderous despotism with which the engravings of the *Histoires des Voyages* familiarised the " general public ". These conceptions were narrow-minded and distorted, but they prevailed amongst readers.

What *conclusion* was drawn from this attitude of the old cultural imperialism ? By what method did people attempt or claim to educate " inferior peoples " ? From what motives did they come to *assimilate* and civilise " non-civilised " peoples ? How did they hope to achieve these aims ?

At this point we approach ideas of law. We must now consider the question of *public order* in the colonies, colonial if not imperial order, in the interest whereof the conceptions, traditions and solutions of the dominant people, supported by the force of the law, must prevail in the colonies. This is in the legal sense *Assimilative Imperialism*.[3]

This is Assimilation, Civilisation in action ; the transformation and adaptation of the subject by the master, *dynamic* not

---

[1] See Herodotus, IV, 106. [But surely the inference to be drawn is that such a condition was abnormal and exceptional ? EOL]

[2] So too Adam Smith, *Lectures on Justice* . . . , 1763 (1896 Ed., p. 14 f.).

[3] R. Maunier, *Loi française et coutume indigène en Algérie*, 1932.

static, civilisation ; the desire to mould the ruled to closer resemblance to the ruler, by a change—which claims to be a change for the better—in his habits of living : and even of dying. This is the conclusion of our cultural imperialism.

The idea was already present, or foreshadowed, amongst the Ancients. Like a god, the *hero* is a civiliser ; his exploits are both destructive and constructive. Aristotle and Isocrates were for assimilation.[1] They maintained that the civilised, in virtue of being civilised, had the right to conquer, but only in order to civilise. The Greek orator Isocrates especially was an imperialist, holding that the barbarians—that is to say the non-Greeks—ought to be conquered in order that they might be hellenised or græcised. He preached the union of the Greek cities in order to colonise the East. Thus, the theory of assimilation was formulated : two thousand years ago.

Let us look at the *object* and then at the *means* of assimilation. The belief in a power and in a duty to re-create man, as a god might do, implies a dual belief : the belief in a goal and the belief in a means ; the belief that it *ought*, and that it *can*, be done.

The *object* of assimilation is an act of faith and a double act of faith. It means that we believe both in the *possibility* and in the *value* of assimilation.

Belief in the *possibility* of assimilation means belief in the *re-moulding* of an entire people. There have been, and not only of yesterday, intemperate assimilators, dogmatic fanatic souls, who believe it a simpler matter to *convert* the ruled on the social plane ; for to civilise is to " convert " in the primary meaning of that word : it implies the turning-about, and the re-casting of a whole human group.

Always and everywhere, people have believed in the ease, or at least the possibility of assimilation. All the great peoples —even the English—have methodically achieved an alteration of laws, manners and customs. They have always sought to *re-form* them on a new plane.

If, however, we want a striking and brilliant expression of this idea, we must turn to the thought current in the " Age of Enlightenment ". It was the philosophers of that day— and foremost among them the French philosophers—who most

---

[1] Aristotle, *Politics*, I, 2 ; G. Mathieu, *Les idées politiques d'Isocrate*, 1925 ; Hegel also says that the Conqueror is the Civiliser, and that Force is Reason : see Cousin, *Introduction à l'histoire de la philosophie*, 1828, Lesson X.

loudly proclaimed faith in the virtue of reformation and education, for they believed that every people can by instruction be
taught how to attain a happier state. They thought it was
possible profoundly to change the state of subject nations. They
were radical ; they were uncompromising ; and many, having
read them, shared their beliefs. It was one of them, Helvétius,
who in his treatise *On Man* [1] affirmed the sovereign power of
education, not only within a nation, but as between one nation
and another. In this respect he compares colonies to : religious
Orders ! Within a religious Order, its laws are omnipotent and
the founders of a religious Order were free to lay down whatever laws they liked ; in the same way the laws in a colony
are all-powerful, as they are in a religious Order. Virtue and
happiness are the result of the legislators' wisdom. He goes
further : he asserts that it is given to the founders of colonies
alone, who are in command of " men free from prejudices "
and from traditions, to discover perfection. The idea underlying assimilation is the idea of the omnipotence of laws, the
idea that societies can be formed and remodelled by virtue of
laws. " Nothing ", he adds, " can in these circumstances
hamper the genius of the founder of a colony in his progress.
Monastic laws are those most free of imperfections, because the
founders of a religious Order are in the position of the founders
of a colony, in that they need take no account of the tastes or
opinions of their future subjects." That seems to me the most
forcible expression that has ever been given to the idea of
assimilation achieved through legislation.—Other philosophers
too have had the same faith in the teaching given to one people
by another. The progress of sociology, the study of types and
degrees, of phases and stages, has forcibly brought home to us
of to-day a realisation of the diversity and originality of civilisations. Any such realisation is denied by the intemperate
reformer-educator. He is a disciple of Descartes ; it is the
Cartesian spirit which inspires Helvétius. The idea of the
philosopher in his well-warmed study, is that good sense exists
everywhere ; that it is " the most widely distributed gift in the
world ", that all men everywhere are dowered with Reason,
which is dependent neither on time nor place ; and that therefore nothing but education is needed to initiate by " the Method "
all who are backward into the ways of Reason. The meaning
of Descartes' *Discours de la Méthode* in this connection, is the

[1] *De l'homme*, 1774, Sect. VII, Chaps. XI and XII (Vol. II, p. 171).

value and the virtue for every mind throughout the universe of the procedures of Western Science, and in consequence the possibility of assimilation.

Belief in the *value* of assimilation, or the necessity of assimilation, represents another act of faith. It is not enough for a change to be *possible*, it must also appear *desirable*, though the one frequently depends on the other. You must see some advantage in bringing reform about, you must believe in the virtue of a change. This is what the French have in mind when they use the phrase " Overseas Frenchmen ". In this respect their idea of the colonial empire is only an extension of their idea of the nation. They cannot conceive their nation apart from the unity and identity which time has brought about. Nor can they conceive their colonial empire apart from the unity and identity which they at least aim at bringing about. Hence, ever since the days of the Ancien Régime, various attempts have been made to fuse the French " over there " with the French at home. Legislation and education have both been employed to obliterate the differences and emphasise the resemblances ; a struggle has been carried on against personalities and originalities in the provinces and in the colonies. In his *Histoire des Voyages*,[1] La Harpe sketched the plan of a league to be formed " by reason and humanity to propagate those virtues useful for the happiness of the world " ; it was to be an association of " non-party people " to civilise, without trying to convert to religion ! And Lamartine [2] had the vision of an Asia re-born and made happy by a great European Congress, which would found cities governed by French laws ; *model cities* whose example would effect the conversion of the inhabitants. We see always an act of faith, always an act of hope. For the last hundred years in Algeria the activities of French legislators and French administrators have been guided by this idea of fusion, conceived as being both possible and desirable. Bugeaud already in a certain sense " created Frenchmen " since he wished the French not only to occupy the country but to associate with its inhabitants, and this association was to involve the reciprocal imitation of French and Algerians. A little later, Changarnier formulated more fully the idea of fusion which he believed to be the prerequisite of all rapprochement. In order to rule permanently it was necessary in his opinion to unite,

[1] *Abrégé de l'histoire des voyages*, 1780, XVIII, p. 530 f.
[2] *Voyage en Orient*, 1835 (Epilogue).

not of course by converting the Musulmans—he had already given up hope of that—but by civilising them. From this there sprang, under Napoleon III, the famous conception of an "Arab Kingdom" based on the idea that Arabs and French could jointly form one single kingdom, one single State,[1] an idea which implied not only association but also civilisation and fusion. We know all about the ensuing experiment.

So it was the French who, in Algeria, both in theory and practice, proclaimed their faith in fusion in its fullest sense. Later we see it prevail throughout the whole French colonial empire. The explorer Domeny de Rienzi had already said, in reference to the peoples of Oceania,[2] "Let us take to these virgin lands . . . the benefits of science, of liberty and of equality of rights . . . Let us exchange thoughts and needs." Jules Ferry, though not the inventor or originator of these ideas, generalised and advocated them in his speeches of 1885.[3] He is the first to suggest that the assimilation of the ruled is not only a right but a duty ; we should most certainly not have found this view held by Bugeaud or Changarnier : the idea that we are *bound* to educate in order to get into touch. In the same year, the same idea was incorporated by the Conference of Berlin of 1885 in a famous international text : thus a public Act recognised a great duty of civilisation. The Conference expressly asserted that, conquests would have amongst their aims, the "civilisation" of distant peoples ; here, for the first time, we find the principle laid down in an official text.[4] The Declaration of 1885 thus repeats the Bull of 1493 which imposed on the conquerors the duty of teaching religion and morals, or the Letters of François I to Roberval in 1540 prescribing his conduct towards the natives and bidding him to "make them live according to reason and regulation" and to show them God. Cultural imperialism thus joins forces with spiritual imperialism.

From this point of view, the colonies form elements of the nation ; the colonies are felt to be like the provinces ; empire and nation are one and the same. The wish is first that the

---

[1] Collected texts, including the preceding, will be found in E. Guénin's *L'épopée coloniale de la France*, 1932, p. 289 f. See earlier writings in the same vein : L. B. Hautefeuille, *Plan de colonisation . . . dans l'Afrique Occidentale au moyen de la civilisation des nègres indigènes*, 1830 ; W. Jablonowski, *Esquisse d'un système de civilisation de l'Algérie*, 1840.

[2] D. de Rienzi, *Océanie ou cinquième partie du monde*, 1836, I, pp. 15, 329 f., 340 f.

[3] See below, Chap. XXIX.

[4] See G. de Courcel, *L'influence de la Conférence de Berlin sur le droit colonial international*, 1935 (thesis).

nation should be unified, then that the empire should be the nation, amplified but also unified.[1]

Such is the aim of assimilation. What, on the other hand, is the method to be? Shall we *impose* or *persuade, legislate* or *educate*?

To impose, or to legislate, is to reform by constraint through the law. From the beginning this was the method preferred by the extremists. The doctrinaires were ready to endorse Sepulveda's *compelle intrare*. Sepulveda, it will be remembered, was the controversialist opposed to Bishop Las Casas. He wished to convert by compulsion and to civilise by compulsion.[2] He held that the European had a right to reform by force the manners and customs of the American Indians, to put an end—and that without delay—to imbecile and inhuman customs. The Swiss jurist Bluntschli in his *International Law Codified* (1885) declares in Article 280 that civilised people have the right to clear by force the path to progress.[3] This is exactly the idea of public order, whether territorial or colonial. In our Empires we all profess—the French even more than others—concern for *law and order*. We reckon that many of our laws should be valid for all, without distinction and without restriction ; the French therefore impose on all inhabitants a territorial law, applicable to all alike, both to rulers and to ruled ; a law of " public order " which none may infringe. Where French law and native custom are in conflict, the French hold that the difficulty should be solved by abolishing or reforming the native custom. Such, in the legal sense, is French cultural imperialism. It means the *abolition* of traditions judged incompatible with French law and order : the abolition of cannibalism, of slavery, of serfdom, of sacrifices and of vendettas . . . when we can !—and the *adaptation*, or transformation, of traditions which may be retained when they are modified or improved. In these two points the French proclaim a *Colonial Order* which must rule throughout the French Empire, and which lays on

---

[1] [The fundamental difference between the French and the British attitude to colonial peoples and the aims of administration, is admirably illustrated in Lt.-Col. W. R. Crocker's valuable and unpretentious book *On Governing Colonies* (1947). EOL]

[2] J. Folliet, *Le droit de colonisation*, 1933, p. 35 f. ; M. Brion, *Las Casas*, 1927, pp. 188–203. Blanc Saint Bonnet, a die-hard monarchist of the last century, also said that " a savage race never progresses of itself to civilisation ", *Restauration française*, 2nd Ed. 1873, p. 293.

[3] Paul Adam in France said : " Imperialism is the fight against barbarism. The Boers were justly defeated if they were daring to evade progress ! " (*Le taureau de Mithra*, 1907, pp. 10 f. and 20 f.).

their subjects the duty of obeying, under penalty, the laws laid down by them without those subjects' consent.

The imposition of these laws is defended on two grounds : *morality* and *convenience*, humanity and security ; in other words, sentiment and self-interest sometimes intrude.

Sometimes *morality* or humanity prompts French hostility to certain native customs, and leads them to impose their own laws. This is why they forbid human sacrifice and religious murder—not always with the success they desire.

Sometimes it is from convenience or for stability that they interfere, although they have frequently promised in solemn texts to maintain and " respect " native customs. It is certainly for practical convenience that they organise a census, and set up a registrar's office in their colonial empire, that they compel the natives to let themselves be counted and to register their names. They have thus broken the *patria potestas* and destroyed the autonomy of the family group ; for in order to register names or count heads, agents of the national government must penetrate into the bosom of the family. Anyone who has lived in a Muslim country will know how outrageous it is to enquire : " How many children have you ? How many daughters ? " Worse still ! To count, to register, to tax, thus to give the State power over the family and the tribe, is to deal a blow at patriarchal and tribal authority, and weaken the ancient and traditional powers of father and chieftain. The French have set up a whole real Constitution in North Africa ; the rights of property, the law of contracts are much more than half French. This has taken place more or less everywhere, more or less fully. They have acted in this way for the convenience and the security of the French colonists, so that wherever their people settled there might prevail the certainty and simplicity of rights, and particularly the guarantee of land tenure.

Persuasion or education has other goals. You believe that you are putting over your doctrines, and you claim that assimilation will be the free choice of the people. Civilisation will come through teaching ; and rapprochement will be voluntary. A hundred years and more have passed since Parieu, the author of a *Course of Political Science*, spoke of " penetration " or the " infusion " of manners and customs from one people to another. By this he meant propaganda, freely and willingly accepted. The theory of the French, since the days of Montaigne and Rabelais, has been to regard the civilising of others as a duty best performed by the medium of *propaganda* aiming to arouse willing acceptance. It is probably with this in mind that the French philosopher, Jouffroy, spoke of " the tree of civilisation which ought eventually to cover the earth with its foliage ". As at home, propaganda in the colonies operates in two ways ; by *word* and by *deed*. *Verbal* propaganda is the pedagogue's business. It is in the matter of deeds and actions that voluntary assimilation takes a curious turn. How can we give the ruled a motive and enlist their self-interest in following and imitating their rulers' ways ? We try various methods which all entail action. By taxes which compel them to work ; by transferences of population, such as conquering peoples have experimented with at various times, in order to blend and mix their peoples with a view of ultimately assimilating them by personal contact. The Chinese and the Incas did this ; the sultans of Morocco also attempted it.[1] This is a kind of semi-compulsion aiming at achieving the civilising of the people by bringing them into touch with others. Was there not, during the French Revolution, an elaborate scheme for transplanting, in order to " republic-anise " them, to the North of France the Provençals and the people of the South, who remained obstinately royalist ? In 1837 too Stendhal proposed planting " two colonies of wise Alsatians " in the inconveniently-nationalist Bretagne in order to rescue that province from its mediævalism. In 1864 Ernest Feydeau published his novel *The Secret of Happiness*,[2] in which by tacitly suggesting models and examples, he praises the peaceful and benevolent colonist—a retired colonel !—who teaches the Arabs industry and virtue. Here is a colonial chapter of morality in action. To dispose the natives to adopt French ways and to follow French laws, however, more generous measures have been tried : rewards and premiums both of an honorary and financial type. When General Faidherbe offered material rewards to the inhabitants of Senegal to induce them to replace their hovels by houses, he was enlisting the people's self-interest in favour of assimilation. He was at the same time demonstrating the infinitely diverse methods which cultural imperialism can devise to allow scope to French genius and ingenuity. " Loyalty " and " fidelity " have their secret ways. But in this case, as in many others, it was ultimately necessary to have recourse to compulsion !

[1] P. Odinot, *Le monde marocain*, 1926, p. 25 f.
[2] *Le secret du bonheur*.

For it is often true that voluntary assimilation produces no result and proves of no value. Persuasion, whether by word or deed, is not enough to civilise or assimilate subject peoples unless reinforced by legislation. On the rubbish heaps of Fostat in the neighbourhood of Cairo you can still see the eloquent ruins of Bonaparte's windmills! When Napoleon came to Cairo and saw the fellahin's women-folk toiling hour after hour turning the handmill and singing the sad grinding-song, he thought he could ease them of this prehistoric labour by building windmills for them. Bonaparte is gone, but his mills are there : long since destroyed. Not until the steam-mill arrived in the valley of the Nile was the ancient handmill superseded.

Behind this cultural imperialism lurks always the idea that *Empires* are *Nations* ; that *domination* must be accompanied by *legislation*, that organisation must be accompanied by assimilation. The Empire like the Nation is conceived as one great "cultural circle" within which there should be cultivated an identity of manners and customs, and a unity of law.

CHAPTER XIX

POWER IMPERIALISM : MAJESTY

Power-imperialism is, in a word, the wish to dominate for the sake of dominating : the "will to power" as Nietzsche called it. This is no doubt an archaic phenomenon. "Primitive" tribes display a passion for conquering just for the pleasure of conquering, of ruling for the sake of ruling. It is this passion which underlies the lust for power, a mania and a rage which the moralists condemn. Hobbes called it "the desire for power", Mandeville "the instinct of sovereignty" and Saint-Cyran coined the happy term "the spirit of primacy" (*esprit de principauté*). This feeling of "amour-propre", that is to say an active and personal *egotism*, in La Rochefoucauld's meaning of the term, may also be a collective egotism, which may be reinforced by and blended with a real craving for *cruelty* : imperial and imperious are one and the same thing.[1] When this manifests itself not merely in the individual, but in the collectivity, and more particularly in the nation, we have power-imperialism or *collective amour-propre*. It is ambition : a noble sentiment according to Garnier-Pagès and Courcelle-Seneuil.[2] Power-imperialism may take two forms, may wear two aspects : the personal and the collective. For this passion may rise to a delirious height in the case of an individual—the most outstanding example being Napoleon—the passion of ruling for the sake of ruling, of aggrandisement for the sake of aggrandisement. But every human group has in some degree a collective desire for glory and for power. Amongst Greeks and Romans Victory was a Goddess ; *Athena, Victoria,* is Power first and only later Wisdom ; Force and Reason ; Glory and Success ! The Goddess is a warrior before being a sportswoman ! The helmet and the sword are her symbols.[3] Collective pride, or national pride,[4] is a characteristic of every human society.

National pride is lust for greatness and lust for power: it

---

[1] A. Spaier, *Cruauté, violence et colère, Revue philosophique*, May–June 1933.

[2] Garnier-Pagès, *Dictionnaire politique*, 1843, s.v. *Colonie* by C. Courcelle-Seneuil.

[3] A. Baudrillart, *Les divinités de la Victoire en Grèce et en Italie*, 1894. *Les lettres du Centurion* by Ernest Psichari (New Ed. 1933) brings these visions together.

[4] Robinet, *Dictionnaire universel des sciences morales*, 1777, sq. s.v. *Orgueil national*, Vol. XXV, p. 684 f. ; Zimmermann, *De l'orgueil national*, 1769 (French trans.) ; Voltaire, *Dictionnaire philosophique*, s.v. *Gloire*.

is *collective dynamism* : the joy in force is in itself a good. Amongst writers it is those who exalt energy, men like Stendhal and Nietzsche, who have been best able to note and render the distinctive characteristics of this phenomenon, and who have told us how—for good or ill—the nations become possessed by this passion for command. They show us imperialism in its narrowest meaning, in its true meaning ; as an instinct which itself supplies its own aim and its own driving power. There is, however, no breach of continuity between power-imperialism, spiritual imperialism, and cultural imperialism, for, as we shall see, all three derive their inspiration from one first principle, the idea of the purity of peoples and races. The idea of their own purity carries the idea of their election and their pre-destined domination, decreed by God, whose designs are to the human mind inscrutable. This idea of *purity*, which came to be secularised one day, as it is in our time—though not yet always, nor everywhere !—proceeded from another idea, that of *holiness* ; from a second idea, too, from that of *primacy* and quality. *Holiness* has been, as we know, the basis of spiritual imperialism ; *primacy*, as we also know, the basis of cultural imperialism. These two concepts sloughed their original charac-teristics, their essential colour as it were, to merge in the concept of purity, the source and inspiration of every form of imperial pride. It is the pure peoples, the great peoples, who are by God endued with the mission of commanding, for the sake of commanding, to the benefit—*incidentally* !—of the whole human race. Pride, however, must inevitably precede benefit. Hence the appetite for command which assails those who crave command of distant countries. In a letter of 1878 Pierre Loti writes, explaining the whim which led him to settle in Tahiti : " I have a horror of everything conventionally called civilisation and of equalitarian theories . . . *To be a seigneur* . . . in countries where the laws are not made for everybody . . ." Cecil Rhodes studied Cæsar's life ; he liked to picture himself as emperor !

So it is true, as Stendhal said, that power is *the greatest of all pleasures*. Auguste Comte too in his *Call to Conservatives* speaks of the *need to dominate* and the *need to win approval*. And Auguste Blanqui in his *Social Critique* denounces Man's " native impulse to invade " and his " universal thirst for usurpation ". Let us, on the other hand, realise that another idea informs the dominating mind ; if Nations and States by exercising power gratify a common desire, if they thereby obtain a common pleasure, they also find therein a common vocation and a common duty. For power must display itself and assert itself. *Noblesse oblige*, we say; Power no less imposes obligation. Strength unexercised is lost; it must be used if it is to be preserved. This is the law of every form of Action; the law that governs every Sport: Pleasure and Duty; Passion and Mission; Greatness and Salvation: the two concepts remain interwoven in the complexity and the continuity of the sentiments of domination.

This being so, power-imperialism has its *attitude* and its *conclusion*—its *attitude* lies in the idea of the *Majesty* of peoples or of kings; the affirmation of their " greatness ", which serves to prolong and to revitalise the idea of the holiness of peoples and of kings. This is the notion of *Glory* in so far as glory is distinct from salvation. It is a reproach to sociology that it has hitherto passed over this idea in complete—or almost complete—silence.[1]—Its conclusion lies in the idea of *primacy*, wherein " power-imperialism " and " cultural imperialism " unite. It is the notion of the superiority of dominating peoples, but is no longer wedded to the transformation of the dominated; it ends by being domination for the sake of domination; it sets out simply to found and preserve an *Imperium* as a thing of value in itself. Primacy serves as an argument for the dominator as much as for the reformer. I am the superior and therefore: I wish to *alter*, or simply: I wish to *rule*; I wish to *convert*, or simply: I wish to *enslave*.

The majesty of peoples and of kings derives from the notion of the divine right of kings and of nations. This is an idea of great antiquity. In the *City of God* (Ch. 12, Book 5) Saint Augustine says that if the Roman *imperium* had succeeded in extending itself over the whole of the ancient world, it had done so by God's decree; God had foreseen and desired the Roman people.

The idea of majesty derived in the course of time from different sources. We can detect three underlying ideas: domination based on *birth*, or on *strength*, or on *growth*.

First, and among " primitive " peoples, the right of command succeeded in asserting itself by virtue of *birth*. God's election of a people to reign over other peoples could establish itself amongst primitive races only by descent: primitive groups are

---

[1] See, however, J. Hirsch, *Die Genesis des Ruhmes*, Leipzig, 1914, but he deals only with the glory of the *individual*. French writers have written similarly on " success."

groups of relations.[1]   They are, or they believe themselves to
be, descendants of a god or of a totem ; the bond that holds
them together is a mystical filiation.   Being the son of my
god, I am myself my god, or the chosen of my god.

This is the vision which was in our day to be the basis of
the " doctrine " of races, revivifying and intensifying the idea
of heredity and of the continuity of the national spirit, an
idea which underlies all " racialism " of whatever type, an idea
already present in the fictions of primitive man.   For the
Ancients, the human group could possess identity, continuity
and the hope of survival only in so far as it was offspring of a
god from whom it derived its dignity and its spirit.   Its heredity
made it holy and made it pure.   The group is god and offspring
of god.   And its authority over the impure or the less pure,
is an end in itself and a good in itself.   The purest are the
strongest since they are endowed with the powers of the gods.
When you yourself are God, to reign is to praise God.   Purity,
a continuation of holiness, has therefore two aspects which,
however, are but one : *mystic* purity and *ethnic* purity.

Mystic purity is the unity of divine spirit.   Blood and soul
are not separate objects ; blood which creates the tribe's
heredity is only the vehicle of the soul or spirit.   Members
of the tribe are relations in virtue of the totem or the god who
enters them with their blood.   Mystic purity is therefore the
soul-relationship or the relationship of soul.

Ethnic purity is the unity of blood.   Mystic purity implies
endogamy, not exogamy.   Members of the tribe, being the pure
and the only pure, can intermarry only with members of the
tribe.   Ethnic purity is maintained by this sacred law of
endogamy.   The blood is the soul, the soul is the blood ; worship
and magic are steeped in blood.   In the course of time, however, the two are separated : the transmission of blood becomes,
by itself, a sufficient bond for the group ; the means, so to
speak, is promoted to the dignity of the end.   This probably
was already the case amongst the *patres Romani*.   It is endogamy
which creates the tribe ; there is no *connubium* or *epigamy* with
the foreigner.   A pure soul or spirit and a pure blood must
be affirmed and preserved.   The Greeks also, who invented the
idea of a barbarian, had the idea of consanguinity too.   With
them, the people and the race were one and the same.[2]   A

---

[1] R. Maunier, *Essais sur les groupements sociaux*, 1929, Chap. III.
[2] A. Rivand, *Recherches sur l'anthropologie grecque, Revue anthropologique*, 1913, p. 230 f.

tribe, and later a City, was an assemblage of the descendants, whether near or distant, of a common ancestor, divine founder, genius or hero. The people was a group of relatives, related to each other firstly in a mystic sense, secondly in an ethnic sense, related both by spirit and by blood. The conception of the "True-born Englishman" to which Daniel Defoe took exception, is only a reminder of this ancient belief.

Another idea arose, however, amongst the Ancients, and in time came to the fore, blurring and obscuring the idea of birth : this was the idea of strength. In the great empires men soon came to sing the glory of the Victor, to make power and strength the very basis of power itself, to identify *strength* with *virtue*. Thus, in the Age of the Great King, Louis XIV, Méré said, at the very opening of his *Conversations* : " The true heroes are the conquerors ! War is the fairest of all honourable occupations : the man most respected is . . . the one-time soldier." This idea had its source in ancient beliefs, since, long before Christianity, religion was wont to apply to God the epithet All-powerful, All-mighty. To reign, or be able to reign, was then the highest form of virtue. The Kings of Portugal came to call themselves "Lords of the Conquest" (1499). The statue of Louis XIV, the Sun King, in the *Place des Victoires*, bore on its pedestal the inscription : " The most barbarous nations came from afar to revere the King, attracted by the glory of his Name " ! (1686). Thereafter, there will be no need, save at the outset, to discuss the descent of a god or a hero, but he must be able to show and to exert a strength sufficient to command respect in order to prove that he has the right and the duty to exert and to preserve it. This brings us to imperialism for its own sake, to authority as the basis of authority, to domination as the guarantee of domination. Amongst the ancient Indians it was written : " the happiness of the subject results only from the strength of the king ".[1] Everywhere in Oriental countries the strength and the virtue of the reigning sovereign are treated as synonymous.[2] Not that the election bestowed by birth was by any means despised. In great States, down to our own time, importance was attached to an original prehistoric investiture. The kings of France claimed to be descendants of the kings of Troy who themselves were sons of Hector—after having been sons of Noah !—and this illustrious

[1] A. Hildebrandt, *Altindische Politik*, 1924.
[2] A. Jeremias, *Die orientalischen Wurzeln der Idee der Weltherrschaft und Gottkönigtum* ; *Oriens, The Oriental Review*, I, Jan. 1926, pp. 14–18.

ancestry confirmed their sacred power.[1] Let us turn again to a book, nowadays forgotten, by a certain Aubery : *Treatise on the Pre-eminence of our Kings* [2] (1649). Here we see the idea that the power of the French kings was a sacred power, created by God, desired by God, devolving on them by reason of their ancient sanctity, and springing in the first place from the fact that they are descendants of the Grecian kings. Their pre-eminence, which is majesty with primacy, comes from their descent . . . or their imaginary descent.

Henceforward, however, in the days of which we are now speaking, power is, by itself, basis and argument : we have reached the stage of *power-imperialism*. Power bestows the right to power ; strength is thought to be inspired by God ; it is not conceived as resting on its own foundations alone, but in the mind of many peoples—and that down to our own times—as based on an alliance with a god ! How many peoples have claimed the right to reign, no longer as *children* of the god—an old illusion, sooner or later forgotten—but assuredly as *friends* of the god ! [3] They are allied with the god, inasmuch as they have entered into a sort of contract with him, a " blood covenant ", in virtue of which the god manifests his protection. We know that amongst the Jews this was the meaning under-lying the ceremony of circumcision : the tie that bound them to their god, and which was symbolised by a bleeding scar. In the beginning the association of the god and his people in filiation was thus symbolically represented.

Filiation, association, both ideas are soon completely super-fluous. The idea which supersedes them, and in our day takes the foremost place, and now reigns in splendour amongst neigh-bouring peoples, is that of *election*. [4] A dominant people is now a mandatory, " mandated " by God without having been obliged ritually to solicit this election ; the chosen people is *nominated* to dominate and to rule. This is in fact the divine right of peoples and of races. The germ of this idea was already present in the Roman mind. They used to divide the territories of the Empire into three parts. The territory of the Roman proper, the *ager Romanus*, land sacred and divine—as the Musul-mans were later to call their territories *dar al Islam*, the country of Islam—land over which Jupiter wished to rule. The second

---

[1] C. Leber, *Collections des meilleures dissertations*, 1826, sq. Vol. X, p. 293 f.
[2] *Traité de la prééminence de nos rois*.
[3] A. J. Reinach, *Revue études ethnographiques et sociologiques*, I, 1908, p. 351 f.
[4] See in general C. van Vollenhoven, *Le droit de paix*, 1932, pp. 26 f. and 49 f.

and third parts the Romans called the *ager peregrinis* and the *ager hostilis,* the foreign territories, corresponding to what the Muslims were later to style " the land of war ", *dar al harb.* The Romans believed it to be their mission to rule everywhere, through their art and through their glory to give peace to the conquered peoples by subjecting them ! Thus in Book VI of the *Æneid* Virgil represents Anchises as saying : *Tu regere imperio populos, Romane, memento* ! [1] Power exercised, benefit conferred, and pride felt in both !

Still more strongly, the Hebrew Bible proclaims the rightful domination of the Jewish people, as the Chosen of Jehovah, over all other nations.[2] Power again, but duty too, for to be " chosen " implies obligation. The Chosen People do not dream of evading their mission : " Cursed be Canaan ; a servant of servants shall he be unto his brethren " (Genesis ix. 25) ! Jewish imperialism was power-imperialism in which an idea of divine majesty served to establish an authority of divine right.[3]

It was another Semitic race, the Arabs, who unleashed this claim and drove it to the extreme. Turn over the pages of the Quran (Sura II, 137 ; VI, 165 ; XIII, 13 and many other passages) ; here the doctrine of *su'ubiyah* [4] reaches its full flowering : authority founded on holiness and majesty. If the Arabs faithfully observed the law of endogamy, not desiring marriage with foreigners—but only with the daughters of foreigners [5]—it was in virtue of the *su'ubiyah,* which is in fact nothing but the idea of election. A chosen people has not the right to bind itself or to ally itself, in any sense, with foreigners, who are necessarily inferior and are also rejected of Allah. This is the source of Pan-Islamism.[6]

---

[1] [Fairclough's translation of this famous passage runs : " Remember thou, O Roman, to rule the nations with thy sway—these shall be thine arts—to crown Peace with Law, to spare the humbled, to tame in war the proud ! " Loeb Ed. of Virgil, Vol. I, p. 567. EOL]

[2] T. Zielinski, *L'empereur Claude et l'idée de la domination mondiale des Juifs, Revue Universelle,* Brussels, Dec. 1926, Jan. 1927.

[3] The idea of the Jewish people's mission still persists ! See Disraeli's novel *Tancred* (1847) and George Eliot's *Daniel Deronda* (1876), second episode.

[4] I. Goldziher, *Die Su'ubijja . . . in Spanien, Z.d.M.G.,* LIII, 1899, pp. 601-20. Ali Abd-el-Wahed, *Contribution à une théorie sociologique de l'esclavage,* 1931, pp. 140 f., 161 f.

[5] [This interpretation of " endogamy " and racial purity, election, etc., will strike the ordinary reader as odd. Professor Maunier kindly explains that the " more advanced " tribes conveniently content themselves with a kind of " semi-endogamy ", absolutely forbidding the marriage of their own women outside the tribe, but tolerating—though not approving—a man's *mésalliance* with a foreign woman. EOL]

[6] C. H. Becker, *Panislamismus, Archiv für Religionswissenschaft,* VII, 1904, pp. 169, 192.

In our own day a similar state of mind is acutely alive amongst the Japanese.[1] The Japanese are an imperial people from self-interest and ambition probably, certainly from pride and from calculation ; but also and above all from mystic dogma. For *Shinto*, the ancient religion of the people of the Rising Sun, teaches that the Japanese is the offspring of God and the chosen of God, and that it is his mission to be the leader of the peoples of the East. Japanese philosophers—not all of them accessible in translation—to-day affirm the Japanese people's right and duty to dominate Asia and to unify Asia against Western Imperialism. Their mission and their election remain acts of faith.

The first aspect of power-imperialism, Majesty, has, as we have seen, been based both on birth and on strength, but also, more recently, on *growth*. By this I mean that in recent centuries the belief has arisen that growth is in itself a good, and that nations have the right to expand for the sake of expanding, and to enrich themselves for the sake of self-enrichment. In 1603 the good French king, Henri IV, granted to the Sieur de Monts the Charter of Acadia, sending him forth " to maintain and preserve (the Crown) in its ancient dignity, greatness and splendour, to *extend* and *increase*, so far as may legitimately be done, the frontiers and limits of the same ". The Charter granted by Charles I to Lord Baltimore for Maryland in 1632 also expresses the " laudable desire . . . to extend at once the Christian religion and the territories of our *Empire* ".[2] From the static idea of strength, we have progressed to the dynamic idea of growth. It is nowadays the fashion to talk of " dynamism ". However great power may be, it cannot stand still ; it must be increased in the name of Progress which is quantity as well as quality. The Law of States is therefore : to conquer in order to grow greater. Nietzsche was wont to say that a man must *overcome* himself and *surpass* himself : " Be brigands and conquerors ! " The apologia of conquest now takes on a scientific disguise : *dynamics* and *statistics* now provide the argument, giving merely a new dress to the thinkers of old. The *pride of numbers* is now much advertised, both amongst new nations and old : calculations of areas and populations are bandied to and fro in discussions between States. Record-

[1] H. Labroue, *L'impérialisme japonais*, 1911 ; G. M. Sangiorgi, *L'imper. giapponese*, 1932 ; J. W. Hall (Upton Close), *Behind the Face of Japan*, 1935. Cf. Inazo Nitobe, *Le Bushido*, French trans., 1927.
[2] G. Gourd, *Les chartes coloniales*, 1885, pp. 230-42.

making and record-breaking has become a recognised mania ! The predisposition to this disease is romantic as well as statistical.

Yet, both in ancient times and in our own, there have been philosophers hostile to the large State. Aristotle, the Stagirite, had already said that great States were badly governed. Ibn Khaldun, Montesquieu, Rousseau above all, and even Renan, all these thinkers and many others as well, have declared that large States could not long survive, and that the sole cause of the fall of mighty Empires was their expansion. This " anti-expansionist " thesis has always opposed the theory that for its own vitality and security a State is bound to grow larger ; that progress lies in increase, and that life is growth. This is true for the body of the nation as it is for the individual. According to Machiavelli and to Hegel, societies are borne along by a movement of growth ; there can be neither progress nor happiness for a great State on any condition other than its continual enlargement. Two arguments are quoted in support of this theory : the one *mechanic*, the other *organic*.

The *mechanic* argument is valid only in so far as we are content to treat the problems of society as similar to material phenomena, and apply to them the laws of matter and in particular the laws of attraction. H. C. Carey and De Greef [1] hold that social progress is governed by the same canons as the movements of matter ; that there exists therefore in every society a natural tendency— and a legitimate tendency—to increase its *mass* ; that the law of attraction operates in drawing small groups into larger groups, to which they are annexed or absorbed. Power-imperialism would then find its justification in the *physics* of social entities.

The *organic* argument is valid in so far as it emphasises— as does H. C. Carey himself—that a society is an organism ; that human groupings, being living bodies, must obey the laws of life and particularly the law that an organism is subject to growth. This is a " divine commandment ". An organism grows and gives off shoots ; these, in the case of States, are the colonies. All evolution involves increase.[2] What is known as " organicism " is thus called in, in favour of expansion and annexation ; and Nature is supposed to have judged and

---

[1] H. C. Carey, *The Principles of Social Science*, 1858-9 ; G. de Greef, *La Sociologie économique*, 1904.

[2] G. Tarde, *Psychologie économique*, 1902, I, pp. 18–22, speaks of a " law of historic amplification " which he expressly applies to great colonial empires. The novelist, Paul Bonnetain, also spoke of an " ineluctable expansion " and of a " fatal necessity " (*Au Tonkin*, no date).

condemned small nations as too small ! The American A. T. Mahan,[1] following the English Seeley's line, showed the European West evolving from quite small Kingdoms into great Monarchies and " planetary Empires " based on world power. This ostensibly scientific argument is merely the continuation and secularisation of the earlier mystical interpretation. Not always, but frequently, this is merely to give old prejudices a new dress more suited to the taste of the day. Greatness can manifest itself only by . . . greatness. The fundamental belief is unchanged, the belief in a Chosen People, dedicated to command, and inspired by God, who is always on the side of the Powers. The same Mahan speaks of Destiny, of obscure forces and addresses a prayer to Providence ! Power-imperialism remains spiritual imperialism ; for it is still based, even in our day, on an act of faith.

[1] A. T. Mahan, *The Interest of America in Sea Power.*

CHAPTER XX

POWER IMPERIALISM : PRIMACY (*LA PRIMAUTÉ*)

Power-imperialism, steeped in Majesty, is infected with Primacy. This is the conclusion, not distinguishable from the position : willed of God, or dictated by Nature ; it is one of the Janus-faces of belief in Majesty and in Election. Progressing from theology to biology, we have quietly passed from a mystic to an ethnic concept. Purity of Soul, purity of Blood, bestow Majesty and lay the foundation of Primacy. The idea of Race thus blends with the idea of Rank.

Famous authors foreshadowed this idea—Bonald, de Maistre and Taine,[1] for instance—the idea that the power of one people over another derives its right from this primacy-integrity, from this primacy-heredity, in virtue of the " primacy " of the pure over the impure. We must repeat it once again : We have here biology-theology and ethnology-theology ! The gods are not dead, nor do they die. Illusions, frenzies remain, both in their creative and their destructive rôles. Some hundred years ago or so, this faith in the primacy of blood gave birth to three terms : *Latinism, Saxonism, Albinism.* This Albinism is the " doctrine of the White Man ", extending his primacy over the entire world. The White Man, in virtue of being white, has the " burden " of ruling over the Non-Whites, even if they might be called civilised. It used to be the fashion to discourse on the duties of a King, nowadays on the duties of·the White Man ; in both cases, the first duty is to rule as a master over his subjects.

Latinism, as Stendhal already explained it, is the idea that the Latins, being great and being pure, ought to rule, not the universe—for in his day the whole universe was not in question —but at least their neighbours. In mediæval times Dante toyed for a moment with the idea of universal or at least European domination by the Latins. His treatise *De Monarchia* celebrates the " world empire " of the Romans.[2] Inasmuch as the Romans of his day were, to his thinking, not only descendants of the

---

[1] On Race, see Taine, *Année sociologique*, X, p. 195 f.
[2] B. Landry, *L'idée de chrétienté*, 1929, p. 179 f.

ancient Romans, sons of Romulus and Remus, but also, through them, descendants of the Greeks and sons of Æneas, the great poet considered them to be the Chosen of God who by their power were to establish the *pax Romana* throughout the entire world. Petrarch also looked on everything non-Roman as non-civilised ; the Popes of Avignon had, for him, settled amongst barbarians in a land beyond the mountains. By this Roman and Trojan myth—from which, as we have seen, the French of that day were not exempt—he formulated a true Latinism which was reasserted just a century ago by Stendhal, who extolled " energy ", and loudly proclaimed his love for the Italians in so far as these descendants of the ancient Romans had preserved the ancient energy of the Roman warrior : that romantic, dramatic energy which he rejoiced to detect in the human insect ; the will to destroy, the will to construct, which was the legacy of the Renaissance to the Neo-Roman. " May heroism save us from boredom, that vice of the bourgeois ! " Mussolini had read Sorel : perhaps he had read Stendhal too ! For it is in Stendhal that we can trace in embryo the idea of universal Latin domination which people call *Pan-Latinism* [1] in order to make clear that it is *all* the Latin nations—blended into one—which ought to dominate the whole world, in virtue of their purity and primacy, and who could do so if they only would, and if they were able to pull together and to unite.

Round about the year 1900, there was a somewhat noisy dispute between the champions of Saxonism and those of Latinism. Edmond Demolins, following Le Play, had published a book called *What is the Source of Anglo-Saxon Superiority?* [2] It was the Germanic peoples, it was the English, who were the pure, the strong and the good. Against this others wrote upholding the superiority of the Latins, not the English. An author—Anold by name—now forgotten because he was swimming against too strong a stream, published a counterblast to Demolins entitled, *What is the Source of French Superiority over the Anglo-Saxons?* (1899). [3] In 1905 an Italian, Napoleon Colajanni, published a powerful book, *The Latins and the Anglo-Saxons*, which proclaimed Latinism in all its grandeur. He claimed that the Latins are superior both in purity and quality, and that the energy that informs them gives them the

---

[1] *Le panlatinisme. Confédération Gallo-Latine et Celto-Gauloise . . . ou projet d'Union fédérative . . .*, 1860, Paris.
[2] *A quoi tient la supériorité des Anglo-Saxons ?*
[3] *A quoi tient la supériorité des Français sur les Anglo-Saxons ?*

right to a great destiny. In our day another voice has powerfully intoned this national theme !

Latinism is not dead, not even in France. Louis Bertrand's romanesque writings aim at demonstrating how greatly France's civilisation of Algeria is a Latin achievement, how French colonisation is " Roman work "—as they always say in Provence —how the French conquests in North Africa bear witness to a great, eternal struggle between African and Latin. A reign of Latin power, of Christian power—if possible !—such is French rule in North Africa. French Latinism is a national much more than a universal Latinism. But there has long existed a universal Latinism, or a Pan-Latinism, properly so called. An anonymous book appeared in 1860 called *The Gallo-Latin Confederation* which formulates the idea of an alliance of all the Latin races, French, Roman and Italian, for a fruitful reign over the entire universe. Such ideas, though confused and obscure, still persist in certain people's minds.

The first place in this series, however, belongs not to Latinism but to Saxonism. The idea exists that it is the business of the Anglo-Saxons to rule non-Saxon peoples, more especially " coloured " peoples, by right of purity, by right of majesty, by right of heredity. This vision is implied, though not clearly expressed—English taste is not for clarity—in Macaulay's writings, especially in his *History of England* (1848). He is one of the first to use the word " race " in a new meaning, in an ethnic, not a mystic, a biologic, not a theological sense. He was one of the first to assert the primacy of the Anglo-Saxon people which God has granted them over the entire earth.

Down to our own day, however, and in our own day, Saxonism takes different forms, two in particular : first, *Gobinism*, secondly *Teutonism*.

Gobinism is, in other words, the theory enunciated by Gobineau.[1] The doctrine of race, in its new sense, is rightly named after this Frenchman—for this aristocratic diplomat was French. It is laid down in his famous book, *Essay on the Inequality of Human Races* (1855). The very title bespeaks the idea of primacy. Long before Demolins, he had made up his mind on the superi-

---

[1] There exists an enormous literature on this subject (a bibliography will be found in a Special Number of the *Nouvelle Revue française*, Feb. 1, 1934, pp 289–310). E. Seillière, *Le comte de Gobineau et l'aryanisme historique*, 1903 ; E. Dreyfus, *La vie et les prophéties du comte de G.*, 1905. E. Seillière's *Houston Stewart Chamberlain*, 1917, p. 48 f., gives an excellent résumé.—The best plan is to read Gobineau's own *Trois ans en Asie* (1855–8), Vol. II, Chap. V, on the Asiatic and the European.

ority of the Anglo-Saxon world, more especially of the Anglo-Norman people. Gobineau had had forerunners in France ; the " racialism " he preached was an old story. Count Boulainvilliers and the Abbé de Mably had already launched similar assertions,[1] but without success. According to Boulainvilliers it is the Aryans—he actually uses the word !—who are the conquerors, while Celts and Alpine peoples are the conquered, doomed to submit to subjection by the Aryans.

Another aristocrat, this Gobineau, was to set these visions of Boulainvilliers to music as it were. History is dominated by two ideas in which we can clearly recognise the two essential elements of power-imperialism : the idea of *purity*, the idea of *quality*.[2]

Purity. The great peoples, the strong peoples, are the pure, unmixed peoples who have been able to preserve their integrity, " to protect their blood ", the peoples therefore who have strictly obeyed the law of endogamy. In many books—a particularly interesting one is called *Three Years in Asia* [3]—an observant explorer constantly recurs to the dangers created by " fusion ". Every form of hybridisation is accursed. A great, strong people owes its strength and greatness always to its *birthright* ; a chosen people should be pure ; individuals of mixed blood are degenerates. Many German writers of to-day,[4] who learned their Gobinism from the Germanised Englishman H. S. Chamberlain, cling obstinately to this belief, chief among them Spengler, author of *The Decline of the West*. According to him, one of the most ominous signs of European decline is the intermixture of populations. It is race-purity which confers primacy.

Quality. Purity may exist without goodness ; there must therefore be quality as well. Power must not be confused with culture. Purity reinforces quality, but the two must not be divorced. Pure peoples are *also* great, good, strong, handsome peoples. Gobineau goes as far as that. For him, beauty and will are associated with purity. It is amongst the Saxons, especially the Northern Saxons, the Scandinavians and the

---

[1] On these forerunners, see Th. Simar, *La formation de la doctrine des races au XVIII* *siècle* . . . , 1922 ; E. G. Detweiler, *The Rise of Modern Race Antagonism*, American *Journal of Sociology*, March 1932.

[2] See A. de Tocqueville's criticism of these ideas : *Correspondance A. de T. et A. de Gobineau,* edited by Schemann, p. 191 f. ; but he asserted that God had willed the domination of the *Europeans* over the entire world (p. 251). He was an *Albinist* but not a *Saxonist*.

[3] *Trois ans en Asie.*

[4] [The author is writing in 1936. EOL]

English—not the Germans !—that you must seek the pure who are the great, the handsome and the strong ! Gobinism is the apologia of the North. Gobineau is ready to define this quality, he analyses it into two factors : the primacy of the North derives from two attributes : *activity* and *liberty*.—The peoples of the North are free and they are active : they are hard-working peoples, productive peoples, sport-loving peoples. The historian Klemm had already distinguished *active* as opposed to *passive* races.[1] Gobineau finds in the love of sport the proof of primacy. The writers of to-day sing the praises of the sportsman, strong man and good, who submits to discipline and exercises authority, the Man of the Tiber whom they contrast with the Man of the Orontes, lover of anarchy and democracy, a human larva, unfitted to rule. Liberty, activity—in work, in games, in battle [2] —these are the signs and the weapons of the best peoples : who strive to create, who strive in games to find an outlet for their energy in prowess and record-breaking. This praise of the winner, this glorification of the fighter, is nothing but the mystic idea of the Ancients once again. Amongst the Greeks the conqueror was a spirit or a demon ; with us, victory is the judgment of God : the conqueror is a minister of God. In ancient times the fighter possessed a " sacred right " ; he was taboo. In the same way primitive peoples imagine that tools and weapons are enchanted things under a spirit-spell ; in the same way, it is everywhere believed that heroes and conquerors in the strife, whether of war or sport, are the Chosen of God.

Purity and quality, according to Gobineau, involve inequality and primacy. It is the peoples *of quality* who will find in domination, for the sake of domination, a means of satisfying that passion of energy which is the very essence of their quality. Gobineau, in short, is, wholly and uncompromisingly, an aristocrat. He wants to see throughout the whole round world the rule of the handsome, the strong and the good : he dreams of a great, universal Anglo-Saxon Empire. He is the self-appointed prophet of domination. In this he sees a double advantage : it implies, of course, authority over others, but also authority *over self*, authority over self *above all*, since authority ought to be in itself a good, since all power is of value for its own sake. You must govern, for the sake of governing *yourself* ; you must exercise

---

[1] G. Klemm, *Allgemeine Kulturgeschichte*, Leipzig, 1843, I, p. 196 f.
[2] In the same spirit : A. Peters, *Psychologie des Sports. Seine Konfrontierung mit Spiel und Kampf*, Leipzig, 1927.

mastery for the sake of mastering *yourself*. It is from this point of view that de Vogüe and Lyautey held that the chief value for France of her overseas expansion lay in the opportunity it gave her to re-temper her sons, and by exposing them to danger to re-steel the slackened character of the contemporary Frenchman.[1] In this pure racialism, though domination is assigned by God to pure and superior peoples who are also the strong peoples, domination is no less in their own interest to increase their pleasure and their virtue : to rule themselves is morally as valuable as to rule others. They have two duties : to preserve their quality, to preserve their purity.

Later there came another writer, also a Frenchman—somewhat forgotten nowadays though I believe he is still alive—a writer whose plaster busts are, it is said, still to be seen standing in state in bookshops beyond the Rhine. He is Vacher de Lapouge, author of the book called *Social Selection* in which he used other arguments to magnify the superiority of strong nations.[2] He maintained that every period of human history should be interpreted as a front-line action of great men and of great nations, that progress can be achieved only through superior types whose " cephalic index " bears witness to their racial quality. He divided men into narrow-heads and broad-heads, the dolichocephalic and the brachycephalic ; the narrow-heads being in general Anglo-Saxons and the broad-heads in general Gauls, Alpines, Celts and Latins. In his eyes, progress was a great . . . Anglo-Saxon achievement. He thought he was able to prove that colonisers were normally men with narrow, not broad, heads. And he talked of the " Imperialist, Covetous, Dolichocephalic Man ". Perhaps he forgot the people of Marseilles and La Rochelle . . . It is not our business here to discuss these views ; we note them simply as beliefs which have exercised influence ; in many countries they are articles of faith. What we must emphasise is the way in which Pan-Saxonism sprang up in France, modified sometimes, often reborn, and subject in our own day to crazy " revivals " !

We know how Gobinism was distorted into *Germanism*. In the countries beyond the Rhine, university philosophers and

---

[1] E. M. de Vogüe, *Les morts qui parlent*, novel, undated ; Lyautey, *Lettres du Tonkin et de Madagascar*, *passim*.

[2] Vacher de Lapouge, *Les sélections sociales*, 1896, *passim* ; *De l'inégalité parmi les hommes, Revue d'Anthropologie*, 1888, p. 9 f.   Cf. *Année Sociologique*, I, p. 518 f. ; E. Hertz, *Moderne Rassentheorien* . . . , Vienna, 1904.   New German editions of Gobineau and of V. de Lapouge by J. Krueper and A. Kirchoff, Frankfurt, 1934.

various writers evolved a theory of the primacy of the German people. Leibniz for one, and Fichte ; most of all Hegel. Nietzsche,[1] too, chanting the praises of the " Superman ", the conqueror, the only man who knows how to " live dangerously " —men like the explorers—destined to rule over weakness and senility. It was, however, one of Gobineau's disciples, the Englishman Houston Stewart Chamberlain, Wagner's son-in-law, who met with the most resounding response. A germanised French emigrant, one Villers, somewhere about 1800 had contrasted the retreating Gallo-Romans with the advancing Germans. A Tyrolese exile in England, a certain William Altner, dreamed in 1815 of federating all the German peoples ; he was the inventor of *Pan-Germanism.* About 1900 H. S. Chamberlain— basing himself on Gobineau—expressed the conviction that the dominators willed by God were the Germans, not the English.[2] According to this writer, heavily infected with the racialism of Nietzsche and Wagner, a very great race of Slavo-Celto-Germans had been evolved in Europe, a race of pure-breds confirmed and preserved by inviolate endogamy. This was the people whom God had designated to dominate the European world, and later the world entire. It is this point which shows Chamberlain to have remained colonial-minded. This is not the place to examine the racialist attitude of the party in power ; this is— or was—solely preoccupied with Europe. We must rather consider the doctrine of Günther [3] from whom Hitler drew his racialist inspiration. Hitler's racialism is a distorted Gobinism, anti-Latin like Günther, anti-Christian like Hauer. There is always the emphasis on purity and on quality ; always the idea of great peoples, who are also the strong peoples, and who ought to dominate, in order to refresh in themselves the strength and virtue of a dominating people : in order to dominate, and in order to dominate themselves. For Power is Perfection and to grow great is only to attain self-realisation. This is why Hitler, who at first was by no means keen on colonies, was bound to come, or to come back, to a colonial programme.[4] A novel of Hans Grimm's, *Volk ohne Raum* (" A People without

---

[1] Nietzsche, *Pages choisies* (*Mercure de France*) pp. 407 f., 415 f.
[2] E. Seillière, *Houston Stewart Chamberlain*, 1917 (and *Revue des Deux-Mondes*, Dec. 1-15, 1903, Jan. 1, 1904) ; P. L. Landsberg, *Rassenideologie* . . . , *Zeitschrift für Sozialforschung*, 1933, 3, pp. 388-406.
[3] H. Günther, *Rassenkunde des deutschen Volkes*, Jena, 1934.
[4] W. E. Muehlmann, *Rassenfragen in Schriften der Gegenwart, Sociologus*, Sept. 1933 ; L. Schemann, *Die Rassenfragen in Schriften der Neuzeit*, Review *Volk und Rasse*, from 1926 onwards.

Space ") bitterly pleads the right of the German peasant to conquer at the expense of the English and the French.[1]

Amongst the Anglo-Saxons, as amongst the French, there had nevertheless been growing for a hundred years another idea aiming at making primacy general and universal : power-imperialism which would thus rule the entire world. This was to be the White Man's rule, not the reign of the Latin or the Saxon or the German, but *Albinism* ; in other words the claim of the White Man to dominate the Non-White. This is in truth *Universal* Colonial Imperialism. It is very striking in the Anglo-Indian poet Rudyard Kipling. In his poems he speaks both of the English and the French, but he speaks too of the White Man who has quality and he speaks of God who vows to end anarchy and barbarism in the universe. The " White Man's burden ", the White Man's task, is mission, right and duty ; it is a White Imperialism, a real Albinism.

The anthropologists had, however, formulated the doctrine a hundred years earlier. They used to assert the White Man's primacy and to predict the White Man's rule. In the earliest controversies about race, Agassiz and Quatrefages stressed the opposition between white and coloured peoples and very firmly upheld the superiority of the white peoples. In the forties a hot dispute developed between the Swiss Agassiz and Anglo-American writers, who were conducting a campaign against slavery. The famous anti-slaver Channing [2] in particular, devoted long passages of his book to a criticism of this scientific —or, rather, pseudo-scientific—doctrine of Agassiz, which asserted that the White Man, solely by virtue of his whiteness, was superior to the coloured, while the coloured peoples, whether " yellow ", " red " or " black ", were by vocation subject peoples. The idea of *subject races*, fatally condemned by their colour to subjection, was thus a postulate of anthropology. An ethnologist, Courtet de l'Isle,[3] used to speak of " races naturally pre-ponderant " and to lay down the " law " of the triumph by selection of the whites over the yellows, blacks and reds. In opposition to Schoelcher, he dwelt on the " un-civilisation " of the African Negro. It is, however, particularly amongst the English that Albinism has flourished ; for the English—in theory, not in reality !—are more Albinist than Saxonist. Many of them

[1] C. Andler, *Le pangermanisme colonial sous Guillaume II, Textes traduits* . . . , 1916.
[2] W. E. Channing, *Slavery*, 1835 ; French trans. 1857.
[3] *Tableau ethnographique du genre humain*, 1847, pp. 13 f. and 27 f.

preach with some asperity, not the superiority of the Englishman as such, but the superiority of the White Man ; the quality common to every white.

Carlyle was the founder of Albinism.[1] According to him the distinguishing virtue of the *Gentleman*, which ought thereafter to be sought and ensued by every man worthy of this title, is : power. He sings the praise of the *Ruler*, the man who reigns over others, the directing-man, who is the true aristocrat ; the praise of the man who is able to find scope for his energy, able by exercising to confirm and renew it. In this he agrees with Stendhal, but he is the first to deduce from these premisses conclusions of an imperial nature. It is he who was the first to speak of " dominating " and of " dominated " peoples. It was he who preached a universal despotism, for the *virtue* and the *advantage*—to be attained at the same time and in the same way—of the white peoples. In this he was mindful of the lesson of the Puritans and Quakers, the founders of English America, mindful of their strong and deep-seated mysticism, which held that the Indian was a " child of the Evil One " and that they owed it to themselves to purify and convert him. They even said that an epidemic which broke out among the Indians was willed by Christ who chose this means of making room for his chosen people : " our people have signed an alliance with God " ! [2] As always, power-imperialism by secret paths rejoins spiritual imperialism.[3] This is why, not long afterwards, Albinism increased with Kingsley, a theologian and a clergyman. Charles Kingsley was a Christian Socialist ; yet he chanted the mighty anthem of force ; even in his sermons he places Force on the highest pinnacle of virtue ; virtue which renews itself by exercise, which would grow weak and dim if it were not re-tempered by the exercise of power. Let us then be strong in the colonies and applaud the stern repression of the Jamaican revolt.[4] This clergyman's homilies were certainly energetic. He spoke sternly of the subject-peoples whom the will of the " Deity " has destined to be ruled, for their own advantage of course, but also for the benefit of their rulers.

If, with the English, colonial imperialism took the form of

---

[1] Especially in *Past and Present* (1843) ; see L. Cazamian, *Carlyle*, 1913 ; C. Cestre, *La doctrine sociale de Carlyle, Revue du Mois*, Nov. 10, 1913.

[2] J. Truslow Adams, *The Epic of America*, 1932.

[3] K. Völker, *Die religiösen Wurzeln des englischen Imperialismus*, Tübingen, 1924.

[4] *Sermons on National Subjects*, 2nd Series, 1852–4. J. A. Froude in his *History of England* (1856–70) admires the " rulers ", even when they are tyrants : he strives to refurbish the glory of Henry VIII.

universal Albinism, we must not imagine that the French kept themselves free from it. Proudhon—mass of contradictions as he was—displayed an intemperate Albinism. In his *War and Peace*,[1] still under Hegel's influence, he thought he had found a solution of the conflict between force and right. Right, he said, is only Force plus Reason. In reality, right force and reason are identical. This is going even further than Pascal ! Victory is thus a gift of God. Conquering, victorious men are the Chosen of God : he does not shirk the word. War is therefore the judgment of God. It is God giving his approval to Reason. If Turkey no longer carries political weight, partition her without remorse ! As far as racialism and Albinism are in question, Proudhon closely approaches the vision of the Greeks who thought the victor was inspired by Niké. " It is the will of God " is the eternal theme. Proudhon formally professed the inequality of races. He held that the domination of all inferior peoples by the superior peoples was necessary. The idea of primacy led this reformer, on one occasion at least, to desire a universal imperialism. An extremely able colonial journalist, Paul Bourde, also said, in almost the same words : " Nature grants the right of freedom to those only who are strong enough to be free . . . "[2]

We shall see too how in our day the idea of universal imperialism has been reversed ; how the Blacks, having learned in the White Man's school, have formed their own conception of universal imperialism ; how, in the course of the last twenty years, they have founded what we may call *Melanism* or *Pan-Melanism*. Melanism is the primacy of the Black Man in virtue of his blackness ; Pan-Melanism is the desire of the Blacks to dominate the entire world, or, at the very least, the whole African world ! In Marcus Garvey, Melanism is very pronounced. He is an American theorist, a hundred-per-cent. negro : his Melanism is an inverted Albinism, similarly founded on the ideas of purity and quality, but in favour and for the benefit of the Black Man.[3] For if it is true that power should belong to the peoples who have preserved the hereditary purity of their race, a day was bound to come when the enlightened Black Man would skilfully use this argument in the name of all his negro brethren !

[1] *La Guerre et la paix*, *Œuvres de Proudhon* (Bouglé-Moysset Ed.), 1927, pp. 21 f., 31 f., 106 f. and 177 f.
[2] P. Bourde, *De Paris au Tonkin*, 1885, p. 88 f. See also A. Rambaud's Preface to the French translation of Seeley's *Expansion of England*, 1885, p. 30 f. : expansion as a natural outlet for *energy*.
[3] See below, Chapter XXXVIII.

CHAPTER XXI

MATERIAL IMPERIALISM : CONCEPTIONS

The Imperialism of to-day is a *material* or temporal imperialism, rather than a spiritual or cultural or power-imperialism. Self-interest is nowadays the impelling motive of emigration and exploitation. The Ancients, however, were also a prey to covetousness and cupidity. It was for their own profit that the Romans built their cities overseas. And the Greeks designed their trade-colonies for commercial purposes, to establish favourable relations and serve as a means of exploiting " new countries ". Aristotle [1] dreamed of a Federation of Greek States under the hegemony of Macedonia to colonise and exploit the countries of Asia. He caught in fact a glimpse of the possibility of developing to advantage the whole Universe ! Amongst the Ancients, at least, such calculations always formerly preserved relations of self-interest and of duty between the colonies and the mother-country. The overseas cities were subjected to a census and to taxes, and if these cities were guarded and protected it was for the benefit of the mother-country. From their foundation therefore colonies were considered as a source of gain. Enumerating the reasons that would lead a man to expatriate himself, Seneca based them all on self-interest : eviction by an enemy, internal troubles in the country, over-population, infertility of the native soil, calamities : let us summarise in two words, necessity or advantage. [2]

The Crusaders too and the Conquistadors, who quite sincerely believed themselves to be Champions of the True Faith, who led the battle for the Spirit, nevertheless sought treasure and thirsted for gold. It was most certainly in the hope of gain that cities and merchants financed the enterprises of the Crusades ; the warriors risked their lives to amass and pile up wealth ; war, in all ages, has desired booty and loot. A sacred trophy is the spiritual symbol ; booty is the price and hire of the risks incurred. " Emprise " is never far removed from " enterprise ". In the Middle Ages, both in East and West, there existed a doctrine of

---

[1] *Politics*, Book VIII, Chap. 8.
[2] " Primitive " peoples also have gone far afield in search of gold, tin, pearls. This is the theme of W. J. Perry (a pupil of Rivers) in his *Megalithic Culture of Indonesia*, 1917, Chap. XXII, pp. 170–9.

booty. Musulmans and Christians alike considered that one of the legitimate aims of war was . . . the quest for products. This was already self-interested imperialism of a kind. Convert by all means, but enrich yourself too : pious sentiment and self-interest were intimately interwoven. On his return from his Third Voyage, Columbus, after all his misfortunes, took refuge in mysticism and wrote his *Libro de las Profecias* [1] in which he suggested that the Christian Kings should conquer the Holy Land . . . with American gold. This was one of the aims of his ensuing voyage : the search for pearls, the quest for gold—for a sanctified purpose ! Adventurers, seekers, and dreamers, if they thought of ruling, thought also of gaining. On a portolano chart of the 15th century, now preserved in the Bibliothèque Nationale, the king of the Mandinga is represented as holding in his out-stretched hand a nugget of gold ! Gold such as the Portuguese Antonio Gonzalez saw for the first time in 1442 on the very banks of the Rio de Oro. The great navigator Jean Parmentier in the 16th century denounced the cupidity of the Portuguese. He saw well enough that the Portuguese—and others too—were not singleminded explorers bent on enhancing the great-ness of the princes who had sent them forth ; that they were diligently seeking in East and West Indies as much a new world to exploit as a new world to conquer. Another great traveller, Peter Martyr, accuses the Spaniards of the same appetite : " a people as greedy as it is insignificant ! " [2] Conquistadors : standard-bearers of the faith, fortune-hunters, bringing salvation, pocketing the profit. All the planners who have woven dreams of conquest, Louis XIV or Napoleon, have thought also of enriching themselves. All who have devised schemes for colonis-ing distant lands, Père Joseph or Richelieu for instance—to name only these two—were thinking of business-houses, offices and ports ; treasure for the princes, profit for the people. [3] The Oriental dream was a commercial dream. Even the moralists had got past being shocked, for, as Nicole [4] says, *cupidity* accomplishes what *charity* would not, and men go to the Indies seeking remedies against disease ! So great a virtue resides in greed for gain !

Those were the days when people looked in published

[1] Manuscripts of the Bibliothèque Colombine.
[2] Peter Martyr, *De orbe novo* (1530), Gaffarel's ed. 1907, pp. 200 and 568 f.
[3] P. Masson, *Histoire du commerce français dans le Levant au XVIIe siècle*, p. 323 f.—there was Razilly's *Mémoire* (1626) proposing to set up business premises in Morocco ; cf. A. Bernard, *Le Maroc*, 6th Ed. 1921, p. 291 f.
[4] Pierre Nicole, *Traité de la charité et de l'amour-propre* in *Essais de morale* (10th Ed. 1709).

pamphlets, or sometimes in unpublished memoirs, to see what were the *advantages* of founding colonies. These words " the advantages " or " the interests " recur more frequently than any other in governors' despatches and colonial memoranda. In an unpublished memoir [1] of the 18th century Kerguelen wonders what interest France would have in exploiting "Austral France ", as it was called, namely, the Oceanic world. At the close of the same century Talleyrand's famous memorandum—which I shall quote later—also weighed the advantages which might accrue from the possession of colonies in the New World. The idea of gain thus comes to the fore. Not only discoverers, not only conquerors, but puritans and members of religious Orders, have abetted or connived at this " materialism "—sometimes, but by no means always, unwittingly. Though the great emigration of the English Puritans at the beginning of the 17th century was chiefly due to the desire for salvation, personal profit was also a factor. The Puritans who sailed away were many, and the reason was—as some of them frankly admitted—that they fled material loss and the serious rise in prices. Inflation helped to recruit preachers ! [2]

Such is the practice, reduced in long-distant times to a formula. The Greeks had already a utilitarian and mercantile *doctrine*. We read in Herodotus that colonies should be multiplied along overseas coasts as a means of averting famine. For in their tiny cities and their infertile lands the Greeks used to suffer from famine. Greek historians knew and stated that expansion brought material benefit to the cities. Another historian, the Roman Valerius Maximus, in his *Memorabilia* (*De Factis Dictisque Memorabilibus*, Book IX, Chap. 1) speaks of overseas territories which will be of interest to Rome. Their value will be that they can make Rome autonomous by supplying her wants, and thus render the city independent of the outside world. Valerius Maximus is wholly opposed to Greek luxury ; for luxury puts you at the mercy of foreigners ; the colonies will be able to provide all necessaries. This thesis is, as it were, the forerunner of the modern ideal of " autarky " ; [3] Valerius wished to see the Roman Empire self-sufficing. We almost seem to hear the voice of one of the speakers at the Economic Conference of the French Overseas Empire, which was held less than a year ago. [4]

[1] *Réflexions sur les avantages que peut procurer la France Australe* (MSS. Archives du Dépôt hydrographique de la marine, 4 pp. ; cf. A. Rainaud, *Le continent austral*, 1893, p. 433).
[2] *Encyclopædia Britannica*, 14th Ed. 1930, Vol. XV, p. 30, col. 2.
[3] J. Nowack, *L'idée de l'autarchie économique*, 1925 (thesis) ; A. Landry, *Autarcie*, *Revue d'Économie politique*, Jan.–Feb. 1936.   [4] [Written in 1936. EOL]

This utilitarian imperialism has therefore, as we see, a long and ancient history. It has existed always and everywhere. It is therefore untrue to describe it, as some have done, as nothing but a " phase " of " capitalism ". This is the doctrine expounded by Lenin in his *Imperialism* of 1916.[1] He refers presumably to utilitarian or mercantile imperialism and seeks to demonstrate that this is only one manifestation of our capitalist era ; one proof of the " monopolist " spirit which, he says, marks the tyranny of Capital. Monopolism and parasitism are, according to him, characteristics of Capitalism the climax of which is colonialism, a product of " excess profit ", a parasitism carried to the nth. Though I find all these -*ism's* somewhat alarming, I do not by any means deny that the colonial phenomenon is a profoundly capitalist phenomenon, nor that it owes its expansion —grown, in our day excessive—to Capital. Businesses require finance ; so too do . . . revolutions. Both need bankers. . . . At all times and in all places, among all human communities, large or small, Tribes, Cities, Nations or States, men have claimed the right to " develop the value " of colonies. The expansion of the most ancient human groups has been dictated either by necessity or by utility. Hear Sir John Falstaff. Hoping to be kept by *The Merry Wives of Windsor* (1602) : " I will be cheaters to them both," says he, " and they shall be exchequers to me : they shall be my East and West Indies, and I will trade to them both." [2]

Though the history of material imperialism boasts both age and continuity, it also shows diversity. Its variations are almost infinite according to climate and terrain, for the needs which give rise to it are always manifold and various. Self-interested imperialism has therefore its *degrees* and its *objects*.

It has its *degrees*, because the material interests which expansion is to satisfy may be less or more important : matters of *necessity* or merely of *convenience*.

Conquest for the sake of exploitation may be undertaken of *necessity* when it is thought—whether correctly or not is here no concern of ours since we are dealing with traditions and points of view—when it is *thought* that the very life of a certain human group depends on expansion, or when it is *feared*—as even the Ancients feared !—that it is threatened by over-population. In either case it is believed that, willy-nilly, distant countries *must*

[1] V. I. Lenin, *Imperialism, the Highest Stage of Capitalism*, Revised Eng. trans., 2nd Ed. 1934 ; *Imperialism and Imperialist War* (1914–17), Eng. trans., *Selected Works*, V, 1935.
[2] [Act I, Scene 3. EOL]

be colonised. The Romans in their day pleaded necessity, as do the Italians of to-day.

Or conquest may be undertaken for *convenience*, for its usefulness or for its facility. Emigration is not thought inevitable or indispensable ; but it provides, or is thought likely to provide, some benefit or advantage. People imagine, for instance, that by exploiting the new country they will be able to increase the production of the old, or the quantity of food supplies available. They are thinking of their comfort or their prosperity.

The love of luxury now takes its place—and often a foremost place—amongst the stimuli to emigration. People have often wished to colonise in order to secure the unnecessary, or what they thought to be so ; to acquire new goods which their fathers had lived without ; to enjoy the luxury of spending ; to follow the fashion and gratify their pride. For the space of two centuries bitter battles were fought for spices ; much courage and guile were displayed to secure plants of clove and nutmeg, simply to satisfy new-fangled appetites which " brought in " most handsome dividends to the trader. The Spice War of the 17th and even of the 18th century—which made the name of Pierre Poivre famous—shows how the degrees of greed can vary.

We have also to consider the *objects* sought by material imperialism. The desires, whether less or more urgent, which increasingly tended to encourage expansion, were very diverse, for the advantages hoped from the exploitation of colonies related to very different needs. It is therefore desirable to distinguish all the interested motives with reference to their particular object.

One major distinction must first be made. There is first the interest in *one's own advantage* and secondly the interest in *someone else's disadvantage*. To impoverish others is relatively to enrich myself ; to weaken others is to strengthen myself ; wealth and power are relative to the wealth and power of others. My good, another's ill, are the two poles of policy ; these are the two targets aimed at in every conquest undertaken in a mercantile spirit.

Present or Future Advantage. Francis Bacon wrote in the 16th century one of the first essays on expansion, an essay which he called *Of Plantations*—that is to say, colonies.[1] The English

---

[1] [Bacon's Essays, No. 33, 1625 : " Planting of countries is like planting of woods ; for you must make account to lose twenty years' profit, and expect your recompense in the end. For the principal thing that hath been the destruction of most plantations hath been the base and hasty drawing of profit in the first years." EOL] French trans. 1742. Richard Hakluyt at about the same time proposed in *A Particular Discourse concerning Western Discoveries* the occupation and exploitation of North America by the English (1584 ; published in 1870 at Cambridge, Mass.).

Lord Chancellor pointed out that it was wise to consider the future, more distant interest and not the present immediate interest only—as colonial exploiters often did and do. The advantage may be a long-term credit rather than cash down !

The *disadvantage of others* may similarly be either present or future. There is no need to remind the reader that colonial wars have been waged to inflict injury on others. This aim has lain behind the struggles between great powers. The Protestant writer, Philippe de Mornay, handed Henri III a long memorandum entitled : *Discourse on the Means of Reducing the Power of Spain.*[1] The very title indicates that in proposing to seize Spanish territory his primary intention was to weaken the Spaniard. When one Empire grows at the expense of another, it enjoys a double profit and a double pride. With Richelieu this became an obsession ; so too with Napoleon. And this it remained . . . down to the days of Louis Philippe when the French sought distant *bases* for their fleets. To wreck houses ; to reduce countries ; this was a work of piety for the conqueror. The consequences were far-reaching, almost infinite. Sentiment as well as self-interest was involved, the eternal aspiration of all human societies, the resort to battle[2] to appease *jealousy*. Material imperialism has its sentimental and emotional side. Self-interest has its own mysticism as well as its own dogma. My interest is countered by . . . the self-interest of my fortunate neighbour. From envy and jealousy I shall enrich myself ; from envy and jealousy I shall aggrandise myself. Let us not linger on this point, for we are getting too close to present-day realities. How to appease jealousy is one of the problems of international government. Honour and pride are blended with self-interest.[3]

Let us rather dwell on the first objective : advantage, the pursuit of gain. But what gain ? There are two primary gains : to *settle men*, or to *acquire goods*.

To settle men in distant places is to put an end to over-population. In this sense, colonisation is in Bacon's phrase " plantation " or transplantation. It is, in other words, long-term emigration, since its main purpose is to settle excess population at a distance. The first, self-interested gain of expansion

---

[1] *Discours sur les moyens de diminuer l'Espagne.*

[2] A typical example is found in R. Pares, *War and Trade in the West Indies, 1739–1748* (*Revue hist. colonies françaises,* Jan.–Feb. 1932).

[3] Prévost-Paradot, *La France Nouvelle,* 1868, Book III, Chap. 3, wished France to create an Empire, but chiefly as " the last resource for our greatness ", to *counterbalance* the great *expansion* of the Anglo-Saxons.

is to settle, or plant, or find a berth for people in a distant land, to create employment, to give work, to offer opportunities not possible in the home country. The Indian Civil Service of the English is primarily designed . . . to supply jobs for younger sons.[1]

This can be carried out on two different lines according as attention is directed to *quantity* or to *quality*—we find the same already amongst the Ancients—to express it in more concrete terms, according to whether you wish to deport to distant places your *excess* population or your *malcontents*.

The excess population are the over-numerous people whom the soil of the Nation or of the City cannot feed, and who are consequently " in excess ". The old problem of feeding continues to cause anxiety amongst all peoples with a high birthrate. Both Romans and Greeks were disturbed by it. In our old countries everything is already occupied : lands and jobs are already allotted : to emigrate to a distance is to find work and well-being. English yeomen dispossessed by the enclosures, workmen continually unemployed, have everywhere populated the lands of the Empire.[2]

The *malcontents* are the deported, the exiles, the sad products of party strife : the " non-conformists " or the " protestants " in the primary meaning of the word. Amongst the Ancients, an end was made of political divisions in the City by the deportation of the defeated. Amongst the Greeks the settlement of malcontents in the colonies was a great stimulus to expansion. In France it was Talleyrand who expounded the theory. He urged that the Government should not only transplant the excess population but deport the malcontents. This was emigration for the sake of emigration.

To settle people abroad was therefore one aim, the other was to *acquire goods* or to " produce " them. In our day this aim takes foremost place. In consequence we no longer seek transplantation as an end in itself, nor emigration for its own sake as a goal to be pursued for the benefit of the City or the State ; we seek rather to *develop the resources* of new countries so as to obtain new goods, and to make new gains ; to acquire goods or, better still, money. We expand to enrich ourselves ; we emigrate, not to populate but to exploit.

[1] [The English reader will already have noted that Professor Maunier has a better grasp of French aims in North Africa than of the aims and achievements of Britain in India. EOL]

[2] D. Pasquet, *Histoire . . . du peuple américain*, 1924, Vol. I, p. 33 f.

To enrich ourselves has more than one interpretation ; it has at least two meanings : to find in the colonies markets for our wares or purchasable goods for ourselves. We desire to *export* from the mother-country and to *import* from the colonies.

Exports. If we favour exports, we hope to find in the colonies opportunities for *sales* or for shipments (*envois*) as they used to call it ; to make these countries markets for the industry of the mother-country. This is the first aim : to gain by selling. This we do from extremely diverse motives : sometimes for *cash*, sometimes for *products*. For *money*, since in the beginning and during the " mercantile " period, the aim was to encourage exports so as to increase the mother-country's stock of gold and silver. We exported for the sake of *treasure*, from hunger for silver and gold ; but the gold and silver were for Princes and States. For *products*, for while the colonies are to be " outlets " and markets, *overflow*-channels for our industry, while we want to load more and more ships with cargo for these countries, while we consider export as in itself a good thing, we want also to encourage the *flow* of goods from the interior. We feel that traffic from *within* to *without* is advantageous in itself, and should be maintained and increased by expansion.

Imports. We look on the colonies therefore not only as outlets and markets. We expect to make purchases from them to get from them some " return ", as they used to say in olden days. We want them to be *reservoirs* and not only overflow channels. We want them to offer or to " furnish " to the mother-country useful goods, or goods believed to be useful : which comes to the same thing. For the last three centuries in particular, we have hoped to draw from the colonies *food*-supplies, raw *materials* or finished *products*, which when imported into the mother-country will give her more comfort and also more power. It has, as we shall see, long been held that importation from the colonies could increase the autonomy or the " autarky " of the mother-country, since the metropolis would thus be able to live on her own resources and be self-sufficient whether in peace or war. She would thus achieve both *prosperity* and *security*. The colonies would serve to bring her both pleasure and power. The traffic between *without* and *within* brings private profit, but at the same time public benefit ; it is interested imperialism because it is interested nationalism.

CHAPTER XXII

MATERIAL IMPERIALISM : DETAILS

We must analyse in detail all the various aims of expansion which in reality are almost invariably intertwined. Mont-chrestien, who was in his own way an imperialist, and in his own way a nationalist, wrote in 1615 the Treatise which I have already quoted.[1] In it we clearly see how closely interwoven are the various interests which justify expansion. If he desires colonies, it is, he tells us, first to enrich the King ; but also to enrich the people, the subjects of the King ; also to get rid of evildoers, to give employment to the poor and the idle, and to remedy over-population ; for in our country, he says, " people are stifling each other ". Thus, many calculations enter in, and many aims. This is a point we must not overlook as we proceed to our analysis.

We have already said : material imperialism is first and foremost *transplantation*. Its first aim is to settle men in a distant country. Amongst the Ancients it already took the form of what we might call *settlement colonies* or transplantation colonies. The Ancients had two needs : to transplant their excess population, and to transplant their malcontents.

Transplanting *excess population*. The first aim of the colonies was to settle excess population on overseas shores.[2] The Greeks were wont in their cities to draw lots for superfluous men, who then went off to build colonies at a distance. The Romans, both under the Republic and under the Empire, pursued a deliberate policy of transplanting to Mauritania their excess men : encouraging emigration by offering free estates to fathers of families who had at least three children. Population policy was therefore familiar to the Romans.

Coming to the West, and first of all to the Middle Ages, we find a similar calculation formally expressed. The unknown poet (perhaps Robert Wace) of the *Roman de Brut*, which is believed to date from the 13th century, puts the following verses into the

---

[1] *Traicté de l'Occonomie politique* (Funck-Brentano's Ed. 1889). Book II, *Du Commerce*, and Book III, *De la Navigation*.
[2] For " primitive " peoples, see O. T. Mason, *Migration and the Food-Quest*, a *Study in Peopling of America*, Smithsonian Report, 1894, pp. 523–53.

mouth of a Saxon chief, who was supposed to have founded a settlement in Brittany about the year A.D. 800 :

> Our folk at home too fecund are,
> Our families too large by far ;
> Too many of us there appear
> And that is why you find us here . . .
> We thus divide the multitude
> For whom our land can find no food,
> For infants more our country yields
> Than beasts to graze upon our fields.[1]

This is probably the first enunciation of the doctrine that colonisation is a remedy for over-population. Thomas More—nowadays reckoned a saint—the great reformer and colonial, was in his own way an imperialist. His *Utopia*, published in 1516, expressly claims for Europeans the right to transplant their surplus population to the New World of America. More also claims the right to conquer all undeveloped territories, because, he says, it is a duty to feed the settlers, and because the occupants of these countries, if the land were to remain uncultivated and undeveloped by the settlers, might become the victims of exploitation and elimination to the profit of more skilful exploiters ! The aim of colonisation is to produce. The idea that it is a right and a duty to develop new countries in the interests of the whole world, is already present to Thomas More's mind. Alfred Mahan's theory of " competent races " can therefore shelter under his predecessors' sanctity. Woe to the inefficient and the unproductive ! There is no right without duty. . . . There is no ownership, no sovereignty except in the general interest of the human race.

At the beginning of the 18th century another national and imperial economist, Melon, or perhaps Mélon, published in 1734 a *Political Essay on Commerce*.[2] In Chapter IV he speaks " Of Colonies ". In his eyes the advantage to the mother-country of possessing colonies was that they supplied a remedy for her over-population, an evil from which the French were then suffering. He wished to see only the excess population exported ; he did not want emigration to be excessive, nor settlement more " intensive " than was necessary. He was colonial-minded, but in moderation. He stressed particularly the point that it was only the surplus population, especially surplus artisans,

---

[1] *Roman de Brut*, verses 6889–922. [*The Encyclopædia Britannica*, 14th Ed. 1930, s.v. *Wace* (*Robert*) dates this Norman French poem as 1155. EOL]
[2] *Essai Politique sur le commerce.*

who ought to emigrate : colonisation was nothing more than a cure for over-population. He was afraid, and others shared his fear, that the State might be weakened by emigration.

Being good at calculation, he concluded that it was a mistake to exterminate the original inhabitants of America, as the Spaniards did, for this policy imposed emigration on Spain, who had to pour in white men to replace the aborigines they had eliminated. In his opinion this was the primary cause of that decadence of the Spanish people which at the time was obsessing everybody's mind. The same view was in those days commonly held in France. The Chevalier de Chastellux was its chief upholder.[1] Colonies seemed to him the panacea for that over-population from which France, like England, imagined she was suffering. We should do like the Greeks, he said, and draw lots to decide whose fate it was to emigrate ! They will be able to live far away : they would not be able to live in the country of their birth ! If a State is suffering from having too many citizens, you must make your choice : either produce more food, or emigrate. If you are to attempt to feed extra mouths, you must produce extra food : if that is not possible, the extra folk who must be fed must be transplanted to distant countries. It is hard for us nowadays to realise how the French under the Ancient Monarchy were haunted by the bogy of over-population. We see that our obsessions of to-day had their forerunners ! [2] We need feel no surprise that Malthus later came on the scene and that his views were faithfully echoed in France. He urged that States should seek a solution for this problem of over-population, that they should take various measures to combat it, especially by means of emigrations.[3] Malthus and his followers were therefore logically advocates of colonial expansion (but only as a very temporary expedient). In 1846 one of the principal disciples of Malthus, the Englishman Thornton, published his *Over-Population and its Remedy*. He advocated emigration on a large scale ; " gigantic " emigration was to be *the* sovereign cure for over-population, the fear of which haunted the people of his time like a tragic nightmare.[4] In 1848 the French made an attempt to transplant the Paris unemployed to Algeria ; the

[1] *De la félicité publique*, 1776, I, p. 46 f.
[2] This was Herrenschwand's theory too : *De l'économie politique et morale de l'espèce humaine*, 1796, II, p. 426 f.
[3] *Essay on the Principle of Population*, 1789 (French trans. 1809).
[4] See also W. Brown, *New Zealand . . . as a Field for Emigration*, 1845 ; Quételet, *Du système social . . .*, 1848, p. 189 f.

plan was half-hearted and was abandoned. The idea which the so-called " Have-Not " peoples are nowadays trumpeting in Germany and Italy, claiming a right to colonies because they have too many mouths to feed, is not an invention of yesterday or the day before. The doctrine has long since taken root in their minds that there is a " Law of Necessity " (*Notrecht*) in virtue of which they are entitled to multiply in distant countries.[1]

Transplanting Malcontents. All who have failed to find happiness or satisfaction in a given state of society : all the maladjusted, who might better be called the " refractory " ; all those whom it used to be the fashion to call " republicans ", " non-conformists " or " dissidents ", can, by settling in the colonies, find a new world for themselves and a new state of affairs. The Ancients had already vaguely thought of deporting the desperate, in order to ease and calm down party strife and guarantee the established order. The Greeks deliberately encouraged, or even insisted on, the emigration of malcontents ; especially those who lacked a proper social status, who were the offspring of parents of different rank ; " class half-castes " as they were called, men who had no fixed position in the city.

Coming down to Renaissance times, we find La Popelinière in France proposing in 1582 the formation of a sort of " Foreign Legion ". He demanded the transplantation to the colonies of rebellious and insubordinate people from whom an army corps could be formed to conquer distant countries.[2] At the beginning of the 17th century English Protestants, persecuted by the Church, betook themselves to the New World, to settle there and find liberty—or so they hoped. They had faith in the right of the oppressed to create a new life for themselves in the desert. But these persecuted folk lost no time in turning persecutors themselves ! In Massachusetts, one of their earliest settlements, and particularly at Boston, a rigid orthodoxy was set up ; non-conformists were hunted down and forced to flee ! So it came about that one of them, a certain Roger Williams, quitted Massachusetts and plunged into the West. By proclaiming the right of all " dissenters " to set forth and find liberty in colonies of their own, Roger Williams gave practical expression to the right to freedom of thought. For him the means of finding liberty was further " emigration "—the right

---

[1] See A. F. von Œrtzen, *Nationalsozialismus und Kolonialfrage*, Berlin, 1935.
[2] G. Chinard, *L'exotisme américain dans la littérature française au XVIe siècle*, 1911, p. 189 f.

to which was still a matter of dispute in European countries
—the freedom to go away, and think and live as he liked.
Colonisation for him spelt liberation.

In his day, this hope was widespread. A somewhat kindred
scheme was born in France under Louis XIV. We must have
colonies, was then the cry, to deport thereto the poor and the
idle and make them of service to the King and the State. A
colonial official, Robert Challes by name, whose writings have
recently been discovered, submitted to the King a plan for
founding colonies in North America to which indigent volunteers
could be sent—for he was not at that time thinking of compulsion
—and an end thus put to idleness and begging.[1] Other writers,
like Vauban for instance, felt uneasy about such a project. On
the other hand, poor Virginie's spiteful aunt is represented as
exclaiming : " Why don't you send these lazy fellows to rot in
our colonies ? " To sink or swim, but anyhow to get out ! In
another spirit, it became the fashion to extol the life, so com-
mendable in its simplicity, which was led by the English emigrants
to North America.[2] It was Talleyrand who first lent authority
to a project of this kind. In a memorandum which he read to
the Institute in the course of the Fifth Year of the Revolution—
a memorandum still deserving attention—he proposed that all
the rebels should be deported to the islands.[3] This procedure
would result in " settling down so many restless men in need of
peace, and so many unhappy men in need of hope ". A problem
which the art of government has so far failed to solve, is to find
a suitable rôle for the discontented. In the gloomy times
through which we are now living,[4] which are not unlike the
gloomy times of M. de Talleyrand's day, colonies may well seem
a peaceful expedient for ridding us of our restless spirits.

A little later we find Benjamin Constant toying with the same
project. His *Politique constitutionelle* points to this as the main
benefit to be derived from colonies. And Stendhal's *Mémoires
d'un touriste* suggest that Mitidja might well be made a refuge for
tiresome people (*mauvaises têtes*), offering them the hope of getting
rich. This is a goal which may seem petty to us to-day. Yet
to them it was the most important consideration. Benjamin

[1] *Mémoires de Robert Challes*, edited by A. Augustin-Thierry.
[2] D. Mornet, *Les origines intellectuelles de la Révolution française*, 1933, p. 390 f.
[3] C. M. de Talleyrand, *Essai sur les avantages à retirer des colonies nouvelles dans les
circonstances présentes*, read on the 26 Messidor, Year V. Reprinted in Bulwer Lytton's
Talleyrand 1868 as an Appendix ; and in *Académie des Sciences Coloniales, Annales*, III,
1929, p. 141 f.
[4] [I.e. 1936. EOL]

Constant in particular was anxious to ensure, not only the removal of the rebels to a distance, but also their reformation. *Removal and reformation* ; he hoped that these tiresome Protestants would succeed in finding in the colonies not alone a new life, but a new soul, and that they would become good citizens once more. " Why don't they try it ? (he asked). It is high time ! " Taine, who had seen the Communards,[1] knew the same fear and the same hope. In the tenth volume of his *Origines*, he preached that colonies were maintained as a convenient place in which to unload dangerous men, in order to preserve the social order at home.

The other facet of material imperialism is *exploitation*, the development of latent values, the *mise en valeur* of " new countries ", to *live on* and *profit by* their accumulated resources. It is moreover a method of permitting the population of the old countries to increase, of allaying the fear of over-population which continued to obsess the large states : a means of finding the wherewithal to feed larger numbers and thus be able to grow greater. Thus the exploitation of new countries was bound up with the " population policy ". But, as usual, the means became in itself an end ; it assumed the value of an end in itself : expansion became a means of self-enrichment. " Why do we come to the Islands ? Isn't it in order to make our fortune ? " Such is the spirit which begins to predominate, as expressed for individuals by Bernardin's Greybeard. President de Brosses was one of those who had more than a glimmering of this. He advocated the colonisation of the " Austral World " not for the purpose of conquering, but very much for the purpose of exploiting it.[2]

There are two recognised ways in which States can benefit. Increase in " national wealth " may be attained either by *tribute*, or by *profit* exacted from the colonies by the metropolitan country. For a long time the exploitation of distant countries was designed to benefit the royal Treasury and increase the royal revenue, which was in early days calculated in silver. " Inflation " of the budget was in the first instance a matter merely of pride. The method was therefore *tribute* levied by means of dues and taxes. There was, for instance, a 20 per cent. tax (*droit de quint*) on the output of the Peruvian mines. Presently, however, people began to look for benefits accruing to the nation and to the King's

---

[1] [Revolutionaries who attempted to seize power in Paris after the Franco-Prussian War. They rose in March 1871 and were suppressed in the following May by the regular French army under Thiers. EOL]

[2] C. de Brosses, *L'histoire des navigations aux Terres Australes*, 1756.

subjects, not merely to the King himself. Men's minds concentrated on *profit* ; national profit, no longer tribute in cash.

So exploitation had various aims ; and various methods to correspond. Two principal methods succeeded each other, since—as I have already said, and as I now repeat—people were at first bent on exporting from the metropolis, and only later on importing to the metropolis. The *colony-as-outlet* was succeeded by the *colony-as-reservoir* ; such was the way in which exploitation developed.

Exportation had two phases : export for *tribute*, export for *profit*.

Export for *tribute*. From Renaissance times the " theory of the balance of commerce ": held the field everywhere. People were anxious to maintain the prosperity and the security of the State by ensuring an excess of exports over imports, with more money coming into the State than going out, thus preserving a " favourable balance ", as it is still called, which was desired especially in order that the King's purse or coffers, that is the Royal Treasury, might be well supplied. This policy was what was called " bullionism " [1] : this, from the point of view of the colonies, meant seeking an excess of exports, so that the Treasury might swell with gold and silver coin, and that the King might watch his reals and doubloons piling up, higher and higher in his nail-studded strongboxes secured with complicated locks ! [2] This obsession kept its grip on the Spaniards for the whole course of three centuries. Their theorists were courtiers too. They all proclaimed—for instance Ustariz, the best known of them—that the only interest which colonial commerce has, is to promote the import of gold and silver into the mother-country, and that the primary aim of this traffic is to fill the Treasury. To extract gold and bring it in their galleons, or else to procure gold by selling more to the colonies than they purchase from them.

That is why, almost to the last, the introduction of foreign products into the colonies was sternly forbidden. A decree of 1614 established the death penalty for anyone bringing foreign merchandise into the New American world, lest this should dam

---

[1] Thus used in the (pseudo-) *Mémoires de Jean de Witt*, French trans. 1709, p. 82 f.
[2] On this subject in general, see G. Schmoller, *The Mercantile System*, Eng. trans. 1896 ; H. Bérindoague, *Le mercantilisme en Espagne* 1929, p. 47 f. (thesis) ; A. Mounier, . . . *Ustariz* 1919 (thesis) ; Forbonnais's Fr. trans. of G. de Ustariz, *Théorie et pratique du commerce et de la marine*, 1753.—For the German Mercantilists see Justi, *Élémens de police*, Fr. trans. 1769, p. 137 (the commercial advantage of colonies). For the Italians : R. Michels, *Les idées coloniales des économistes classiques italiens du XVIIᵉ siècle et du XVIIIᵉ siècle. Revue des Sciences politiques*, Oct.–Dec. 1931.

the return-flow of gold and silver.   For the popular superstition about the value of treasure-hunting had invaded even the steps to the royal throne.   To dream of treasure remained the mainspring of action both for nations and kings.   In vain La Fontaine raised his voice against this superstition : the aged artist would not have been able to convince either king or commoner of his day !   We are again, as always, face to face with *faith*.

Export for profit.   Export for profit was destined to come, but very slowly ; traffic, export for the common good, for the advantage of the subject : this idea gained ground in the 17th and still more in the 18th century ; and this was the achievement of the " economists ".   It was well said by Montchrestien that " foodsupplies rather than money " should bring wealth.   The exploitation of the " islands " ought to be to the advantage of the general public, not merely of the King, as heretofore.   Men and ships should be adventured for food and products, rather than for gold and silver, and the export of such goods could bring a fair profit to the King's subjects.   Montesquieu was to say the same thing in still stronger language, not only in his *Esprit des Lois*,[1] but in a work too long overlooked, his *Reflexions on the Wealth of Spain*.[2] In his opinion, the main reason for Spain's collapse was her obsession with gold and silver ; the fact that the sole aim of all her colonial commerce was the enrichment of the Treasury, and that she amassed such vast quantities of gold and silver as finally to lower the value of the precious metals.   This produced a rise in prices to the detriment of the public.   The gain of kings is not their subjects' gain : " A great Treasury does not make a great people."   It is the common good, the " common profit " of the whole kingdom which should be sought.   The *Instructions* of 1765, established under Choiseul, were inspired by Montesquieu : the " doctrine of bureaux " in this connection meant export for the benefit of the nation.[3]   At the same date Forbonnais sees as the sole purpose of colonies " to increase the revenues of the country which founds them ".[4]   Pure selfishness, therefore, underlay this " colonial pact ", but it was nevertheless also a national pact.

We find in England the same conception as in France.   It is expressed by a professed mercantilist, Joshua Gee, whose work

[1] *Esprit des Lois*, 1748, Book XVI, Chaps. 21–3 ; *Considérations . . . ,* published in the *Revue historique litteraire F.*, XVII, 1910, pp. 287–305 ; and Ch. Vellay's edition.
[2] *Considérations sur les richesses de l'Espagne.*
[3] A. Daubigny, *Choiseul*, 1892, p. 239 f.   See also Diderot-d'Alembert's *Encyclopédie*, s.v. *Colonies* by Forbonnais, who connects *commerce* with *opulence*.
[4] *Principes et observations œconomiques*, 1767, p. 68 f.

MATERIAL IMPERIALISM : DETAILS 229

Trade and Navigation of Great Britain Considered (1738) was translated into French in 1749. For him the advantage of colonies lies in the maintenance of the mother-country's industries : colonies are the markets, the outlets, which increase the activity and prosperity of the home country's manufactures, provide work for the poor and idle, and solve the problem of unemployment, which even at that distant date was becoming a nightmare to England. The aim was therefore to stimulate a nation's industrial activity by opening new markets in the colonies. One of the last of the French mercantilists, a certain d'Heguerty, published in 1754 an " Essay on the Interests of Maritime Commerce." [1] He clings obstinately to the belief that the aim of trade with the colonies is to bring in gold and silver ; but he contends that it should also serve the interests of navigation, and yield a commercial profit, and that the industries of the mother-country should find openings in the colonies. New *shipments* would bring new *returns* and the chief advantage of an export trade would redound to the national, and not, as of old, solely to the royal interest.

It is, however, the work of Adam Smith which most strongly emphasised the idea that the profit derived from colonies should accrue to the country as a whole, to the nation in its entirety, and that the purpose of exportation should be to give scope to a country's industrial activities. His *Inquiry into the Nature and Causes of the Wealth of Nations* (1776) expounds his great conception : that the progress of an industry is determined by the extension of its markets ; the extension of markets is the driving power of any society, for it is this which begets division of labour and specialisation of production. The march of progress on the material plane can therefore be, in part at least, promoted by trade with the colonies. In Book IV, Chapter 7, of the *Wealth of Nations*, Adam Smith writes very fully about colonies. He sees in them two main advantages for the nation as a whole. First, the increase of *enjoyment*, since food supplies will come from distant countries to the mother-country as a means of exchange and in payment for her exports. Secondly, the growth of *industry*—and this is the fundamental thing—since the colonies, he says, are markets, and since trade with them will offer a remedy for the over-production of the old country. Overproduction means over-population ; only new markets can

---

[1] *Essai sur les intérêts du commerce maritime*, reprinted in the *Discours politiques*, II, 1766, p. 11 f.

create new employment. You might imagine you were reading a work published to-day ! Colonisation was thus to become a means of growth and enrichment for all the old countries, an instrument for expanding the nations' *productive powers* ; cure for poverty, balm for despair.

Having sought for exports, people turned their attention to *imports*. For the benefit of the mother-countries, men looked to find in their colonial empires either food-supplies, or raw materials, or products to satisfy their wants. Colonies would no longer be *outlets* only, but *reservoirs*, not markets but warehouses and granaries.[1] This material imperialism has in our day become as much, or even more, preoccupied with importation than in olden times with exportation.

It is of course true that the eagerness to bring imports to the mother-country is not a phenomenon of yesterday. At first the overriding concern was with food-supplies. For, as early as the 18th century, people had come to maintain that " tillage should take precedence of exchange "—as had been the case amongst the Ancient Romans—instead of the search for commercial profit. Towards the middle of the century this was the current opinion. Then we find certain thinkers taking the opposite view, and maintaining that the profit from colonies lies in exchange, not in tillage. The mercantilists fired the first shot. D'Heguerty, of whom we have already spoken, wrote that plantations ought to be encouraged, the cultivation of tobacco for instance in Louisiana, to make the French independent of English tobaccos. A century earlier, a royalist-minded theorist, Hay du Chastelet, ventured in a *Treatise on French Policy* [2] (1669) to propound an unexpected paradox. He contended that the " habitant ", that is to say the colonist, of the islands should be able to live on the resources of the country, and that his food should no longer be a burden on the homeland ; and further, that these distant lands should be able also to produce " things necessary or useful to the State ". This was to demand that these distant colonies should serve to furnish many food supplies to the Kingdom at home, and should also provide subsistence for the colonist. French and English vied with each other in preaching this theory.

Du Chastelet had been anticipated by Vauban in a work which was not, however, published during Vauban's lifetime,

---

[1] Both had been discussed under the Restoration : Molé had dealt with the outlet- and Lainé with the reservoir-question. See M. Dubois and A. Terrier, *Un siècle d'expansion coloniale*, 1902, pp. 102 f. and 117 f.

[2] *Traité de la politique de France*, Chap. XII, pp. 238–59.

and which ultimately appeared only in 1840, a *Memorandum* namely *on the Colonies* which formed a fragment of the work known as *Idle Thoughts*.[1] In this Memorandum Vauban, who died in 1707, said that in the colonies the most urgent task was that of clearing the ground for cultivation, and that both colonists and soldiers ought to be sent to till the soil. Such Physiocrats as were colonial economists upheld the same doctrine. What should be sought in every country, near or far, is the sheer produce of agriculture. One of them in particular, that same Pierre Poivre who was Governor of the Île de Bourbon and of the Île de France, laid this down in his *Voyages of a Philosopher*.[2] This great colonial spent many years in overseas countries, he lived at times in China and Cochin-China, he travelled in Malaya, Siam, India and the Moluccas ; he had been a spice planter ; he had laid out splendid gardens. Like Mercier de la Rivière, sometime Governor of Martinique, he was therefore a colonial, but not of the settler type. He had every right to theorise about the conduct of colonies. To colonise, he said, is most certainly to civilise, inasmuch as you extend agriculture in distant countries, and agriculture is the first step towards all progress ; inasmuch also as you encourage an increase in population. In the philosophy of the Physiocrats these are the two aims of every economy : agriculture and population. New countries in particular were to find prosperity through tillage and " peoplement " (*la " peuplade* "), while the old countries would enjoy larger food supplies and live in greater ease. Anticipating Bugeaud's ideas, Poivre proposed that soldier-colonists should be sent to the " islands " to bring all land under cultivation according to a plan. Since, said he—and this was a point of view already half-seen by Hay du Chastelet and Vauban—the colonies ought to support their colonists, and further they ought to be able to re-victual the royal squadrons. It was all wrong, he contended, that, as was then the custom, the mother-country should have to supply the colonies and the ships' crews. People living in the colonies should take their own measures both to support themselves and to furnish supplies to the King's sailors. It was therefore essential to develop the colonies ; and the first

---

[1] *Mémoire sur les colonies* in *Oysivetés*, 1843, IV, pp. 1–43. Cf. Deschamps, *Histoire de la question coloniale en France*, 1891, p. 224 f. and the work of my assistant J. Y. Le Branchu, *Les idées coloniales de Vauban et le Canada, Annales du droit et des sciences sociales* II, 1934, p. 329 f.

[2] *Voyages d'un philosophe*, 1767. New Edition, with biography, in the Year V by Dupont de Nemours. Henri Cordier and M. Alfred Lacroix have devoted well-deserved studies to Poivre.

dividend they should pay would be to make themselves self-supporting ; later, their shipments to the mother-country would enable her to support a larger number of the King's subjects at home.   Turgot, who gave a great deal of thought to the colonies, was not inclined to disagree.[1]

Not long afterwards this idea was considered orthodox in England, where the first " colonial economists " made their appearance earlier than in France, chief among them James Mill, father of John Stuart Mill.   He maintained that the chief profit from colonies lay in what was *received from* them, not in what was *sent* to them, in imports, not in exports ; in the subsistence of the colonies and their mother countries ; in the bringing into production of new areas which—according to Ricardo—must be tilled in order to feed the ever-growing populations.

This idea rapidly gained ground when large-scale industry developed in England, when England was obliged to give up feeding herself, and her people were forced to depend on supplies from overseas.   This was the " Industrial Revolution " which begot a *revival* of the imperial spirit amongst the English.

Later, another need made itself felt : the need to import not food only, but *raw materials* for manufacture to maintain the nation's *industry*.   When Colbert was ruling France in the King's name, the French began for the first time anxiously to look towards the colonies to discover those " primary products " necessary to feed the factories which were springing up throughout the country.   " Colbertism " was based on the conviction that both by legislation and restrictive methods the import into the mother-country of unworked materials must be encouraged. But this line of action was not formulated as a doctrine till nearly a hundred years after Colbert.   The French had to wait till half-way through the reign of Louis XV before the Englishman, Joshua Gee, of whom I have already spoken, casually—incidentally !—enunciated the opinion that the advantage of possessing colonies was that it freed the mother-country's industry from paying foreign tribute, furnished her with essentials and food and, above all, supplied her with the iron she so badly needed, thus releasing her from bondage to other countries.

This was, however, only a doctrinal episode.   In France especially we must have recourse once again to the Physiocrats and read particularly *The Friend of Men* by the Marquis de

---

[1] Schelle's Ed. of the *Œuvres de Turgot*, III, *passim*, especially pp. 548 f., 563 f., 684 f., and IV, p. 89 f.

Mirabeau. This book saw the light in 1756.[1] It is in the writings of this Liberal that we find—somewhat to our surprise ! —the first exposition of the idea of *autarky*, a word whose present-day fate we know ; the idea, according to which it is desirable to ensure the Nation's industrial autonomy (the word was becoming current exactly at this moment), by making it self-sufficient and self-supporting, above all by means of colonial production, by having " products of our own soil ". This famous work ran into numerous editions, and the idea, if not the names, gripped the public. Let us have colonies to be independent of foreign trade ; let us thus obtain provisions and materials necessary for the inhabitants of the mother-country, emancipating them from the payment of foreign tribute. We ought, he asserted, to get from our own colonies, without having recourse to foreigners, all the goods needed to satisfy the taste of " the people "—which may thus be accounted as necessaries—and all objects of common use or need. This is the reason why he wanted to see the colonial countries colonised and developed ; and why he also wanted freedom of intercourse and increased exchanges between the Kingdom and the Islands. Bestow Luxuries on the colonies and receive Necessities in exchange. Such is *industrial progress* for the *nation*, the rule and the reason for great colonial empires, whether English or French. Mirabeau's tradition became firmly established during the century following and formed the cardinal principle of Jules Ferry. For Ferry's patriotism and his colonialism were bound up in industrialism ; not only in his speeches of 1882 and 1885 but still more in his work of 1890, *Tonkin and the Mother Country*.[2] In it he writes that colonial policy is the daughter of industrial policy. Exploitation of the colonies is the means of promoting industrial development at home, of securing therefore for the home country the ores and the materials to foster its industrial progress. This

---

[1] *L'ami des hommes*, Part III, Chap. 6, on colonies.

[2] *Le Tonkin et la Mère-Patrie*. See Alfred Rambaud, *Jules Ferry*, 1903. Martin Aldao's thesis on Ferry's colonial doctrine (1933) is completely valueless.—This is not the place to write the still-unwritten history of those disciples of Ferry who after '85 formed the " Colonial Party " and who, like their master, failed to distinguish between *greatness* and *profit*. See in general J. Pélissier, *Profits coloniaux*, 1892 (with portraits by F. Regamey), and *Les colonies et la vie française*, 1931, p. 196 f. Let me quote particularly : Un Marin, *Les colonies nécessaires*, 1885 ; Amiral Aube, *Marine et colonisation* . . . , 1886 ; A. Rambaud, *La France coloniale*, 1886 ; H. Mager, *Les cahiers coloniaux de 1889* . . . , 1899, and *Les droits coloniaux de la France* . . . , 1890 ; Eugène Étienne, *Un programme de politique coloniale, Questions diplomatiques et coloniales*, XI, 1901, pp. 65–82. See *Eugène Étienne, Son œuvre coloniale*, 1907 ; as early as 1890 he had in a speech spoken of " *Empire* ". So had J. Chailley ; on him see Lyautey, *Paroles d'action*, 1927, p. 458 f.

is, he says too, " an irresistible movement ", to which we must yield if we hope to win in the international competition, if we wish to ride the winner in " this great steeplechase ", this life-and-death struggle between the great powers.   You must have colonies to supply you with the elements and essentials of industry. Let us have no more " bourgeois and parsimonious conquests " ; let us win whole continents ; let us obey the " fatal laws of the economic State " ; let us shake ourselves free from " the doctrine of self-effacement ".   We must grow great ; we must grow rich —or perish.   In another of Ferry's books, *Tunisian Affairs*,[1] the historian Alfred Rambaud, who writes the Preface, also main-tains that it is essential to secure colonies, above all for the sake of industrial progress, since the struggle between the nations is a battle of producers, and since, if this be true, the productive power of the country must be reinforced by the help of the colonies.   His fears for France are isolation and inaction, the " policy of the chimney corner ", and he wants to see throughout the world " the expansion of the French name ".   He attempts to demonstrate that the French Republic is capable of acquiring the finest Empire of all.[2]   These propositions still remain the key to our action to-day.   In 1886 people were asking—What use are colonies ? [3]   Not simply in order to make profits, for we could make profits equally well at the foreigner's expense ; but to augment the power and prestige of our country, and thus indirectly increase its ability to produce.   The real profit is greatness, and to be rich you must be strong.   Let us rejoice to have come on the scene in time : late-comers will be sorry for themselves.   Prophetic words !   Let us skip ten years.   When M. Albert Sarraut published in 1923 his great work entitled *Development of the Resources of the French Colonies* [4] he was able to demonstrate forcibly and fully that the advantage of large colonial empires lies in the support they give to industry and the assistance they render to the producer.   The inaugural lecture he delivered in 1935 to the French Colonial Conference was curiously in tune with the above-quoted speeches of Jules Ferry.

Having got so far, we find that the idea of importation has led us on to a more far-reaching conception which we must finally deal with ; *manufacture* in the colonies.   For we reach the

---

[1] *Les affaires de Tunisie*, 1882.
[2] These ideas were to a certain extent set forth by Renan as early as 1870 ; he drew, up a whole colonial programme in *La monarchie constitutionelle en France*.
[3] C. Gide, *A quoi servent les colonies*, Revue de Géographie, 1886.   Later, Gide became violently anti-colonial, carried away by ideas about the " rights of peoples."
[4] *Mise en valeur des colonies françaises.*

point of demanding that the colonies shall supply us with finished products, manufactured goods, not merely with raw materials ; that there shall be in the colonies production in the narrower sense ; that the colonial empire must not make its aim, or its sole aim, to supply us with food and raw materials, but must also and above all furnish us with manufactures. This is the idea which has ultimately held the field, though not without protest, as we shall see.

For the proposition that distant countries will be, or ought to be, sooner or later, industrial countries, met for a long time, and still meets, formidable opposition. It was the traditional policy of the French Monarchy to employ every legislative and administrative device to prevent industrial production in the colonies and to forbid the *habitants*, whom we should nowadays call the " colonists ", to manufacture any goods which the home country was able to produce. Industrial rivalry between the recent colonies and the metropolis still remains a problem, highly charged with electricity. This could be clearly seen at the recent French Colonial Conference ! Under the Ancient Monarchy the problem was quashed by almost absolute prohibition. This policy was known as the Colonial Pact or the " *Exclusive* ". Under it the colonies were forbidden not only to trade with foreign countries, not only to trade with each other—to carry on what was called " colonial intercourse "—but also, and above all, to manufacture ; forbidden, that is, to convert their raw materials into finished products. Such was the attitude of mind which prevailed amongst the theorists, amongst the English in particular, but also amongst the French. That Joshua Gee, of whom we have already spoken, demanded that no industrial implement should be sent to the colonies : no tool, no loom, no machine. He wished to see the colonies denied every industrial facility so that manufacture in these distant countries might be made impossible ! And d'Heguerty, whom we have quoted above, another upholder of the Exclusive, demanded that the colonies should be forbidden to refine their sugar-cane, or to " clay " (that is, to bleach) their sugar. This seemed to him a matter of so grave importance that he begged that sons of the colonists might be brought to France as hostages, to ensure that their parents would observe the prohibition ! A hundred years before, Hay du Chastelet had made the same suggestion. He had also wished to see the colonists' sons transferred to France to make sure of their fathers' obedience and of their loyalty to the King. Such was the spirit of exploitation and domination which then reigned in the French Empire !

Even much later, at the beginning of the reign of Louis XVI, the author of a great work, the *Dictionary of Moral Sciences,*[1] Robinet—a writer to-day forgotten—also desired to restrict arts and crafts in the colonies. He demanded that the colonies should confine themselves to growing food and mining ores, but he did not wish—and this just a few years before the Revolution of 1789—to see the colonies allowed to develop their own production or manufactures.

It was not only in actual legislation or practice that from then on the spirit of the " Exclusive " persisted ; it continued to dominate public opinion also. To prevent the industrial development of the colonies, solely in the interest of the mother-country, remained the general desire. Let us recall how in 1760 the importation of Indian printed cloth was forbidden ; and how a whole outburst of liberal protest was necessary to persuade the King to reverse this decision and open the doors of his kingdom to these *indians* as they were called.[2] Let us remember how down to our own day the English have striven to prevent the spinning and weaving of cotton in Egypt and India : how, by every possible means, direct and indirect, overt or subtle, they have endeavoured to prevent these countries from acquiring the right to manufacture their own raw materials on their own soil.[3]

Though colonial production has down to our own times been confronted by deliberate opposition, it has nevertheless been steadily gaining ground. For a century or so, the idea that it should be permitted has been advocated by many thinkers.

Vauban, in the work which I have already quoted, expresses the wish that not only soldier-cultivators should be sent to the colonies, but artisans and craftsmen ; and he believed that these

---

[1] *Dictionnaire des Sciences morales.*
[2] E. Depitre, *La question des toiles peintes . . . ,* 1912.
[3] [The author's information would seem on this point strangely out of date. The first cotton mill in India, financed and controlled mainly by Indians, was started in 1853. By 1914 India was the fourth greatest cotton manufacturing country in the world.

The manufacture of jute in India started in 1855. In 1875 the Bengal Iron and Steel Co. was founded. In 1907 the famous Tata Iron and Steel Co. was founded with Indian capital and under Indian management, and with full Government encouragement fulfilled orders from Japan, China, Java, Ceylon, Burma and the Straits Settlements.

By 1916 India possessed complete fiscal autonomy. By 1929 India held sixth place in world trade. See Vera Anstey, *The Economic Development of India,* 1936, and Hubbard, *Eastern Industrialisation,* 1935. The student would be well advised similarly to check the facts about Egypt, which was of course never a British colony. EOL]

distant countries should not only feed but clothe their colonists, and in fact become as self-sufficient as possible. Thus long before our time Vauban desired to see colonisation by industrial workers. But it was not until last century that the thought of *industrial colonisation* grew up in France, the thought of working and manufacturing raw materials, apart from merely mining ores and procuring raw materials. This was the great scheme of Saint-Simon's followers. If they have earned a special place in this study of history, it is because they were the very first to foresee and to desire the creation of an industrial type of empire. Their dream was to encourage industries everywhere ; for to them that seemed the sign of progress. The new era was to be one of production and organisation. Their motto was : " Everything through industry, everything for industry." Their newspapers were called *The Producer* and *The Organiser*. To encourage the exploitation of the " globe " as a whole, and thus promote universal progress, universal happiness and the civilisation of the globe as a whole : this was the vision of these great dreamers for whom to colonise was to civilise.

Saint-Simon's first disciple, Père Enfantin, wrote in this sense in his two books, *The Colonisation of Algeria* (1843) and *Political Correspondence* (1849). He was the prophet of industrial colonialism ; he preached the development of values (*mise en valeur*) everywhere. The aim, he says, of the " new policy " is the development of the entire globe, " the opening up of works of a pacific nature " which will put an end to works of a military nature. From war to work : that is the evolution. The idea of universal industrialism, universal productivity, is Père Enfantin's scheme. " To develop, not to possess ", should be the aim of all expansion. Colonisation must not be in any sense a method of subjugation ; what it must do is to fertilise, in other words advantageously to develop, latent values. The motive for colonising the globe is to diffuse Industry. Enfantin's socialism was imperial because it was industrial.

Such was the purpose. But the method was to be not violent subjection by conquest, but " occupation ", or what he also calls " protection " ; in other words domination for the benefit of all, having as its aim the fertilisation of the entire globe to the advantage of all the dwellers thereon, the advantage both of the rulers and the ruled. He expressly says that he wants " no more soldiers " ; it seems to him that government by the military has had its day ; he claims that what is now required is govern-

ment by the " industrialists ". Colonisation is therefore synonymous with industrialisation ; it is an instrument whereby the
progressive peoples will authoritatively bestow progress on the
backward peoples. When Enfantin produced schemes for cutting
through the isthmus of Suez or contructing a railway to Baghdad
—two suggestions of delightfully prophetic genius—his aim was
to point out how the linking of one continent to another would
help to promote the advantageous development of the entire
world. His ideas had an undercurrent of obscure mysticism ;
he felt himself inspired, he spoke freely of God's great design of
calling the West to the East. Great Empires were for him
instruments of a spiritual nature as well as a material nature ;
they were to be the means of binding together East and West.
By this contact the West would re-learn from the East both
strength and faith. In this Enfantin was definitely of one mind
with Spengler.

From this point, material imperialism came to be based on
the general *universal interest.* Having begun as a national, it has
become more and more a universal or international phenomenon.
As we have seen, Enfantin hoped that the great colonial empires
would lead to universal communion ; he foresaw the Suez Canal
as the principal factor in this communion.

It was not, however, until a little after his day, that this
idea of universal benefit came to be generally accepted as the
chief argument in defence of material imperialism. John Stuart
Mill, for instance, saw the chief advantage of colonies as lying
in the use of them to place the resources of the entire world at
the disposal of all nations to their benefit and advantage. And
nowadays this is the favourite argument adduced by the Anglo-
Saxons to prove that the possession of colonies is legitimate.
The whole human race is the gainer when the best men reign
and they are the ministers of Progress. If then, they say, colonisation ends by expelling from their countries inferior peoples—
well called " incompetent "—who are unable to develop their
own resources, why, that is because it is in the interest of the
entire world that these lands should be developed.[1] " It would

---

[1] Gourd, *Chartes coloniales,* 1885, I, p. 104. The argument occurs already in
Thomas More's *Utopia* (1516). See particularly the American, Mahan, quoted
above, and his Preface to Theodore Roosevelt's *American Ideals,* 1897. It was this
same argument that Lord Northcliffe in 1922 flung at the Australians, who imagine
they can keep their doors closed to foreigners : The world will not tolerate Australia's
standing empty. People the country or open it ! See also W. Willoughby, *Race
Problems in the New Africa* 1923 : he who does not develop does not possess ! The
resources of the world belong to the world.

have been a crime ", said the Connecticut Charter in 1633, " to have left so fertile a country uncultivated ! " The philosopher Secrétan, a Protestant writer, asserts in his book, *The Rights of Humanity* (1890),[1] that it is legitimate to expropriate primitive peoples who do not know how to fertilise their land, and who therefore have no right to keep it. The rights of one single people must not override the rights of all peoples ! [2] The expropriated peoples are condemned not as *infidels*, after the manner of Marc Lescarbot in 1612, but as *incompetents*.

This is the ultimate point at which material imperialism arrives : colonisation based on the benefit of the entire world ; justified in the interest of the human race. Berrichon, in his Preface to the *Letters* of the poet-adventurer Rimbaud, writes : " to colonise is to develop values for the human race ".[3]

The extension of progress ; the diffusion of comfort : such is colonisation, which is civilisation.

[1] *Droits de l'humanité.*

[2] Paul Bourde similarly wrote : " The earth has been given to humanity ; if one part of it lies fallow, the whole of humanity suffers injury . . ." (*A travers l'Algérie*, 1880, p. 48 f.). See also, in the same sense, the Protestant E. Babut, *La revue Franco-Annamite* II, Aug. 1, 1930 : " the peoples colonised were not fulfilling their duty to other peoples by developing their land ; if they are punished it is because of their *incompetence* ". A partisan of the *Rights of Man* also admits that it is a *duty* to develop—by humane methods—resources which the savage is too ignorant to exploit ; Ruyssen, *Cahiers des droits de l'homme*, 1925, p. 489 f.

[3] In his Preface to the *Lettres de J.-A. Rimbaud*, 1899, Paterne Berrichon thus attributes a colonial doctrine to Rimbaud (especially pp. 39-40). The strange adventurer Gaston de Raousset-Boulbon, who would have liked to give Mexico to France, had written in 1854 : " A people has no right to have its fields infertile, its mines fallen in, its frontiers barred ; you must perish or march with the times . . . Mexico is a country where civilisation can be introduced only by violence." H. de la Madelène, *Le comte G. de Raousset-Boulbon*, 1856, p. 117 f.—This was also the view of Paul Leroy-Beaulieu : " Not leave half the globe to ignorant and impotent men " but educate them and bring them on by " skilful and affectionate initiation " (*De la colonie . . .* , 4th Ed. 1891, p. 819 f.)

CHAPTER XXIII

MATERIAL IMPERIALISM : ASPECTS

Such in its evolutions and transformations is material imperialism. To see it better, let us take a concrete case of to-day. We shall then grasp that such a state of mind is very much a " complex ", as people call it nowadays, and we shall bring together items which we have been separating for the purpose of our analysis. The special case which we shall choose is that of the English people. For it is amongst the English that we can find the crudest expression of the opinions and feelings which make up material imperialism. The English Empire has justly been called the firm of " John Bull & Company ".[1] The spirit inspiring the enterprise is the search for profit. Yet Anglo-Saxon imperialism shows diversity of opinion and complexity of feeling. Less than a century ago there were English theorists who were opposed to all expansion. The liberal doctrines of Manchester pleaded against expansion. Thus Cobden, about 1835, like the French economist Jean-Baptiste Say a little earlier, denied the usefulness of colonies. This is the point from which Anglo-Saxon imperialism had to start !

Anglo-Saxon imperialism had its *ends* and its *means* which give it a place apart.[2]

Its *ends* ; there are two aims which appeared almost simultaneously : *nationalism* in the first place, *productivism* in the second ; both of them more marked than in other countries.

First *Nationalism*. It is amongst the English that we can best observe how material imperialism invariably seeks the benefit of the mother-country. Anglo-Saxon interest is the motive and the driving force, unconscious and conscious at the same time : at once instinctive impulse and cold calculation. This is the *Jingoism* that has been so much talked of : so called from the name of the supporters of the conquest of Afghanistan in 1878 who had adopted the name of Jingoes for themselves after the legendary sovereign of Japan who was supposed in former times

---

[1] Max O'Rell, *John Bull & Co.*, 1894.

[2] J. Gazeau, *L'impérialisme anglais, son évolution* : *Carlyle, Seeley, Chamberlain*, 1903 (thesis). L. Hennebicq, *L'impérialisme occidental Genèse de l'impérialisme anglais*, 1912 ; Earl of Cromer, *Ancient and Modern Imperialism*, 1910 ; Mary Kingsley, *West African Studies*, 1901, Chaps. 21–2.

to have annexed Korea ! [1] From the beginning of the Victorian era this was the creed of a great colonial, Sir Stamford Raffles,[2] who was Agent to the Governor-General of the Malay States. In a Memorandum of 1808 he pleaded with the East India Company to retain Malaya which it was then desirous of abandoning ! He emphasised not only the importance of Malaya as a military base and for the protection of the sea-route and the future of " sea-power " ; but also and above all, the value which the development of its resources would have for the industries of Birmingham and Manchester. It was its value to the mother-country which provided his sole argument. In the light of to-day [1936. EOL] a prophetic view indeed !

During the thirty years which followed, the English displayed a nationalist-utilitarian frame of mind ; you find it in Wakefield, in Butler, in Torrens, who have been the great theorists of the exploitation of distant countries for the sole benefit of the mother-country. Wakefield was the founder of the Australian system of land-tenure. Colonisation was one of his major interests, for in it he saw a means of increasing the population and of developing industry. *Populationism*—the word has been coined —and *industrialism* are the two pillars of Wakefield's colonialism.[3]

It was Sir Charles Butler who a few years later gave reasoned support to these ideas in a famous speech delivered in 1843 to the Chamber of Commerce.[4] According to him, colonisation is a vital necessity for England. From it she derives two advantages : *supplies* and *employment*. As Adam Smith had already pointed out—though only incidentally—the possession of colonies permits England to increase her citizens' consumption, while it enables her to provide employment for the poor and idle. It is a well-known fact that as early as 1843 England was face to

---

[1] [This amusing derivation of the word Jingo is, of course, as fantastic as it is entertaining.

The Oxford English Dictionary records the first known occurrence of the word in 1670. It was derived from conjurors' jargon.

By 1694 *By Jingo!* was in common use as a strong asseveration.

In 1874 a music-hall song made a popular hit with the lines :

" We don't want to fight, but by Jingo if we do
We've got the men, we've got the ships, we've got the money too."

From this popular song the name Jingo was applied in disapproval to those who supported Lord Beaconsfield's policy of sending the British Fleet into Turkish waters in 1878 to oppose the Russian advance. EOL]

[2] R. Coupland, *Sir T. Stamford Raffles*, 1926.

[3] E. G. Wakefield, *View of the Art of Colonisation*, 1849. Cf. A. Siegfried, *E. G. Wakefield et la doctrine de la colonisation systématique*, 1904 (thesis) ; W. Blommaert, *Vorloper van . . . Wakefield*, *Mélanges Pirenne*, 1926.

[4] C. Butler had already published *Responsible Government for Colonies*, 1840.

face with the great dramatic problem of unemployment ; that the " Industrial Revolution " was an accomplished fact and that from then onwards, for every English " man in the street ", emigration remained the inevitable alternative to poverty. Charles Butler endeavoured to prove his point by a significant parable. There are two poor men in one parish : a labourer and a weaver ; both are out of work and are in receipt of Poor Law relief, a burden on the parish. One of them, the labourer, emigrates to Australia. He becomes a colonist and is able to produce not only the grain and meat he needs for himself, but a surplus of grain and a bale of wool. Then he bethinks himself of his unfortunate unemployed friend at home, and he says to himself : " I shall send him the wool to make clothes for me, and the sack of flour in payment for his work." No sooner said than done. The weaver is able to return to his loom—there is one less unemployed, with work and payment assured. The final result for the country is that instead of having to support two out-of-works, she possesses two workers who support each other, and who will live in comfort by exchanging all the products of their toil.

It is thus that a man of action formulates the national interest : consumption goods and employment. These remain in our own time the two vital needs of England !

Shortly afterwards Robert Torrens, author of the Australian *Torrens Act*, himself entered a plea for the Empire.[1] Like Wakefield and Butler, he saw in it a procedure for the increase of consumption and still more for an increase of industry. For, like many other Englishmen of his day, he felt fearful of overproduction. He was afraid of industry's producing an excess of goods, which, according to the theory of markets, could be counterbalanced only by increasing the products of cultivation. This was the purpose which the colonies ought to serve. So, some hundred years ago, Torrens perceived that expansion might prove an antidote to mechanisation, and that an excess of industrial " mechanism " might find conpensation and solution in the imperial scheme ; for the English at least, in an increase of overseas territories.

From the point of view of aims, this was the nationalist idea. But it was also the *productivist* idea ; since production is the chief advantage of expansion, the idea was to be able to develop,

---

[1] R. Torrens, *Colonization of South Australia*, 1844. [See Footnote p. 717. EOL]

without risk or danger, the productive power of England. Productivism or utilitarianism was therefore the thing. It soon afterwards began to take on a mystical and dogmatic tinge. The exploitation of new countries, conceived not only as a means of achieving prosperity and security, nor as a remedy only for the evils of industrial mechanisation, but as a power and a duty, which in the eyes of God—ever present to the English mind—justifies the colonisation and expropriation of the conquered peoples. The desire was, of course, as with Enfantin, to render the whole world fruitful, in the interest of England—it need hardly be said—but in the interest also of the inferior peoples, and so to the universal advantage. Productivism is thus not identical with nationalism ; it is in a certain sense international, and it can be reduced to two factors : domination-as-exploitation and domination-as-obligation.[1]

First and foremost the idea is domination for the sake of advantage : in the interest of the English, but also, so they would wish to assert, in the universal interest. What makes their rule legitimate in English eyes, is that its aim is to develop new countries for the benefit of distant peoples. This idea is in fact a very ancient one ; we have only to recall that amongst primitive peoples, and in our day amongst the Musulmans, the possession of the soil is justified by the development of its values. In Muslim law the ownership of a title to land is to render it fruitful, to " bring life " as they say, to the " dead earth ". This is the idea which the English have amplified and translated into a universal design. Domination imperatively required for exploitation, rendered legitimate by exploitation for the benefit of the Universe. We have already said that Sir Thomas More, author of the *Utopia*, had proclaimed, as early as 1516, the justice of expropriating the lands of backward peoples to develop then in their owners' stead. He contends that expansion is a business undertaking ; that it has no value—the very word implies this—except in so far as it develops latent values. This conception forms the foundation of the right, soon felt to be a duty, to expropriate primitive and inefficient peoples, these " incompetents " as they were to be called, who do not know how to administer their inheritance, and ought then to surrender it into English hands.

[1] John Stuart Mill has expressly said in his *Political Economy* (1848, Book V, Chap. 11, para. 14) that the *universal* point of view must prevail. This is why he too is a productivist : anxious to increase the productivity both of capital and of labour.

Secondly, the idea of *obligation* emerged, a new facet of this universal *productivism*. Some thirty years ago, at the beginning of the century in which I write, the English reached the point of maintaining with Kipling, the poet of Empire, the right and also the duty of the white Anglo-Saxon to render fruitful the world in its entirety. In 1899 Rudyard Kipling published a famous poem in seven verses entitled *The White Man's Burden*, the task of the White Man which is to bring distant lands into cultivation ; a duty, he says, of " devotion ", an obligation, willed by God, to cultivate new countries in the universal interest, spreading everywhere prosperity, security and comfort—namely, civilisation, as the English understand it. Saint-Simon's idea and Enfantin's idea of universal economic imperialism strikes a new note in Kipling : a trader's Saint-Simonism ; to civilise is to increase production in order to increase consumption in the interest first of the ruling people but also, as Kipling expressly says, in the interest of the ruled.

In a book significantly entitled *The Bridge Builders* he well shows that the White Man's job is to foster the increase of food supplies and products, so as to offer the entire world, new countries as well as old, both comfort and leisure : civilisation is propaganda for comfort and leisure. It is thus an extension of the machine. He writes vibrantly and lyrically of the first appearance of the machine and the ship amongst primitive peoples : he sings of the " golden harp " of the telegraph wires which brings order and thought to every quarter, and which is the path of moral duty. For the White Man's work is not done when he has spread acquaintance with the machine ; he must teach coloured men the science of comfort, the science of leisure ; the science of the good and the beautiful. If this poet of conquest is preoccupied with economics, he is preoccupied also with ethics and æsthetics. To rule in order to gain, does not satisfy him ! [1]

If these are the *ends* of this Anglo-Saxon imperialism : first, nationalism, secondly, productivism conceived as a moral duty ; what are its *methods* or its instruments ? There are two in particular which set it in a class apart, for England has displayed them better than many other countries : aristocracy and liberalism.

First *aristocracy* : a vision, a melody in many keys, that

---

[1] For the " imperial poets " see A. Haslam, *Anthology of Empire*, 1922 (selected extracts). Apart from Kipling's chief poems, it is worth noting Laurence Hope's fragments *The Masters* (p. 237).

Anglo-Saxon power, granted by God, desired by God, is the power of *gentlemen* ; power, unlimited and unchecked, to rule in Anglo-Saxon interests and then in the universal interest. The conception of a *gentleman* is one born to rule in virtue of precedent and tradition. The Anglo-Saxon is a *ruler*, one who should regulate, one who should reign. The patriotic song *Rule, Britannia* is not new ; it was first sung in 1740 ; it was written by the poet Thomson, author of *The Seasons*. Gentleman, Governor, are titles of honour. When all the English were singing the famous song—which they still sing to-day—*Britannia, rule the waves !* it was the idea of the gentleman which spread through the entire Empire.[1] This instinct of aristocracy has its ancestral roots in the English mind ; in the course of time it passed through two phases. It was first a development of *feudalism*, as the English call it, that is to say of the feudal spirit ; the gentleman was the feudal lord. This deep-rooted, English feudal spirit permeated the whole Empire ; it is this feudal spirit which we can still find as late as Kipling. We can see it in the tale where the Tharauds have drawn a bold portrait of Dingley.[2] A gentleman, he says, ought to have a hard heart ; and his power, desired of God, implies and justifies his cruelties in the present and future interest of the subjugated peoples ! Ancient tradition, living on in every Englishman, explains why in England imperialism displays a vigour and a complexion which it has not shown in French countries ; the gentleman is still a feudal lord.

Another idea has in our day superseded feudalism in England ; it is the *Darwinism* of the English. For nowadays the aristocratic instinct of the English is justified by Darwin. The struggle for existence, the survival of the fittest, take place between nations. All expansion is a struggle ; rivalry between nations is a natural law ; and the extension of the great countries is only the testimony to the success of the better countries. As early as 1884, Seeley [3] applied the law of evolution to the great colonial empires ; humanity is attracted to truly planetary Organisms ; such is its true destiny which makes the vocation

[1] Charles Dilke (*Problems of Greater Britain*, 1868) goes so far as to predict the expansion of the English people throughout the entire world by the absorption of the dominated peoples. He believes that in a hundred years three hundred millions of men will be English.

[2] [The novel *Dingley, l'illustre écrivain*, laid the reputation of the Tharaud brothers. EOL]

[3] J. R. Seeley, *The Expansion of England*, 1884. A. Rambaud's French trans., 1885.

and the destiny of the English people. Karl Pearson, the founder of the science of biometry, in his book called *National Life* (1900) taught that the expansion of the great empires in itself denotes progress, a gain in the vital sense, inasmuch as it desires the disappearance of backward peoples for the benefit of the more advanced. Colonisation may entail elimination. If there are peoples in distant lands, who have hitherto survived without learning how to utilise their soil to advantage, the laws of order and vital progress command their elimination !—From Feudalism to Darwinism : from the traditions of ancient days to the conceptions of modern times ; this is how the impenitent English justify their aristocratic instinct !

Secondly, however, there is another characteristic more markedly developed amongst them than amongst the French. It is their *liberalism.* For a long time, a very long time, the writers have been teaching that expansion is possible only through liberty. While the doctrine of restriction and exclusion has persisted in France, the doctrine of colonial liberalism has long since carried the day in England. This has been especially the case since the American colonies won their freedom. That was a lesson the English never forgot ! Nor must we forget that the Protestant spirit—as we have already said—was a liberalising agent in the English Empire ; that the original colonists were nonconformists who departed to seek liberty in distant lands ; that the old colonial law was a law of liberty ; that the Quakers who founded Pennsylvania were liberals ; that the states of New England set up parliamentary constitutions ; that in the 17th, and still more in the 18th century, the colonies already possessed a Parliamentary Legislature subject only to the royal veto. So the English are liberal by tradition, as they are imperialist by tradition. In Bacon's Essay of 1597 on *Plantations* this liberal doctrine finds expression. He was an enemy of the restrictive commercial system which then reigned even in his own country, and he held that expansion could be profitable only if the colonies were granted freedom of external relations. The doctrine and the tradition of liberty established itself in England before it came to France, and more firmly in England than in France. We see this especially in Adam Smith, who wished to see the whole world transformed into one great trading republic, a universal circle for the free exchange of products and ideas. This is why liberty has reigned in England for a century and more. That is why, close on a hundred years ago, a Parliament, properly so called, a legislative Parliament with full powers, was set up in Canada.

We find among the English therefore both economic and political liberalism, in every sense, in every plane, in thought and in action. Thus the idea increasingly gained ground among them in legislation and administration that the guardianship of the colonies should develop into an association, and domination should be superseded by partnership. Let us be quite clear about it : partnership of White Man with White Man ! partnership of the colonies and the mother-country ; not partnership between the White Man and the Coloured. There was at least emancipation of the King's possessions from the power of the King ; an emancipation which, as we know, was never reached in France ; for even in Algeria the central power is the legislative power ; it is still France who gives her own laws to Algeria.

The British Empire is thus a home of liberty. Two canons are to-day well established in it : *home rule* and *self-help*. Home Rule, that is autonomy in the real sense ; the right of a colony to legislate, of itself and for itself. Self-Help is the corollary of Home Rule : the right to live and thrive, of itself and for itself, without the right to make any claim on the Crown. This is autonomy on the material plane ; the necessity of existing by its own effort according to its own good or ill fortune. The bond between the Crown and the countries of the imperial domain is no longer a material bond, but a spiritual bond ; a bond of loyalty and faith between King and his subjects overseas.

Judged by its aims and by its methods, Anglo-Saxon imperialism is thus material imperialism. Yet let us not forget that the English still cling to their theology which is a mystical conception of expansion ; mystical in regard to its ends and also in regard to its means. The Italian Disraeli,[1] a Jew converted to Christianity, who was the first to set imperialism in motion, had been moulded by the Unitarians ; Joseph Chamberlain was also a Unitarian. The Unitarians were a rigid sect born of exiles, a sect whose mysticism was concentrated and enduring ! For an Englishman who is, or wishes to be thought, a gentleman, it is always God who has desired the exploitation of the entire world, for the benefit of the entire world ; it is God—Franklin said so—who has desired the diffusion of comfort

---

[1] [It was the grandfather of Benjamin Disraeli, Lord Beaconsfield, who emigrated to England from Venice in 1748. The son, Isaac, and the grandson Benjamin were English-born though of foreign descent. EOL]

and leisure ; it is God who in the Anglo-Saxons has granted the world the image and model of civilised man ; for God is on the side of gentlemen and gentleman-peoples.   Every English-man meditates on Holy Scripture, and for him expansion is only an amplification of the ancient struggle between Jacob and the Angel !   Kipling says so in a stirring *Song of the English* :

Clear the land of evil, drive the road, and bridge the ford . . .
By the peace among Our peoples let men know we serve the Lord !

Thus, to give peace to inferior peoples is to obey the command of the Almighty !   In the Anglo-Saxon's devotion to the Bible the material and the spiritual blend and mingle.

CHAPTER XXIV

PATERNAL GUARDIANSHIP : CHRISTIANITY

The paternal authority which one people exercises over another has its *motives*. On the other hand it has also its *degrees*. Let us note the evolution of paternity, how it has changed its aspect and how we can observe, in the colonial sphere, the same evolution of paternal power as we see in the family sphere. For we can trace an almost perfect parallelism between the two. Paternal power *between nations* has followed the same course as did paternal power *between relatives* amongst the Romans and elsewhere. It has progressed from authority to humanity, from correction to protection, from the absolute to the relative, from the unlimited to the limited, or from the immoderate to the moderate ; from the interest of the dominator to the interest of the dominated ; to put the matter in a nutshell : from *power* to *duty*. In his first *Treatise on Civil Government*, Locke said, in 1689, that paternal power is paternal duty rather, and that in its beginnings it rests—like all government—on the *tacit consent* of the children. So it was to be with colonial power. At first we meet power for the sake of power, especially in all power-imperialism ; for power, in itself and for itself, was the initial aim of domination : to rule for the sake of ruling, to grow great for the sake of growing great. On both planes it becomes more and more, not power for the sake of power but power for the sake of duty ; authority-as-function, authority-as-mission, since then both on the family plane and on the colonial plane, authority is exercised more and more in the interest of the dominated, for the profit—we might almost say, for the happiness—of the dominated. For a minor needs a guardian. This is the condition to which I have given the name " Paternal Guardianship," not paternal power ; a form of paternity which is not the right of almost unlimited direction, the right of almost untempered correction, but a duty of protection and an intention of training : a *guardianship* in the same sense as in law between individuals.[1]

[1] " A nation which has a colony ", says Waxweiler, " is like a guardian to whom children are entrusted : it is in charge of the soul " (Preface to *Études Bakango*, by A. de Calonne-Beaufaict, 1912, p. 151). Much earlier, Courtet de l'Isle had used the word : colonisation is a " work of guardianship " : " Accursed be the unfaithful guardian ! " (*Tableau ethnographique du genre humain*, 1847, p. 28 f.). In 1857 Gladstone spoke of the English as the guardians of the Indians and of their *duty* towards them. Leroy-Beaulieu also uses the word.

Let us sum up in a few words this transformation by which *authority* has passed into *humanity*.

The idea of paternal guardianship demands definition. It comprises two elements : *obligation* and *moderation*.

Obligation means, in this context, power governed by duty ; the authority can rightly be used only for the good of the person under authority, just as the guardian should act only in the minor's interest. Conditional, directed, power is an instrument only ; a means, no longer an end.

Obligation and then *moderation* ; for direction implies limitation ; power disciplined and subordinated ; action of which the actor is no longer sole lord and master : being a means and not an end, having a purpose outside and beyond itself, the authority must be *controlled*, either by legal or by moral power ; it will be regulated, it will be restrained, by external action. In the language of to-day we might speak of a power as much directed as directing.

If these are the constituent elements of paternal guardianship, we should point out that this idea has had its precedents or antecedents. We noted these in speaking of spiritual or, it may be, of cultural imperialism. From these points of view obligation was already accepted in a certain sense and to a certain degree. For those who preached spiritual imperialism, and those who advocated cultural imperialism, proclaimed that the dominators had a God-given mission to teach and to civilise. The idea of duty imposed was by no means lacking in those bygone times. But this duty was a duty either to self or to God, not a duty towards others ! It was for God, or for a man's own salvation, that man believed himself bound to convert : primarily for God, since man was laying claim to a mission confided by God to His chosen people. It was not, as it is to-day, a duty towards others, towards the people governed ; a duty which creates and regulates the power. Henceforward the dominator is only guardian and protector, or " governor " in the original meaning of the word, that is to say preceptor and educator. This is a modern, recent idea : on which we shall enlarge.

Consisting of these elements : obligation and moderation, the new idea has its consequences which are effects *sui generis* : authority thus regulated has not the same virtues as had the unlimited authority of old.

The consequences are three facts which have come to rule the relationship between dominant and dominated peoples :

first, *legislation* by the paternal power ; secondly, *emancipation* from the paternal power ; thirdly, *partnership* with the paternal power.

Legislation by the paternal power. From the new point of view, the authority is controlled and limited and hence regulated. In private law, as we know, the evolution of the paternal power has been in the direction of restraint by the legislature and of intervention by the magistrates ; there has been a modifying of the paternal power first by the City and then by the Nation. A similar idea has gained ground in the colonies ; regulation, by public opinion at least, comes to govern colonial power, the opinion of foreign countries in particular, and sometimes by the legislative powers with which the League of Nations has been endowed. Colonial legislation is therefore governed *by opinion* and also already by outside *regulation*.

Emancipation from the paternal power. From the new point of view—the parallel is exact—all power is temporary and must come to an end. Guardianship is in its nature provisional ; it must cease when the minor attains his majority and achieves his emancipation at the wish either of the father or of the law. In its new meaning, authority, which is a means of protection and of training, must one day cease. The abolition in the course of time of paternal power by the emancipation of the dominated peoples must be contemplated, for in virtue of their training they will have been promoted to the right of governing their own destiny.

Partnership with the paternal power. When, on the family plane, paternity becomes guardianship and protection, and when it is tempered by moderation, it happens that the child is gradually allowed to participate in this power. It is fitting that the minor, who will presently come of age, should be *prepared* for the exercise of power by partnership and education. We can study in Roman Law and in the ancient law of France : the partnership in the jointly-owned family property of French communities where the sons shared their father's power (*communautés taisibles*) ; the partnership particularly of the eldest son, the future heir, who has been called the " recognised heir " (*héritier institué*), in the rights and actions of the *paterfamilias*. Similarly, on the colonial plane, the idea is foreshadowed of a partnership between dominated and dominant. A partnership, we must understand, incomplete and imperfect, a partnership still subject to domination ; a partnership between unequals, not between equals. Yet it was, to a certain extent, a partnership, *hierarchic* not *equalitarian*; such a partnership as might exist between father and son, between dominant and dominated. It was a partnership on the lines of most " companies " and " enterprises " run for profit !

I propose briefly to trace the development of this state of mind or point of view ; and to show how, especially in France, the idea of *protection* as the fundamental attribute of paternity was first mooted and then confirmed.

There were in France two great moments in this evolution ; in the first, the idea of protection rested on the interpretation of *Christianity* ; in the second, on the interpretation of *Humanity*. Christian protection, humane protection, the one foreshadows the other, beckons the other to follow.

Christian protection was originally understood in the Roman Catholic not in the Protestant sense. The work of the Protestants in the colonial sphere lay in promoting equality, not merely humanity, which served only to temper authority. The rôle of the Protestants thus was to provoke the emancipation of the subjugated peoples, which is the dream of our time. But in the Roman Catholic conception it was the idea of humanity which was revealed as an influence moderating the old dominating power. From now on when I speak of Christianity I am speaking of Roman Catholicism, not of Protestantism.

Can we assume that the Ancients, and the Greeks among them, that people of moderation, never even dimly thought of moderating the right of the strong ? The Greeks conceived not only the idea of a common law amongst Greeks, and peculiar to Greeks, which regulated the relations between civilised men, between one city and another, but they also had the conception of a universal law of peoples, which governed the relations between Greeks and Barbarians : the idea of rights and duties of a moral or natural nature which limited the authority of Greek over non-Greek.[1] It was, for instance, forbidden to devastate the property of conquered peoples, even if they were overseas Barbarians ; it was forbidden to murder envoys or non-combatants. There already, at least ultimately, the Greek world recognised a natural law, a *law of peoples* which governed the relations of the Greeks with all non-Greeks. It remains true, nevertheless, that in Western countries opposition to the ancient abuses of

---

[1] G. Glotz, *Le droit des gens dans l'antiquité grecque*, 1917.

domination was the work of Christians, and that in France protection was in the first place Christian protection.

In the French Middle Ages we meet with a curious document whose author is believed to have been inspired by King Charles V. It is called " The true Régime and Government of Shepherds and Shepherdesses ", composed by " the rustic Jean de Brie ", the Good Shepherd.[1] The good shepherd takes thought for, and shows kindness to, his flock ; he respects their *natural law*—the very word is used—the law which Nature has taught to all animals. He ensures their obedience by " gentle correction ". Here is already an appeal for moderation, an appeal also for docility. There is a lesson both for masters and for subjects. This is, as far as I have been able to discover, the first time that the idea is proclaimed that government should be exercised with gentleness. We know that the public mind had grown accustomed to this thought two centuries later. In the 16th century this was so : the people expressed it in their own way. There was in those days in Rouen a kind of procession which was known as the *Montre*, in which the great events which had taken place were recorded in the form of mummeries and parodies. One year, amongst the chariots which formed the procession, a sphere appeared, over which several sovereigns quarrelled bitterly ; and the chronicler records that they " maltreated (*margouilloient*) these poor men roughly enough ". This was a satire expressed in action or representation. These innocent spectacles brought home to the general public, for whom these jests were displayed, the idea that authority ought to be tempered, and thus public opinion was prepared to lend an ear to the preaching and exhortations of the great authors of whom we are about to speak. It was their voice which was raised in the name of Christ against all the abuses of cruel conquerors ; it was their voice which called authority " tutelary ".

It was heard first in Spain. As early as 1514 the Augustinian Peter Martyr lamented the cruelty of the conquistadors and thundered in Biblical style against the massacre of the natives of America.[2]

---

[1] *Le vrai régime et gouvernement des bergers et bergères*, 1379. See Ch. Lenient, *La satire en France au Moyen Age*, 1859, p. 221 f.
[2] *Extrait . . . des îles Trouvées* (1514), French trans. 1533 ; cf. G. Atkinson, *Les nouveaux horizons de la Renaissance française*, 1935, p. 204 f. [This Peter Martyr is not, of course, the theologian Vermigli, but Peter de Anghierra, 1455–1526, member of the King of Spain's Council of the Indies from 1524, and author of the treatise *De Orbe Novo*. EOL.]

Two other great names must be cited, Bishop Las Casas and the monk Vitoria.

Bartholomew de Las Casas was born in 1474 and died in 1566. He lived for fifty years in America and was Bishop of Chiapas in South Mexico. He was really the first who in the name of Roman Catholicism demanded both by word and deed the protection of the conquered peoples.[1] He was the author of a work published in 1552, entitled *Story of the Destruction of the Indians*. This was translated into French in 1579. Las Casas had presented it to Charles V as early as 1542 : and this is the date which should be remembered as the first revelation of humane feeling against the cruelties of the Spaniards in the New World of America. The great religious Orders followed his lead. Before he became a bishop he had been a Regular of the Dominican Order. This was the first movement of the religious Orders, which, in the history both of Christianity and of Islam, moderated the power of the State. For good or ill they hampered the State in colonial countries.

We must consider the work of Las Casas as revealed both in his *thought* and in his *acts*.

It was Las Casas' *thought* which raised a protest against the conquerors' assumed right to conquer and to occupy. He produced a number of arguments, dressed up in legal form, subtly and bitterly pressed so as to reinforce each other, in order to make out his case that there exists no right of conquest, and that conquest accordingly can be justified and legitimatised only by the benefit and happiness of the defeated people. He proposed to Charles V, all-powerful sovereign, that the Inca should be reinstated on his throne and that the reign and the power of the Divine King of ancient Peru should be restored.

The denial of the right of conquest : this was the first, the intellectual aspect, the rational side of Las Casas' thought ; we might say that it was the legal aspect too. But there is another aspect : the human aspect. No longer a denial of legal right, but a deeply-felt, often violent protest in his sayings and writings against all the sins of the first conquerors : a protest, thought to be for publicity reasons exaggerated, against the acts and deeds of men like Pizarro and Cortes. This was the beginning

---

[1] Las Casas, *Tyrannies et cruautés des Espagnols*, French trans. 1579 ; *Œuvres de Las Casas*, French trans. 1822, especially I, p. 333 f., and II, p. 201 f. Abbé Grégoire, *Apologie de Las Casas* ; M. Brion, *B. de Las Casas*, 1927.—E. Nys, *Les publicistes espagnols du XVIᵉ siècle et les droits des Indiens*, 1890 ; B. Atkinson, *Les nouveaux horizons de la Renaissance française*, 1935, pp. 158, 206 f.

of criticism of the abuses in the colonies, the battle against the harshness and cruelty of the conquerors,[1] a battle which has continued without ceasing down to our own day. Las Casas was able to carry his protest to the steps of the throne itself. He fearlessly took part, in the King's presence, in an open discussion with the defenders of the old, uncompromising imperialism ; with Sepulveda, the theologian, who upheld the right of conquest and with whom the Bishop was to carry on in 1560 a controversy that has remained famous. The chroniclers report that the eloquence of Las Casas carried the day and that humanity won the hearts of the courtiers—for a moment ! [2]

From his thought, we pass on to his *action*. Las Casas was a man of action ; he was the first reformer of West Indian legislation. As early as 1515 he undertook the risk of travelling to Seville from Peru. He obtained audience of the King and lodged in the name of equity, in the name of Christianity, an eloquent and daring protest against—what he called—the destruction of the American Indians. The two conceptions, equity and Christianity, were blended in his mind, and both comprised in the one word : humanity. In his declaration he laid stress on the goodness of the natives. Before the assembled Court, in the presence of all these refined people he professed his faith in " the good savage ", and proclaimed his vision of " the natural man ", virtuous and happy. He asserted that before the Spanish Occupation, the American Indians had been an immense, infinitely numerous people whom the conquerors by their ferocity had in a few years destroyed. He preached the duty of converting the natives by gentleness and kindness. He later made a second journey during which he once again emphasised his ideas before the Court ; and during which in order to bring relief to his beloved Red Indians, he had a scheme for organising for America the trade in negroes purchased in Africa. It was he who proposed at the Grand Council for the Indies to transplant to America a coloured labour force so as to reduce the excessive exploitation of the Red Indian labourer. Las Casas was a man of his own epoch. He had no thought of *liberating* the natives of every country ! He sought merely to *mitigate*

---

[1] Recent protests have been lodged against certain exaggerations of Las Casas : R. Levillier, *Las Casas, Revue d'histoire moderne*, No. 3, 1932 ; J. Babelon, *Fernand Cortez*, 1928, also speaks of the " pious calumnies " of Las Casas. Cf. also *Nouvelle Revue historique de droit*, 1926, p. 159.

[2] In the legislation designed to protect the natives and on Charles V's great —but little-respected—ordinances, see [Peter Martyr, *De Orbe Novo*, Gaffarel's edition, 1907, p. 599 f.

abuses ; to improve and temper the lot of the natives under the authority and domination of the conquerors ; for a good King ought to govern for the happiness of his subjects. But the Good Shepherd remains a Shepherd still, a Shepherd or a Driver ! As with Jean de Brie, the good-shepherd idea persists.

Francis of Vitoria was also a man of his own epoch.[1] As in the case of Bishop Las Casas, we should look in vain for any desire of his to emancipate the American natives. But by his preaching and by his writing he sought to stir men's feelings in their favour. Francis of Vitoria never visited the New World himself. He lived in Spain and published in 1575 a book which included two essays on the Indies, at least one of which has been translated into French.[2] Vitoria's work therefore lay in the field of thought, not of action ; it consisted chiefly in intellectual protest against the absolutism of the conqueror. In his capacity of Professor of Law, it was he who—even more effectively than Bishop Las Casas—laid the foundations of the new attitude of mind in which authority must allow itself to be tempered by humanity. His demonstration was governed by two ideas.

Denial of the Right of Occupation by the conqueror. We have already met this in Las Casas, but Vitoria demonstrates and illustrates it better. He asserts the natives' right of possession and claims for them an unlimited legal right, against which the right of the conqueror cannot prevail. By almost infinitely numerous arguments Vitoria confirmed the title of the first occupants to their property, their incontestable right to the occupation of their own soil ; a right which cannot be annulled at the wish of the conquerors. In this connection he indulges in numerous passionate diatribes against the arrogance of princes who found empires and who dream of ruling the whole universe —though the Kingdom is not of this world ! If Vitoria is the champion of the native it is because as a theologian he conceives Christianity as comprising *humility*. The conquerors are the proud and haughty, the chief of sinners, seduced by the Demon to destruction ! Thus the spirit animating Vitoria is profoundly Christian.

Vitoria not only denied the right to possess the new countries, but he also maintained the *Limitation of the Right to Govern* them.

---

[1] A good exposition of his views will be found in J. Folliet, *Le droit de colonisation*, 1933, p. 50 f. Cf. Q. Albertini, *L'œuvre de François de Vitoria et la doctrine canonique de la guerre*, 1903 (thesis).

[2] Vanderpol, *La doctrine scolastique du droit de guerre*, 1910, Appendix.

He placed restraints on legislation and jurisdiction in a colonial country ; and he based his strictures on legal grounds, for he was a jurist as well as a Christian. The first argument he advanced was liberty; according to his reasoning every man possessing a right based on natural order, willed by God, granted by God, possesses liberties which cannot be violated : liberty to live in his own land, to govern and administer himself . . . The Law of Nature is the Law of God, and it guarantees to peoples " the option of disposing of themselves ". Ought the natives then to be emancipated ? By no means, for according to the law laid down by God, there exist the liberties of other peoples. The " savages " would be in the wrong if they attempted to prevent foreigners from entering their countries, from travelling about and residing there : it is a natural right of all men, in all places, to trade, to cultivate, to possess.— And here is something which goes rather far ! It is always arrogance on the part of backward peoples to attempt to prevent more advanced people from settling in their country. Hence arise conquests and colonies !—The natives ought—as it was later expressed—to " allow passage and freedom of action " to the foreigner ; nothing more and nothing less. The Europeans are not justified, according to Vitoria, in imposing foreign occupation and legislation on the natives' land.[1] The law of liberty reigns everywhere, the gift of God to man, inasmuch as man has been created by God.

Vitoria, however, jurist though he was, was above all a Christian ; and the limitation on the right to govern backward peoples did not invalidate the duty imposed by God on the conquerors to convert the natives to the Christian faith. The one justifies the other . . . The conquerors' duty is the duty to convert. For God has not granted liberty of belief and thought ! From this point onwards Vitoria remains the very firm champion of spiritual imperialism. You must first, he says, attract the natives by persuasion ; you must preach and teach and try to indoctrinate them by moderation. But if this does not suffice and if the natives, spurred on by the Demon, resist in their obstinacy these efforts at conversion, you have then the right, and the duty, to have recourse to force ! You must

[1] Lagarde took this question up again : *La colonisation et les droits indigènes, Travaux juridiques économiques, Université de Rennes*, XIV, 1935. James Lorimer in his *Institutes of the Law of Nations*, 1883-4, Book II, Chap. 2, recognises only the pure duty of *humanity* in the civilised man's treatment of the savage ; no equality, no common right, no contract, no obligation. This is the doctrine which long prevailed.

pursue the *spiritual conquest*. Vitoria's denial of the right to legislate does not prevent his asserting the right to preach and to impose the True Faith in the name of God. Liberty to live, but not to think. Liberalism does not, therefore, spell emancipation.

Through the labours of Las Casas and of Vitoria, the new-born idea of protection in the Christian sense was able to gain ground in Spain. So true was this that in 1545 the Emperor Charles V gave " New Laws " to the colonies, and by his Great Ordinances imposed on the Spaniards a more humane code of conduct towards the American Indians. He forbade flogging ; he forbade the separation of a husband and wife for work, which was a usual practice. He demanded—these are the very words of the text—that " care should be taken " of the natives ; he wished that consideration and protection should be shown them. Little as these laws were obeyed, owing to distance—a phenomenon familiar even in our own day !—they bore witness for the first time to moderation and humanity. Better still : the conquerors themselves, even the most cruel, confessed their sin and crime : in the Memoirs of Cortes, great destroyer and great slayer as he was, it is written—in *one* place !—that the savages' " affection should be gained ". This was to subscribe, just once, to that moral ideal which every Christian ought to serve.

If the Spaniards were the very first to set up this ideal [1] it was the French who after them revived it. Benzoni, translated into French by Chauveton, a Protestant, had, no doubt, a share in the matter. They both condemned the Spaniards in the name of Christian virtue : and Chauveton went so far as to speak of " the law of peoples ".[2] At the beginning of the age of Louis XIV there were many writers in France, inspired most probably by Las Casas and Vitoria, who asserted the obligation of showing consideration for the natives, of tempering authority in the name of Christian duty. There was Lescarbot, for instance, the lawyer-adventurer who went to Brazil in 1612, and in recounting the hardships of his escapade wrote that the natives should be " humanely treated ". The word " humanity " is thus recorded in French for the first time in an unquestioned text.

---

[1] Humboldt, *Essai politique sur le royaume de la Nouvelle-Espagne*, 1811, I, p. 422 f., gives an extract from a long memorandum presented in 1799 to the King of Spain by the Bishop and Chapter of Michoacan to ameliorate the lot of the Mexicans.
[2] Benzoni, *Histoire nouvelle du Nouveau-Monde*, French version by H. Chauveton, 1579. Chauveton, *Bref discours des Français en Floride*, 1579 ; cf. G. Atkinson, *Les nouveaux horizons de la Renaissance française*, 1935, p. 208 f.

" To treat humanely " from Christian motives the unfortunate backward people inasmuch as they are creatures of God and the Christian's Rule constrains him to respect them.[1] Three years later, in 1615, the economist Montchrestien, imperialist though he was, and a partisan, as we know, of domination, also wrote in one passage of his *Treatise* that you must treat the natives humanely, you must conquer them, and educate them, but with gentleness, in harmony with the Christian spirit. Fifty years later, the great historian of the Antilles, Jacques du Tertre, insisted at length—not merely in a word or two—on the duty of showing consideration for the natives, of treating them kindly and of combining Christianity with humanity.[2] Thus over three centuries ago protesting voices were raised in France against colonial despotism. Later, when Joseph de Maistre, fanatical upholder of authority, spoke with reprobation of those " European brigands " who conquered the New World, he was only reviving and refreshing the indignation of the old theologians.[3]

[1] This text is conveniently available in E. Guénin, *L'épopée coloniale de la France*, 1932, p. 53 f.

[2] G. Chinard, *L'exotisme américain aux XVIIe et XVIIIe siecles*, 1913, p. 51 f.

[3] It was almost a tradition in France to denounce the failure of the Spaniards. In the *Théâtre de Clara Gazul* (*La carrosse du St. Sacrement*) Mérimée illustrated the vanity, futility and venality of the viceroys of Peru ; of one, for instance, who took an Indian half-caste, La Périchole, as his mistress, about 1760. For the facts, see M. Radiguet, *Souvenir de l'Amérique espagnole*, 1856, p. 132 f.

CHAPTER XXV

PATERNAL GUARDIANSHIP : HUMANITY

From protection based on the Christian motive, men advanced to protection based on the motive of *Humanity* ; *humane protection* succeeded Christian protection. The idea arose that it is fitting to protect and educate the natives, for their benefit and for their happiness and in virtue of their human rights. This idea still exists on two planes : the plane of interest and the plane of feeling. Those who defended the idea of paternal guardianship or of paternal obligation, despiritualised as it now was, based their arguments on interest and on sentiment. They pleaded the duty of the rulers both on the grounds of its *usefulness* and on the grounds of its *equity*. This has produced in the West in the course of two, or perhaps three, centuries, a quite new type of imperialism : *paternal imperialism* which imposed on the rulers the mission, duty and function of ruling in order to educate in accordance with the idea of humanity, which is the secularised version of Christianity.

The *criticism of colonial abuses* which we met in Las Casas and Vitoria becomes legal criticism, a demonstration of the *rights* of the dominated in relation to the dominators. Criticism of abuses was ere long almost imperceptibly to lead to criticism of rights. For the mind has a natural inclination to proceed from questioning the abuse of rights to questioning the rights themselves : to discuss the ends after discussing the means. This whole mental attitude, which we shall sum up in a few words, gently eases the transition to other mental attitudes. It opens the way for those who contend that the domination and exploitation of distant countries is not strictly *justified* in law ; that it is consequently right in the immediate present to restore autonomy to the ruled and re-establish dignity and equity amongst them.

Humane protection, or the assertion of humanity, has had two moments in the past. There were first the *forerunners*, who in the 16th and still more in the 17th century affirmed the natives' human rights. Later there were in the 18th century the *founders* who reasserted the affirmation of the forerunners but were in a position really to put the new ideas into action.

The *Forerunners*. These were the men who, especially in

France, were the very first to do battle with the abuses in the name more of human than of Christian law. Not that the ideal of Christianity was effaced or outworn amongst them all ; far from it—we shall presently be speaking of some who cherished it ; but henceforward it no longer took the first place. It was the idea of humanity, creating a right common to every human being, which gave the forerunners their inspiration.

Here two names stand out with exceptional brilliance : the names of Rabelais and of Montaigne ; they initiated the idea of educating the natives and associating them with the conquerors, basing their idea on the moral duty of humanity.

In the third book of *Pantagruel*, which appeared in 1546, Rabelais [1] told how the Utopians used to found their colonies. Their womenfolk were excessively fertile, and one day King Pantagruel was forced to convey a first colony to Dipsodie, an overseas country. The colonists included, he said, " professors of all the sciences, in order to refresh people, and adorn the said country ". To *people* and to *adorn* : those were the two aims. He insisted also that the newcomers—who were to establish themselves without striking a blow ; this was an essential condition !—should treat the original inhabitants with great gentleness. He would dream, he said, that a day would come when the Dipsodians—in other words, the dominated—would regret not having earlier heard the fame of King Pantagruel ! Could we, in our day, say more ? The Dipsodians must be pleased with the Utopians, they must be happy that they have come, they must prefer their new subjection to their ancient liberty. Such was good King Pantagruel's dream ! This is, I believe, the first expression of the secularised idea of humanity, and it occurs in a French book. [2]

But it was Montaigne's *Essays*, published in 1580, which asserted and confirmed, in many passages, the dominators' obligation to act with gentleness ! In Chapter 31 of the first Book, writing " Of Cannibals ", the great sceptic fearlessly pointed out—before many other writers—the relativity and instability of civilisations. There is no such thing, he contends, as " more civilised " and " less civilised " : " each calls barbarous any

---

[1] R. Maunier, *L'idée d'association dans la doctrine coloniale de la France, Revue de l'Institut de Sociologie* (Brussels), XIV, 1934, No. 2 ; M. Besson, *Rabelais et les débuts de la colonisation française, Grande Revue*, April, 1933.

[2] A. Lefranc, *La notion et les sentiments d'humanité dans la littérature française du XVIe siècle (Congrès sciences historiques*, 1927, pp. 30–40 ; and H. Pirenne's comments following).

customs other than his own " ; and if we are superior to the American natives we are superior in malice, not in wisdom ! Here we have already the formal admission that domination is not founded of right on superior civilisation, as cultural imperialism would have it ; that each people, whether savage or primitive, possesses its *own* civilisation which is quite as valuable as ours. In Book III, Chapter 6, " Of Coaches ", Montaigne drew his conclusions from this relativity of civilisations. He was led to deny the conquerors' right always and everywhere to boast of their cultural superiority. Reprobating the Spaniards' crimes in America, he says " it was an infant world . . . nor have we won it over by our justice and goodness, nor subdued it by our magnanimity " ; we ought " gently to have cleared away all that was barbarous ".[1] By goodness . . . by gentleness . . . the virtue of humanity finds expression in the words.

It was Montaigne and Rabelais in France, writing at the same time as Vitoria and almost at the same time as Las Casas— the dates are almost exactly coincident—who secularised the old idea of gentleness, that originally sprang from a religious motive ; humanity in itself, man's duty to his fellow-man ; the idea that all these natives of distant countries, being human, have a claim on their guardians, who are bound to treat them with goodness, to " win this infant world with equity ", to make the governed content by seeking as far as possible their happiness. Childhood demands guardianship, requires protection. Authority there must be, but authority tempered by humanity.

These great minds had their echoes, even in their own day. They were not alone in pleading for kindness. Chroniclers and even poets recommended that the natives should be won by gentleness. In his *Discourse against Fortune*,[2] addressing the conquerors of the New World of America, Ronsard, for instance, begs them to remove " the cruel halter " which they have fastened round the native's neck ! Brantôme too asks that they should live with the natives in all equity.[3] In England too the Lord Chancellor, Francis Bacon, whom I have already mentioned, demanded that all natives should be " justly and graciously " used. The Chancellor, the colonial writer, the author responsible for the first essay *On Plantations* was also, as we know, a professed moralist ; in his little essay, he is mindful of it.

---

[1] [E. J. Trechmann's translation, Oxford, 1927. EOL]
[2] *Discours contre fortune.*
[3] L. Deschamps, *Histoire de la question coloniale en France*, 1891, pp. 39 f. and 51 f.

It was not until the following century that this humane attitude found opportunity to translate itself into practice and policy. There were, under Louis XIV, writers who in their turn defended, more or less eloquently, more or less obscurely, the idea of Rabelais. But there were also men of action who by the power of laws made the protection of the native a *reality*.

In 1623 a certain Emeric La Croix—at one time quite forgotten, but nowadays very famous because he was a forerunner of the doctrine of our League of Nations—published the *Nouveau Cynée*,[1] a pamphlet in which he proposed that Algiers should be occupied by a colony of European traders ! But, to what end ? First to put a stop to the raids of the Barbary pirates ; but also, he said, to " pacify the inhabitants " after they had submitted, and teach them peace by making them " give up a tormented existence " ; and lastly to pacify the Maghrib territories and put an end to the cruelties of the Algerians. This Emeric La Croix is far from being a champion of conquerors. Three centuries before the time, he advocated the occupation of Algiers, but it was firstly in the interests of security, and secondly in the interests of humanity to pacify the inhabitants, to teach them the French idea of order by transplanting to these countries the laws of the French King. He teaches that the earth is the common property of all ; the right of the conquerors can be based only on the advantages they can offer to their future subjects. The vision and the plan of conquest is associated with the duty of civilising and raising moral standards.

The year 1664 saw the creation of the French East and West Indies Co., to exploit Malagasy. A lawyer called Charpentier was appointed by the King to draft, in harmony with the royal ideas, a prospectus for public circulation. The author of the prospectus was thus—and this is a point we must bear in mind —the mouthpiece of the King. It is the King's attitude which we shall find in the prospectus and in the Company's charter.[2]

As regards the Malagasy—the " Malgaches " as they are called in French—the prospectus already informs us that the King insists that they must be governed " gently ". We may reasonably suppose that Charpentier borrowed the words *gentleness* and *gently* from Montaigne. In the Charter, a statute of thirteen articles, drawn up by Charpentier, we see how the King

---

[1] P.-Louis Lucas, *Un Plan de paix . . . Le Nouveau Cynée d'Emeric Cruce*, 1919 (thesis).

[2] E. Guénin, *L'épopée coloniale de la France*, 1932, p. 81 f. ; J. Bouruet-Aubertot, *Louis XIV, businessman*, 1931, p. 121 f.

set himself to instil principles of humanity into the government. Article 7, for instance, insists that "no wrong be done to the earlier inhabitants" and that they be treated "with equity and justice". This is more than mere advice ; it is the moral rule which, at the King's desire, is to inform the relations between governors and governed. Means to ensure that these provisions of the charter should be observed were not forgotten ; it was intended that all natives should be given facilities for claiming their rights. It is further ordered that the Charter should be posted up throughout the whole of the Island,[1] not only in the French text, but "in the language of the country". (?) The good intention was there. The King wished all the native inhabitants to know the terms of the Charter and at need to invoke it. A little further on, he says, or Charpentier says for him, that the inhabitants must be treated "with humanity and tenderness". This is the first text of a legal statute in which the word humanity is to be found. The authors had the idea, and here it appears, for the first time in a legal text, at the end of the Charter of 1664 worked out for a colonising Company. Let us then turn the limelight on the obscure name of Charpentier, linking with his the glorious name of the Great King who inspired the Charter or better still was its dictator, in every sense of the word. Let us remember, too, that as early as 1611, the *Instructions* of the King of Portugal to the Governor of Angola enjoined him "to live in peace and friendship with the inhabitants", and to command the obedience of their chiefs "by gentle and courteous means". So the legislators had their say.[2]

Vauban, who came shortly afterwards, also demanded—in a passage of the work I have already mentioned, and which was prior to 1707, the year of his death—a "stern morality" in the conquerors. There were thus some spirits, few in number but not isolated, who proclaimed the duty of humane and moral conduct in the relationships between rulers and ruled. In his letter of 1503 to the King, Columbus advised "good methods of procedure". And the Memorandum of Quiros to the King of Spain on the *Terra Australis*[3] warns him to treat the natives "gently and with friendliness". This being so, we need not be

---

[1] [La Grande Île ou l'Île Dauphine.]

[2] *Outre-Mer*, 1934, p. 338. Two hundred years later, in 1814, Governor Macquarie gave orders to treat the New Zealanders with equity and humanity. (Eyriès, *Abrégé . . . des Voyages*, V, 1823, p. 442.) In France, the Royal Instructions of 1816 for Senegal also counsel *kindness* and *friendship*. Cf. G. Hardy, *La mise en valeur du Sénégal*, 1921, pp. 12 f. and 315 f.

[3] E. Charton, *Voyageurs anciens et modernes*, 1869, III, p. 102 f. ; IV, p. 230 f.

surprised that the legal commentators, habitually the last to arrive on the scene, presently felt able to write the new principle into their rigmaroles. Pufendorf, a disciple of Grotius, author of a treatise, *The Law of War and Peace*,[1] which Barbeyrac translated into French in 1731, writes in Chapter III of his first Book [2] that there rests on all conquerors the obligation " to respect the rights of the natives ". He even goes further—as commentators with their passion for deduction always love to do ; having arrived later, they go further—he is not afraid to question the intrinsic and basic right of conquest. He draws his conclusion from the relativity of civilisation which Montaigne had illustrated, and says that he cannot see any ground on which a right of conquest can be built. At the very least, conquest must be redeemed by great duties. The conquerors must be made to recognise an obligation, not only to respect the natives and treat them with consideration, but an obligation to make them content, to promote their happiness and desire their welfare. A little later we read in Montesquieu [3] that conquest " leaves always an immense debt to be paid " if it is " to justify itself towards human nature ".

Already the distinction which Rabelais had made, had been clearly drawn between the two aspects of this duty of humanity, the *passive* and the *active*. In the passive sense, there is the obligation to respect and show consideration towards the natives ; to abstain from cruelties. This obligation does not satisfy Rabelais or Pufendorf. For there is, secondly, obligation in the active sense : to take pains to make the natives happy and to make a genuine effort on their behalf.

We now pass on from the *forerunners* to the *founders*. Domination is going to imply obligation : both in the passive and in the active sense. These are the two concepts which the commentators will set out to illustrate. They are going to sermonise, which had not before been done, on this duty of humanity and they will discover different bases for it : a basis of *utility* and a basis of *morality*.

A basis of *Utility*. Without seeking any other motive, it is in the interest of the conquerors to agree to show consideration to the natives. Travellers had not failed to observe that you might stand in need of the natives, and it was therefore just as

---

[1] *Droit de la guerre et de la paix.*
[2] Vol. I, p. 388 f.
[3] *Esprit des Lois*, 1748, Book X, Chap. 4 ; cf. Chap. 11.

well to secure their goodwill ! For some barter with them is essential and it is better that they should sell or give willingly ! Thus, from sheer self-interest of course, the explorer is inclined to exercise moderation in his demands. In Volume X of his *Last Voyage* [1] James Cook says that he always took pains to be considerate to the natives and not to arouse their resentment ; for you need them and it is interesting to instruct them. The *Instructions* issued to him for his second voyage, ordered him to form ties of friendship with the natives by treating them with civility. This is why on one of his ships he brought back with him to England a native of Tahiti called Omai, whom he eventually took back to the Society Islands, armed with provisions and instruments—like Robinson Crusoe !—to educate his compatriots and make agriculturists of them. At the same period another great navigator, Chevalier de Bougainville, also remarked that you must not ruffle the South Sea Islanders, for you want to enlist the necessary practical collaboration from them. To this end Bougainville also brought back a native with him to France, a man called Aotourou who has left us his opinions on the life of the French Court. He also was re-embarked for home but he died on reaching Mauritius [2] without having regained his native country.

There is no conqueror of recent times who has not perceived that it is in his own interest to make friends with and educate the natives. The type of conqueror who works by destruction and extermination is " out of date " to-day. [3] Brazza, for instance, said : " To make good use of the natives, to identify their interests and ours, to make them our natural allies, that was in my opinion one of the most important aims of my mission." " Our natural allies " : the phrase should be remembered, for it implies partnership *in* and *under* domination ; convergence of interest, consideration, conciliation, though under the authority, the limited authority, of the ruler.

If, however, we are looking for the real father of colonial " humanism " we must find him concerned with the basis not of utility but of *morality*. Less than a hundred and fifty years

---

[1] French 32⁰ Ed., pp. 229–30 ; cf. Vol. XI, pp. 9–10 ; on Omaï, Vol. XVIII, p. 45 f.—See, a little later : *Voyage of the Valiant* (1797), Ed. Müller, p. 144, in which Cook says that you must make the savages like you, you cannot provision yourself sword in hand ! In our own day Lyautey said that to avoid setbacks " let our first contact continue to be just and beneficial ". *Lettres du Sud de Madagascar*, 1935, p. 145 f.

[2] [Île de France.]

[3] [This statement of 1936 reads as irony in our post-Hitler day. EOL]

ago, people were anxiously seeking a moral justification for benevolence towards the natives ; they succeeded in making a real moral duty of this consideration, an obligation of a moral nature. Without going so far as to contemplate equality or liberty for them, without, that is to say, drawing the conclusions that might fairly have been drawn—and were, later, to be drawn—from the doctrine of Montaigne's *Essays*, they were already firmly linking humanity to morality.

Most surprisingly, we find Napoleon doing just this ! He had been, at least in his youth, a disciple of Rousseau, and it was probably of Rousseau that he was thinking when, in planning his Egyptian expedition he dreamed of transplanting the spirit of the West into the valley of the Nile. We know from his writings that he believed himself commissioned by God to bring Western civilisation to the Egyptians. Idea and action were both his ; he formulated the humane doctrine and he put it into practice ; he proclaimed it on his arrival, and he made it a reality during his brief stay in the country.

In his *Proclamations* [1] the idea of humanity, based on moral duty, is very amply expressed. First in the Proclamation of the 4th of Messidor of the Year VI (June 22, 1798) to his soldiers made on the *Orient* as she sailed from Toulon towards the Egyptian coast, he said :

Soldiers, you are about to make a conquest whose effects on civilisation and world trade are incalculable. The Beys and Mamelukes who exclusively favour English commerce, who have heaped insults upon our merchants, and who tyrannise over the unhappy inhabitants of the Nile—within a few days of our arrival, they will have ceased to exist.

Here we have the idea of the good fight against all tyrants, of the liberation . . . by Western intervention, of oppressed peoples.

The peoples [he added], with whom we are going to live are Muhammadans ; this is the first article of their faith : " There is no God but Allah, and Muhammad is the Prophet of Allah." Do not contradict them ; act with them as we have acted with the Jews, and with the Italians ; pay the same respect to their *muftis* and *imams* as you have paid to the rabbis and the bishops.

---

[1] *Correspondance de Napoléon*, Vol. IV, p. 269 f. ; C. Cherfils, *Bonaparte et l'Islam*, 1914 ; F. Charles-Roux, *La politique musulmane de Bonaparte, Revue études napoléon*, Jan.–Feb. 1925, and *Bonaparte, Gouverneur d'Égypte*, 1935. Napoleon later said : " My Egyptian proclamations were mere charlatanism, but of the highest type . . . All these things were said merely to be translated into beautiful Arabic verse . . ." But did he not also say that he would have embraced Islam for the sake of gaining the empire of the East ?

But it is at the end that his idea is most clearly defined and emphasised. Still speaking to his soldiers aboard ship, he continues :

> For all the ceremonies prescribed by the Quran, and for the mosques, show the same tolerance that you have shown for the convents, for the synagogues, for the religion of Moses and for the religion of Jesus Christ. The Roman legions were in the habit of protecting every religion. You will find here manners and customs different from those of Europe. You must get accustomed to them. The people we are going amongst treat women differently from us, but in every country the man who violates a woman is a monster. Looting enriches only a few ; it dishonours us and destroys our resources . . . —Napoleon's counsels are a fine blend of utility and morality— . . . it makes enemies for us of people whom it is our interest to have as friends.

We see the idea of friendship already dawning here ; and Napoleon gives partnership with the Egyptians as the object of his occupation of Egypt.

Then, when he disembarked at Alexandria, he addressed the Egyptians in his Proclamation of the 14th of Messidor of the Year VI (July 7, 1798), promising them liberation . . . by good government ; that is, perhaps, the true form of liberation ! Then Bonaparte speaks, Member of the National Institute, General Officer Commanding in Chief :

> For many a long day the Beys who govern Egypt have insulted the French nation and affronted our merchants : the hour of their chastisement has come. This gang of slaves, purchased in Georgia and the Caucasus, has tyrannised too long over the fairest quarter of the world ; but God, on whom all things depend, has willed that their reign should cease.—This was the mission entrusted by God to the Liberating Conqueror.—Peoples of Egypt, men will tell you that I come to destroy your religion ; do not believe them ! Reply that I come to restore you your rights and to punish the usurpers, and that I have more respect for God, his Prophet and the Quran than for the Mamelukes. Tell them that before God all men are equal ; only wisdom, talents and virtue create differences between them. . . .

Later on he promises that " all the Egyptians will be called to administer all the posts . . . " This is good and this shall come to pass : genuine partnership of interests, collaboration in legislation and administration ; and the French subjects in Indo-China are now in 1936 demanding in fact only just that, the majority at least !

All the Egyptians will be called to administer all the posts ; the wisest, the most learned and the most virtuous shall govern and the

people will be happy . . . Qadhis, shaikhs, imams, chorbajis, tell
the people that we are the friends of the true Musulmans. . . . But
woe, and thrice woe, to those who take up arms for the Mamelukes
and fight against us ! There will be no hope for them : they shall
perish.

Admonition followed by a curse in the true style of the *suras*
of the Quran. He has the right, he has the force ; the master
is a friend, but the friend is also the master ! Obey, so that
we may make you happy ! Liberation—Domination, that is the
meaning of the address. Domination for the benefit of the
governors, domination for the benefit of the governed, according
to the laws of equity.

By his proclamations, but no less by the *applications* thereof,
Napoleon founded a régime new for an Oriental country. Short
as was his stay in the valley of the Nile, he put into action the
statute announced in his proclamations. From the very first he
established collaboration between Egyptians and French both in
the administration and in legislation. He set up a *Mixed Diwan*,
namely a Great Consultative Council, consisting of both Egyptian
and French members, to give legislation the right direction.
Both sat together to organise the common welfare. He issued
several decrees to ensure due honour and respect being shown
to officers, officials and " the clergy ", that is the qadhis and the
imams whom he set out to flatter. The word is there : the
policy of *respect and consideration. (la politique des égards)*, of which
we still speak, is present in the legislation of the young conqueror.
He concluded an alliance with the Sharif of Mecca ; he established a Commission " to ascertain the improvements desired by
the people of the country ". To consult, to suggest ; to propose,
rather than to impose ; to seek the common good by common
consent : these had been the ideas of Rabelais. Assuredly
Napoleon's shade in the Other World will be somewhat surprised to find it so ! Yet these two great minds both saw the
vision of a reign whose aim should be the welfare of the subject,
they thought of consulting him, not of working out his happiness
without his knowledge and in his own despite !

These are ideas which in our own day might advantageously
be revived !

Napoleon not only made a reality of laying the foundation
of a partnership between Egyptian and French, he set himself
also to improve Egyptian civilisation. Collaboration ; Civilisation. He opened schools ; He tried from the very beginning to

organise primary education for all.   He was therefore the very
first to seek to educate and instruct the African.   He wanted
also to encourage industry in order to increase prosperity.
Lastly, he wanted to improve the lot of women.   His idea in
erecting windmills in the neighbourhood of Cairo—windmills
now in ruins—was to put an end to the laborious toil of the handmill which fell on the Egyptian woman.   Collaboration and
civilisation ; by these, Napoleon the General was the founder
of colonial *humanism*.   And if, thanks to his work, the expedition
to the Nile was the first ethnographic expedition, it was also in
its effects the first democratic expedition.

Thus, in the course of time, the old conception of paternal
domination was modified and humanised.   Authority was profoundly transformed both in thought and deed.   Men progressed
from power to duty.   Not yet as far as equality and liberty ;
there still remained domination and still direction ;   still the
subjection of the governed to the governors, but for the protection and development of the former.   Education—Domination ; conquest for the benefit of the conquered : in a word,
government for happiness.

BOOK VI
PARTNERSHIP

CHAPTER XXVI

REFORM OF DOMINATION

How was the spirit of domination combated in the colonial empires of the West ? How did men pass from the age-old conception of domination to the new concepts of partnership and emancipation ?

These were reached by gradual modification, by evolution. Domination was blunted and effaced in three stages, the first of which was transitional : *reform, partnership, emancipation.*

We shall deal first with *Reform*, since people, especially in France, reached the stage of proposing to reform, not merely to modify, ancient authority in colonial administration. Reform thus marks an immediate transition to a new line of action, in course of which domination is to be abolished. Reform means contesting, shaking, the foundations of the old power. We must in this distinguish the *aims* and the *agents*.

First, the *Aims*. When men desired to reform colonial power, they wished to clip its wings, but not to destroy it : to modify it and to lessen its abuses. They criticised its excesses and its abuses ; they did not discuss its rights : the first attack on ancient despotism. Abuses may be of many kinds ; in this case there were three varieties : abuses by the conquerors, by the administrators, by the exploiters.

Abuses by the *Conquerors* : " brutalities " and " cruelties " were speedily denounced, as we know, in the case of the Spaniards. Examples of cruelty have been enshrined in the sermons of monks and friars from the moment they were known,[1] then in the *History of Voyages* [2] and also in the legal texts.[3] When he was in exile at Kingston, Bolivar wrote his *Letter from Jamaica* (1816) recalling the atrocities of the early conquerors, which he said " seemed to pass the bounds of human perversity ". In France,

[1] See in Prévost, *Histoire générale des Voyages XII*, p. 170 f., the sermon of the Dominican Montesino in San Domingo in 1512. He preached in the presence of the Admiral and was ordered to " stop his invectives ".

[2] *Ibid.*, XII, pp. 128 f., 153 f., 179 f.

[3] Gourd, *Chartes Coloniales*, 1885, II, p. 228 f. (New England).

these things were already discussed in the days of the Old Monarchy.[1]   Then, under Louis Philippe and the Second Empire, there were debates, still unforgotten, about the cruelties of the fighting in Algeria.   In 1845 there occurred the " Dahra Affair ", one of the first cases where public protest was made against the conduct of a colonial conqueror.   The commander of the French Battalion, Colonel, later Marshal, Pélissier, had, we must remember, conducted lengthy but unsuccessful negotiations with the natives before exterminating them by fire ! [2]   Public opinion was vigorously indignant at his conduct.   This moment saw the birth of the newspaper as a new power, which was henceforward to control the acts and deeds of generals.   There followed an interpellation in the House of Peers led by the Duke of Moscova. Marshal Soult, the Minister of War, who at first wished to plead Not Guilty, was compelled to admit that a wrong had been committed and General Bugeaud was driven to venture an apologia for Pélissier in the paper *Moniteur Algérien*.   The newspaper articles were violent and the memory of them persisted. So the conqueror has become subject to public opinion ; a rostrum has been] set up where every act is judged.[3]   This is a new state of affairs, there is a new code of conduct to which the early conquerors had not been obliged to conform.

Abuses by the *Administrators* may arise from their legislation and methods of government after the occupation.   A wave of opinion very soon arose in Algeria against the abuses of government.   In 1856, under the Second Empire, another unforgotten episode occurred : the " Doineau Affair ".   Doineau, Captain of the Arab Bureau, was administering the town of Tlemcen. He instigated the murder of an *agha* in a stage-coach.   He was condemned to death, but the sentence was commuted and he served in fact only five years in prison.   The newspapers launched a campaign against this leniency.   Since then, the newspaper, the novel, and the pamphlet, have given the French colonial administration a bad time.[4]

[1] P. de Vaissière, *St-Domingue*, 1909, p. 190 f.

[2] [A whole Arab tribe had taken refuge in a large cave at Dahra.   Pélissier had large fires made in the entrance, and the entire body of recalcitrants perished from suffocation.   EOL]

[3] See the typical book of P. Vigné d'Octon, *La gloire du sabre*, 1900.   M. Irisson d'Hérisson also criticised the conquest of Algeria in *La chasse à l'homme, Guerre d'Algérie*, 1891.   See in general Yves de la Brière, *Guerre coloniale et théologie catholique, Études*, Sept. 5, 1935.

[4] A.-H. Canu's book, *La pétaudière coloniale*, 1894, is a violent attack on the " vultures " (*corbeaux*) of the Administration, " a regular gang of malefactors ". And E. d'Arvay's novel *Vers la colonisation*, 1902, p. 172 f., is an indictment of the bureaux.   See also Urbain Gohier, *La Révolution vient-elle*, 1906, pp. 169 f. and 293 f.

Repressions and punishments carried out in the colonies have in the past excited disapproval amongst the English too. The events following the Sepoy War or Indian Mutiny of 1857 were acidly denounced both in English and French newspapers, especially in the *Journal des Débats*. In this same connection the *Revue des Deux-Mondes* itself wrote that in the colonies men should act not as " rapacious drovers " but as " benevolent shepherds of men " ; this phrase echoes the Christian image of The Good Shepherd.[1] We also meet with denunciation of excesses committed by native authorities retained in power by the French, which, it is sometimes said, are aggravated and even fostered by the French.[2]

Lastly, abuses by the *Exploiters*. These include all excesses committed in developing the resources of a country to the injury of the inhabitants ; the abuses by the colonists, neither by the soldiers nor by the government offices. In our day this takes the first rank among protests. Thus there is the abuse, or what is reputed to be the abuse, of forced labour in the colonies, especially if it is used in private interest. This is now forbidden by the new laws. It is now also forbidden even where used in the public interest, and for the benefit of the State and not of the individual. Recently a chorus of maledictions was raised over the Congo-Ocean railway from Brazzaville to Pointe Noire, for this line took a heavy toll of human life ! [3] Even under the Old French Monarchy people were denouncing the over-severe labour imposed on slaves in the " American Islands ". The institution of slavery itself was not at that time questioned, but people wished to see it humanised. The missionaries for their part also hurled curses against the traders, the fur-traders, and the trappers, who bartered their " fire-water " with the natives, and carried on a traffic in brandy. In 1702 a missionary in

---

[1] *Journal des Débats*, Oct. 24, 1857 (Xavier Raymond) ; *Revue des Deux-Mondes*, May 1858. There were also great polemics in the English papers of 1919 on the subject of General Dyer's terrible repression of the insurrection in the Panjab. The *Morning Post* raised a public subscription for him ! [The English student will be well advised to acquaint himself with the actual facts of the unfortunate occurrences in the Jalianwala Bagh. After full debate, the House of Lords completely vindicated General Dyer's conduct at Amritsar and their opinion was corroborated in the libel action, O'Dwyer v. Nair, before Mr. Justice McCardie and an English jury, and since then by informed public opinion. EOL]

[2] Thus : Pierre Bertrand, *Le Progrès Civique*, Oct. 29, 1921.

[3] A clamorous piece of reporting by Albert Londres, *Terre d'ebène.—La Randonnée de Samba Diouf* by the brothers Tharaud is a revelation of the forced recruitment for the French army. The enlisted men were known as " volunteers with a halter round the neck."

Canada, Father de Carheil, lodged a violent protest against the sale of liquor to the " overseas savages ".[1]

If these are the *aims* of reform, who are to be the *agents* ? They are diverse, and in every country they are of three categories : the *dominators*, the *dominated* and the *outsiders* : three groups in whose heart the reforming spirit is bound sooner or later to spring to life.

The *Dominators*. It is they, we must admit, who have been the first to criticise the abuses of their own power ! Self-criticism or self-questioning ! A confession of sin, by the country which has committed the sin ! You cry *mea culpa* with two voices : a personal or a collective voice ; the voice of an individual or of a group. Societies exist to-day created for the express purpose, proclaimed in their statutes, of bringing about the reform of abuses.

In considering those rulers who seek to reform their rule, let us note their *methods* and their *motives*. *How* and *why* do they desire to reform the exercise of their own authority ?

Let us first deal with their *methods* or their *means*. Sometimes they have acted semi-officially, and sometimes officially. In the first place, and more especially, they have acted semi-officially. It has been particular individuals who have campaigned against blunders . . . or against horrors. In Portugal, an imperial poet, the famous Camoëns, wrote about 1555 a whole pamphlet, *Disparities in India*,[2] a pamphlet which is a catalogue of the " follies " of the Portuguese in Hindustan. Here, for the first time, we meet a satire on the colonist. The result was that Camoëns was exiled to China. In Spain, Baltasar Gracian in his *Criticon* of 1653 very severely condemned the ways of his compatriots in the colonies. They deceive the Indians, he said, by a bogus trade in worthless glass, and the French play a similar trick on the Spaniards " who are, so to speak, Indians to them ". They thus take from them their silver and their gold. The individual writer was presently succeeded by the group. First the writers, then groups of persons, later societies, worked amongst the rulers for the reform of colonial abuses. First pamphleteers, then journalists, and in our day newspaper reporters.—It is above all the literary folk who for the last half-century and more have taken the field with their novels or " enquiries " or " mis-

---

[1] F. Parkman, *The Old Régime in Canada*, 1898, pp. 372 f. and 483 f. It was missionaries again who in about 1905 denounced the Germans' cruelties in the Cameroons. Chazelas, *Cameroun et Togo*, 1931, p. 59 f.

[2] *Disparates na India.*

sions " against the sins of the rulers.[1] Important books devoted to the various countries of the French colonial Empire, have revealed how far this criticism of abuses has been displayed, especially in novels.[2] It was Victor Hugo, the " patriot of humanity ", who spoke in *Les Misérables* in 1862 of " Algeria too harshly conquered and with more barbarity than civilisation, as was India by the English ". Amongst the Netherlanders a celebrated writer, who took the pseudonym Multatuli but whose real name was Dekker, exercised considerable influence. He had lived for a long time at Amboina ; he was recalled as having shown himself too sympathetic to the natives ! He published in 1862 an extremely famous novel, *Max Havelaar*, which is the ancestor of such novels of to-day as are more or less anti-colonial.[3] In it he voices his indignation over the cruel excesses of slavery and forced labour. His name will be remembered both in Holland and in France because of the movement which he started.[4]

After the writers came the groups and the societies, formed to combat the errors of authority. They were not in the first instance founded specially for this purpose. When the Lyons Academy for instance opened a large congress in 1783 to discus, " The Consequences of the Discovery of America ", the rival dissertations struck a questioning protesting note : thus Auget de Montyon contended that far from being purely a benefit to mankind, the discovery had been a real disaster for the human race, and certainly a fatal catastrophe for the original inhabitants of the New World.[5] Later came the *ad hoc* associations founded with the expressed intention of " protecting " the inhabitants of the colonies, by protesting against the failings of their govern-

---

[1] We must not draw up a Bibliography : there would be too many entries ! In England T.E. Donne, *The Maori*, 1927 (Chap. 26, *The Barbaric White Man*). In France one of the most typical is J. Viot, *Déposition de blanc*, 1932 (against the Dutch in New Guinea). The action of *women* in this connection is very marked as is to be expected : there are Andrée Viollis and Denise Moran, for instance. The rôle of the sex in revolutionary and reform movements has yet to be studied.

[2] The *cartoon* and the *film*, as media for criticising abuses, would need to be studied. It was Tony Johannot's picture, reproduced in engravings, which immortalised the Dahra affair. In our own day, see Crapouillot's *Atrocités coloniales*, 1935 ; the film *Ombres blanches* produced by Metro-Goldwyn (1929).

[3] *Encyclopædia Britannica*, 14th Ed. 1930, s.v. *Dekker, E. D.* [There is an English trans. of *Max Havelaar* by W. Siebenhaar with an Introduction by D. H. Lawrence, 1927. EOL]

[4] One of the best accounts of this attitude of mind is Lapie's *La Justice par l'État*, 1899, p. 140 f.

[5] Montyon, *Conséquences qui ont résulté pour l'Europe de la découverte de l'Amérique*, 1792 ; B. Fay, *L'esprit révolutionnaire . . . ,* 1925, p. 132 f. D. Mornet, *Les origines intellectuelles de la Révolution française*, 1933, p. 396 f.

ments. In this spirit the Anti-Slavery societies played their part. In 1882 the *Indian Rights Association* was established in the United States to intervene in favour of the Indians with the government.[1] And in France the *Society for the Protection of the Natives* was formed in 1880 which, however, died out in 1884.[2] Twenty years later a persevering campaign was waged in the *Revue Indigène* of M. Paul Bourdarie. In 1898, under the ægis of the Permanent International Peace Bureau, Miss Ellen Robinson founded in Turin a *Committee on Relations with Weaker Races*. With a questionnaire of a dozen questions it opened an enquiry into methods of abolishing " abuses ". In 1900 a devout Roman Catholic, Paul Viollet, a Frenchman, founded an *Association for the Defence of the Natives*. Other societies were started in other countries with the same object. In 1913 these groups, eleven of them in all, amalgamated in an International Bureau of Natives' Defence Leagues which, as was natural, was set up in Geneva. For these protesting societies were nearly always Protestant, even if not so in origin. Most of them were led by pastors or professors.[3] Since the War [i.e. 1914–18. EOL] other committees have been set up in various countries.[4] The Roman Catholics have here developed a very active rivalry with the Protestants.[5]

Reform was also tackled *Officially*. For the authorities were long since somewhat disturbed by these attacks of individuals. We have long had *confessions* of sins and errors by their authors. The Emperor Charles V made vain attempts at reform. The " Reformers " whom he despatched were unable to put an end to abuses. Nuñez de Vela acted with great vigour in 1543 ; but after two years of hard struggle the famous Carvajal had his throat cut ![6] In 1746 the Spaniards sent one of the King's Counsellors, the economist John de Ulloa, to the colonies to investigate all the abuses reported by Baltasar Gracian. We

[1] F. W. Hadge, *Handbook of American Indians*, I, 1907, p. 608 f. (bibliogr.).

[2] *Bulletin* edited by A. de Lamothe. There are, or have been, also the *Anti-Slavery & Aborigines Protection Society*, the Swiss *Ligue pour la défense des indigènes*, the German *Gesellschaft für Eingeborenenschutz*. Many South American societies run a Bulletin called *Pro Indigena*, 1909.

[3] In this connection and for this attitude of mind, see the Protestant Ch. Gide's lecture *Le devoir colonial*, 1897 (Anduze). His nephew, André Gide, is also a Protestant : his *Voyage au Congo*, 1927, is an anthology of abuses.

[4] On these new groups, see G. Gautherot, *Le communisme aux colonies*, p. 83 and note 1 and *passim*.

[5] E. Dermenghem, *Les catholiques et les abus coloniaux*, Vie Intell., Nov. 1928 ; J. Folliet, *Morale internationale*, 1935.

[6] Prévost, XIII, p. 145 f. ; cf. p. 228 f. on the reformer Pierre de la Gasca who was sent, without success, in 1549.

possess Ulloa's report ; it is an authoritative admission that reforms were urgently needed.[1]

For the last hundred years and more, there have been in France many occasions on which official admission was made of various abuses in the colonies. On the question of slavery a Commission sat for five years, from 1837 to 1841, whose reports and documents were made public. A little later, both in 1845 and in 1856—as we have said—the Chambers themselves declared that many excesses must be stopped.

Such are the methods. Let us examine the *motives* of the reformers amongst the ruling race. The motives are of two kinds : the interest of the colonists and the interest of the subjects.

The interest of the colonists. For in the first instance—and we tend nowadays to forget this—it was in the interest of the emigrants, the occupiers, the exploiters, that protests were raised against abuses of power. This was the principal reason for the emancipation of the South Americans.[2] Captain Basil Hall had seen the struggle in 1818, in 1824 and in 1830 ; in his *Voyages* he says that it was fought to get rid of restrictions and exactions and to attain liberty and justice. In the French colonies, it was the colonists, the civilians, who fought against the soldiers. They led an attack on the " military régime ", which form of government is of course everywhere necessary at the beginning. For the military are always tempted to perpetuate their authority : " Here I am and here I stay ! " is a soldier's motto ! In this Lyautey has been a remarkable exception ; he wanted to see civil government established as soon as possible. This was the quarrel of the " Arab bureaux " in French Algeria. Daudet's books, his *Tartarin* in particular, sounded the charge against the *képi*. Military power, which is at the same time judicial power, has always, since the days of Montesquieu, offended the French sense of what is right, for it unites instead of separating the two forms of authority.

The satire most certainly struck home. Later, pamphlets appeared, written by the colonists themselves, recounting their misfortunes, and proclaiming their discontents. The civil power then became the object of a fresh attack. A book—now forgotten—called *Twenty Years in Algeria* by Villacrosse [3] shows that

---

[1] James Bryce, *South America*, 1912, II.
[2] See : M. André, *La fin de l'empire espagnol d'Amérique*, 1922.
[3] A. Villacrosse, *Vingt ans en Algérie, ou tribulations d'un colon racontées par lui-même . . .* , 1874. The rôle of the *légistes*, who defended the laws, was also marked in Algeria. Larcher, Professor of Law, was a resolute opponent of the administration.

the " Algerian trouble " is by no means a new thing.   It is the
very depressing story of the disappointments of a colonist.   A
more recent book by Le Goupils is a pendant to it.   Le Goupils [1]
was a professor who went among the Kanakas of New Caledonia
as a planter.   The title of his book is eloquent : " *How you Cease
to be a Colonist.*"   He shows no tenderness towards the French
administration ! [2]

In our day, however, it is not the interest of the colonists,
but above all the *interest of the subjects*, which has made the ruling
peoples spring to attention.   We have got to the stage of
denouncing and stigmatising all the excesses of domination and
exploitation which affect our subjects : abuses of punishment or
of repression : brutalities and cruelties which have aroused a
fine fury of indignation : often sincere, sometimes artificial : for
journalists and writers like to talk of horrors : " drama " and
" crime " yield first-class headlines !   It is much easier to flatter
the public than to guide it !   Publicity plays the rôle of a Reformer,
it is Æsop's parable of the tongues, in more than one sense.

Thus it was among the rulers themselves that criticism of
abuses first made itself heard, but later it was taken up by the
ruled.   Outbursts of indignation are contagious.   It was inevitable that protests and questionings expressed at home should
catch the ear of subjects abroad.   The progress of our own
enlightenment inoculated our subjects with an attitude of mind
apt to demand reforms, to ask questions and to make claims.
For some thirty years now, the discussion of French errors has
been as lively in French-dominated countries as at home in
France.   It began first amongst the civilised, sometimes the
ultra-civilised, sometimes the pseudo-civilised, who thanks to
the French themselves are legion in the French colonies : later
it filtered down to the semi-civilised or the uncivilised or even
what it would be nearer the mark to call the " pre-civilised " ;
so it arose first amongst the " advanced " and then amongst the
" backward ".

We thus find it amongst the Annamites and the Javanese
as the civilised, sometimes ultra-civilised.   With the spread of
education there has arisen amongst them a great impatience of
abuses real or false, long-standing or imaginary : this is not the
place to judge.   In olden days in Annam, civilisation was

---

[1] H. Le Goupils, *Comment on cesse d'être colon. Six années en Nouvelle-Calédonie*, 1920.
Cf. Marc Le Goupils, *La crise coloniale en N-C, La science sociale*, Oct. 1905.

[2] See also : A. Vollard, *La politique coloniale du père Ubu . . .* , 1919 (reprinted
in *Les réincarnations du père Ubu*).

represented by the mandarins alone, who were by upbringing conservative, and by tradition upholders of the *status quo*. With the spread of education it is the students who have led the van in the drama of struggle. In speeches, in newspapers, constantly suppressed and constantly reappearing, they have raised public protests, but always under the inspiration and at the instigation of French " directors ". In Java long since—and long before the same thing occurred in French Indo-China—there has been a reform movement amongst the students, Javanese or Sumatran, young men who have long been studying, not only in Batavia but in Holland too, and especially in Leyden where they are to be found in great numbers. It is through this contact of the East Indies with the Netherlanders that the Malays indirectly caught the infection. In Algeria, complaints about French errors began to be heard from the very beginning of the occupation : that was in 1883 and they are fighting by 1936 ! [1]

A still graver problem confronts authority : the wave of protest is seen, sooner or later, in semi-civilised or non-civilised countries ; amongst peoples who are still in a state of barbarism or semi-barbarism, but who nevertheless assert their claims. Sometimes they do so by insurrection, sometimes, at the later stage, by published writings.[2] For education is penetrating even to them, and as in more advanced countries it is by speech and writing that they give expression to their opinion. This is so with the Kabyles of Algeria. Both the Kanakas and the Bantu peoples, " primitive " though they remain, have things that they desire and things that they demand.

With the Kabyles, it is a very old story. From the very moment of the first French conquest in 1857, poems were to be found amongst them in which the French were freely and acidly judged. I have before me at this moment a Kabyle poem which passed from hand to hand a few years after the 1857 occupation.[3] It runs :

The day when we learnt " Good evening " (that is to say the day when we learnt to say " bonsoir " in French), we received a blow on the jaw, and were surfeited with locked prisons :

The day when we learnt " Good day ", we received a blow on the nose, blessings ceased for us ;

---

[1] Sid Hamdan ben Othman Khodja, *Aperçu . . . sur la Régence d'Alger intitulé en arabe " Le Miroir "*, French trans. 1833, Paris, Goetschy, 456 pp. This is a prosecutor's indictment of French errors.

[2] See the early, moving petition of the Cherokees to the American Congress in 1829, recorded in Tocqueville's *Démocratie en Amérique*, 1835, II, p. 308 f.

[3] J. Liorel, *Kabylie du Jurjura*, 1892, p. 503 f.

The day when we learnt " Thank you ", we received a blow on the throat, we inspire less fear than a sheep ;

The day when we learnt " Pig ", a dog was of more account than we ;

The day when we learnt " Brother ", we received a blow on the knee, we walk shamed to the breastplate.

Thus in the form of a recitation this poem was handed on in mosques and on the march, passing by day and night from mouth to mouth : a protest against the French.

The Kanakas of New Caledonia, a completely primitive people who remained cannibals by tradition, long ago staged the revolution of 1878 and also set up claims. We know this from Louise Michel, the famous revolutionary, known as the " Red Virgin " who was deported from France to the Kanaka country after the Commune. She was a very gifted woman and wrote a very pleasing, little-known book *Kanaka Legends*.[1] In it she records the grievance of the Kanakas which is similar to that of the Kabyles, and which indicates the aspiration of these Melanesians to kind treatment and progress.

The same aspiration is found amongst the Bantu of Central and South Africa. We know this from a work by the Bantu writer, D. Jabavu—a graduate of course !—who has drawn up a list of the Blacks' grievances against the White Man.[2] These grievances take different forms with the advanced and the backward native. The backward natives, still dominated by their own traditions, have their grievances : taxes and work, the requisitioning of supplies, in fine, the whole machinery of government which is not theirs and which, it is easy to imagine, seems harsh to them and weighs heavily on them, inasmuch as it imposes on them a new scheme of life. The advanced natives have other complaints, and we meet their opposition in French countries ; they want jobs, they want positions, they want salaries and pay ; they want lots of things and lots of different things. The distinction between the two types is very marked in South Africa, but in the French Empire too. Arabs and Berbers have different cravings. They create different problems requiring different solutions.

As agents of reform, however, we have to reckon nowadays not only with rulers and ruled, but also with *outsiders*. The

---

[1] Louise Michel, *Légendes Canaques*, pp. 49–50.
[2] In : L. Schapera, *Western Civilisation and the Natives of South Africa*, 1934, Chap. XII, pp. 285–99.

opinion of foreigners is a great, new factor in colonial empires.[1] Account must now be taken of foreign opinion. So we have now got the grand-stand or the strangers' gallery looking on and criticising like spectators at a game ! There is a public who hisses the actors. The setting and the climate has completely changed. No empire is any longer a closed retort in a laboratory.

These outsiders, you may be sure, are often interested rivals ; peoples who possess colonies of their own, or who would like to ; the " have-nots " who come to criticise from motives of self-interest or ambition. The " haves " criticise each other ; the " have-nots " criticise the " haves ". It is nothing new for the English to run down the French, or for the French to make mock of the English. We can hear Balzac saying that if the French Empire is admirably governed and administered, the English Empire is the scene of excesses and mistakes ! " England," he says, " is an infamous guzzler of treasure against whom India will cry out for all eternity ! "[2] It is the mother instinct of " mother-countries " which thus finds voice.

In our day, it is the foreign countries properly called " have-not " or, to use the fashionable phrase, " disinherited " countries, which are without colonies,[3] states without empires, which sit in judgment on our old empires ; covetous countries, they might be called, which may be either European or American. Countries too which do not want to, or are unable to, become imperial countries. Such is the tribunal of opinion, and it is an international tribunal. Sweden, Norway, Denmark and Switzerland are our vigilant judges, Switzerland particularly, where over a quarter of a century ago they founded the " Swiss League for the Defence of the Aborigines ". Northern countries and Protestant countries : for religion always takes a hand ! The acts and deeds of nations are nowadays severely criticised in neighbouring countries and in distant countries. The gallery is the universe.

The action of outsiders in reforming colonial abuses has also employed two methods or two means : the semi-official and the official.

Semi-official, especially at the outset : in these countries,

---

[1] Thus we find de Tocqueville in his *Démocratie en Amérique*, 1835 (II, p. 297 f.), sentimentally shedding tears of pity over the " sad picture " of Red Indian misery.
[2] H. de Balzac, *Maximes et Pensées*, 1856 (Hetzel), p. 120.
[3] The great question of to-day is, as we know, whether equality and community ought not to regulate the relations between nations. Democracy between States : the tendency is logical : many " plans " have been drawn up to this end. See J. M. Bonn, *The Economic Equality of States*, *Economica*, Nov. 1935 (solutions proposed).

whether rival or disinterested, it was individual writers who
investigated the colonial empires : people who had no " mandate " but who were skilful in sowing seeds of indignation.   Under
the Old French Régime, a Swiss who was in San Domingo
criticised very sharply the French administration there.[1]   Some
thirty years ago there was the famous case of the Belgian Congo.
The agitation about the " Congo Affair " was led in England,
America, France and in Belgium by the opinion which a group
of writers unleashed against the blunders and crimes of the Congo.
There was the well-known American humourist, Mark Twain—
his real name was Samuel Clemens—there was the French Pierre
Mille, there was finally the Belgian Vandervelde, who between
them created a movement for the reforming of the status of the
Congo.   This ended in 1908 in the Congo's being annexed by
Belgium.[2]   The " Independent State " became a colony . . . to
the great advantage of the inhabitants.

Later, the action of outsiders was taken *officially*.   There
were public conventions and agreements, between one State and
another, usually made in Geneva, drawn up to limit for present
and future the authority of the great colonial empires.   At the
moment of writing, the great empires have thus lost all real
autonomy ; for they are no longer free to decide or to legislate ;
they are tied by engagements ; they are subject, though of their
own free will, to outside control.   The *contract* has superseded
the *statute*.   The actual beginning of this may be seen in conventions of some considerable time ago ; those of 1885 and
1890 : the Conventions of Berlin.   Actually also in some of
more recent date : the Treaty of Saint-Germain in 1919 which
aimed, amongst other things, at the abolition of slavery in the
colonies.   Like the agreement of 1885, known as the Act of
Berlin, the Treaty of Saint-Germain consecrated the outsider's
intervention in the government of colonial empires.

It is, however, the League of Nations and the International
Labour Organisation which have set the seal on this intervention.
An International Colonial Law has thus been created.[3]   By
means of conventions or " recommendations " the outsider has
thrust his oar in, now by forbidding, now by reforming, practices
current in the colonial empires !   On the expression of international opinion there follows international legislation.   Colonial

---

[1] P. de Vaissière, *St-Domingue*, 1909, p. 168 f.
[2] See especially : Pierre Mille, *Le Congo Léopoldien*, 1905 ; E. Vandervelde, *La
Belgique et le Congo*, 1909 ; and on the same lines O. Mirabeau's novel, *La 628-E-8.*
[3] G. Scelle, *Précis de droit des gens*, I, 1932, p. 142 f.

law is no longer . . . colonial, I mean thereby confined within the colony : we have got heteronomy, not autonomy. In this way the reform of abuses has made much speedier progress in the last twenty years than it had done before.

We are face to face with a new fact, a new status, a new World ! Let us emphasise this. States and empires have had to surrender their isolation ; they are no longer closed circles. The outsider's influence has nibbled away their power. They can no longer pass their own isolated laws, they can no longer conduct their separate administration ; they are governed by a common international law. A law accepted and endorsed ; a law deriving from a contract or from a convention, but a law which, like Rousseau's Social Contract, hamstrings the liberty of the contracting parties in the future. No one's house is now his castle ; no one is any longer master in his own house.

CHAPTER XXVII

REFORM OF EXPLOITATION

The movement for colonial reform was first directed against the abuses of domination, but it was directed also, as we have said, against the abuses of exploitation.[1] The attack was first made against one particular abuse of exploitation : slavery and forced labour. This was an abuse in a new sense, and considered an abuse only in new times. In olden days it was an accepted institution, whose existence was long unchallenged ; one day it suddenly became a crime to be expiated. It was the *Antislavery* or Abolitionist movement which infused morality into the question of legality. Two ideas were behind the movement : slavery was held to be a sin of a religious nature because of the *brutality* and the *indignity* which were its accompaniments ! [2]

Brutality, or cruelty. The exercise of brutality was early condemned in the physical and corporal interest of the slave. Brutality is a sin against humanity in that it causes suffering and often death.

Indignity, or humiliation. The institution of slavery was condemned also in early times as a crime against both the spiritual and corporal dignity of the person or individual. In distant countries, and they were not a few, where the slaves were happy and well cared for by their masters, and lived free from anxiety or fear ; in countries where there was therefore at least in the ordinary way no question of brutality, there always nevertheless remained indignity and humiliation in the status of the slave. Servitude in itself, slavery in itself, was a crime against the person, inasmuch as God had given to man the gift of liberty. The American Channing condemned slavery in the name of human dignity, of natural law, and of divine law ! every man is god, being created in the image of God.[3]

Yet slavery found those to defend it. It found its defenders

---

[1] First and foremost *commercial exploitation* : the struggle is an old one, conducted by the colonies themselves against the *Colonial Pact* and in favour of free trade relations : M. M. Miller, *American Debate*, 1911, Vol. I, Chap. I, has given the description of it for the English.

[2] See in general, E. Ghersi, *La schiavitù e l'evol. de la politica coloniale*, 1935. Cf. M. N. Work, *A Bibliography of the Negro in Africa and America*, 1928.

[3] W. E. Channing, *Slavery*, 1835, French trans., 1855. Cf. E. Laboulaye, *La liberté religieuse*, 1858, p. 231 f.

especially where slavery was being attacked. They fought a long and hard battle with the opponents of slavery. Its champions were at first triumphant champions and later shamefaced ones. Triumphant champions pleading that it was a moral and legitimate institution. Then, more and more—a sign of the new times—pleading that it was necessary and useful ; in other words, " pleading guilty ", admitting that it ought to be abolished—but not just yet. We see in our own day the same development on the subject of forced labour.

The champions of slavery, then, especially in the last century,[1] pleaded that it was moral and legitimate. Quite a number of people, not only among the merchants trading in Nantes and Bordeaux, but also as we shall see among the writers, defended the institution in the name of the right to govern with which God had invested rulers.

Melon, the famous author of the *Essai politique sur le commerce*, and himself a native of Bordeaux, includes in it an intolerant, exaggerated apologia for colonial slavery. Let us, however, in preference read a forgotten work of the obscure moralist Abbé Janson " Concerning the Duties Appropriate to Every State of Natural and Civil Society ".[2] Chapter XXV discusses the Slave Trade. The author contends—and this was in 1787, the very year in which the society known as Friends of the Black Man [3] was founded—that the Slave Trade is always legitimate, on condition first that the slaves are sold by their own masters and not by traders, and secondly that the slaves are given religious instruction so that they may be Christianised, and thirdly that they should thereafter be humanely treated. These things being granted, the slaves, being their masters' property, might be sold. The coloured labourer could then be treated without scruple as an article of merchandise for sale. Such was the accepted opinion of the day. Fifty years later a new debate began. Even after 1830 several authors were still to be found pleading in favour of negro slavery as a moral institution. Adolfe Jollivet, for instance, who styled himself the " Negrophobe Deputy ", fought against emancipation with more than twenty pamphlets

---

[1] On this controversy under the Old French Régime : P. de Vaissière, *St-Domingue* . . . , 1909, pp. 154 f., 190 f. and 212 ; L. Deschamps, *Histoire de la question coloniale en France*, 1891, p. 328 f.—For Spain, G. Scelle, *Théories rélatives à l'esclavage en Espagne au XVIIᵉ siècle*, *Revue hist. doct. écon.*, V, 1912, pp. 200–27.

[2] *Des devoirs propres à chaque état de la société naturelle et civile*, p. 375 f. More recent Christian authors have, in the same spirit, stood for tempered slavery : Bautain, *Philosophie des lois*, 1869, p. 89 f.

[3] *Amis des noirs.*

written between 1840 and 1848, especially one of 1842 called *English Philanthropy*. He remained a fanatical advocate of slavery.[1]

A case was also made out for the *necessity* and for the *usefulness* of Negro slavery, if no longer for its moral justification.[2] The champions of the institution were now shamefaced, recognising the immorality of slavery, but maintaining that the common interest required its retention for at least a long time to come. Benjamin Franklin was, on religious grounds, an enemy of slavery, yet in his *Memoirs* of 1790 he declared that it would be necessary for a long time to keep the slaves : first, because of the need for labour, and secondly because of the indemnity which would have to be paid to their owners if they were set free. These two arguments were dished up again and again after Franklin's time. At about the same time a very distinguished colonial, Moreau de Saint-Méry, replying to Abbé Grégoire, was saying that slavery should be *softened* but not *abolished*. If you are going to introduce a Declaration of Rights for us here, said he, then good-bye to the colonies.[3]

In Jollivet's time, in the 1840's when slavery was about to be abolished, controversy was still vigorous ; and self-interest continued to make its voice loudly heard. As early as 1790, when the first attack was launched against the institution, the defenders of vested interests, whether traders or colonists, had raised a loud outcry : Dubuc, for instance, a merchant of Nantes, and Abeille, a trader of Marseilles. The latter published in 1790 a book entitled *A Rapid Survey of the Colonies*,[4] in which he defended slavery on material grounds. The chief defender, as we have just said, was Moreau de Saint-Méry, who proclaimed himself an enemy of free labour, because of the need to exploit the American islands, which would be reduced by abolition, so he contended, to ruin and despair. Forty years later the same plea was advanced. Toussenel, a disciple of Fourier's, said : we must regulate but not abolish. Abolition would ruin the Antilles to the benefit of India. Let us not be taken in by English designs ; and let us tide over the transition by timely forced labour ![5]

[1] *De la philanthropie anglaise.* Cf. also Granier de Cassagnac, *De l'affranchissement des esclaves*, 1837, and *Voyage aux Antilles*, 1840. He was a declared champion of slavery.
[2] On the controversy after 1789, see P. Gaffarel, *La politique coloniale de 1789 à 1830*, 1908, p. 6 and *passim.*—And the curious memorandum of L.-N. Baudry de Lozières, *Les égarements du nigrophilisme*, 1802.
[3] A. Elicona, *Moreau de Saint-Méry*, 1934 (thesis), pp. 84 f., 98 f. and 106.
[4] *Aperçu rapide sur les colonies.*
[5] Toussenel, *Les Juifs rois de l'époque* (1846), 3rd Ed. 1886, II, p. 239 f.—Stendhal in his *Mémoires d'un Touriste* of 1837 (Ed. C. Lévy, I, p. 15 f.) is very reticent. He assures us that the slave, being free from care, is often happy, " but Europe will teach him that he is unhappy."

Though it is less than a hundred years ago since the supporters of slavery found their voice, there had long been opponents of the system or at least would-be reformers of it. The reformers wished to see it abolished and done away with.

We have already seen that there were opponents of slavery in ancient times. Let us recall that there were among the Ancients men who preached freedom for the slave.[1] It was certainly the recollection of the Stoics, Greek and Roman, which in the century before last quickened men's minds anew. Zeno and Epictetus had condemned slavery as a product of war and an offence against right. The Roman Seneca was the first, after the Stoics, formally to state, as he did in his *Letters*, that the slave is a man and not a thing, that he is a person with a soul in his body, that he should have the dignity due to his humanity and that he cannot therefore be an object of traffic. He should be treated as one of the family. Here we meet the concept of the indignity of slavery.

In modern times we find Montesquieu, in the middle of the Age of Enlightenment nearly two centuries ago, fighting slavery in the name of morality and of human dignity.[2] For in 1740 or thereabouts public opinion was prepared for this line of thought by the revived memory of the classics. An obscure movement seems to have been at work in men's minds. The year 1740 saw Marivaux's comedy, *The Isle of Slaves*,[3] heavily charged with the spirit of reform. He pictures some masters and slaves landed together on a desert island where the slaves seize power. They rule over their former masters, not in order to oppress them, as the masters had formerly oppressed the new rulers, but in order to educate them and cure them of their wickedness ! " We are not avenging ourselves on you," said the slave-chief, " but we are correcting you " ; and in the play after the lapse of three years the new slaves are set free, as many at least as have purged themselves of their pride. The dénouement of the play is conventional enough, but the plot is revolutionary. The very foundation of slavery, the very principle of the system is undermined in the name of dignity and of freedom, these rights of the human race.

How was this movement able to manifest itself ? It had its *methods*, its *motives* and its *effects*.

---

[1] P. Allard, *La philosophie antique et l'esclavage* in *Études d'histoire et d'archéologie*, 1899. Cf. C. Turgeon, *Les théories esclavagistes de l'ancien Orient, Travaux jurid. et écon. Université Rennes*, Vol. X, 1930.

[2] E. Jameson, *Montesquieu et l'esclavage*, 1910 (thesis).

[3] *L'Île des esclaves*. See C. Lenient, *La comédie du XVIII* siècle, I, p. 383 f.

It had its *methods* or perhaps rather its *agents*.   There were individual agents and collective agents, single persons and groups of persons who drew up various arguments and set various procedures in motion.   They appealed to that " sensibility ", that delicacy of feeling, to which at the time all hearts were susceptible, addressing themselves to sentiment and to emotion.[1] This writing and these speeches induced feelings of pity and worked up indignation.   More and more, society everywhere tends to be influenced by these deliberately prepared " campaigns " ; this is a subject worth the attention of sociologists.

Writings.   Some of these writings were *Novels* which, like *Paul et Virginie*, exercised great influence on sensitive souls. Others were *Pamphlets* which appeared at the two critical moments of which I have spoken when slavery was seriously attacked : first, round about 1790 and again round about 1840.   They were for the most part short pamphlets which served up *ad nauseam* a re-hash of all the moral arguments against slavery. But repetition is a recognised device of the preacher.—Novels and pamphlets, later plays and operas.[2]   Marivaux's comedy bears witness that opinion was publicly worked up.   From the first moment, as early as 1789, comedies and tragedies began to flourish, spreading amongst the general public the philosophic arguments first canvassed in the *salons*.   The theatre was the route by which the reforming spirit, generated in Society— sometimes at Court—reached the wider public.   Round about 1840, at the second critical moment, a comic opera met with great success : it was Scribe's *Black Code*,[3] produced in 1842. It represents in three acts the well-known story—already included in Raynal's *History of the Europeans in the East and West Indies* [4]— of the son of a Negress who, at the very moment when he is about to be sold, discovers his father !   Tears were shed over this half-caste rescued from his fetters : the distant ancestor of all the half-castes of fiction ! [5]

Lastly, there were *Poems* which were assigned their part and played it.   In 1823 the French Academy had set this subject for their annual Poetry Prize : " Ought slavery to be abolished ? "

---

[1] A typical work of this kind was Joseph La Vallée's *Le nègre comme il y a peu de blancs*, 1795, written for the express purpose " of making the Black Man loved ".
[2] See in general, E. Servais, *Les sources de Bug-Jargal* . . . , 1923 (Liège).
[3] *Le Code Noir.*
[4] *Histoire des Européens dans les Deux-Indes.*
[5] Addison's *Spectator* (1710–11), No. 11, tells the story of the Englishman who sells his native wife into slavery.   This story was also incorporated into Raynal's large book.

A little later in England Byron's narrative poem, the *Giaour* (1830), told, for the benefit of " ladies " in their " country-seats ", the story of a Muslim slave, the unfortunate girl Leta, who was killed, sewn up in a sack and thrown into the sea for having appeared to be in love with a Christian, a slave like herself. In revenge the Christian slave shortly afterwards slew their master. It appears that this story was true, and that Byron when in Greece had witnessed the occurrence. These poems, read in the great houses, opened the hearts of " gentlemen " to emotion and indignation. In America too, Longfellow tuned his harp for the cause of liberty.[1]

The writers had thus paved the way for legislation against slavery. But the *orators* also played their part : *speeches* are more potent to move and stir the mind than written words. *Campaigns* were organised for the purpose of arranging meetings, where speeches would arouse public sympathy and pity. These campaigns were known in Anglo-American speech as *Crusades*. Thus, a hundred years ago, Baron de Staël, the occluded husband of the famous letter-writer Madame de Staël, preached with great effect his Mission or Crusade. He travelled over the whole of France making speeches against the slave-traders ; he organised an Exhibition in Paris displaying the iron fetters which were made and sold in the city of Nantes for the cruel use of the traders.[2] By using these new methods of arousing pity—proclamation and display—the Baron was assuredly the forerunner of those " Demonstrations " which attract millions of audiences and spectators in the United States to-day.

These campaigns presently took on a protective colouring and not, as at first, a personal colouring. For societies were founded *ad hoc* to bring about the abolition of colonial slavery, and they fought their battle with both the written and the spoken word. This was necessary in the interests of " efficiency ". These Abolition Societies flourished in England and in France : the most important of them, to which we shall return later, was called, as early as 1787, *Friends of the Black Man*.[3] Very frequently, especially in the Anglo-Saxon countries, these campaigns were the work of women enthusiasts. It was women who played in this matter the leading rôle. Who will be able to gauge the influence women have exercised—influence of the first import-

---

[1] H. W. Longfellow, *Poems of Slavery*, 1842, and *Christus*, Part I.
[2] Comtesse J. de Pange, *Mme de Staël et les nègres*. *Nouvelles Littéraires*, April 2, 1932.
[3] *Amis des noirs*.

ance—in preserving, on the one hand, and on the other, in transforming established custom ? In the anti-slavery literature women's writings attained great success. In 1788 there appeared a poem by a clergyman's daughter, Hannah More, on *Slavery*, which roused the public to feelings of strong disapproval of the system. A year later in France the famous Olympe de Gouges wrote a drama in prose which was acted at the Théâtre-Français. It was a three-act play which created some stir, called *Negro Slavery or the Fortunate Shipwreck*.[1] Above all, there was the brilliant work of the American lady, Mrs. Harriet Beecher Stowe : *Uncle Tom's Cabin* (1852). Contrary to the general belief, this was not a work of imagination, but a collection of real facts with a slight touch of " romance " added in order to win people's sympathy.[2] In 1853 she published *A Key to Uncle Tom's Cabin*,[3] in which she relates the chief actual occurrences on which her famous book is based. Every country was moved and touched by *Uncle Tom's Cabin*. The readers of it were past counting ! [4]

These were the methods employed. Now for the *motives* and the *aims*. What were the motives and what were the arguments for fighting against Negro slavery ? Let us treat separately, as we have done above, the *usefulness* and the *morality* of the institution. The champions of slavery had pleaded first that it was moral and secondly that it was necessary. The opponents of slavery were bound to take up these points, but in the reverse order, dealing first with its alleged usefulness or necessity, and secondly with the question of humanity or morality.

Its *usefulness*. The 18th-century economists condemned the institution of slavery in their own interests. They therefore play the first rôle in the evolution of opinion. The French Physiocrats denounced forced labour as contrary to the progress of nations ; and they considered servile labour as less productive and less effective—" efficient " as we would say nowadays— than free labour. The Marquis de Mirabeau pleads for liberty

---

[1] *L'esclavage des Nègres ou l'heureux naufrage.*

[2] French trans. by Mme L. Belloc.—In the same spirit : Hildreth, *The White Slave, A New Picture of Slavery in America*, French trans. by F. Normand, 1870. In his *Mémoires*, under the date Aug. 23, 1853, H. de Viel-Castel describes Mrs. Stowe as a " thin little woman ", " a republican blue-stocking ", and says that *Uncle Tom's Cabin* is " the book of Protestant hypocrisy ", and " the gospel of philanthropic societies " ; despite his malevolence, he is not far wrong.—See a bitter criticism of Mrs. Stowe by Ch. Maurras, *Revue encyclopédique*, 1896, II, p. 518 f. : " What a lovely book might be written," he says, " in praise of slavery ! "

[3] French trans. *La clef de la Case de l'oncle Tom*, by Old-Nick and Ad. Joanne.

[4] See Edith E. Lucad, *La littérature anti-esclaviste, Étude sur Mme Beecher Stowe*, 1930 (thesis).

in work. So does a colonial Physiocrat, of whom I have already spoken, the worthy Poivre, who was Governor of Mauritius and Reunion. In 1767 he published a book called *Voyages of a Philosopher* [1] in which he sums up his colonial experience. He condemns Negro slavery, from the point of view of self-interest, inasmuch as the system was completely outworn and as a means of exploitation unproductive. [2]

Half a century later, Jean-Baptiste Say, famous upholder of the liberal spirit, attacked the principle of forced labour, still from the point of view of efficiency and productivity. Under the bourgeois King of France in the 1840's, the discussion I have been speaking of still hinged on utilitarian arguments, and the two parties opposed each other sharply and bitterly. [3]

Later, motives of *humanity* and arguments of *morality* made their appearance. Taking their stand on considerations of human dignity and kindness, people took up the fight, in speech and writing, against the enslavement of coloured folk. This line of thought developed simultaneously amongst the Anglo-Americans and the French.

With the Anglo-Americans the Puritan spirit was at work. Puritanism and Protestantism together roused them—as early as 1800—to condemn slavery on moral and humanitarian grounds. The dissenting Protestants known as Quakers were the very first to take up arms against American slavery. A certain American, John Woolman, for instance, published *Considerations on the Keeping of Negroes* in 1854. In this book he makes a strong appeal to humane feeling and pleads with passion for the liberation of the slaves. [4] A little later he found supporters amongst his fellow-countrymen. The Quakers had been for a century established in the New World, and the Quaker spirit had been transplanted with them. It was through Woolman's influence that even before the War of Independence a strong repudiation of Negro slavery had grown up in the United

[1] *Voyages d'un philosophe.*

[2] About the same time the Scot John Millar also condemned slavery from the point of view of its usefulness in his *Observations concerning the Distinctions of Ranks*, 1771, and his *Origin of the Distinction of Ranks*, 3rd Ed. 1781 ; 4th Ed. with Life by J. Craig, 1806. See, on the same lines, de Tocqueville, *Démocratie en Amérique*, 1835, II, p. 323 f.

[3] Bibliography in : *Commission . . . Esclavage, Rapport* (1843) pp. 11–16. See in particular, G. de Beaumont, *Marie, ou l'esclavage aux États-Unis*, 1836, *L'Abolitioniste français*, Bulletin de la Société d'abolition . . . de l'esclavage, 1845 ; (Gougenot des Mousseaux) *Des Prolétaires . . .* , 1846. A. de Tocqueville, *De l'abolition de l'esclavage in Études écon. polit. et littér.*, 1866 ; G. Bonet-Maury, *La France et le mouvement antiesclav. au XIXᵉ siècle in France, Christianisme et Civilisation*, 1907.

[4] See W. Riley, *Le génie américain*, 1921, p. 17 f.

States.[1]   As early as 1671 the English Quaker, George Fox, was condemning slavery.   In Georgia a Wesleyan, J. Oglethorpe, forbade all slavery in that state.   And it was the Quakers who in 1790 had the courage to found under Franklin's presidency the *Pennsylvania Society for Promoting the Abolition of Slavery* which sent a memorandum to Congress.   A Frenchman, Hector St. John de Crèvecœur, who had settled in America, published in 1782 a work which was widely read, *Letters from an American Farmer*, in which in the name of morality he very firmly attacked the institution of colonial slavery.[2]   The great names of the close of the century which made their mark in 1782 and 1789 in this fight against the indignity of servitude, are those of Jefferson, who later became President of the United States,[3] and above all the name of the English Wilberforce.[4]   These two, and many others, needed only to adopt the Quakers' themes.   The Quaker faith was a battering ram which profoundly and permanently shattered the institution of American slavery.   It also served the cause of the North against the South in the Civil War.   The American Anti-Slavery Society founded in 1833 in Philadelphia—always Philadelphia—certainly had this end in view.

These Quakers exercised an influence even on the French themselves.   For one of the founders, the chief founder indeed, of the *Friends of the Black Man*,[5] the famous Brissot,[6] had lived in London where he had met the Quaker Clarkson.   Clarkson was his teacher and through him taught the French.[7]   Necker, Raynal, Grégoire and Condorcet amongst others—Petion de Villeneuve, for instance, by his *Discourse on the Slave Trade*[8]

[1] This is recalled by Lady Simon in her book on *Slavery*, 1929.—See also Jacques Lambert, *Histoire constitutionnelle de l' Union américaine*, II, 1934, pp. 267 f. and 364 f. (bibliog.), who notes the character, at once self-interested and religious, of the Abolition movement. Cf. also M. M. Miller, *American Debate*, II, 1911, pp. 49 f., 98 f. and 156 f.

[2] H. C. Rice, *Saint-John Crèvecœur*, 1932 (thesis), *passim*.

[3] Jefferson, *Notes on Virginia*; a résumé of these will be found in Fay, *op. cit.*, p. 85.

[4] R. Coupland, *Wilberforce*, 1923.—Napoleon was influenced by him, as is shown by a document of his dated 1789, in which Wilberforce's arguments are summarised : Masson, *Napoléon inconnu*, II, 1895, p. 60 f.

[5] On this Society, see C. de la Roncière, *Nègres et négriers*, 1933, p. 145 f. ; L. Deschamps, *Les colonies pendant la Révolution*, 1898, pp. 15 f., 41 f. and 50 f. ; L. Cahen, *La Société des Amis des Noirs et Condorcet*, *Révol. franc.*, June 14, 1906.—Saint-Just was anxious to see the negroes set free, repatriated to their native Guinea, and supplied with land and implements.   He thus anticipated the creation of Liberia.   (*Œuvres de Saint-Just*, 1834, p. 419.)

[6] J.-L. Primo, *La jeunesse de J.-P. Brissot*, 1932, p. 216 f.   See his *Mémoires* (1754-1793) published by C. Perroud in 1912.

[7] Thomas Clarkson, *Summary View of the Slave Trade*, 1787 ; *Essay on the Impolicy of the Slave Trade*, 1788.

[8] *Discours sur la Traité des Noirs*.

(1790)—formed a large and influential group to campaign against the Slave Trade.[1] Their action secured the passing of a law in 1793 abolishing slavery. This abolition was merely a gesture showing how effective had been their agitation. Grégoire's writings came a little later.[2] What his action was everybody knows.

There were two other writers in France who followed, at some distance, the Quaker inspiration which had reached them through the Revolution : Victor Schoelcher and Charles Daïn. Schoelcher was a representative of the people in 1848, after having been a member of secret societies. In speeches and pamphlets he campaigned for twenty years against the enslavement of black workers.[3] The ultimate abolition of slavery which was carried through in France in 1848 was the ample reward of his efforts. But a less well-known name, that of Charles Daïn, ought not to be forgotten.[4] A Phalansterian [5] and a disciple of Fourier, this native of Guadalupe joined Schoelcher in the fight under Louis Philippe to bring about abolition. He preached, he published, he worked for fifteen years from about 1833 onwards, the year in which a great European Congress was opened in the name of Fourierism. He pleaded eloquently before this Congress the cause of abolition.

Such having been the methods and the motives of the battle against unlimited authority, it now remains for us to enquire about its *effects*. What influence had the struggle for Abolition on laws and institutions ? How did people, in practice, succeed in reforming authority by limiting its abuses—whether from self-interest or from sentiment ?

Under the Revolution, and in some places even before it, people had succeeded in getting slavery forbidden. But how many, many times had popes and emperors forbidden it already !

---

[1] In connection with this movement we have, in the very year of the Revolution (1789) (Pruneau de Pommegorge), *Disc. de la Nigritie*, p. 207 f. ; Frossard, *La cause des Esclaves nègres et des habitants de la Guinée* ; Bernardin, *Vœux d'un Solitaire*, 1789. In Abbé Dulaurens' *Arretin Moderne* (New Ed., I, p. 97 f.) we most unexpectedly find a plea for the Negroes. Mercier in his *Néologie, ou Vocabulaire de mots nouveaux*, records his disapproval of the words *Négricide* and *Négrier* (II, p. 364). See Anna J. Cooper, *L'attitude de la France à l'égard de l'esclavage pendant la Révolution*, 1925 (thesis).

[2] Abbé Grégoire, *De la littérature des Nègres* . . . , 1808 ; *De la Noblesse de la peau, ou du préjugé des blancs*, 1826.

[3] Especially his *De l'esclavage des noirs et de la législation coloniale*, 1833.

[4] *De l'abolition de l'Esclavage* (extract from the *Phalanges*), 1836.

[5] [The " Phalanx " was the name adopted by a body of American Transcendentalists who tried the experiment of a model socialist community for education and agriculture at Brook Farm in Massachusetts (1841–47). Their central building was known as the Phalanstery. EOL]

Many papal bulls had formally abolished slavery in Christian countries.[1] Impotent bulls, as ineffective as the famous document of the Emperor Charles V, known as the Grand Ordinance, which he issued in 1542 in response to the pleadings of Bishop Las Casas, and which announced the abolition of slavery throughout all Spanish territories. We have to wait till the French Revolution to see Negro slavery effectually abolished. Here we find two stages : first, prohibition of the *Slave Trade*, and secondly, prohibition of the *Employment* of slaves. The purchase and sale of slaves was first forbidden ; later—and this was more difficult—the employment of slaves.

The two stages, however, were completed within a few years in Western countries, in France and England over a hundred years ago. In France a first decree in 1793 was inoperative ; a second and effective decree dates from 1848. Article 6 of the Constitution ran : " Slavery cannot exist on any French territory." In England a law of 1833 forbade slavery in every form. The Convention of Saint-Germain in 1919 which solemnly proclaimed the abolition of slavery by all countries only recalled the prohibition pronounced first of all by France.[2] The abolition of slavery has been almost completely realised in the French colonial Empire. In law, if not quite always in practice, slavery is in the French colonial empire a thing of the past. If we must admit that there still are slaves in the Algerian *sudd*, in the towns of the M'zab and in Morocco, they exist against the wishes of our governments, the fact being that the *habitants* cling to their long-established customs and conspire to defy French laws.

The effects of the Anti-Slavery campaign have subsequently acquired a new aspect and a new value. When once slavery was abolished, the spirit of reform was free to attack yet another institution, which is a continuation of earlier slavery, namely, *forced labour* in the colonies. Under the Old French Monarchy, Governor Poivre, when in the Mascarene Islands, issued a decree in 1771 which greatly moderated forced labour by limiting both the weight and the size of the loads which porters might be asked to carry. This was—though the fact is generally ignored, especially at Geneva—the first step towards the modern movement against the hardships of forced labour. For it is only

---

[1] Pius II, for Guinea, as early as 1460 ; Urban VIII in 1639 : Benedict XIV in 1741 and Gregory XVI in 1839.

[2] [Ineffectively in 1793 ; effectively, not until 1848, fifteen years after England. EOL]

within the last fifteen years [1] that the spirit of protest has re-awakened, in new guise, to contend in the name of morality and humanity against colonial forced labour and has stirred the International Labour Organisation [2] to action. The evolution, or revolution, was completed in a few years, mainly between 1926 and 1930. It was marked by three stages, following each other at short intervals. There was first the Convention of 1926, passed by a very large number of States, which condemned forced labour in principle and on moral grounds, implying consequently the intention of abolishing it in time. Next came the 1929 Commission, which instituted an enquiry into the methods and abuses of forced labour in the colonial empires and published the famous Grey Book denouncing many excesses and drawing up arguments in favour of putting an end to forced labour.—Finally, there was the Convention or Resolution of 1930, which laid down two legislative rules for limiting compulsory service in the colonies. In the first place for the present : forced labour for *private* purposes is to be completely abolished in all cases and in every country. That is to say that no individual trader or colonist may henceforward make use of compulsory labour. Under the Mandate system the Mandatory is also absolutely forbidden to employ the expedient of forced labour. In the second place, there must be, says the Resolution, the abolition in due course, but with the least possible delay, of all forced labour even for *public* and Government purposes. In discussing France in particular, the Commission was forced to recognise that forced labour for public purposes might still be necessary— in the interest, of course, of the inhabitants themselves. To get rid of porterage, you must open roads ; to make roads you must have workers ! We come back again to the old battle of Necessity *versus* Morality . . . in many rounds ! But the Resolution demands that in time, and in as brief a time as possible, compulsory labour in the colonies shall cease, not only when performed for individuals but for governments also. Liberty for all ; Dignity for all ; *Dolce far niente* for all.

We see from this that unlimited authority is to-day dead and buried. Public opinion, worked up by pious propaganda, no longer tolerates the thought that disguised slavery in the colonies should interfere with the free activity—or inactivity—of the

---

[1] [Written in 1936. EOL]
[2] J. Fayet, *Travail et Colonisation*, 1931 (thesis) ; R. Mercier, *Le travail obligatoire* . . . , 1933 (thesis).

inhabitants.   People nowadays would endorse Proudhon's dictum in his *First Memorandum on Ownership*,[1] which might well serve as exordium to the collected discussions of the I.L.O. : " What is slavery ? " he asks.   " It is murder.   For the power to deprive a man of thought, of will, of personality, is a power of life and death . . . to make a man a slave, is to slay him ! "   That is how in France—always in France—the new spirit clothed itself in words.

[1] *Premier Mémoire sur la Propriété*, 1840.

CHAPTER XXVIII

HIERARCHIC PARTNERSHIP

From the plea for reformation of colonial power, men arrived at a new concept, the *partnership* or association of rulers and ruled : the idea of working out conjunction and union between them.

Partnership in the colonies has three phases or three stages which shade into each other. For it rests on an idea of *humanity*, on an idea of *equality* and on an idea of *fraternity*. Humanity, equality, fraternity : these are the three motives in this desire for partnership. Let us not look too closely to see whether for the inferiors humanity might not cloak resentment and protest against the superiors ; affection for the under-dog being— repressed hate for the superior : giving vent to the need of revenge, so fundamental a human need : raise up the savage, in order to cast down the civilised . . . It might well be so ! [1]

This idea of partnership was indeed included or formulated in the reformations of which we have spoken. About the year 1600, the " Inca ", Garcilaso de La Vega, who wrote a History of Peru,[2] spoke of the " reciprocal assistance ", as between relatives and good friends, which, he thought, might exist between masters and subjects : " mutual assistance ", as we should say, which, whether you like it or not, is a form of partnership. As in our day Savorgnan de Brazza writes in his *Correspondence* : " To make good use of the natives, to identify their interests and ours, to make them our natural allies, that was in my opinion one of the most important aims of my mission." To identify the interests : that is, in one sense, partnership.

The idea of partnership was first formulated in a spirit of *humanity* as a means of moderation. It was hoped thereby to introduce humanity into the relationships, in law and in practice, between rulers and ruled. In its first phase partnership remains *hierarchic* : there is no equality, but there is humanity and modera- tion ; there is partnership, but between un-equals, not between equals. There is collaboration and co-operation, but of the superior with the inferior. This, then, is what we might call the

---

[1] This is the thesis enunciated by the psychologist Max Scheler in his studies on sympathy : *L'homme du ressentiment*, French trans., pp. 111 f. and 121.

[2] French trans., *Histoire des Yncas, rois du Pérou*, 1704, II, p. 147.

first phase or stage of partnership : *hierarchic collaboration,* a prelude to that *equalitarian collaboration* which is full and complete partnership. When we speak of the conquerors educating the natives of a colony, we understand collaboration in the former sense ; for every form of education implies collaboration and acceptance ; since educator and educated must combine their effort ; but it is the hierarchic co-operation of a superior with an inferior, or, if you prefer, of a teacher with his pupil. Hence the relationships envisaged by this new mental attitude are no longer the patriarchal relations of father to son, but the relations of teacher to pupil, or of guardian to ward. The ruler is no longer a father, but a master ; he is the guardian, not the lord ; and the atmosphere between rulers and ruled will be that of the *school* and not of the family. The ruler is an instructor. In an article under the word " Colony " in his *Dictionary of the Moral Sciences* (1780) the forgotten Robinet, whom I have already quoted, says that the relationships between a colony and its metropolis should be conceived as " relations of apprenticeship ". The phrase expresses the position well. The rulers are educators and instructors ; we have got partnership, but it is hierarchic, not equalitarian. It is from this point of view that in his day people spoke of showing *consideration* for the natives ; as, a hundred years later, they were to talk of showing *respect (égards).*[1] Restif de la Bretonne wished people to be just and humane and not to " segregate " the natives as if they were " brutes or wicked people ". A hundred years later, Paul de Rousiers, a disciple of Le Play, was to speak of *patronage* towards the backward peoples.[2]

A new spirit was abroad, expressing itself in new words. In the speech of the 18th century words made their appearance to underline the change in men's ideas. The word *philanthropy,* which the Greeks had coined, and which had long been forgotten, reappears in the language in Diderot's day, and was in common use to define human relations, especially the relations between primitive and civilised peoples.[3] You meet the word philanthropy everywhere ; and when Abbé Grégoire wrote his *Letter to Philanthropists* [4] he conferred on the word the freedom of the city. Philanthropy was humanity. It was then that, with

---

[1] Restif de la Bretonne, *Le thesmographe,* 1759 : *Des Colonies et des Nègres,* pp. 324–66.
[2] P. de Rousiers, *La colonisation et les conditions de prospérité coloniale, Science Sociale,* I to III, 1886–7, especially II, p. 347 f.
[3] [The Oxford Dictionary records *philanthropy* in English in 1608. EOL]
[4] *Lettre aux philanthropes.*

Beccaria and with Howard, people began to think of " humanising " gaols and prisons, and trying to reduce the severity of punishments.[1] But another word, *friendship* (*amitié*), to describe the relations of rulers and ruled, appears in the writings of the time. As we have said, Garcilaso de la Vega, the "Inca", spoke of *kinship* and of *friendship* between Spaniards and native Americans ; the two conceptions were in his mind allied. He forms the transition between the two concepts kinship and partnership. The word friendship frequently recurs in various pamphlets about the colonies. The word *alliance* is also used in them. During the Great Century a traveller, François Piquet, nicknamed " the Canadian ", was famous for his persistent and obstinate advocacy of a policy of " alliances " between the French and the Red Indians of Canada ; [2] a new thing and a new word freely used by others after him. The word " to tame " (*apprivoiser*), which is often on our lips, is no coinage of yesterday either. De Pauw used to say that we ought to have tamed the American natives by gentleness.[3] The word we use to-day, *partnership* or *association*, and which I shall make use of too, is much more recent. It made its first appearance, at least in its intention of describing the relations between rulers and ruled, at the very end of the century before last, that is to say, in the colonial field. It was Robinet, of whom we have spoken above, that unrecognised forerunner, who in 1780 expressed a wish for the " association " of coloniser and colonised.[4] In 1801 a certain Charpentier de Cossigny, having an idea of organising settlements on Madagascar, proposed to " carry civilisation " thither, and to *associate* a rustic, but worthy, people with his own nation . . .[5] A little later we find the word passing into works of importance. There is, for instance, a book of Count de Laborde called *The Spirit of Association in the Community* [6] in which he foresees a partnership between rulers and ruled. There was, too, the great economist, Count Rossi, who published his *Course of Lessons in Economic Policy* [7] in 1837, in the second volume of which he is the first to draw a complete picture of a doctrine of

---

[1] F. Alhoy, *Les bagnes* . . . , 1845, p. 82 f. and *passim*. On this subject too there were protests from those who clung to the past (p. 315 f.). Cf. in general Seligman's *Encyclopædia of the Social Sciences*, VII, s.v. *Humanitarianism*.

[2] A. Chagny, *Un défenseur de la Nouvelle-France* : François Piquet, *le Canadien* (*1708–1781*) . . . , 1913, Montreal.

[3] C. de Pauw, *Recherches philosophiques sur les Américains*, I, 1774, pp. 99–100.

[4] *Dictionnaire universel des Sciences morales* . . . , s.v. *Colonies*, XII, 1780, pp. 380–95.

[5] P. Gaffarel, *La politique coloniale* . . . *de 1789 à 1830*, 1908, p. 329 f.

[6] *L'esprit d'association dans la communauté*.

[7] *Cours d'économie politique*, II, 1841, Lessons 13–15, especially p. 337.

association not only between colonies and their mother-countries but also between " natives " and conquerors. De Laborde and Rossi are the heralds of that spirit which in our day is the prevailing one. In 1836 the geographer and explorer Domeny de Rienzi expresses the wish to assimilate the peoples of the Pacific by *association*.[1]

To illustrate this idea we must separate its *conception* and its *application*.

Its *Conception*. There occurs a transposition, a transformation of legal relations. The ruler was the father or the lord, he now becomes the " master " or the " patron ". The governor becomes the " governor " in the old sense of preceptor.

This scheme was adopted first by the civilian officials and then by the soldiers : these conquerors and destroyers took up their position for a battle the aim of which was the education of the " non-civilised " by the " civilised ". Under the Great King, Louis XIV, one isolated voice was heard, that of the traveller-adventurer, Robert Challes, whose *Memoirs* have recently been published.[2] A document of his of 1684 is unfortunately lost and only extracts from it are preserved in the author's *Memoirs*. In it he had set out a complete colonisation scheme for the New World of America. He explained how, in his opinion, the operation ought to be conducted. " In it I pointed out," he says in his *Memoirs*, " how few fortifications would need to be erected ; I described the manners and customs of the savages dwelling in these places and their essential innocence." Here we detect the " theory of the good savage " long before Rousseau, and we find it held by an adventurer—a sailor, and therefore well known amongst the common herd—who found it easy to live " on good terms with them *and to make friends of them* ". As far as we know, this is absolutely the first text where the word " friends " is used to express the relation between the dominant and the dominated. " Thus," he adds, " this is how they might be incorporated into the colonies, in spite of distance, and I pointed out the normal loyalty of these peoples, and that if their attachment was to be secured they would have to be treated with reciprocal good faith." So our adventurer wants to establish a friendship ; he also wants the natives to be incorporated, or as we should say fused ; incorpora-

---

[1] D. de Rienzi, *Océanie*, 1836, I, pp. 15, 334 and 340 f. Dumont d'Urville had said that a colony ought to " bring profit to its distant masters without the native subjects suffering unduly " (*Voyage pittoresque autour du monde*, 1835, II, p. 272).

[2] *Mémoires de Robert Challes*, published by A. Augustin-Thierry, p. 263 f.

tion : otherwise association, partnership, not only of interests but of feelings : society of a moral nature.

Robert Challes's voice found for a long time no echo, at least in France. We must betake ourselves to the Quakers to find thoughts of partnership and friendship. These Quakers, who were dissenting Puritans, used to address each other as " Friend ", and amongst the French they were known as the Sect of Friends. The word philanthropy, as we have already said, and the word friendship are Quaker words, expressing their love of the human race. Under Quaker influence words appear, and re-appear, which become current in the philosophy of the Age of Enlightenment : the word charity, the word benevolence and the word which the Utopist Abbé de Saint-Pierre called *beneficence*. Protestant moralists had for a hundred years been preaching the duty of benevolence " towards every reasoning being " in virtue of the reason which is in him.[1] These gentle reformers, the Quakers, always pacific and consequently enemies of tyranny and destruction, appealed to the tearful sentimentality of the times, and awakened in fashionable drawing-rooms humane feelings towards native populations. Quaker dress became fashionable in France ; the Quaker was received in society ; he preached to the public, he dictated public opinion.[2] Even Voltaire, and after him André Chénier, was steeped in the Quaker spirit. Rousseau defined Man as " a compassionate and sensitive being " ; he counts pity the highest of virtues : " Men, be humane, that is your first duty ! " for people of every age and of every rank. It is true that he also said later : " So-and-So loves the Tartars, so as not to have to love his neighbours." The Quaker spirit even infected the economists—these champions of self-interest, these men by profession insensitive—most of all the Physiocrats themselves ; Le Trosne and Turgot are examples. In a short memorandum of 1776 Turgot went so far as to wish that the status of " allied provinces " should be created to replace the old status of " subject provinces " in the relationship of the metropolitan country to its colonies. He had in mind, of course, the white colonists or *habitants*, but here was the idea of partnership which was bound to spread contagiously and work for the

---

[1] R. Cumberland, *De legibus naturae* . . . , 1672 ; and after him S. Pufendorf, *Des devoirs de l'homme*, 1673. Molière's Don Juan says to the poor man to whom he is giving alms : " I give it to you for the love of humanity ! " Cf. D. Mornet, *Les origines intellectuelles de la Révolution française*, 1933, p. 111 ; and B. Fay, *L'esprit révolutionnaire*, 1925, p. 11 f.

[2] Edith Phipps, *The Good Quaker in French Legend*, 1932.

advantage of the " natives ". Still more, Le Trosne, who in two successive works, *Social Order* and *Social Interest*,[1] both published in 1777, pleaded against the " Colonial Pact ", or " The Exclusive " as it was called, against the subordination of the colonies to the metropolis in material affairs.[2] You must, he says, allow liberty and equity to prevail in the relationship of the colonies to the metropolis ; you must treat the colonies " just like provinces "—the phrase occurs also in Turgot within a year of the very same time—you must make them henceforth an integral part of the mother-country, or at least partners of the mother-country, and consider them as internal not as external affairs. The French Empire was thus *fused* with the French Kingdom and not *annexed* by it. We have here already the conception of Great France.

The year 1780 or thereabouts was therefore the first moment when the civilians—it is still of them that we are speaking—worked out and formulated the idea of hierarchic collaboration, aiming at the education of the native. There was a second moment, round about the year 1830, when slavery was also being for the second time attacked. The idea of partnership or association was now based on sentiment, not as with Turgot, on self-interest ; society was to be bound together by ties of friendship. Two authors proclaimed this doctrine : De Laborde and Enfantin.

De Laborde published in 1821 a work entitled *The Spirit of Association in all the Interests of the Community*.[3] He was speaking in it of the inhabitants of San Domingo and demanding a change of legislation on their behalf. For San Domingo, he writes, " is now civilised ", and therefore liberty should be conferred on it, not in order that it might be separated from France, but in order to bring it into partnership, to form, as he says, " an alliance of this country with its former metropolis ". This was to be an alliance in which self-interest would be blended with sentiment ; for the new state of affairs would be less burdensome than subjection ; sentiment and self-interest were mingled and combined.

It was Enfantin, however, Saint-Simon's chief disciple,

---

[1] *Ordre social* and *Intérêt social*.
[2] See especially *De l'intérêt social*, 1777, Chap. IX, p. 695 f.
[3] *L'esprit d'association dans tous les intérêts de la communauté*, 2nd Ed. 1821, especially Vol. II, Chap. 3, Sect. I, p. 44 f. See books of our own day on this hierarchic partnership of interests : J. Harmand, *Domination et Colonisation*, 1911 ; E. Seillière, *Mysticisme et Domination*, 1913, Chap. I.

" Père Enfantin ", who preached the partnership of colonies.[1] This advocate of industrial Socialism was obsessed by two ideas : industrialism and partnership, both conceived as universal. He dreamt of industrialising the entire " Globe " ; spreading progress, diffusing comfort, to the whole Universe. But he dreamt also of establishing in every continent the partnership of peoples and nations. Industrialism and partnership are two ideas which Saint-Simon and Enfantin wished to see applied, not only to the relations of civilised States, but also in a not-distant future to the relations of those States with clans and tribes. This is why Enfantin was the first protagonist of the Protectorate régime —like the conqueror Lyautey at a later date—which was then by no means a feature of common law ; for he wanted to see established, even in Algeria, not colonies administered at first by soldiers and based on unlimited domination, but protectorates which by definition represent collaboration of Peoples or States, a partnership *de facto* as well as *de jure* between governed and governor, between protected and protector. Enfantin was thus the first to formulate a practical concrete plan, expressly for Algeria and for Egypt, for setting up a partnership with a view to protection. His greatest desire was that communal administration should be left in the hands of the colonists ; that the native organisation should not be destroyed ; he also wanted to see that indigenous jurisdictions and civil tribunals should be preserved. He thus sets out concretely and precisely, with illustrations, his idea of partnership in a protectorate : a hierarchy, but an organised hierarchy. It was Enfantin who hit on the very charming word to describe the relationships which he hoped to see realised : *affamiliation*, an intimate association in the sense of kinship and brotherhood between rulers and ruled. After his day, and perhaps under his influence, Guilbert said that you should not colonise " without the fusion of races and interests ".[2] In 1838, in a Report presented to the Chamber, Dufaure also speaks of " creating a people, a friend of France, which later perhaps will become identified with France . . ." What more can be said, even in our own day ? In a certain writing of this time we find everything down to the phrase " a *sacred mission* to defend and propagate civilisation " in the interest of Algeria which is to be treated as an " adolescent girl ", not

---

[1] Enfantin, *Correspondance politique*, 1835–40 (*Lettres écrites du Caire et d'Alger*) ; *Colonisation de l'Algérie*, 1843. See G. Weill, *Les Saint-Simoniens colonisateurs, Revue bleue*, March 14, 1896.
[2] A. Guilbert, *De la colonisation du Nord de l'Afrique*, 1839, p. 323 f.

as an " exploited slave ". Such is the mission of the French people.[1]

So the civilians of recent times have found—often unsuspectingly—a model in Enfantin. All the declarations made in the last fifty years, all the suggestions for French republican policy in the colonies—from Paul Bert, de Lanessan, Burdeau, down to Sarraut—are but echoes of Enfantin ; especially the idea of hierarchic partnership, the collaboration of master with pupil or apprentice, of " institution " in the earliest sense of the word—the sense in which Calvin speaks of " Christian Institution "—in other words, the teaching of the inferior by the devotion of the superior, education, in fact, which—as we must repeat—implies association and acceptance. Edmond About wants to make " these fine Africans " into " genuine allies ", " acquired by France ", " who accept our benefits ".[2] Paul Bert, too, the first French Resident in Tong-King, in a famous speech in 1886, fifty years, that is to say, after Enfantin, said that the solution for France was to establish a Protectorate : a protectorate not domination, legislative and on the executive plane. From this Republican standpoint partnership and protectorate are synonymous. It is a Republic between nations.[3] Another Republican, Burdeau in 1891, in reference to Algeria, reported on a " policy of rapprochement ", saying that the French aim—later, he even said French duty—was to improve the natural ways and manners of the inhabitants, " to vivify their native institutions, and transform them without violence, bringing them into line with French ideas ".[4] We here recognise the famous formula attributed to Waldeck-Rousseau, but antedating him by ten years ; the evolution of the manners and customs of the inhabitants " in their institutions " ; evolution, not revolution. It was Burdeau who gave expression to the idea that partnership and education

[1] E. Carrey, *Récits de Kabylie*, 1858, p. 81. Jules Duval also said : " to gain the liking of the natives by positive benefits " which " are *due* to them, members as they are of the human *family* ". (*Réflexions sur la politique de l'empereur en Algérie*, 1866, pp. 16 and 106.)

[2] E. About, *Le XIXe siècle* (1883), Edition of 1890, p. 349 f. The Marquis de Morès in his famous speech in the Theatre of Tunis in 1896 also announced a " Franco-Islamic Alliance ".

[3] S. H. Roberts, *History of French Colonial Policy*, II, 1929, p. 439 f. ; L. Dubreuil, *Paul Bert*, 1935 ; J. Chailley-Bert, *Paul Bert au Tonkin*, 1887. Very shortly afterwards, de Lanessan spoke of *respect* (*égards*). And that great writer Jules Boissière wrote in 1896 of the Annamite that his " co-operation ought to be deserved " : *La société annamite et la politique française* in *l'Indochine avec les Français* (no date), pp. 16, 118 f. (a remarkable essay).

[4] A. Burdeau, *L'Algérie en 1891*, 1892. Similarly Charles Benoist, in the same year (*Enquête algérienne*, 1892, p. 207) : " . . . to the natives of Algeria, as men, you owe justice, as ignorant men, you owe them charity."

would be able insensibly and progressively to transform the manners and customs of the country by rapprochement—by " taming " them, as we should say—insinuating but not imposing our point of view. In the codicil to his Will, written at the very end of his life, Cecil Rhodes also inclined to feel " a great wish for association between races " [1] in the near or distant future.

Amongst civilians, but indeed amongst *soldiers* too, association has long been practised. In speaking to his soldiers, and addressing his appeal to the ordinary man, Napoleon, though he was first and foremost urging a tempering of domination, showed himself also as the prophet of association and partnership. In various passages of his two proclamations he speaks of equity and tells the Egyptians that he has come to give them liberty and equity. He thus gives evidence of two attitudes of mind : first, and above all, he wants moderation, tempered domination. But at moments he also wants rapprochement and partnership of French and Egyptians.

It was chiefly Bugeaud, however, who preached association or partnership amongst the soldiers. In his Memoirs, in his Letters, even in his Circulars, in his capacity as Governor of Algeria [2] he expressed firmly and formally—and this was nearly a hundred years ago—the attitude of which we are speaking. Thus, in a letter to a friend, he dreams of " a pacific blend of the two peoples under one and the same government ". " *Pacific* blend ", what could that be except a fusion of Algerians and French ? " We must identify them with ourselves," he also said, " in such a way as to form one single people under the paternal government of the French King.[3] We must blend them into our Society." He wants thus to forge a sentimental link between the Algerians and the French. Here is something better still : the Circular addressed in September 1844 to the

[1] [I can find no such phrase in any of the four Codicils (1901–2) to Rhodes's Will, the last of which was signed on March 12, 1902, just fourteen days before Rhodes's death.

In the Will itself (July, 1899) the only words even approximating to this quotation refer solely to closer understanding between British and Americans. They run : " I also desire to encourage and foster an appreciation of the advantages which I implicitly believe will result from the Union of the English-speaking peoples throughout the world and to encourage in the students from the United States of North America . . . an attachment to the country from which they have sprung . . ." EOL]

[2] Bugeaud, *Le peuplement français de l'Algérie*, 1933 (a collection of his speeches), especially p. 187 f.

[3] C. Frégier said the same thing about the Jews (*Les Juifs Algériens*, 1865, pp. 13 f. and 15 f.) : " To *transsubstantiate* conquered and conqueror into one people " ; to melt them down in the course of time " in the same crucible ".

armies. In it he orders officers and soldiers "to make known to them (the Algerians) our kindness and our justice, to treat them with kindness, equity and humanity". He speaks, too, of "urbanity", "the hallmark of every civilisation" which ought to govern all their relations with the inhabitants. "Reconcile therefore," he says again, "the interests of the Arabs with the interests of our policy." This impenitent disciple of Fourier, when himself in the position of a conqueror, committed himself to proclaiming partnership with the Algerians. Thirty years later, in 1873, Francis Garnier said to his sailors : "You will take pains to make the flag which shelters you loved and respected . . . by showing yourselves in all circumstances just and kindly."

The *Application* of this doctrine in his case followed hard on the conception ; practice corroborated principle. In earlier days practice sometimes preceded theory. In the legal records of earlier times we find decisions which in fact imply a partnership between rulers and ruled. The tendency preceded the doctrine, the unexpressed principle was older than the expression of the principle ; partnership was practised before it was formulated. Let us see, in a few words, how partnership or association is shown, genuinely and concretely, in the application of this principle. We have seen it, in isolated cases, in the old days ; we can see it as the normal thing in these new times.

There are precedents for it in ancient times. In the *Assizes of Jerusalem*, the Code of the Latin or Levantine Orient, the feudal and seigniorial code of the time of the Crusades, we find decisions which favoured partnership in colonial territory. There was, for instance, the institution of Mixed Tribunals where Syrians and French sat side by side—as they cannot to-day !—an anticipation of Napoleon's Mixed Diwan. It was also the custom for the Crusaders freely to employ native officials as well as Syrian cooks and servants.[1]

A little later, in papal bulls, the spirit of partnership and association already foreshadowed, blossoms forth again. In the Bull of 1493—in which almost all our ideas are implicit— Alexander VI [2] gives the Spaniards the right to rule the New World of America on two conditions : that they shall teach religion and morals, by education and by conversion. Moral education, which obscurely implies association, is here present in spirit and in embryo.

---

[1] H. Lammens, *La Syrie, précis historique*, 1921, I, pp. 235–71, and the large book of R. Grousset, quoted above.

[2] [See footnote, p. 22, n. 1. EOL]

Later, but still in olden times, came the Colonial Charters, which, while granting the right to rule distant countries, laid down conditions which figuratively displayed the same spirit. The Will of Queen Isabella recommended the King " not to consent to the Indians . . . suffering any injustice . . . but on the contrary to ensure that they be humanely treated." [1] The first Statute for Virginia in 1611 imposed on the colonists the duty of protecting the Indians and punished kidnapping with death.[2] Finally, we know the instructions given to La Pérouse by Louis XVI under his own hand, conjuring him to act always with moderation and always to endeavour to *obtain friendship* by good treatment. La Pérouse in his own *Relation* says that he went " to spread enlightenment ", to " make the islander happier "; to " teach him the ways of society ", to " make him a citizen ", to accustom him to work and dedicate him to progress.[3] Colbert granted concessions in Canada and Madagascar subject to the condition that the natives should be treated with consideration, that they should be educated and transformed—which of course involves their collaboration.

It is our modern times, however, which have seen an upsurge of decrees and laws which have by legislation enforced the practice, though not explicitly expounded the doctrine, of partnership. For the last fifty years, laws and decrees in the great empires have been fragmentarily and sporadically inspired and imbued with this unexpressed ideal : there has been the application but not the enunciation of it. Both the French and the English have been instituting Protectorates and multiplying their number for almost the last hundred years—a form of government of which Lyautey was a great advocate. The very conception of a Protectorate implies the collaboration of the two peoples ; and the increase in their number bears witness to the partnership attitude of mind. In its conception a colony still remains a domination since authority is there legally undivided, yet even in the colonies decisions inspired by the same spirit— though their promoters may not be consciously aware of it—have been increasing in number. We thus find partnership or association in practice though not declared in theory ; legislation favouring but not proclaiming it ; just as in Australia and New

[1] In the same spirit is the narrative of the *Voyages avantureux du Capitaine Jean Alfonce, Sainctangeois . . . Plus le moyen de se gouverner . . . envers les Barbares*, 1578.
[2] Yardley, *Before the Mayflower*, 1931, p. 142.
[3] Texts will be found in A. Eyriès, *Voyages modernes*, 1823, I, pp. 3, 53, 101 and 267.

Zealand we find " socialism minus the doctrine ". This takes place in three different spheres : *law, economics* and *theology.*

On the *legal* and political plane there has been association, in the legal sense, between rulers and ruled. It is first to be seen in *legislation.* Especially in French territory, there has been a multiplication of Mixed Assemblies and Councils, on the lines of Napoleon's Mixed Diwan, within which French and Natives meet and discuss together and take decisions by a joint vote. Rulers and subjects sit thus together in Algeria, in Tunis, in Indo-China and in Madagascar and, very recently even in the islands of the Pacific. There is association in *jurisdiction* too. We can name more and more tribunals which might be called mixed or composite which dispense justice to the old inhabitants ; tribunals like those in the olden Kingdom of Jerusalem, where rulers and ruled take their seat side by side, or which have at least their quota of assessors and supplementary officials drawn from the ranks of the subjects. The assessors have full voting rights and are legally judges in the full sense. Finally, there is association in *administration.* More and more, the kings, the chiefs, the sultans, the *qaids* are called to exercise power, to consult and to take decisions. More numerous—though still not as numerous as they would like—are the local, native officials. They have their rank in the administration, and in due course mount the ladder of promotion in the official French hierarchy, invited to govern jointly with the officials of French birth. In every country this raises a great problem.

On the *economic* plane also, rulers and ruled have already been able to co-operate. For a long time the natives were servants only, employees ; that prepares the ground for partnership and association in organising the common life. When people in Indo-China talk of " the rule of the ' boy ' ", we can well see that this servant, the " boy ", has considerable influence in the house and that familiarity—sometimes even intimacy !— often grows up between him and his master. In material matters association is more properly displayed in two institutions : the civil service (*le salariat*) and society. Natives of the colonies tend more and more to become salaried civil servants ; they are " employees " in the European sense, with the liberties and the privileges of the salary-earner. Being no longer slaves or servants, they have rights corresponding to their duties. Their whole status is controlled and guaranteed by government ; they have the legal right to lodge protests and to lay claims. The civil service, imperfect though some may consider it, is a step towards partnership. In certain countries, such as Algeria, Tunisia and Morocco, *Society* has been able to bring about a community of interests. In the countries of the Maghrib, social intercourse amongst civilians is frequent between Algerians, Moroccans, Tunisians and French ; in Libya between Italians and Tripolitanians ; social intercourse in the pastoral, cultural and even commercial spheres ; these are the results of a community of interests. Throughout the Maghrib, from Tunis to Fez, the *Mugharsa* is practised, an agricultural agreement, in which contributions and profits are pooled.

Lastly, on the *theological* plane, association or partnership arises from the admission of natives to the ranks and functions of the clergy. They take their share in Christian rites : they were first accepted as catechists, then as priests, and later as bishops. In the spiritual sphere they are our peers ; and it is often through their work that the Christian faith is spread. There is therefore collaboration in propaganda and in teaching ; association in preaching, as also in exploitation and legislation. At this point we have passed beyond *hierarchic* partnership and are already approaching partnership *in equal terms*. The pupil has become a master or a patron ; co-operation takes place between equals, and a white priest even owes respect to a yellow or black bishop. Such is the effect of religion. Hierarchy works in both directions and not in one alone : the social inferior may become the ecclesiastical superior. Black and White have at least the same function and the same mission. This is society in its perfect form which always demands that a man should move amongst his equals.

CHAPTER XXIX

PARTNERSHIP OR ASSOCIATION ON EQUAL TERMS

Hierarchic partnership is thus an introduction to equalitarian partnership, complete and ideal partnership or association between equals ; a genuine *society*, as the Ancients so well expressed it. Amongst the Hellenes society was represented by a perfect circle. The meaning was that society implied the equality of all its associates. We note that this concept in the colonial sphere has both its ancient and its modern history.

Its *ancient history* : the people of old sometimes in their colonies practised association on equal terms.

The Egyptians, that self-conscious—we should say " nationalist "—people, who for a long time kept foreigners at bay and aimed at living as in a closed retort, who in early days forbade anyone to emigrate ; this aristocratic and " autarkic " people, if there ever were one, underwent, at one period, a change of attitude. It was in the reign of Amenophis IV, Amenhotep, King of Tell-el-Amarna, that for one fleeting moment—for some reason to which we have no clue—the Egyptians conceived the idea of the equality of one people with another, and in particular the equality of the ruling people with their subject people. King Amenhotep was probably the half-breed offspring of an Egyptian father and some foreign woman. It was a half-breed who was the very first to suggest the equality of foreigners. He sought to set up a common cult, a syncretism for all men, Egyptians and foreigners, without distinction of race or colour. This half-breed and reformer seems vaguely to have conceived the idea of equality as a concomitant of the idea of humanity. It was he who first set going the notion of " the human race ".[1]

The Greeks and the Romans tackled the question better. The Greeks at one point failed to distinguish between distant peoples ; but later they enlarged their idea of social ties and thus for the first time came forth from out their own city walls. It was they who in a certain sense first conceived the idea of humanity ; they who first dreamt of philanthropy ; they even

[1] S. Dairaines, *L'Égypte . . . XVIIIe dynastie* (thesis), 1933, p. 118 f. ; cf. J. H. Breasted, *The Earliest Internationalism*, 1918.

at times advanced so far as to conceive identity and equality between peoples or nations.[1]   Aristotle identified *natural law* with *universal law*.   He formulated the concept of this natural law as a law common to all men in all countries, valid for the whole human race, without distinction of race or colour.   We need not therefore be surprised that his illustrious pupil, Alexander the Great, the conquering Emperor, dreamt at one time of universal empire, of a universal monarchy, in which under his power equality should reign between the Greeks and the Barbarians of overseas.   He dreamt of monarchy, but a monarchy based on the equality and identity of all his subjects.

So it came about that, under the new inspiration of the Greek philosophers, the Romans later took equality to be the rule regulating the relations between peoples and peoples. Cicero—who, as we know, was never anything but an echo— also expresses, especially in his treatise *De Republica,* the idea of universal empire, the idea of universal common law ; civilisation and legislation for the whole world to apply to all human beings, Romans, Barbarians and Aliens in equality of powers and duties. It was this common law applicable to the whole universe, which they called *Jus Naturale* as distinct from the *Jus Gentium* and the *Jus Civile.*[2]

The *Jus Civile* was the law of the conquering Romans ; the *Jus Gentium* was the law of the conquered aliens ; the *Jus Naturale* was the law of the as-yet-unconquered barbarians ; and Cicero wished to see it based on the idea of equality.   Marcus Aurelius eloquently echoed Cicero.   Though these were all theories without an immediate future, the fugitive expression of ephemeral dreams, they lingered on as memories to be re-born centuries later.   Pondering on the idea of equality from the modern angle, we shall observe that in Western lands the ideal of the Ancients was destined to recover its vitality.

Its modern history.   The idea of equality to be attained by the partnership of rulers and ruled, has two phases.   First, it was *Christianity* in the West which created equality in the relations of colonisers and colonised, by asserting the identity of peoples and races and overlooking questions of mind and colour.   Islam, also, the conquering religion, which imposes on its adherents the duty of waging Holy War on all Unbelievers, occasionally

[1] A. Bonucci, *La legge comune nel pensiero greco,* 1903 ; cf. Lucian, *Demonax,* 10.
[2] F. Senn, *De la justice . . . ,* 1927. Cf. Aranglo Ruiz, *Gaius,* 1934, p. 74, on the *society* of natural law which might exist amongst all men.

conceived for a fleeting moment the idea of equality. Amongst learned Muslims dissidents were found, who preached the equality of the Believer and the Infidel. It was, however, far more through Christianity that the assertion of equality was fostered, and that the legal rights of rulers and ruled came to be based on an idea of equal partnership.

In Christianity itself there were two currents : Roman Catholicism and Protestantism.

Roman Catholicism paved the way. It is itself founded on two doctrines both of which must in time lead to equality : the doctrine of Creation and the doctrine of Redemption.

Creation. All human beings are bearers of the same blood, and have been created by God from the same clay by one single creative act. In all of them there are therefore two elements : the Divine and the Human. This doctrine was inevitably bound to lead in time to the assertion that there is an identity, a " oneness " of all Mankind, regardless of colour. This identity was likewise bound, also with the lapse of time, to lead to the assertion of Equality. As soon as men cease to believe that the End of the World is close at hand, this conclusion is unavoidable.[1]

Redemption. There is not only the Creation but the Redemption. All human beings, having similarly sprung from the hand of the same God, moulded by Him of the same clay, it is for all of them that Sin was committed, it is for all of them that Salvation is desired. Redemption is a universal, essentially humanitarian idea and " catholic " in the exact sense of the word. Salvation is open to all the human race ; redemption shines for the benefit of all. For all : the same Fall ; for all : the same Salvation.

These primary dogmas acquired equalitarian virtue by what might perhaps be called a kind of spiritual fertilisation. New ideas lent wings to Equality by unveiling and unmasking it. No longer *theological* ideas—as were those of Creation and Redemption—but rather *sociological* ideas ; social conceptions concerning the human race, which infusing themselves into the primitive dogma, called to life all those results which had lain obscurely and confusedly dormant in the Christian dogma. These new ideas, which so to speak brought theology to bed, were the ideas of *nationhood*, of *virtue* and of *happiness*.

The idea of *Nationhood*. All Western theologians, especially at the time of the Renaissance, came to think of primitive peoples

[1] See *Les démocraties modernes*, 1921, pp. 74 f. and 85 f.

as Nations, as bodies endowed with rights.[1]   They anticipated our contemporary attitude of mind.   The inhabitants of the New World of America form Nations, of the same dignity as our own Nations, who ought to have the same powers and the same duties.   A Tribe is a Nation ;   why draw distinctions ?   So spoke Francis of Vitoria, the theologian, who was the fore-runner of the League of Nations ; [2] barbarous tribes possess power and a government, they are assuredly nations ;   we must not confine the word to our own civilised States.   All human groups, however humble, are certainly nations.   Barbarian peoples have towns and in them order is established, says Vitoria, they have matrimonial regulations, they have magistracies and properties ;   and so they are—the actual word was to come later—just as civilised as we.   It is fitting that they should be treated on an equal footing.   Thus theology—the sociology of Roman Catholic Spaniards—by applying the concept of Nation to primitive peoples awakened the pagan dream of equality.

The idea of *Virtue* also helped theology to lay stress on equality. Primitive peoples are virtuous and kindly ;   issuing from the hands of God they are pure and holy.   The whole " theory of the Noble Savage " is implicit in this attitude of mind.   This is an immense subject, on which we shall not attempt to enter.[3] This is Rousseau before Rousseau's day ;   a theme taken up once again in our own time by the so-called Religious Ethnology : savages possess humility and simplicity, they are nearer to God than the arrogant peoples who call themselves civilised ;   fresh from the Revelation they know the True God, they are the True Believers ;   and people exert themselves to prove that the Pygmies of Central Africa worship One God,[4] and one alone.   So the

[1] E. Nys, *Les origines du droit internationale*, 1894 ; J. Brown Scott, *La découverte de l'Amérique, et le droit des gens, Revue de Droit international*, XII, Jan.–March 1930, pp. 33–58.   And above Chap. XXIV.

[2] This has been clearly seen by R. P. Delos, *La société internationale et les principes du droit publique*, 1929, pp. 213 and 222 f.   See C. Barcia Treller, *Francisco de Vitoria, Recueil Cours Acad. Droit international*, The Hague, XVII, 1927, II, pp. 136–94.

[3] Amongst the Ancients : A. O. Lovejoy, *Primitivism* . . . in *Antiquity* (to be continued), Baltimore, 1935 ; See in general, G. Chinard's works above quoted ; P. van Tieghem, *Bulletin Société histoire moderne*, June, 1922 ; P. Hazard, *La crise de la conscience européenne*, 1935, II, p. 223 f. ; H. Fairchild, *The Noble Savage, a Study in Romantic Naturalism*, 1928.   Even to-day this theory has its adherents : G. Elliot Smith, *Human Nature*, 1927, and Preface to C. Hose, *Natural Man, a Record from Borneo*, 1926 ; G. Landtsman, *The Kiwai Papuans* . . . *Instance of Rousseau's Ideal Community*, 1927.   See new texts in G. Atkinson, *Les nouveaux horizons de la Renaissance française*, 1935, pp. 145 f. and 161 f. ; J. Macmillan Brown, *Peoples and Problems of the Pacific*, 1927, I, p. 215 f. ; Aldous Huxley, *Beyond the Mexique Bay*, 1934 ; or, in France, P. Gauguin, *Noa-Noa*, Ch. Morice's edition 1924, pp. 35 and 83.

[4] This is in particular the theory of the Reverend Fathers W. Schmidt and W. Koppers.

vision of the Noble Savage had been first accepted by the theologians before taking hold of the philosophers.[1] For the theologians, this theory had the merit of " exalting the humble "
and casting down the mighty, of magnifying the small in the
teeth of the great !   And the sculptures which adorn the tympanum over the doors of our cathedrals, showing the mighty
being dragged off to Hell by horned devils, were wont to preach
the equality of ranks and races.   The work of the carver, the
meaning of which could be grasped by all, prepared the ground
for the *doctrine* which was preached.   Bishop Palafox de Mendoza,
a successor of Las Casas, wrote a pamphlet in 1650 called *The
Virtues of the Indian.*[2]   He believed that in it he had proved, not
only that the American Indians were exploited and unhappy,
but that they were nearer to God by reason of their greater
kindness and virtue.   Amongst French theologians the idea of
the virtue of primitive men gained much ground in the following
century.   A much-read book of popularisation, *A Course of
Sciences*[3] by the Jesuit Father Buffier, speaks with complacency,
again and yet again, of the " natural equality " between men,
based on the virtue which they have all received of God.   If
any men deserve to be beloved of God it is assuredly those who
are nearest to Him, primitive men, who are purer and holier.
This Reverend Father speaks precisely the same language as the
Encyclopædists : [4] a sign of the times and token of a " current "
of contemporary thought !   Napoleon, too—the Christian Deist
who had read Rousseau—in his Proclamations repeatedly said
that all men are equal . . . in the sight of God !   Speaking to
the Egyptians, he held out to them a gleam of hope that he was
bringing them equality as well as equity.

The idea of *Happiness* came to reinforce these thoughts in
the minds of various men.   The teaching of Rousseau—a thinker
imperfectly de-Protestantised—that savages, being more virtuous,
are also happier, is only the old doctrine of salvation desired by
God for the whole human race ;   desired particularly for those
who are nearer Him and more beloved of Him.   Happiness,
associated by the theologians with virtue, belongs therefore by

---

[1] And, as always, it is pushed to extremes, people went so far as to talk of the
noble animal ; the beast alone is pure . . .   See G. Boas, *The Happy Beast in French
Thought* . . . , 1933.
[2] *Virtutes del Indio*, French trans. *L'Indien ou portrait naturel des Indiens*, 1672 (reprinted
in Vol. II of Thévenot, *Relations de divers ouvrages curieux*, 1686).
[3] *Cours de Sciences.*
[4] *Encyclopédie* by Diderot and d'Alembert, Geneva Edition, 1777, s.v. *Égalité*
(Droit naturel), XI, p. 963 f.

preference and by privilege to the primitives. This is the vision which colours the *Narratives* of French missionaries in Canada, these *Edifying and Curious Letters* [1] which paint a full-length portrait of the noble savage. Later, Abbé de Lamennais, a democrat and republican though a priest, who long remained in the bosom of the Roman Church but was at last compelled to leave it, has expressed better than anyone the equality founded on the happiness which God has granted as a reward to primitive man. Equality by happiness, for happiness, which goes to the humble and the small.[2] In his *Politics for the People* [3] Abbé de Lamennais sketched a universal federation between all peoples in accordance with the motto of the French Republic : Liberty, Equality, Fraternity. " All fractions of the human race," he says, " are gravitating towards unity." [4] It is therefore fitting to establish " justice and charity " between all peoples for their happiness, without distinction of race or colour. All peoples throughout the world—he recurs to this in several chapters—have the right to happiness ; they have the option and the capacity of finding happiness ; we must therefore not reserve the right of attaining happiness to the nations of the West alone. Proudhon—who was a Christian—would have spoken of " the capacity of the primitive peoples ". It is the Christians—for, once a Christian, always a Christian !—who talk in this vein.

Yet, as I have already hinted, it was Protestantism which imposed this equality in so far as it influenced the relations between the home countries and the countries overseas. There had been, it is true, in the Roman Church, dissident sects, heretical groups, who had perceived the idea which we find held by every Protestant : the idea of the sanctity of each individual endowed by God with the ability to discover for himself what is good and what is virtuous ; the idea, consequently, of mental and spiritual equality. Hence sprang Quietism, hence—more important still —sprang Jansenism : " heresies " which marked the transition from the Roman Catholic Christian to the Protestant Christian. It was the latter who was to take up arms as the champion of equality.

Let us distinguish in non-Protestant circles and non-Protestant

---

[1] *Relations—Lettres édifiantes et curieuses.*
[2] For this whole period, see M. Gibbs, *Le roman de Bas-de-Cuir*, 1927 (thesis), pp. 15 f. and 79 f. and Gustave Aimard, *L'Ami des blancs* (novel), 1879.
[3] *Politique à l'usage du Peuple.*
[4] Reproduced from articles in *Le Monde* (1837), 1838. Cf. also P. J. Buchez, *Traité de politique et de science sociale* (posthumous), 1866 ; Buchez was a Christian Socialist who dreamt of the federation of " all the peoples of the earth."

minds three stages : *proclamation, propagation, transference* ; or, to phrase it differently, the transplantation of the Protestant spirit to the non-Protestant mind.

Proclamation begins with the earliest movements of the Reformation. The two objects of Luther's Reform, in every country, were Individualism and Equalitarianism. Individualism—even in certain sects anarchism—was the affirmation that every individual has the option and the *capacity* to find faith and therefore salvation for himself.[1] This is a conception which can be subdivided into two : Universal Spirit, Universal Salvation.— *Universal Spirit :* all human beings have in the spirit by the gift of God, the power of discovering for themselves the Way or the Path by the free study of the sacred Scriptures. From this position there follows the protest against the authority of the clergy, whether high or low, and the assertion that every believer has the means of achieving his own salvation without the intervention of any dogmatising Body. The sons of Adam, dowered by God with one and the same spirit, being thus Sons of God, possess the Means and the Way—a Universal Spirit giving access to *Universal Salvation*. For the sin of Adam, committed for all his descendants, demands salvation for all his descendants. The Redemption wrought by Christ must benefit the whole human race. From the first, this vision led John Calvin to the vision of equality.

Individualism introduced Calvin to *equalitarianism*. From his doctrine of universal sin and universal salvation, he formally deduced the right of subjects to rebel against oppressive masters. The right of insurrection and revolution, this right of the individual, thus passed from the realm of theology into that of sociology. Liberty of thought prevails on every plane, and in Calvin's view the People are justified in judging the King. A day will come when the Black Man, taught by the Protestant Missions, will also invoke this right of rebellion in virtue of the unity in spirit and in blood between all human beings. Individualism and equalitarianism are one and the same thing. Liberty of thought is no exclusive privilege of the White Man! The Protestant Church is by definition established on the idea of universal priesthood ; all believers are pastors since all possess the Spirit ; holiness, purity, dignity are recognised as inherent in each Believer. It is on this point, more than on any other,

[1] See in general, C. Borgeaud, *The Rise of Modern Democracy in Old and New England*, 1894 (in its relations with the " universal priesthood ") ; G. P. Gooch, *The History of English Democratic Ideas*, 1898.

that Protestants are alienated from Roman Catholicism.   The idea of universal priesthood abolishes legitimacy, humiliates superiority.   It is Protestant equalitarianism, born of Protestant individualism, which leads to that Protestant solidarism which has been expressed this fifty years ;   solidarity, interdependence in law and in practice, amongst all human beings.   All possessing the same spirit, marching along the same road to the same salvation, have necessarily a common interest, a common duty, a common future and a common dream.   Here we already have Woodrow-Wilsonism in almost complete form.

To convince ourselves of this, we must turn to the *propagation* of Protestant dogma, especially in the colonial empires.   It is a striking fact that from the earliest days of the Reformation the Protestant levelling spirit first spread in the colonial countries ! First in Holland, and very shortly afterwards in New England, in the early years of the 17th century, less than fifty years after the Reform, the new ideal took root.   This is a fact which deserves the student's attention :   in the colonies, especially amongst the English, stress was from the very beginning laid on this aspect of Protestant teaching :   equality desired of God, established of God, between all human creatures regardless of colour.   In these countries it was the dissidents, the persecuted *Dissenters* who very logically, very straightforwardly, laid stress on equality.   That was, no doubt, why they were persecuted !

Two sects in particular played a decisive rôle in this matter. First those people known as *Congregationalists*, according to whom all the faithful assembled in the Congregation, having the same spirit, had also an equal right :   every one of the faithful was a pastor and none had need of other pastors.   Each Congregation thus enjoyed autonomy ;   being directly under God's guidance, it needed no interpreter in addressing God.   Priesthood of the faithful ;   this principle, by Luther only half-suspected, became in the course of the century the master-principle of the Congregationalists.   Authority in the reformed churches was thus undermined.   It was precisely this sect which was driven from England to Holland, and whose leader, John Robinson, took up his quarters in Leyden in 1609.   You can still see, piously preserved in Leyden, the house where he long lived and the courtyard where he used to preach.   It was he who in 1620 sent the famous *Mayflower* across the Atlantic with the first Protestant emigrants to found the colony of Plymouth.   It was a flock of poor, persecuted folk who set out in the hopes of discovering both liberty

and equality out yonder, and of being able to organise themselves on equalitarian lines in harmony with the profession of
faith of the Congregation.   Fifteen years later, one of them, a
certain Roger Williams, son of a tailor, who had been for a
time a Church of England chaplain, was persecuted in his turn,
and in 1636 quitted Salem, near Boston, to find at Providence [1]
a patch of free land where he might be able to live in equality
with a few friends.   Roger Williams is still famous in America,
mainly because he was the first to preach equality in the relations
between natives and colonists.   Long before the Quakers, he set
up equality, in contrast to authority, as the principle that should
govern relations with the Indians.   Thus Roger Williams was
the founder of American democracy in its equalitarian aspect.
In the New World he created an Anglo-Amerindian common
law.[2]   Protestant dogma, spreading directly through dissident
groups, especially amongst the John Robinson sect, thus opened
a new era in the colonies.

Secondly, the *Presbyterians* exercised a similar influence.
Their name explains itself : they are people for whom every
Believer is a pastor : holiness resides in every Son of God, the
minister is only a guide and guardian, who holds his title by
right of election, who is nominated by free choice, who is account-
able to his flock and is in duty bound to prove himself a Good
Shepherd.   The ancient idea of the Good Shepherd underwent
a regular *revival* amongst these sectaries.   Equality within the
flock, equality between different flocks ; no authority whatever,
whether without or within.   These Presbyterian dissenters, persecuted emigrants to North America, introduced amongst the
colonists there the spirit of partnership in their relations with
the natives.   The first Protestant attempts, even those of French
Protestants, to establish colonies in the New World, were the
work of Presbyterians.   Coligny, for instance, and Jean Ribaut,
setting out for Brazil in 1562, were Protestant democrats.   Lau-
donnière, too, who went in 1564 to Florida—only to die there
—was Presbyterian in spirit.   The founders of the English
Virginia Company (1612), which was one of the earliest of
English expansions in the New World, were also Dissenters, Presbyterian in spirit, who stressed the equality of all human beings.

Lastly, *Transference* of the Protestant dogma.   By this I mean

---

[1] [This was the first settlement in Rhode Island.   EOL]
[2] D. Pasquet, *Histoire . . . du peuple américain*, I, 1924, pp. 69 f., 86, 96, 338 ;
M. M. Miller, *American Debate*, II, 1916, p. 17 f. ; Perry Belmont, *Political Equality* ;
Religious Toleration from Roger Williams to Thomas Jefferson, 1927.

the spirit of the Protestants revealing itself in others, non-Protestant, as it were by infection or inoculation. Equality, consequently, desired for itself, sought for its own sake, disentangles itself from theology and links itself with sociology. Several very great names meet us here.

Locke is the first of them.[1] At Oxford Locke was a pupil of a Puritan, named Owen, who greatly influenced him ; we know of his relations with the Quaker, William Penn, who was, like him, sent down from the University ; we know that he gave birth to a new English doctrine of democracy. He was the famous disciple of an obscure preacher whose ideas were incorporated into the pupil's writings. "Natural Law" . . . "Social Contract" . . . "Sovereign People", these three ideas of Locke were to be the three ideas of the *Declaration of Rights*, and people would seek to realise them, not only in the relations between civilised people, but in the relations between civilised and non-civilised. *Natural Law* was already a conception of the Ancients of which Locke revived the memory. The *Social Contract* was the concept of the Dissenters, the super-Protestants. It underlay the famous *Compact*, the contract made between the emigrants of the *Mayflower* by which they undertook to give, of their own free will, law and order to the country. Finally, this Contract implied the *Sovereign People*, in whose name all these democratised Protestants were to make the Revolution of 1776. Locke, the inspirer of their Revolution, remains the exponent of a Protestant dogma. After him, and under his influence, Thomas Paine and Edmund Burke pleaded in the name of law and justice for the autonomy of the colonies. The former, an excise man who was dismissed from the excise, was a Liberal who wanted *self-government* for the Anglo-Americans ; the second desired, as he said, *equality* throughout the *Empire*. He uses the word and defines it as an *association* . . . like to-day. He had only White Men in mind ; but assuredly, the seed he sowed is for the Black Man too !

Second in importance is Rousseau, this ex-Protestant, from Geneva, but, as I have said, imperfectly cleansed of his former Protestantism.[2] It has been remarked by Lanson[3] that

[1] *Two Treatises on Civil Government*, 1690, re-edited by H. Morley. Cf. C. Bastide, *John Locke . . .*, 1907 ; E. Laboulaye, *Locke, Législateur de la Caroline, Revue de législation et de jurisprudence*, XXXVII, p. 225 f. See M. M. Miller, *American Debate*, 1911, I, p. 125 f.

[2] G. Vallette, *J. J. Rousseau, Genevois*, 1911.

[3] G. Lanson, *L'unité de la pensée de J. J. Rousseau, Annales J.J.R.*, VIII, 1912, pp. 1–31 ; cf. E. Faguet, *XVIIIe siècle*, p. 391 f.

Rousseau's doctrine was " an imperfectly secularised Quietism ",
being a protest by the governed against the ruler.   One blood, one
spirit, throughout the whole human race, equality and liberty
of the Sons of God in the state of nature ; these sons of God
who are free to submit themselves—so it be voluntarily and
under contract—to a sovereign power always set up by themselves, always controlled by themselves.[1]   This Genevan, reared
on the Greeks and Romans, reading Plutarch in his childhood [2]
and later influenced by Francis of Assisi ; pagan and Christian ;
Protestant still tainted with catholicity, was a profound believer.[3]
His philosophy is theology ; in his thinking he drew inspiration
both from the Ancients and from the Christians, and amongst
the Christians from the Protestants, while he was directly and
intimately steeped in the teachings of Locke, his master.   His
direct Protestant borrowings were austerity and simplicity, and
finally equality, in which his vision and his mania centred.   In
1740 he had composed an opera which was never produced, called
The Discovery of the New World (*La découverte du Nouveau Monde*) :
in it the contact of races makes it evident where virtue lies !

Last of the three great ones comes Kant, who founded
Western democracy in Practical Reason ; he was a Protestant
riddled through and through with Protestant dogma.   In his
Doctrine of Right [4] he was the first to say that colonies are causes
of evil and destruction, that no one has the right to plant colonies
(*jus incolatus*) amongst the inhabitants of distant countries, except
after the conclusion of a Contract voluntarily agreed on.   It
was Kant who, with elaborated doctrine and carefully constructed
system, worked out in detail the idea which Roger Williams
had preached a hundred and fifty years before : the idea of
agreement, freely reached, regulating the relations between
native and colonist.

Coming to more recent times, no one can hope to understand the contemporary colonial policies pursued by civilised
States,[5] and in particular in the French Empire, who does not
know that its very foundation has remained Protestant.   For
those who created the attitude of mind which has in recent
times prevailed, and to which willy-nilly everyone is constrained

[1] E. Seillière, *Mme Guyon et Fénelon, précurseurs de J.J.R.*, 1918 ; *J.J.R.*, 1921.
[2] A. Oltramare, *Plutarque dans Rousseau, Mélanges Bernard Bouvier*, 1920, pp. 185-96.
[3] E. Seillière, *Les origines romanesques de la morale et de la politique romantiques*, 1920.
[4] 1797, cf. Aulard's Ed., Sect. LXII, p. 167 f.
[5] " A negro is as good as a white man ", said the Protestant missionary E. Casalis
in *Les Bassoutos*, 1860, p. 11.

to pay homage, the spirit of Jefferson and Woodrow Wilson, have unquestionably been Protestants. The first of them, Jefferson, one of the authors of the Declaration of Rights, who was a profound believer in the Sovereign People and the Social Contract, was a dissenter among his Protestant brethren. In the Declaration of Independence in 1776 he stigmatised colonial abuses, anathematised despotism, and proclaimed equality of rights. Woodrow Wilson above all, the doctrinaire of the Fourteen Points,[1] on whom the eyes of all " oppressed " natives were turned, considered himself chosen of God to effect their liberation. He is incomprehensible if it is forgotten that he is a Protestant. Not only did he boast several Scottish ancestors, but he was the son of a Presbyterian minister. In his *Memoirs* he tells us how strong on him was his father's influence ; his thought drank deep of Presbyterian spirit, though this was only one of its draughts. For he tells us that the two Treatises of Locke had made a profound impression on his mind. What he sought and what he dreamed for States and Empires was, he says, " the reign of Law based on the consent of the governed sustained by the organised opinion of mankind ". The 14th of Wilson's Points is the equality of the large States and the small, within the League of Nations. Here we are back to Vitoria's point of view. Here Roman Catholicism and Protestantism are in accord ; theology is the key to it all. Finally, if we want to understand a man like Sun Yat-sen, Father of the Chinese Revolution, it is important to remember that he was by training a Protestant.[2] His father was a Christian convert of the London Missionary Society, a preacher of the Protestant persuasion, and he himself was a convert also, having been instructed in their doctrines by the Protestant American missionaries in Hawaii, when he was a student in Honolulu. His wife was a Protestant too, like her sister Madame Chiang Kai-shek. All in all, it is true to say that the Founder of the Three Fundamental Principles —Nationalism, Democracy and Socialism—who was into the bargain a reader of Rousseau—was in the fullest sense a product of the Christian Missions ! The Chinese Revolution is the spiritual work of the Americans ! Through them, it goes back to the Protestant dogma of olden days, to Locke and to Rousseau, inasmuch as it is the assertion, the orchestration of Equality !

---

[1] *Encyclopædia Britannica*, 14th Ed. 1930, IX, s.v. *Fourteen Points*.

[2] G. Soulié de Morant, *Soun Iat Sènn* ; H. Bond Restarick, *Sun Yet Sen, Libérateur de la Chine*, 1932.

CHAPTER XXX

SECULARISED EQUALITY

We have been able to trace partnership on equal terms (*association égalisée*) in its antiquity, and then the first signs of it in modern times. We have studied how the idea of equality in the relations between dominant and dominated peoples, developed in Roman Catholicism and in Protestantism. Let us pursue this idea and see how it became secularised, and how, in relation to the colonies, the transition came about from Roman Catholicism and Protestantism to radicalism and democratisation. How equality led to fraternity and to community ; to association and fusion, by the power of thought and the virtue of love. The last phase of equality is *secularised equality* : humanised equality leads to fraternity and brotherhood.

How then did equality become secularised ? How was the transition made from theology to sociology, providing a humane, secular basis for equality ? There were three great phases in this transition engineered by three sets of agents : those who *foretold*, those who *proclaimed*, those who *applied*.

Those who foretold secularised equality were those who preached equality for its own sake in the relationships of peoples brought into contact. In the very heart of the Middle Ages we already find advanced spirits who, independently of theology, conceived equality in a universal sense for the whole human race. In the 14th century a certain Honoré Bonet, a prior of Salon-en-Provence, author of a book called *The Tree of Battles*,[1] issued a pamphlet in which a Turk—already !—read the Christian peoples a lesson. Here we have the malevolently-critical foreigner, or the remonstrating barbarian, whose type is rampant of late.[2] This Turk, being a Turk, steps forward to plead, not in the name of our Christianity, but in the name of equality itself, that a Turk is as good as a Christian, and an Oriental as good as a Westerner. He comes to offer advice to the West, pointing out that the West is not always first, does not always enjoy primacy, and that Reason and Virtue may have their home in other places too !

[1] *L'Arbre des Batailles.*
[2] C, Lenient, *La satire en France au Moyen Age*, 1859, p. 253 f.

In his *Caractères* of 1687, La Bruyère would seem to be the very first to expound secularised equality founded on the fact of the relativity of civilisations. The mere fact that conquerors are conquerors does not make them superior—far from it. The East can well teach the West, in virtue of—what we should call —the "relativity" of civilisations. Each has its truth ; each its social system ; the one is as good as the other, and for its own folk better than the other. My system is for me the best. Here La Bruyère thus proclaims the *equality of civilisations* : one people is as good as another, one custom as good as another. There is no shadow of inherent superiority or inferiority as between one nation and another. Reason, he tells us in the well-known chapter of the *Caractères* " Concerning Strong Minds " (*Des esprits forts*), " reason is of every clime ", and " wherever there are men, there is right thinking ". Thus he preaches the Universality and the Relativity of Reason, Unity and Identity of mind. Similarly Chevalier de Méré in the Third of his *Conversations* (1682) says " Everyone has by nature the same mind, or very nearly " ; a worthy man is as likely to be found " in the depth of the Indies " as amongst us at home. Equality comes to be based on common Reason. " What should we say if the Siamese wanted to convert us and were to send us their *talapoins* as missionaries to teach us their doctrines ? " This idea recurs in the philosophers of the 18th century, the idea that the Eastern nations would have every right to send to teach us religion and morals and to civilise us, if they felt the wish ! It is only out of tolerance that they do not ; and because they show more respect for our beliefs than we for theirs. Equality thus embraces tolerance ; to feel equal, is to feel tolerant. Reason condemns Imperialism, spiritual and cultural imperialism alike.

An obscure creator of a Utopia, or of an " imaginary voyage " to those lands where happiness and virtue dwell, a certain Tyssot de Patot, author of *The Voyages of Jacques Massé* (1710), speaks still more firmly on the same lines. This imitative author was captured by this idea, already vulgarised and commonplace, that an Oriental was as good as a Westerner and a non-European as good as a European,[1] and that a pagan too was as good as a Christian ! This was going rather far and was no longer fashionable ! Secularised equality, emancipated from theology, was soon to smack of heresy !

[1] On a contemporary of Tyssot de Patot, J. E. Bernard, see G. L. van Roosbroek, *Persian Letters before Montesquieu*, 1932.

Shortly after, this was markedly the case with Fontenelle. He it was who was the chief prophet of this attitude of mind. In his *New Dialogues of the Dead*,[1] published in 1721, there is a dialogue between Montezuma, the last King of the Aztecs, and Fernando Cortes, who had defeated him. In it, Montezuma defends this very equality between nations and on the grounds of Reason. Cortes repeated how much stronger the Spaniards were! " But," replied Montezuma, " the most civilised countries have had their coarse and savage superstitions, arousing well-deserved disgust. We do not make mock of the superstitions of the Americans ; Europeans have their superstitions too ! The Athenians, the founders of Reason, these children of Athena, had traditions which show a curious similarity with those of the American natives." The idea was : Identity, therefore Equality. It was this thought which led people at this period to seek out the analogies between various civilisations, to discover resemblances between various traditions in order to draw together and to equalise different peoples. If Reason is of every clime, superstition, Anti-Reason, is found under every sky. The argument advanced by Montezuma's shade is a secular argument ; it is sociological, not theological. " If, on the other hand," he says—still pleading against Cortes in this dialogue between phantoms—" if, on the other hand, the Spaniards have had their arts and crafts which made them great and made them strong, the Mexicans also had their own arts which were quite as well worth while as the Spaniards'." This comparison was pursued all through the century, between the arts, manners and customs of various peoples, to emphasise over and over again how the ruled might be no less valuable than the rulers. Thus : the Aztecs had a history, unwritten, it is true ; a history with their own historians ; they thought, they wrote in their own appropriate way. They had an art of construction—like the ancient Egyptians : architecture without machines, which has left imposing monuments. In what sense then have the Spaniards a right to claim to be superior ? " Well," he says— and this is the bombshell !—" the sole superiority of the conquerors lay in their ships." It was by force alone that they were superior ; by their ships, not by their talents. The " free-thinker ", Fontenelle, with little of the Christian left about him, thus undermined European pride. The value of peoples lies in

[1] *Nouveaux Dialogues des Morts.*

what they create ; works of the spirit, works of toil, are of the
same rank in every climate.   The Spaniards' superiority lay in
—their cannon !

Next comes Voltaire, another destroyer ; [1] a mighty echo,
no inventor, but a marvellous populariser.   In various tales he
shows that our European pride is foolish and vain ; that the West
could learn from the East, and that "culture " is not the exclusive
privilege of our little upstart peoples who owe respect to much
older peoples.   His *Letters of Amabed* permit an Indian to pass
judgment on the claim of the West to be of more weight and
value.   The antiquity of the Indian people—here we meet the
antiquity argument which was presently to be flourished in favour
of the Chinese, the Mexicans, the Peruvians and others—the
antiquity of the Indian people is in truth far higher than the
slight antiquity of the Jewish people of which the Westerners
boast so much.   If civilisations are to be rated in proportion to
their age, it is not in the West that you will find the Chosen
People but in the East, amongst the Indians, the Egyptians, or
in the further West among the Mexicans, the Peruvians ; above
all, amongst the Chinese, whose great antiquity was beginning
to be suspected in Voltaire's day.   " On the other hand," the
Indian goes on, " Europeans often lack certain industries which
have long flourished in our Hindustan ; they were obliged to
go forth and seek in these burning countries arts which they did
not possess.   They owe these far-off peoples many of their
products : spices and perfumes for instance, coffee and cotton
. . ."   What the Americans nowadays call " primitive man's
contribution ", which they humbly acknowledge,[2] has been
already clearly set forth by Voltaire.   Not all the arts are of
Western origin—far from it !   Many have been learnt from the
despised natives of other continents.   Finally the Indian says :
" Europeans are always hairy ; they are carnivorous ; they eat
meat ; we think them barbarians ! "   Voltaire skilfully lets us
see the Indian gloating over the barbarous ways of the foreigner,
puffed up with pride because he feels himself to be the better.
With barely concealed malice Voltaire lets his Indian talk of
our missionaries.   These missionaries are barbarians ; for they
slaughter hens, which for a Brahmin is a savage deed !   Every-

---

[1] See in general, L. Drapeyron, *Voltaire et la question coloniale, Revue de Géogr.*,
March 1894.
[2] A learned amplification of this theme in J. G. Frazer's *Golden Bough*.   See
abridged Edition, 1923, Chap. 23, *Our Debt to the Savage* ; and G. Wharton James,
What the White Race may Learn from the Indian, 1908 (Chicago).

thing is turned against the European, even his pride ! [1] No
one is essentially better than another ; but each thinks himself
better. Let us be tolerant . . . and grateful too, towards these
Orientals to whom we owe so much, and who are quite as good
as we !

With Voltaire we leave the prophets of equality in the lay-
man's sense, and come to *those who proclaim it*, the propagandists
who won over public opinion. Their names would be many,
and the series is continuous. My intention is therefore only
to point out, by reference to authors at intervals of time, how the
idea progressed during the last century. The " communist "
Morelly was not slow to echo Voltaire, the lord of Ferney :
" Nature is constant and invariable . . . Nothing therefore
which can be adduced about the difference of manners and
customs between savage and civilised peoples can prove that
Nature varies . . . " [2] Always Identity, always Equality. Next
Condorcet : Annexed colonies " bar the system of confraternity ;
there must be freedom of relations in the interest of all the
powers ; without which the spirit of independence will necessarily assert itself." [3]

Proudhon in whom, as in so many other " thinkers ", we
can detect several different attitudes of mind existing concurrently ; Proudhon, who was later to sing of war and boast of
conquest, yet proclaimed—and indeed better than any other—
about 1850 in three of his writings, the *Idea of the Revolution,
Justice in the Revolution*, and *War and Peace*,[4] the equality which
ought to reign between the nations of East and West, between
rulers and ruled. In connection with the labour of slaves, he
says in *War and Peace* that human dignity must be respected in
every race and that Man, everywhere, is called to enjoy the right
to liberty. This was a democratic, not a theological vision,[5] an
idea, according to his own phrase, of the Revolution. In the
first of these books he says that the relations between people
and people are " the free and universal interpretation of races
under the sole law of contract ". Like Kant and Rousseau, he

---

[1] Even our " mechanical devices " which the pseudo-Iroquois, Igli, was criticising
at this same period ! (Maubert de Gouvest) *Lettres iroquoises*, 1755.
[2] *Code de la Nature* . . . , 1757.
[3] *Bibliothèque de l'homme public*, VIII, 1790, p. 157 f.
[4] *Idée de la Révolution, Justice dans la Révolution, La Guerre et la paix.*
[5] V. Considérant had also said, in his *Manifeste de la Démocratie pacifique* (1842)
Edition of 1847, pp. 66 and 72, that " States and Peoples are ' living personalities ',
each possessing its own right to free existence in the ' Society of Nations '."—It is not
clear whether in this passage he had non-Europeans in mind or not.

wants a Social Contract drawn up between equals, even if it were in the relation between the primitive and the civilised. In the same book he says : " Man, of whatever race and colour, is really a *native of the Universe* " ; from this there would follow a universality of rights and duties for all mankind. He made no doubt precautionary reservations, no doubt he wished transitional stages, and in speaking in *War and Peace* of the universal call of Man to the right of liberty and to the right of equality, he pointed out that progress in this evolution must be slow ; that the old, existing state of affairs must not be shattered in one day ; that liberty and equality must not be suddenly, unexpectedly, brutally hurled at all subject peoples. " You must improve slavery before setting free the slave ; it would serve no purpose to emancipate the slave merely to make him into a proletarian, for that would be worse than slavery." But a day ought to come, and it ought as far as possible to be hastened, where liberty with equality would reign between the nations of every colour.

To attain this goal, these infant peoples must be educated. " All that we have to do in the colonies, we of superior race *vis à vis* those of inferior race, is to raise them to our level, to try to improve them, fortify them, instruct them and ennoble them." Is not that an expression, in very striking terms, of the *education* and *partnership* whose aim is to make the inferiors in the course of time the equals of the superiors ? Equals—in dignity particularly : " To be conscious of dignity in yourself as in others, is the very essence of Society." Justice is therefore respect for the dignity of others, a respect based on the identity of the human spirit in all men. This is the point of view which produced the " policy of consideration and respect " (*politique des égards*).[1]

In the 60's at the very moment of Proudhon's death, his ideals won over the middle-classes, the " bourgeois " ; the conservatives were converted into reformers ! It was not only the Utopia-minded and the Socialists who foretold and proclaimed these ideals. It was the " Republican Party ", and the humbler middle-classes, the " *petty bourgeoisie* " which professed the equality of the colonies ; and with them the " moderate " party. Edmond About, for instance, whose conservatism no one can question, says

---

[1] In his *Philosophie de la Révolution* (1850) J. Ferrari, an Italian domiciled in France, who was in many ways close in thought to Proudhon, proposed to promote the equality of the whole human race by " a universal agrarian law."

in his work *Progress* [1] of 1865 that what he calls "autonomy"
should reign between White and Black—this is neither more
nor less than equality for Mankind. "This old Negro in his
rags," he says, "is your equal! This Negro is a legitimate
sovereign, inviolable and sacred." I doubt if anyone in our day
would go further : the Negro-Sovereign is the statue of Equality!
"There is," he adds, "no question of degree in this matter of
human dignity"—About uses the word under the influence of
Proudhon. This universal attribute of dignity takes its place in
the new portrait of Man.—Jules Barni in *Lessons* delivered in
Geneva in 1864–5 condemns conquests, still in the name of
human dignity.[2]

It is easy to understand that it was amongst working people
that these ideas took root, in the Workers' Associations which
appeared under the Second French Empire. When these associations started, they did not think of asking themselves any questions
about the rights of the native in the colonies. The equality
clause, however, soon appeared in the statutes of the International ; the "International Working Men's Association"
founded in London in 1867, recorded in its statutes that "this
association will recognise as the basis of its conduct towards all
men, truth, justice and morality without distinction of colour,
creed or nationality". In this "proletarian" setting, the
equality of peoples is an act of faith.

Coming nearer to our own times, it is amongst the Republican
or Radical Party in France—which once reigned there, but reigns
no longer—that we must seek the prophets and apostles of this
ideal. In the first Republican "programmes", in the Clémen-
ceau programme and in the Gambetta programme of 1869,
there was no question of coloured races, the talk was of Europe
only and no mention of the colonies was made. We have to
take a leap to discover amongst the Republican party the assertion of equality in the colonies, the transference to them of the
Rights of the Citizen. It was somewhere about the year 1880
that the party began to show itself conscious in its manifestos
and in its programmes that the Rights of Man were articles of
export to distant countries ; that the Declaration of 1789 had
spoken of the Rights of Man before it mentioned the Rights of
the Citizen, and that this declaration was valid for the whole
world. But in fact it was not until much later, not until after

---

[1] *Le Progrès.*
[2] J. Barni, *La morale dans la démocratie*, 1868, Lessons 13 and 14.

1900, that the doctrine assumed its full and ample form in France. This was thanks to Victor Augagneur, Governor of Madagascar, and to Albert Demangeon, author of a chapter in colonial policy in his work *Republican Policy*.[1] Equality for secular reasons, in the name of the rights of man, between former rulers and subjects had now come into the picture and the theory was vigorously pursued.[2]

As we saw in another connection, we see here that the *application* had preceded the formal announcement of the doctrine; that the secularised ideal of equality had first found those who realised and those who *applied* it; for in France under the Revolution and under the Directory we have seen the law formally create equality in a legal sense between ruler and subject. We have seen equality, without the doctrine of equality. One of the very earliest decrees of 1790 had, it is true, stated that equality held good only for France itself and by no means for the colonies ! But a decree of 1791 soon followed, according citizen rights to free-born coloured men ; consequently not—not by a long way —to all the inhabitants of colonial countries ; it granted these rights to mulattos or to half-castes, called " people of colour ", provided they were born of parents who were not slaves. This decree was annulled in the same year, but a new decree of 1792 soon gave once more the same solution of the problem. And under the Convention a decree of 1794 proclaimed—for a short time !—equality of rights between rulers and subjects. All the inhabitants of the colonies were French citizens, even pure-blooded Negroes !

[1] V. Augagneur, *La politique coloniale républicaine*, in *Questions pratiques de législation ouvrière*, 1908.—A. Demangeon, *La politique coloniale* in *La politique républicaine*, 1924, p. 417 f.

[2] A. Sarraut, *La mission civilisatrice de la France* in *Le Panorama : Grandeur et servitude coloniales*, 1931, and the vol. of the *Rights of Man*, quoted below. Cf. H. von Gerlach, *La politique coloniale*, *Thèses présentées au xxvᵉ Congrès Universel de la Paix* : " there are no superior and inferior peoples . . . we must civilise backward peoples to emancipate them in the future ". A. Sarraut speaks of " the Declaration of the Rights of Man interpreted by St. Vincent de Paul ". See also his Preface to M. Olivier, *Six années de politique sociale à Madagascar*, 1931.

CHAPTER XXXI

ORGANISED FRATERNITY

In the days of which we are speaking, secularised equality, no longer rooted in theology, but based instead on sociology, had formally led to a yet more advanced idea—that of fraternity, the common brotherhood of all Mankind. No longer hierarchic partnership, no longer partnership on equal terms, but, if I may so express myself, *fraternal partnership* in which a feeling of brotherhood should reign ; community in the moral sense, coloured by an element of sentiment and passion ; a common aspiration towards an ideal vision and a shared affection. Fraternity is thus much more than the equality of the 1789 slogan ; for it embraces three several conceptions : *reciprocity, intimacy* and *unanimity.*

Reciprocity or *Solidarity* : means rights and duties accepted in both directions and for the benefit of both : for the benefit of the White and of the Non-white. The new inhabitants and the old inhabitants are to have reciprocal powers and reciprocal duties. The legal bond between them is to be bilateral. "We must help each other" is to be their motto. Equality was a passive fact ; Brotherhood is to be an active fact.

Intimacy or *Sociability* : means the desire for close and intimate relations ; the wish for, and pleasure in, mixing socially together, and in forming friendships ; the inclination to be bound together in affection : love is to prove better than duty, and fusion better than partnership. In this sense, fraternity means proximity, intimacy.

Unanimity or *Uniformity* : means the conjunction of feeling and the identity of aspiration, arrived at by a lengthy process of education and fusion. There is a wish that a time may come when the accord of feelings, what the Greeks called symphony or harmony, the fusion of souls and accord of hearts, may be granted to men as to the gods themselves.

Community or *Brotherhood* is the creation of a social being, the formation of a collective spirit by the devotion and the absorption of all the members into one body.

Fraternity which has its three aspects, has also its three phases— a *Hellenistic* phase, then a *philosophic*, and lastly a *democratic* phase.

During the *Hellenistic* age the Greeks, in a happy moment towards the end of their evolution—which had begun with the

closed city of early days—had a lightning-like perception, an
" annunciation " or " revelation " in the religious sense, of active
brotherhood between all human beings. The Stoics had conceived the idea of universal man, " citizen of the world ", an
idea which implied a sense of devotion, of mutual obligation
between peoples to establish a symphony between nations. Such
was the spirit of Zeno's " cosmopolitanism ". This is thought
to have been an extension of the Chaldean cult, the worship
of the Heavens, which burn and shine for all Mankind.[1] It
is, however, something more ; the search for love between men
of all places ; the abolition of any feeling of distinction between
peoples ; the brotherhood of all men, dreamt of for a far-distant
future. The words which the Ancients coined, philanthropy
and harmony, *homonoia* and *concordia*, the union of hearts, as the
Stoics called it, these represent a partial vision of fraternity.

The *philosophic* phase came two thousand years later, in the
" Age of Enlightenment ", when the " human race " was re-
thought and re-felt. A foreigner who came to France, a certain
Anacharsis Cloots, preached a Universal Republic animated by
love of the whole human race. Before Saint-Simon, before
Auguste Comte, he dreamt of a deified Humanity, the object
of worship, like a God. This was the Great Being of Enfantin,
possessing identity and continuity, whose *animus* is Brotherhood.
In 1790 this same Anacharsis Cloots presented at the bar of the
Constituent Assembly an " Embassy of the Human Race "—
amongst them a Chaldean and an Arab, two Oriental interpreters whose names have been preserved : Chafis and Chammas.
This was an affirmation of the Brotherhood of Humanity, staged
with all the theatrical accompaniments beloved in Revolutionary
days. In the same spirit Sieur Lequinio in 1792, drawing his
inspiration from the Ancients, styled himself, not without pride,
a " Citizen of the Globe ". This was in a work which he called
Prejudices Destroyed ! [2]

In the Declaration of Rights, not the Declaration of 1789
which is obsessed solely with equality limited in the first place
to the European world,[3] but in the Declaration of 1793 which

---

[1] J. Bidez, *La Cité du Monde et la Cité du Soleil, Bulletin Académie Royale Belgique,
Lettres,* 5th Series, Vol. XVIII, 1932, pp. 244–91. Cf. L. Dugas, *L'amitié antique,*
1804, p. 141 ; W. Shücking, *Der Kosmopolitismus der Antike, Zeitschrift für Sozial-
wissenschaft,* X, 1907, p. 519 f. ; M. Mühl, *Die antike Menschheitsidee,* 1928 ; W. W. Tarn,
Alexander the Great and the Unity of Mankind (*Proceedings of the British Academy,* 1933).
[2] *Les préjugés détruits.*
[3] See in general, Gaston-Martin, *La doctrine coloniale de la France en 1789, Cahiers
révolutionnaires français,* III, 1935.

was mainly the work of Robespierre, what do we read ? " Men of every country are brothers, and the different peoples should aid each other according to their power, like citizens of the same State." [1]   Here is the conception of active brotherhood implying duties, desiring mutual aid between peoples. It was Volney—of whom we shall be speaking again later—who in 1790, three years earlier, had drawn up the draft of a decree which says : " The Assembly looks on the universality of the human race as the basis of one single and identical society whose object is the peace and happiness of all."   When Volney published some years later his well-known reverie called *Ruins*, his nineteenth chapter bore the heading : " General Assembly of the Peoples ", and in it we read this apostrophe : " O Nations ! Let us in future form but one single society, one large family . . . ! "   This is friendship, but brotherly friendship, which as the Greeks had already seen, is the most perfect form of friendship.   " Let us then live as one single family under one single code, the code of Reason." Volney predicts, before Auguste Comte, that at some future day all Mankind will be governed by one Assembly of a universal nature like the Council of our League of Nations ; an Assembly in which the representatives will be ranged according to their costume and the shades of their skin " down to the tattooed representatives of the Pacific islands " ; and the law-givers will say to all these deputies that God wishes them to be all free and all equal !

When—perhaps a little later—another forerunner, Abbé Grégoire, wrote in his *Memoirs* that " the various nations are sections of the one large family " ; when he wrote that " there are indefeasible rights possessed by suffering humanity, without distinction of faith, climate, colour or race " ; when he spoke of "the human family" and when he proposed—still in 1793— a Declaration of the Rights of Peoples, to proclaim liberty, equality and fraternity between the dispersed peoples ; finally, when in the same document he said that " men and peoples are brothers " he was anticipating the spirit of our present time, he was singing in beautiful language the ideal of brotherhood ; he was preluding the *democratic* phase of to-day. The Theophilanthropists had also said : " Our love ought to embrace the human race in its entirety." [2]

[1] *Œuvres de Robespierre*, Vermorel's Edition, 1866, pp. 271 and 276.
[2] This whole upsurge of feeling explains better than anything else the instructions issued, and arrangements made, by the Directory : P. Roussier, *La politique coloniale du Directoire, Congrès Sciences historiques*, Warsaw, 1933, II, p. 317 f. ; J. B. Chemin, *Manuel des théophilanthropes . . . et amis des hommes*, Year VI (1798), p. 53.

In this *democratic* phase, as we may call it, the idea of brotherhood has become firmly rooted in men's minds for the last century or so. As usual, there was first the *proclamation* and then the *propagation* of it. It is these collective " currents " which we are looking for ; what concerns us as much as, or more nearly than, the proclamation, is the propagation and circulation of the new sentiments and feelings.

Proclamation. French socialist doctrine has been current this hundred years. It was Socialism, and after that Positivism, and after that Humanitarianism which proclaimed the brotherhood of the colonies.

It was through *Socialism,* and particularly in France through the old Utopian French socialism, that the new ideal of fraternity made headway, thanks to the propaganda of the Saint-Simonians.

In the very forefront stands Saint-Simon himself. In his *Exposition of the Doctrine,* of 1828 and 1829, in which he coins the well-known phrase " man's exploitation of man ", he touches on the relations between Black and White ; and in the fourth Lesson of the course he shows the transition that may be hoped for " from antagonism to partnership " for the whole Universe.[1] In his own words, " the circle of partnership ought to extend to the human race in its entirety, so as to improve the moral, physical and intellectual condition of Mankind ". The problem was to abolish the domination and exploitation of man by man ; the plan was to transform the world into a vast workshop, " working under one common law towards the fulfilment of one common destiny ". This was no longer equality pure and simple ; for here there is a duty throughout the human race to render mutual assistance and mutual affection under the same law to the same end. What ought to rule the relations of man to man is " a bond of love between all living things ". In his *New Christianity*[2] he also writes : " All men ought to behave like *brothers* one with another." Here we have the express and formal proclamation and publication of the ideal of brotherhood. One of the " Disciples of the Messiah ", a certain Olinde Rodrigues, published in 1831 some *Letters on Religion and Policy.*[3] In them he upholds the idea of " the unity of the human races as opposed to the dogma of royal races ". Before Auguste Comte, he tried to found a Religion of Humanity ; the aim he proposed for this religion was to be the happiness

---

[1] Especially : I, p. 144 f. ; II, pp. 105, 171 and 178.
[2] *Nouveau Christianisme.*   [3] *Lettres sur la religion et la politique.*

of the species and the constitution of a universal community, the Society of Humanity.

The supreme preacher of fraternity, however, was Enfantin, who in his *Political Correspondence* continued the work of Saint-Simon as propagandist for partnership. I have already pointed out that he sought to establish not only partnership but *friend-ship* with the coloured peoples ; he wishes " the peoples to be made partners and to be put in families ". He was speaking therefore of an *affamiliation* between French and Algerians ; brotherhood between East and West, since, he said, while the Orient would have much to receive from the Occident, the West would also have much to receive from the Ancient East, since she it was who would restore to us strength and faith. Strength and Faith would return from the East. Here is the prophetic expression of many hopes of our own day ! A follower of Saint-Simon, Ismail Urbain, actually embraced Islam a few years later, the better to be able to fraternise.[1]

The idea of fraternisation was present also in *Fourierism*. It spread speedily to Algeria. Fourierist circles sprang up there in the 1840's. In Algeria there arose a colonial Fourierism which was also a doctrine of brotherhood ; and it laid the foundations in Algeria of *indigenophilia* or *arabophilia*—these words are not of my invention—to express the sentiment of fraternity between French and Algerians. On the occasion of a Fourierist banquet near Algiers in 1848 one of the speakers exclaimed : " The foundation of many Phalansteries [2] will rally the Arab race and will be the signal of universal brotherhood among the peoples." [3] After-dinner enthusiasm no doubt, but the words nevertheless gave expression to a new ideal. So Bugeaud, when he was speaking, as we have seen, in his letters and in his circulars, of treating the natives with consideration, of respecting the natives and displaying equity towards them, was speaking under the inspiration of Fourier who had for a short time been his teacher. Above all, when he said in one single passage—which I have intentionally reserved till now—" Let us make ourselves beloved of them, to form a single people ", it was Bugeaud the Fourierist who was speaking. He was predicting and prophesying fusion through brotherhood, in the bond of blood and in the bond of love.

---

[1] See : (I. Urbain) *Indigènes et émigrants*, 1863.
[2] [See footnote 5, p. 293 above. EOL]
[3] V. J. Czynski, *Colonisation de l'Algérie, d'après la théorie de Charles Fourier*, 1839.

Another of Fourier's disciples, who however never went to Algeria, Victor Considérant, also abandoned himself to the dream of brotherhood. In a work called *Policy in General and France's Rôle in Europe* [1] and published in 1840, Considérant spoke of " the fraternity of peoples " and of " the policy of humanity ". Finally, he spoke of summoning all peoples to a great Unity, by a bond at the same time spiritual and physical, of the inter-racial union of the sexes : making, as we should say, an appeal to the heart. At the same moment as fraternity between *classes* [2] was being preached, fraternity between *peoples* was being preached also.

Lastly, we must take note of Pecqueur, one of the inventors of " Collectivism ", who in 1838 formally proposed " methodic hybridisation " between different peoples. To his mind the only way of re-establishing equality between master and subject was to make them into a unity ; equality without unity is a fiction. If you are in earnest in trying to establish equality you can succeed only by creating a unity, a liaison, in every sense of the term, between the one people and the other.[3] He wished to see Equality achieved by Unity, and to this end the institution of a very comprehensive cosmopolitan partnership, brought about by reciprocal marriages between the peoples ; marriages of both types, between Frenchmen and native girls, between native men and French girls. Pecqueur expressly desired this as a condition of full reciprocity. This idea was in those days extremely novel, it pushed the original idea of identity from which he started to its logical conclusion : Unity by Fusion in one crucible ! A historian, who was also a prophet—Michelet, I mean—foretold in his *History of France* [4] the foundation of a Half-Caste Empire where continual intermarriage would maintain fraternity.

The same ideal was pursued by *Positivism*. In his *Discourse on the Sum Total of Positivism* [5] in 1848, Auguste Comte vigorously sang the praises of the idea of the universal partnership of Man.[6] In one of his writings, to which I shall be alluding later, he goes so far as to wish to see separation as well as liberation of the

[1] *De la politique en général et du rôle de la France en Europe.*
[2] M. Chevalier, *Lettres sur l'organisation du travail*, 1848, p. 318 f. Chevalier was another ex-follower of Saint-Simon.
[3] *Des intérêts du commerce* . . . , 1838, II, p. 328 f., 401 f., 435 f. and 507 f.
[4] Vol. XVII (1878), p. 180.
[5] *Discours sur l'ensemble du positivisme.*
[6] Conclusion, p. 384 f. ; cf. *Appel aux Conservateurs*, pp. 8, 27, 34 and 40. Henri Martin, the historian, presently wondered whether the diversity of peoples ought to last or to be extinguished : *De nationum diversitate servanda, salva unitate generis humani,* 1849 (literary thesis, Paris).

ruled ; diverse currents of thought are, as we know, wont to flow through the same mind ! In this book, at least, he wishes partnership and fusion between master and subject : peaceful and universal love. If the West, he says, represents the *élite* of humanity, an *élite* at whose head France stands, this fact imposes on the West, and particularly on France, more duties than privileges ; superiority of civilisation is a burden, not an asset. Thus he dreams that the West, with France as leader, shall undertake the regeneration of Mankind, under the " presidency " of the French people. The white race, superior to other races, should thus exercise its strength and its talents to organise and unify Mankind ; but not too soon, as he expressly stipulates : his dream is only a dream of the future. A day will come when, throughout the entire world, one Universal Committee shall reign—a Universal Parliament, as he says !—which will consist of sixty members : with deputies from the " backward " as well as from the " advanced " peoples ; there would be four yellow men and two black. For the Universe, partnership in the community would be brought about by the West in the distant future.

Under Napoleon III there was no need for anyone in France to be a Positivist or to be a Socialist, to be a follower of Comte or of Fourier, in order to assert and proclaim community and fraternity in the countries overseas. It was Fourier of course who had founded indigenophilia or arabophilia in Algeria, but within a short space of time the idea had gained ground and prevailed to such an extent as even to affect Napoleon III. Perhaps as an ex-*carbonaro* he was mindful at the moment of the fact that he had himself conspired against reigning sovereigns ! He devised for Algeria what has been called the " Arab King- dom " : the idea was that Algeria could govern itself in an association under a protectorate which would be based on community and fraternity between Algerians and French.[1] The Emperor's dreamings bear on them the stamp of their origin in sects and chapels, and show that the moderates were already champions of brotherly love. We have a striking example of this : there was a journalist, or rather there were two journalists, who in the very time of Napoleon III formulated this doctrine of fraternity in a private writing : de Girardin the founder of the halfpenny press and Clément Duvernois who had collaborated

---

[1] A. Fourmestraux, *Les idées napoléoniennes en Algérie*, 1865, and the work of J. Duval above quoted.

with de Girardin in a pamphlet called *The Civilisation of Algeria* which came out in 1860. Particularly in the section of this pamphlet drawn up by Clément Duvernois, the emancipation of Algeria was announced as a distant goal ; for the present, what he desired was colonisation, but by freedom. He demanded the creation of an Imperial Viceroyalty for Algeria, endowed with full powers so as to pursue a completely new policy in that country, a policy which should not be, as in the days of the generals, a policy of tyranny. What you must do, he said, is not to expel or " drive back " the old inhabitants as they did at first ; nor yet, as they have tried to do, to " assimilate " or " Frenchify " the Algerians, imposing the adoption of French manners and customs on them by law ; what you must do is to civilise them, to educate them, to draw them to you by teaching them ; you must set going sociable familiarity between them and the French, the only thing which will put an end to hostility. The better to attain this end, he made the daring suggestion that the French colonists should be placed under Algerian rule ! We must, he said, administer the country for the native, not for the colonist ; for the natives are in the majority and the colonists form a minority. If, therefore, we want partnership in Algeria, our administration must be for the Algerians ; our government must be conducted in their interests. He speaks thus of the " fusion of interests " and already also of the " fusion of races " ; he even uses the word " crucible " to indicate the intimate intermingling of the two populations. Algeria is for him a crucible—we should nowadays say a " melting-pot "— where the blending of the two peoples would be consummated. " It is a simple thing to civilise the native " ; you need only to enfranchise the natives, teaching them at the same time to come along with you, trying to draw them towards you, forming and transforming them to associate them with you in their own interest and fusing them with you in feeling.[1]

Ten years afterwards came the Third French Republic, and the number of writers grew who dreamed of the Society of colonisers and colonised. Edgar Quinet in his work entitled *La République*, published in 1872,[2] similarly said : " Every durable victory has brought about the fusion of human races." He believes that he has already noticed in the Roman domination

---

[1] The proscribed Ferrari, of whom I have already spoken, in his *Histoire de la Raison d'État*, published in Paris in 1860, predicts the civilisation of the entire globe by the union of all the peoples of the Universe by the year 3500.

[2] p. 248 f.

of the Greeks, that even in olden times there could be no civilisation or unification save by fusion and intermingling. " Colonisation is then the partnership and association of two human
races." In opposition to Gobineau, who had written fifteen
years before, he goes on to maintain for the first time the superiority in the social sense, of mixed or blended nations, such, he
says, as the old French nation. Gobineau asserted the superiority of " pure " races ; for him mixed peoples, hybrid peoples,
were inferior. This idea was absolutely opposed to the association and fusion of peoples in contact with each other on distant shores. Edgar Quinet took the exactly opposite line : the
superior peoples, the most civilised peoples, such as our own
French people, are hybrids, half-castes, bastards, in whose blood
different spirits and different talents are combined. There is
no expansion without mixing, and mixing is a sign of progress.
It was Quinet therefore who instilled into democratic opinion
the idea of brotherhood in its fullest sense, by the fusion of soul
and blood ! Father Hugo noisily echoed him : " God offers,"
he said, " Africa to Europe . . . not for conquest but for
fraternity." [1]

The same spirit, moreover, reigned all around. When, towards the end of the reign of Napoleon III, the *Ethnographic
Society.* [2]—still flourishing in our day—was founded in France,
it took for its motto a Latin phrase :

Corpore diversi et mentis lumine fratres (diverse in body and brothers
in the light of the mind).

In other words—to translate very freely— : " Humanity is composed of different bodies (viz. of different peoples) but in one
spirit founded on fraternity : " a scientific but also a democratic
motto. When President Légitime in Haiti pleaded for the
autonomy of his island, he recalled in his Declaration of 1888
this motto of the Ethnographic Society and commented on it
in these words : " God, the Master of us all, has neither
privileged class nor superior race." The old concept of equality
in the name of God revives in the black man's brain to translate
the new concept of brotherhood in the name of Unity. One
of the admirals in Cochin-China, Jauréguiberry, in his instructions of 1879 formally foresaw an association of equals : he

---

[1] *Discours sur l'Afrique,* 1879, Extracts in the *Monde Colonial illustré,* May 1935.
—According to F. Vermale's report, *Au Sahara,* p. 15, Father de Foucauld was not
innocent of similar visions.

[2] *Société d'Ethnographie.*

desired an Assembly composed half of natives and half of French.[1]

Let us take a leap to the beginning of our own century. In 1902, a now-forgotten writer, d'Arvey, published a book called *Towards Colonisation* [2]—labour as completely as possible wasted—in which he hopes to promote in the future a complete " fraternal division " of all the wealth of French civilisation, by means of domination transformed into partnership.

Though this author, and others, were out of touch with the public, voices crying in the desert, there has been nevertheless *propagation*, infiltration into the public mind, of the brotherly colonial spirit. Its popularisation was mainly the work of the newspaper, but other factors have played their part—speech, pamphlet, play and screen.

A book achieved considerable success under the First Empire, Joseph Lavallée's *The Negro with whom few White Men can compare.*[3] His intention was to melt the heart of his readers—especially his women readers—over the Negro's fate ; to " make the Negro beloved of the white man " ; a romantic work, before the word " romantic " was in vogue.

Plays and *novels*, however, were what gripped the public. Under Louis Philippe, while the struggle to abolish " slavery " was on, *The Well-Doing Mulatto* [4] was put on the stage, representing the mulatto, a better man than the white, who is able to save the white man and learn to love him. Roger de Beauvoir published in 1838 a most successful novel, *The Chevalier of Saint George*. This is the triumph of the gentleman-mulatto, the apotheosis of the half-caste, a song of praise for the mingling of races : having been " lionised " and promoted to be an elegant of the boulevards, he gives a lesson of magnanimity and generosity to a pure-bred French Baron ! A successful author, Anicet Bourgeois, produced in 1848 a seven-act play to which all Paris is said to have flocked, *The Black Doctor.*[5] This is the portrait of a valiant Bourbon mulatto who becomes a doctor and saves the life of a young girl who is a hundred per cent. of noble birth. She consents to marry him secretly. Her mother gets the deceitful son-in-law thrown into the Bastille ; he goes mad. Oh, the cruelty of the aristocrat ! the cruelty of the White Man ! The valiant mulatto was acted by Frederick

---

[1] Le Myre de Vilers, *Institutions civiles de la Cochinchine*, 1908, p. 2 f.
[2] *Vers la colonisation.*
[3] *Le nègre comme il y a peu de blancs.*
[4] *Le Mulâtre Bienfaisant.*   [5] *Le docteur noir.*

Lemaître ; we can well imagine that he made the part an emotional success. The elder Dumas, who had a natural instinct for knowing which way the wind was blowing, was bound to come along next and join in the chorus. He published his mulatto novel under the title of " George ". A mulatto who has made a fortune comes back to Port Louis from Mauritius and vainly fights a losing battle against the cruel prejudice felt towards people of mixed blood. In a moment of exasperation he avenges himself by provoking a Negro revolt. He is defeated and condemned, but the loveliest of the white ladies rescues and marries him. The same theme eternally recurs : the final marriage of the black man and the white woman, or the mulatto and the white woman ; an attempt to bring about a union of soul and body, a joint society of black and white. The play and the novel thus jointly conspired to propagate the new ideal. There thus sprang up a whole *colonial drama*, preaching the idea that progress means fusion, that there is no civilisation save by uniting the peoples by interbreeding : a half-breed drama—if I may use the phrase—which preached hybridisation for the happiness of Mankind. This was a plan conceived by Bernardin who was a reformer of burning enthusiasm, and not yet the venerable patriarch whom we see near the cedar in the Jardin des Plantes. In 1789 he published *Dreams of a Recluse* ; [1] one of his dreams was to achieve the unity of the human race by encouraging the intermingling—I quote his very words—" of the lovers of all nations ". Through love—and it was sexual love he had in mind—the union of enemy peoples was to be brought about. Similarly Jefferson, dyed-in-the-wool Puritan, champion of equality, but champion also of fraternity, hoped for fusion to result from nuptial mating between all peoples. In 1808 as President of the United States, he wrote a letter to the chief of the Cherokee tribe, in which he said that the " American ideal " —to use a phrase of President Roosevelt's—was to create from two peoples one single people by repeated intermarriages between White people and Red Indians.[2] Fusion in the social sense was allied to fusion in the sexual sense. Talleyrand, great aristocrat as he was, when an *emigré* exile in Philadelphia, used to take his walks with a native woman on his arm ; this same Talleyrand, who later married an Indian woman, was thus, as always, in practice a free-thinker, a liberal and a progressive.

[1] *Les vœux d'un solitaire.*
[2] Perry Belmont, *Political Equality*, French trans. 1927, p. 143 f.

BOOK VII

EMANCIPATION OR LIBERATION

CHAPTER XXXII

WAYS AND MOTIVES—MEANS AND AIMS

It is now our business to enquire how, in the opinion of the colonial peoples, we have advanced from the earlier attitudes of mind—domination and partnership—to the new one which we must now discuss : *Liberation.* How we have tended to hope for and to foster the emancipation of the subject peoples ; the idea of ultimate emancipation came first to the rulers, often not until later to the ruled. We now no longer find, as hitherto, moderating and reforming spirits, " associators "—if I may risk the word—but " dissociators " and emancipators, who have been trying to promote the separation of the colonies from their masters and their " tyrants ". Let us in general terms take a look at the landscape from a slightly higher point of view ; let us enquire by what ways, for what motives, by what means, for what objects, this attitude of mind has developed. Our plan is to search out the *paths, motives, means* and *objects* of the emancipator's ideal.

By what *paths* has he arrived at the idea of emancipation ? There are two : an old one and a new. Partnership has been capable of leading to liberation ; but domination was also able, and not too recently, to lead by hidden tracks to liberation. Partnership and Domination both paved the way to emancipation.

Partnership or *Association* led thither in accordance with the rationalist spirit of France which is ever ready to push an idea to its ultimate conclusion. The French arrived at the conception that partnership or association in its true sense is friendship ; and friendship is freewill and liberty. The Ancients had already said that there is no friendship, that there is therefore no Society in the perfect sense, except through free-will and liberty. Society or friendship is a *contract* from which either party ought always to be able to withdraw, a bond which either party ought always to be free to break ! The right of secession or separation is included—if you pursue the idea to its extreme—

in the concept of society and of friendship.   The right to retreat :
that is the idea which is bound to germinate as soon as you base
the relations of ruler and ruled on the concept of partnership.

Domination : through domination it was also possible to
catch a direct glimpse of emancipation : this was an ancient,
not a new path.   I have shown that domination may imply
obligation, may imply education ; this may be a power, it may
be a duty.   You may flatter yourself that you are dominating
no longer for the sake of dominating, that you are ruling no
longer for the sake of ruling, but in order to teach, in order to
educate.   You may pride yourself on conceiving your authority
as a mission, as a task, picturing the legal relations of ruler and
ruled as those of teacher to pupil, rather than those of father to
son, holding that colonisation is for protection and education.
Now all education is due to come to an end ; that is the difference
between a teacher and a father ; the father remains a father for
ever, while the teacher ceases in time to be a teacher.   Education
bears within it the idea of a time limit, the idea of an end.   Education is therefore authority which ought in due course to cease,
or domination from which there should be ultimate release.
Not the right of retreat, but assuredly the right of exit.   We have
thus arrived at the conception that the emancipation of colonial
peoples must come : either because their education has been
effective, or because it has proved wholly ineffective.   In the case
of success, when education has fulfilled its aim, it is obvious that it
is finished.   This is the language of all the texts of the Mandates.
Zaghlul Pasha, the Egyptian liberator, professed to realise that
the Egyptian people were indeed for the moment in need of
education ; he did not therefore wish at the beginning of his
great movement that emancipation should take immediate
effect.   In his Manifesto of 1919 he quite explicitly stated that
the liberation of the Egyptian people should come only when
their education and transformation were complete—be the day
near or far—for a people " ignorant of its rights " needs to be
still ruled.[1]   Others, however, have maintained that this education, which is the aim of domination, should have an end in every
case, even where it has achieved no success.   If it has met with
a check, if the subject people prove impossible to transform, or
" beyond doubt " ineducable, even in these cases the ruling
people ought some day to relinquish power.   The Inca, or
rather the half-breed Inca, Garcilaso de la Vega, attributed in

[1] Foulad Yeghen, *Saad Zaghloul*, pp. 39 and 116 f.

the 16th century an astonishing proposal to one of his ancestors, a famous King of Peru, the Inca Huayna Capac.[1] The Inca is said to have found the inhabitants of the province of Manta, a country remote from Cuzco, so backward—or, alternatively, so " brutish ", as the French translator of our author phrases it— that he is reported as having said : " Let us withdraw from this country, the inhabitants are so obstinate that they do not deserve to have us to govern them ! " He would have abandoned them to their fate as being ineducable or " non-assimilable " by their successful conquerors. Domination may thus serve to introduce emancipation either by its success or . . . by its failure !—In French lands during the 13th century, at the height of the Gothic period, the poet Rutebeuf sang of the dispute between the Crusader and the renegade Crusader who had cast off the Cross.[2] The Renegade chides the Crusader for dashing off to invite danger and risk in distant lands. Is it not more seemly, he asks, to live in peace, not to go seeking war at the ends of the earth, not to go picking quarrels with the Infidel ? For safety and for love of peace is it perhaps not better to stay at home ! You can almost hear the voice of one of the characters, Numa Roume- stan : "But this Algeria in Africa is so far away ! " Rutebeuf's conclusion is that it is a man's duty to take the Cross ; but he has in fact overshot the mark.

So much for the paths that lead to liberation ; but what are the *motives* for it ? Motives there are many ; they are diverse, they are continuous ; they re-appear, they break out anew at times and in places far apart. We can detect two types of motive : those that are expressed and those that are not.

Unacknowledged or *unexpressed* motives have their home in the Unconscious and are therefore rather driving forces or springs of action than true motives. Alternatively, if they are conscious, they are concealed. The most important of these unacknow- ledged motives are *calculation* and *envy*. The wish to abandon colonies often arises, as a matter of calculation or for reasons of envy.

Calculation may occur in the mind of the rulers, or more probably of their neighbours, the outsiders, the rivals. This would be calculation based on self-interest ; present or future. Interested calculation, resting either on hope or on fear, hope of advantage, fear of injury, desire of profit or fear of danger.

---

[1] *Op. cit.*, II, p. 391.

[2] C. Lenient, *La satire en France au Moyen Age*, 1859, p. 64 f. ; G. Cohen's Trans- position in *Université*, No. 2, Feb. 1936.

Calculation in hope, or hope-calculation ; this was frequently present in the French mind : for the national interest or for the colonial interest, for the benefit of the rulers or for the benefit of the ruled, it seemed prudent to abandon the colonies to their fate. The prospect of peace or the prospect of profit seemed to be better assured by abdication and renunciation.

Calculation in fear, or fear-calculation sought to flee from some anticipated danger : the fear of adventure, the fear of disaster, in a word the dread of risk. This motive helped to foster in French countries and particularly amongst the French, thoughts of abandonment. The thrifty and peace-loving Frenchman has often been fearful of venturing overseas. When the poet Rutebeuf makes his Renegade say to the Crusader that it would be better to live at home in peace and safety than to go picking quarrels with the people over there, he is talking prudence in true *bourgeois* style. He thus portrays the " average Frenchman ", miserly and timid, who does not willingly surrender his sons or his ha'pence, who is afraid of risk and danger and will be ready to listen to the advice to quit. Montesquieu, prudent bourgeois that he was, is not far from thinking on these lines.[1] Financial timidity and cowardice in war, fear of expenditure, fear of disaster :[2] repulsion or counter-impulsion have always been at work and have been exploited in French Parliaments by all the enemies of French expansion. All the parties without distinction united in 1885 against Jules Ferry whom Clemenceau denounced in the name of the shopkeepers. However misguided Clemenceau was, let us admit that he had the Right as well as the Left behind him, in arguing that the cost of planting the French flag at Tong-king was too great. The same thing had been said at the time of the conquest of Algeria. At the beginning and for many years there had been protests against the occupation of Algeria. Bugeaud himself opposed it ; and his main reason was . . . fear of the expense ![3] It was *envy* too that made people preach the advantage of quitting Algeria. The envy of the people at home, the envy of foreigners and finally the envy of the subjects, called in those days the " enslaved " (*asservis*).

The envy of the *people at home* : colonies are a means of

---

[1] *Lettres persanes*, 125.

[2] This is very marked in a pamphlet of N. L. Planat's : *De la nécessité d'abandonner Algérie*, 1836 (a long extract in E. Guénin, *L'épopée coloniale de la France*, 1932, p. 21 f.).

[3] Valet, *L'Algérie devant le Parlement*, 1924 (thesis). See also V. Demontès, *Papiers du Gen. Berthezène*, 1917 (thesis), pp. 3 f. and 48 f.

acquiring riches ; large fortunes have been " gained " from the colonies ; they are the nurseries of the new rich who are always hated as upstarts. So you can always be sure of stirring up public opinion, particularly the opinion of the people and of the " small man ", by eloquently haranguing against expansions which are said to be for the benefit of the few. This feeling is nothing new ; it was there in the days of the French kings when the financier and colonial Jacques Cœur was condemned and despoiled for having, it was alleged, made his fortune overseas at the expense of the public. Envy of other men's success, envy of other men's gains, this was the unexpressed motive of the opposition to expansion raised by the people at home.

The envy of *foreigners*, enemy or friend, distant or near, who are the self-appointed critics of imperial peoples. This attitude of mind runs wild to-day ; without it the League of Nations would be incomprehensible. It is the work of the countries which lack colonies, the Have-Nots, as they call themselves, who are always ready to challenge the enterprises of the Haves. This is not the place to express a judgment ; we bear witness merely, it is enough to have mentioned the matter.[1]

The envy, finally, of the *ruled*. These subject peoples, however great their thirst for liberty, are also moved by spite. For power, bringing success, bringing profit, is jealously regarded by those at whose expense it is won. Power, success, profit, these are all one and the same in the eyes of the onlookers. This feeling impels them to revolt. This is an element in the famous " inferiority complex ". Let us dwell no longer on these unacknowledged motives.

Declared, *expressed* motives are more obvious. Envy and calculation are camouflaged by party policy, by anti-colonial prejudice : whether this be doctrine or conviction ; dogma at any rate always takes a hand. Speaking for a system, propaganda must be carried on, converts must be made ; motives are deduced, reasons are brought forward : propaganda makes the policy ! This is the diffusion of a dogma or of a " principle " in which a person believes . . . or pretends to believe. This is the meaning of a saying attributed to Robespierre but in curtailed and mangled form.[2] He did not say—it was in 1791 in the

[1] Let us nevertheless quote a Pole's bitter indictment of French West Africa which provoked protests : Gisicki, *Blancs et Noirs*, 1935. In a less degree the American R. Leslie Buell had criticised the French in *The Native Problem in Africa*, 1928, discussed by *L'Afrique français*, July 1928.

[2] L. Deschamps, *Les colonies sous la Révolution*, 1898, Appendix. The text is found in Robiespierre *Œuvres*, Vermorel's edition, 1866, pp. 47–8.

Assembly—" Let the colonies perish, rather than a principle ! "
what he actually said was : " Let the colonies perish, if they
seek to force us to decree what best suits their own self-interest."
In other words : the nation's will ought to carry the day, even
if it were in favour of coloured people.   Dupont de Nemours had
expressed himself in the same sense.   And Robespierre also said :
" Let the colonies perish, even if it cost us our honour and our
liberty ! "

We must however draw a distinction.   Speaking of moderation and partnership in the course of our talks, we have said how
much these movements owed to convictions and beliefs ; and
we have also noted that it was a matter of deliberate policy to
seek to promote moderation and partnership.   The Roman
Catholic desire to moderate, the Protestant, the Radical and the
Democratic desire to create association or partnership, these
were without doubt dogmas and policies.   They were policies
of long standing which begot new policies of which the three
main ones were Liberalism, Democracy and Autonomy.   This
gives us three phases to consider.

First, *Liberalism*.   It was at first in the name of a desire for
freedom, especially material freedom, in the name of economic
liberalism that people wanted, a century or more ago, to emancipate the colonial countries.   Liberalism was both material and
utilitarian ;   the dogma and ideal of the economists, all at that
time out against the State and wanting to see an end put to all
domination everywhere, as a matter of self-interest—the interest
of the mother countries or the interest of the colonies.

Secondly, *Democracy*.   In our day it is in the name of the
democratic idea that men have sought to bring about the liberation of the colonies.   Domination of any kind, even tempered
domination, even domination moderated and humanised by
partnership, is tainted by authority : a father, a chief, even a
guardian or a director, is incompatible with Democracy.
Equalitarianism in the total sense, in perfect taste, is needed
and it will take several variant forms :   from more or less " bourgeois " radicalism down to collectivism and even communism.
There are many precise points to be noted.

Lastly, *Autonomy* :   the idea of nationality transferred to the
colonial countries.   This is now more and more the ruling
concept—whether we like it or not—of liberty for the nations :
collective liberalism according to which peoples have a right to
freedom.   Nationalism, as it is called, was invented in France

a century or two ago. It is patriotism, born in France and handed on by the French to their subject peoples. It is at the very least a desire for autonomy, for I think I may claim to have shown that French-dominated countries have not so far developed a national spirit.[1] The idea of the nation, the idea of the fatherland, *la patrie*, " the country " has not appeared until very recently in our time, and then in brief flashes only, amongst all these backward peoples. But they have at least the idea of autonomy ; they hold that we owe them freedom, that a people has, as such, the right to decide its own destiny, since men and peoples are equals.

By what *means* do people propose to emancipate the colonies ? This is a question of time : some want liberation in the *present*, by *revolution* if necessary ; some want it in the *future* by reformation and by evolution. Revolution or evolution : these are the alternative means involving the time factor.

We must, however, distinguish more exactly, more concretely, between these means, first the *methods* and then the *agents* to be employed. Taking the *methods* first : how do you set about liberating all subject peoples by means which are, as I said, either evolutionary or revolutionary ?

Amongst these so-called " enslaved " and " oppressed " peoples, there are many advocates of a reformation and a transformation, and they plead therefore for an emancipation in the course of time. They want liberation in the future, a liberation which would require preparation and gradual introduction through partnership and education. In our day, amongst French subjects, this attitude of mind seems the more prevalent, if an opinion may be offered ! This was the idea formulated in France by Théophile Gautier. Speaking of Algeria, he very much wanted partnership in the present, partnership linked with domination ; but for the future, albeit the distant future, he wanted emancipation. And in a great Congress of the League of the Rights of Man, which was held in 1931—I shall revert to this Congress, for it is a document revealing contemporary trends of thought—in the course of which the subject of colonisation was discussed, we are not surprised to find that opposition to expansion was manifested in various forms. There were present at this Congress enemies of expansion ; there were also defenders of expansion. Men like Victor Basch and Albert Bayet reckoned that it was advisable to preserve the association for the present,

[1] R. Maunier, *Coutumes algériennes*, 1935, Chap. 8.

to promote education, and arrive some day—probably some distant day—at emancipation.[1] Some wanted immediate "evacuation"; others also wanted evacuation in the future but in the not-too-near future.

So much for Evolution; there remains Revolution. Emancipation is demanded at once, without delay, without patient waiting: liberation as the outcome of a revolution. The revolutionary-minded foresees, rightly or wrongly—an everlasting French North Africa is not to be contemplated—that the colonial empires will resist; he therefore thinks that he must win liberty, not without striking a blow, but by effort and by combat. This attitude of mind was anticipated by various writers, who were nevertheless moderate-minded. People have for a long time been prophesying that a revolution would break out, sooner or later, to put an end to colonial empires. There is a well-known, frequently quoted saying of Turgot's in his *Reflections on the Progress of the Human Mind*,[2] a speech which he delivered in 1748 at the Old Sorbonne which was then still a theological college. He said: "Colonies are like fruits which cling to the tree until they have received sufficient nourishment; then they detach themselves, they germinate and produce new trees." We well know the driving force exercised by this published prophecy, according to which in the fullness of time the colonies must inevitably be set free! Nothing grips and moves people like a prophecy! Nothing is more infectious; other prophecies always follow! After Turgot, many people predicted emancipation in either the near or distant future. In his Memorandum of 1765 Choiseul, for instance, said: "The American Revolution is not the only one which will happen." Auguste Comte later expressed himself on the same lines. In the last major work of this great thinker, his *System of Positive Policy*, he says: "How slight is the efficacy of all incorporations that are not spontaneous, is a point proved, as we well see in Algeria. Not Algeria alone, but Alsace also, clearly prove the growing impotence of a long foreign domination against any really pronounced nationality." And he considered the British Empire as a "probably temporary exception". He daringly concludes: "I here venture to proclaim the solemn hope which

---

[1] *Ligue des Droits de l'Homme. Le Congrès National*, 1931 (Part II).
[2] Schelle's Ed. of the *Œuvres de Turgot*, I, p. 141; cf. p. 222. In his *Voyage en Syrie et en Égypte*, Year VII (1799), Volney also said, Vol. II, p. 459 f. (written in 1789): "Sooner or later, the chains will slip from the hands of the masters of these artificial empires . . ."

I entertain in the name of all true Positivists, that the Arabs may energetically drive the French out of Algeria, unless the French are wise enough to restore it to them with dignity." [1] " Let us forestall revolts by always keeping in view the ultimate emancipation of *all* our colonies."—" I shall always be proud to remember that in my childhood I ardently wished for the success of the Spaniards against the armies of Napoleon." Renan also said that the colonies ought to hive off " like the sucker of a plant which bears within itself its germ of life ".[2]

The spirit of willingness to resign is here very pronounced ! [3] It was a counsel of despair : to give up because the loss of the game was foreseen. Prediction was auto-suggestion ! [4] It is better, other writers said, to abandon with a good grace what we must, sooner or later, give up in any case ! This was the view of a liberal author, the historian Laboulaye, in a delightful pamphlet no longer read nowadays, *Le Prince Corniche* of 1868. He puts these words into the mouth of what he calls a " Liberian ", that is to say a Liberal :

The white race has long been mistress of the world, to-day the black race claims its share of the inheritance ; it will get it, Africa belongs to the black race.   To colonise is not to send our generals and prefects abroad ; if we want to keep our conquests a little longer, it will be by peace, by liberty, and by hard work, but we must foresee that a day will come when revolution will bring emancipation . . .

" The old divided Europe will soon be a matter of past history."[5]   When people talk to-day—and not only in French !— in a tone of hopeless despair about the great decline of the white races, they are saying nothing new : they are merely saying it less well !   In his *Life of Washington*, Guizot applauds the revolt

---

[1] *Système de politique positive*, II, p. 463 ; IV, pp. 419 and 471 ; *Catéchisme posit.* p. 373.   But in Vol. III in a Letter to the Tsar he recognises the Russian conquest of the nomads !   Cf. A. Baumann, *Le progr. polit. du positivisme*, 1904, p. 92 f.   For the authors more or less in favour of Arab independence, see J. Caillat, *Le voyage d'A. Daudet en Algérie*, 1922, pp. 132 f., 158, 180 f.   Théophile Gautier was not far off.   The Englishman, Richard Congreve, a disciple of Comte, proposed the abandonment of India in his *India* of 1857, Fr. trans., *Ordre et Progrès*, 1858, with a long Preface on the same lines by Pierre Lafitte.

[2] *La monarchie constitutionnelle*, 1870, pp. 54–6.   Baron Hübner in his *A travers l'Empire britannique*, Vol. I, 1886, predicted the secession of Australia.

[3] So in C. Dumas's book, *Libérez les indigènes ou renoncez aux colonies*, 3rd Ed. 1913.

[4] Even Gobineau succumbed to the prophecy that the Indian people would free themselves : *Essai sur l'inégalité des races humaines*, 1855, New Ed., Vol. I, p. 33.

[5] 1868, pp. 285 and 289 f.   The Englishman Bannister, who appears to have written in French (*Appel en faveur d'Alger et de l'Afrique du Nord*, 1833), also pleaded for the liberation of the Algerians.   And Toussenel (*Les Juifs rois de l'époque*, 1846), New Ed., II, p. 165 f., wished France to quit Algeria for the sake of peace.

against oppression and believes in " a day . . . showing a hand divine " which will set free the suffering peoples !

These are the *methods* of the liberation movement ; it has its *agents* too. Here we must be somewhat insistent in order to correct an error fixed in men's minds. For those who have struggled for emancipation are not primarily nor chiefly the ruled, the oppressed ; first and foremost, and earlier than the oppressed, the champions of emancipation were the rulers, and also, again earlier than the ruled, the foreigners. The rulers, the foreigners and the ruled were the three agents or actors who worked to promote the emancipation of the subject peoples.

The *rulers* were working against themselves ! Comte, Laboulaye and Renan foresaw, and desired simply because they foresaw, the abandonment of the colonies. In our day it is especially the writers and in particular the novelists, the man of letters and the woman of letters, who have fought against " colonialism ".[1] So in the rulers there is a mood of abdication ; the defeat of hope, the relaxation of will. The phenomenon is not new ; during the American War the English Whigs sided with the Americans !

The *ruled* needed to do nothing but echo their rulers ; they could only go one better ! There were people in France who did not hesitate to contend that subjects have the right to rebel and to secede. Why indeed should the governed be more in favour of the ruler than the ruler himself ? In a writing of the Emperor Napoleon we unexpectedly find—but he was young at the time and full of Rousseau and the date was 1786, though it was not published till a hundred years later—that the future Dictator, who later asserted that " Corsica must be treated as a colony ", maintained that the Corsicans had the right to free themselves by overthrowing the power of France ![2] Did he not on behalf of his Corsican compatriots complain of French arrogance ? He ended by very formally demanding autonomy : " Voices from our home country, which will make themselves heard ! "

Finally, *foreigners* are in our day agents of liberation. It is not a question of enemies who play their good or evil game by

---

[1] Thus in France, Romain Rolland, René Maran, and André Gide ; Victor Margueritte and Henri Barbusse ; and amongst the women, Denise Moran and Andrée Viollis as well as Valentine de Saint-Point. In America Upton Sinclair, and at an earlier date Herman Melville.—There have been many " refutations ". Julien Maigret has replied to Gide, Gaston-Joseph and Blache to Maran.

[2] F. Masson, *Napoléon inconnu*, 1895, I, pp. 141-2 ; II, pp. 73-4 and 85-6.

stirring up sedition in French countries. It is a question of those who claim to feel no hostility, but only the desire to set subject peoples free from the exploitation and domination of other peoples. This is not a Moscow invention ; there have long been foreigners anxious to intervene to liberate " the oppressed ". Did not the Americans found in 1771 in New York a society of the " Knights of Corsica " to bring about by armed intervention the liberation of the Corsican people ? The French generously heaped coals of fire upon the Americans ! In the days of the American War of Independence, at the suggestion of the French minister, M. de Vergennes, they gave most valuable and effective aid to help to liberate the Americans ! [1] The " right of the peoples was proclaimed . . . by the foreigner " ! [2] This was the meaning of the Monroe Doctrine of 1823 : all European States were forbidden to establish or to re-establish colonies anywhere in the American continent.

For what *objects* and with what *results* do people wish to see the emancipation of subject peoples ? Let me repeat : when we speak of emancipation or liberation, we refer not to one procedure but to two different procedures : sometimes *liberation-through-partnership*, sometimes *liberation-through-separation*. Many French subjects, the majority indeed, have no other thought than to obtain freedom of self-government, while, very wisely, preserving the advantages of French protection, and retaining the security and prosperity which they well know are of French creation ! They do not at all want *autonomy* in the Greek sense, as do the partisans of liberation-through-separation, the " separatists " of the finest water, they want only *isonomy* ; the liberty of government, the right to have an Emperor, or perhaps an independent Parliament ; above all, the right to have two Chambers, like the French. They want the simulacrum or façade of government, with all its powers and none of its duties. They want the right to make laws, but not to undertake self-protection ; to live for themselves, but not by themselves. For they want to feel *free* but not *deserted* ! This would be liberation-with-limitations. This is what people wanted, in the century before last, for the white colonists, or the *habitants*, when they complacently pointed to the freedom of the ancient Greek

[1] B. Fay, *L'esprit révolutionnaire* . . . , 1925, pp. 60 f. and 126 f.
[2] The Americans again organised a whole orchestrated newspaper campaign to provoke sedition in Cuba. M. M. Wilkinson, *Public Opinion and the Spanish-American War, A Study in Propaganda*, 1932 (Baton Rouge, Louisiana).

colonies.[1] The Greeks were everything; it was a sort of mimetic argument, so to speak.

Other subjects of France, however, go further. What they dream of is *liberation-through-separation* : the right to follow their own destiny in their own way without the support, too dearly bought, of the alien. This would be true *autonomy*, not mere *isonomy* : the right to decide their own form of happiness, each in his own home, each for himself, each self-dependent. They want no more interference by a foreign guardian, a censor who offends their pride ! At the most they will perhaps tolerate advice which they will forgo as soon as they think they know as much as—perhaps more—than their advisers, their paid, not paying, advisers. Liberation-through-separation which might become—pursue the idea to its logical conclusion—*liberation-in-opposition* ; the right to face conflict or war with the dethroned protector ; the right at least to have contrary interests, opinions, feelings.

Liberty, with or without protection, isonomy or autonomy : in every case there is always a demand for less alien authority, always the craving for a greater degree of dignity.

---

[1] A competition held in 1745 by the French Academy of Inscriptions. On this controversy see A. Maury, *L'Ancienne Acad. des Inscr.*, 1864, p. 352 f. Especially de Sainte Croix, *De l'état et du sort des colonies chez les anciens peuples*, 1779.

CHAPTER XXXIII

UTILITARIANISM

Amongst the motives for emancipation deriving from policy—or prejudice—we have assigned first place to Liberalism, meaning thereby mainly *emancipatory materialism and emancipatory utilitarianism*; for if the liberal economists raised their voice against colonies, they did so for reasons of necessity or of practical utility. Self-interest is either *present* interest or *future* interest. Doctrine takes heed of future interest, and keeps its eye on the question of duration; opinion concentrates on present interest and the problems of the moment. For the comfort and convenience of those living to-day, that they may bear fewer burdens and be exposed to fewer dangers, people come to thinking of the abandonment of colonies. Whether it be present or future interest there are always two factors : *necessity* and *utility*. Sometimes the suggestion of giving up the colonies arises from the vision, or it may be the pre-vision, of *necessity*, a need so vital that it is compelling, that to ignore it is a sentence of speedy or lingering death ! Sometimes the suggestion arises from considerations of *utility*. For comfort or for convenience, it would be, people think, more advantageous, or less disadvantageous to . . . liquidate the colonial Empire. Sometimes you *cannot*, you *ought not* to keep the colonies ; sometimes it is *unseemly* to keep them and you *must not*, though you might do so without fatal effects.

First, *Necessity*. This reason has been advanced, especially in France, but under two forms or for two motives. First, the argument runs that you *cannot* keep the colonies and that they are bound to be lost, whether you like it or not ; the second argument runs that you *ought not* to keep them ; you could keep them but not administer them, but you could not administer and develop them without ruining yourself. In this second argument the colonies are impossible to administer, but not impossible to retain. Both arguments are based on necessity.

The colonies are *impossible to keep.* It is inconceivable, people sometimes say, or it will in the future be inconceivable, that we should remain master of so many subjects ; you cannot deny, they say, that great Empires must come to an end, that is a Law. Inescapable fate will lead to the abandonment of your colonies.

Such was the idea of an old English author, the great statistician, William Petty ; as early as 1680 he said that sooner or later the colonies would be lost.[1] The disheartened forecasts and despair-laden prophecies which we found in France are to be found in England too. Half a century after William Petty, a moderate-minded Frenchman, the Marquis of Argenson, in his *Considerations on the Government of France* declared that sooner or later people would have to quit the colonies ; strangely enough, he predicted the secession of the colonies in America, especially the English colonies there. Amongst the Germanic professors of " cameral sciences ", that is to say sciences of administration, there were also " colonial defeatists ". The best known of them, a certain Sonnenfels, who published in 1763 a *Treatise on Civil Administration* also predicted that sooner or later, whether people liked it or not, the great colonial Empires would dissolve from the sheer impossibility of subsisting.[2] We should call it : Dissolution, after Evolution and through Evolution.

A little later, we find in France an author of the middle classes, who is thus better able to interpret the common current of opinion which we seek to learn from the writers : he is Sebastian Mercier, editor of the *Tableau de Paris*, who also wrote in 1878 a book called *Tableau des Empires ou notions sur les gouvernements*.[3] In this book he reveals himself as an anti-colonial in discouragement ; he sees the revolt of the colonies coming, as an inevitable fate.[4] The colonial Empires, he says, are impotent to govern and consequently impotent to preserve their colonies in the future, by reason of the distance separating colonies from their mother-countries. This fact, which he perceived before Jean Baptiste Say, the difficulty of governing distant countries,[5] this fact, which continues even in our day to chafe us extremely—and that in spite of radio and aeroplane—is for Mercier a reason for fore-seeing secession ; this is bound to come, for sooner or later the minor comes of age and thus emancipation follows. He means by this that distant countries which have been for a long time under tutelage, will become puffed up by their education and

[1] See N. Le Gendre's reply, *Traité de l'opinion*, IV, 1741, p. 464 f.
[2] A. W. Small, *The Cameralists*, 1909, p. 570 f. For Italy, see R. Michels, *Il concetto coloniale nette teoria degli economisti classici italiani, Riv. di Pol. Econ.*, May 1932.
[3] For France in general see H. Sée, *Les économistes et la question coloniale en France au XVIII* siècle, Rev. hist. colonies fr.*, 1929.
[4] Part II, Chap. XIV.
[5] A frequently recurring theme, especially in Montesquieu, is the inconvenience of too-large States : H. Barckhausen, *Montesquieu . . .*, 1907, p. 197 f. Shaftesbury had already said that large Empires were " unnatural " (*Characteristicks . . .*, 1737, I, p. 113).

transformation ; they will become conscious of the new power which they have been able to acquire and thus, one day, they will free themselves by revolution. Very shortly afterwards, Volney proposed that the French should give up Louisiana : let us, he said, quit these far-off possessions " burdensome, illusory, impossible to retain ". True power consists in " not expanding beyond one's sphere of activity ".[1] The same attitude of mind meets us a little later in England. The orator Fox said in a speech that there was no use in counting on the British Empire's lasting ; it was better to anticipate its dissolution. Canada's autonomy was sooner or later bound to come.[2]

The colonies are *impossible to administer*. It might be possible, some said, to keep the colonies ; there was no decree of Fate compelling their abandonment ; but to retain them would be to incur deadly damage. The ultra-liberal economists—chief among them Jean Baptiste Say—considered the colonies impossible to retain and impossible to administer without decisive injury. They justified this opinion by two great arguments : criticism of the *means* and of the *results*. Both by the means employed and by the results produced, colonisation seemed to them to spell the ruin of the State. As early as 1803 Jean Baptiste Say figures as an anti-colonial. He not only mercilessly condemns the methods of expansion prevailing under the Old French Monarchy—what was called the *Colonial Pact* or the " Exclusive "—but he condemns colonisation in itself. He believes that there is no means of preventing the foundation and maintenance of large overseas Empires from being hurtful to the colonising nations.[3] For, he says—and this is an argument already brought forward by Mercier—a country is not well governed when it is governed from a great distance. Knowledge and promptitude are essential to government ; you must know, and you must be able to act quickly. You can neither know nor act if you are attempting to govern an unlimited domain. All empires strive to escape from a centralised power, only to fall in every case under the despotism of local tyrants. All governors of distant countries, whom the central authority cannot control,

[1] G. Chinard, *Volney et l'Amérique*, 1923, p. 134 f.   Roederer was also in favour of quitting (*ibid.*, p. 163 f.)—Volney was already speaking of the French inaptitude for colonisation, *Tableau . . . des États-Unis* (1795), *Œuvres*, Didot's Ed., p. 699 f.
[2] E. Réveillaud, *Histoire du Canada*, 1884, p. 326 f.
[3] *Cours complet d'Econ. polit. pratique*, 2nd Ed. 1840, Vol. I, Part IV, Chaps. 22–6 —See H. Oppenheimer, *J. B. Say et la colonisation*, 1930.—Charles Comte shared these views, *Traité de Législation*, IV, 1827, Chaps. 22–3. See also Filangieri, *Science de la législation*, Fr. trans., Book II, Chap. 22 and V. Scialoja, *Economia Sociale*, p. 378 f.

are kinglets or petty tyrants, a law unto themselves. We have seen it : why deny it ? For Say, and for others after him, this is a strong argument against all expansion. So he concludes that it would be better, if not to abandon the colonies without conditions and without restrictions, without worrying about their fate, at least to give them freedom in the course of time, conferring on the inhabitants the right to administer their country themselves.[1] There would thus be two successive phases : first, the association of mother-country and colony, as long as the colony is in the position of a minor needing protection and upbringing ; secondly, the emancipation of the mature colony which has attained its majority, preserving only, as did the Greeks, spiritual ties and symbolic links, so as to maintain the façade of an Empire.

Criticism of the methods we have found in Jean Baptiste Say ; criticism of the *results* we find in many other writers. Even if you claim, they say, that it would be possible at a pinch to administer the colonies from a distance, and overcome the grave handicaps of every distant government, there would nevertheless ensue such effects and such dangers, that you must abdicate. The glory and the grandeur would be too dearly bought ! So maintains Abbé Pradt in a work called *The Three Ages of Colonies, or their Past, Present and Future*.[2] As regards the Past he condemns the procedure of the Colonial Pact. For the Present and the Future, he dwells on the risks and perils inseparable from the possession of far-away countries. There is first the question of distance, which always entails the self-emancipation of the governor and raises him to the rank of a small-scale petty tyrant. Here the Abbé recalls the old saying : " God is very high up and the King very far away ! " He has, however, another reason too : the mania, he says,—he is writing in 1801—the mania of the French for transplanting the rules of Republican government to the colonies ; the passion for assimilation, as we should say ! This is to ignore the elements of place and time, and the Abbé says so quite bluntly. It shows failure to appreciate the temporal and the relative, and how arrogant to transport manners and customs unchanged. This is a fatal danger, in governing these distant lands. That is why the future abandonment of the colonies is imperative. No fight can be put up against blindness, for no power can escape it, the government

---

[1] P. Leroy-Beaulieu, *Colonisation* (1874), 4th Ed. 1891, pp. 137, 819 f. and 841 f. He also saw the colonial phase as an *educative* one destined to come to an end . . . after several generations.

[2] *Les trois âges des colonies, ou de leur état passé, présent ou à venir*, 1801–2.

either relapses into weakness or develops into tyranny. The colonies thus become " reasoning beings " ; by assimilating them you teach them to desire advantages, to claim rights ; you educate them for liberty !—There is prophecy !

For the Abbé, dogma comes to reinforce policy. Societies, he says, are in a sense living beings, they have their childhood and their manhood. Colonies which to-day are children, will grow up and become nations ; their " evolution " is education under guardianship for liberty. It would therefore be a mistake to treat the colonies in the future as if they were going to remain children for ever. The laws ought to keep step with their progress. Their development ought therefore to be watched so that the right moment for autonomy may be chosen. He uses " autonomy " in the Greek sense : liberty for the colonies to legislate for themselves. For, he says, they must be constituted as independent States—this is the first time that the word State has been used to describe colonial status—independent States enjoying their own natural limits, possessing their own form of government, preferably—so it seems to him in 1809—a monarchy. They must be Sovereign States, sole masters of their own destiny, sole judges of their own welfare—*there* are anticipations of the prophecies of to-day ! [1]

Half a century later, Taine was taking the same view of France's future, suggesting that she should quit the colonies on the ground that it was impossible to administer them ; in this, he was echoing the predictions of the liberals. [2] In his correspondence, posthumously published, we find this liberal anxious to limit the powers of the State : anti-State, anti-colonial, the two positions are interconnected ; liberalism is the negation of imperialism : " The State's function," he says, " is to protect its subjects, not to expand itself." He sees a danger in the policy which Napoleon III pursued, of emancipating near countries and civilising distant ones, thus allowing the French State to play " the part of a knight errant " and indulge in an orgy of pride. It is not the business of governments to play a large rôle ! In the foundation of the French colonial Empire, which was then, round about 1880, beginning to be sketched out, he detects the wholly characteristic French love of distraction, which no doubt shocks his austerity ; the desire to divert the citizens by glorious achievements, the Republic's inclination to provide a spectacle

---

[1] For " anticolonialism " at the time of the French Restoration, see P. Gaffarel, *La politique coloniale de la France de 1789 à 1830*, p. 15 f. (General Foy and the Agrarians.)
[2] (Taine) *Sa vie et sa correspondance*, III, 1905, pp. 321, 331, 333.

for the French people : what Plato called *theatrocracy*. This would reduce the government to the rôle of an *impresario*, whose colonial conquests would be designed, amongst other things, to amuse the electors ! This, according to him, is an error *de jure* : for expansion is a violation of the rights of the individual ; but it is also an error *de facto*, for it is irresponsible and injurious to the serious purpose of government which is to protect, not to amuse.

The basis of these ideas is probably always the belief in an inescapable, fate-decreed relinquishment, a belief which in certain minds acquires a mystic tinge. In the Germany of to-day [1] . . . or perhaps, rather of yesterday . . . this becomes a mystical fatality. In his *Decline of the West*,[2] Spengler predicted the inevitable dissolution and collapse of the great Western Empires. Imperialism is " the symbol of the end " of the great States ; the law of civilisations is to grow great and perish ; this fate is ordained by God ; this is *kismat*, as the Muslim calls it, which decrees—as the Berber Ibn Khaldun declared over five hundred years ago—the end of every human Empire.[3] " The expansive tendency," says Spengler, " is like a delirium : a demoniac spirit, which takes possession of Empires to lead them to perdition."

Thus, down to our own day necessity has been cloaked as Fate. French writers, however, more often prefer the secular argument of utility, based on comfort and convenience. People say, or used to say : " Even if we can keep, even if we can administer, distant countries, it is not, on balance, worth while encumbering ourselves with them. This attitude represents a more tolerant, moderate opposition, they are weighing the *lucrum* against the *damnum*, the advantages against the drawbacks, but they claim that the drawbacks far outweigh the advantages ; they work out a balance-sheet in which the liabilities exceed the assets. Colonisation is therefore bad business : an enterprise which, so to speak, " does not pay ".

Voltaire's view is the same, notably in his *Essay on Manners and Customs*.[4] The occupation of the New World has had, he says, both good and bad results ; and on the whole the advantage is very questionable. This was the first time that anyone calcu-

---

[1] [Written in 1936. EOL]

[2] *Der Untergang des Abendlandes*, 1918 ; revised ed. 1922. Eng. trans. by C. F. Atkinson. French trans., I, 1931, p. 74 f. Hitler's adherents at first considered colonies " an expensive luxury " and a " dangerous mixture " : A. Rosenberg, *Der Mythus des 20sten J.h.s.* Cf. R. Guignard, *Outre Mer*, 1934, p. 350 f.

[3] Ibn Khaldoun, *Prolégomènes*, Slane's trans., 1862, I, p. 342 f. *et passim*. Cf. Brooks Adams, *La loi de la civilisation et de la décadence*, 1898.

[4] *Essai sur les mœurs*, Chaps. 141-54.

lated on these lines. His temperate mind was, as we know, apt at calculation : he could reckon to the last ha'penny, and "balance" a profit and loss account. In this case, he does so most skilfully. Advantages and disadvantages certainly abound. Amongst the advantages are the products which have been brought to Europe, cochineal, cinchona, tea, chocolate, coffee ; a new luxury which has enriched and refined our continent. Amongst the disadvantages are : the depopulation of the Spanish possessions, the spread of diseases—which he names—the rise in prices which since Bodin was known in France to be due to the Spaniards' exploitation of the silver and gold mines, especially in Peru. Undoubtedly therefore the loss exceeds the gain.

Soon, however, people were able to advance more closely-reasoned arguments. They made exact and concrete calculations to prove that the assets were outweighed, and more than outweighed, by the deficits. Two arguments in particular were brought to bear : the reduction in the mother-country's strength and the increase in the mother-country's burdens, due to the possession of distant countries.

Diminution in strength. The Empire weakens the mother-country. However great the gain may appear to be, this is the price that must be paid ! In the prosopopoeia of Book IV of the *Lusiads*, a colonial poem in which Camoens lyrically celebrates the Portuguese Empire, the poet depicts Vasco da Gama's embarkation. He introduces an old man who warns the adventurous navigator of his mistake : " You would be better to stay at home. What are you going to gain, what is Portugal going to gain in these distant lands ? It is pride which is luring you, not advantage. Your enterprise will weaken our country, depriving her of men and goods." Later, care was taken to distinguish the two ways in which the strength of the country would fatally suffer : *population* and *activity*. These are the two elements in a country's strength which should be concentrated, not dispersed.

Population. It had long been asserted that colonies depopulate the mother-country. Emigration weakens the State ; in every country the first factor in the greatness and strength of the State is the number of its men. In his *Political Essay on Commerce*,[1] Melon, who was both a " mercantilist " and an "interventionist ", based his argument against large colonial empires on this population question. He contended that the possession of colonies weakens the State by depopulating it, by robbing it of the active

---

[1] *Essai politique sur le commerce,* 1734.

and productive elements which ought to be conserved, and not at any price transplanted. In Chapter IV of this *Essay*, called " Of Colonies ", he says : " The error of the Spaniards, and one which was in time their ruin, was first the extermination of the natives." Not that Melon was worrying about the humanitarian aspect ; at the very beginning he says that he is considering " the question of utility alone ", but from the utilitarian and material point of view, this was a mistake ; for the original inhabitants had to be replaced by Africans or Spaniards and so Spain herself was depopulated. Melon considered this the prime cause of Spain's ruin. " If Spain," he says, " had in Europe all her American subjects, America under foreign rule "—and here he drives home the readiness to emancipate—" would be of much more use to her. Holland wisely sent only her surplus population abroad. Only such artisans as are superfluous at home ought to be exported to the colonies. The progress of the colonies ought then to be slow, but it may be assured and useful. But if the homeland set about peopling her colonies with speed and intensity, she would weaken herself by sending away too large a proportion of her population." This was bound to be the great argument in France at the time of her conquest of Algeria, and it was used by the anti-conquest party, the Agrarians, who looked then, as they do to-day, with disfavour on colonies, and fought against the taking of Algeria. A deputy called Delacroix was particularly anxious ; he contended that Algeria would tempt Frenchmen away, and would depopulate the Kingdom of France to the advantage of Algeria. This danger has recently and frequently been denounced by the French Press. " France," they tell us, " is one of the countries where the population has ceased to grow ; by reason of her falling birthrate she cannot dream of transplanting men into a distant country without robbing and weakening herself. Let us think of ourselves and remain in our full numbers on our native soil."

In addition to population, there is *Activity*. To persist in colonising is not only to depopulate the State, but also, or at least so they say, to impoverish the State.[1] We are bound to send to our colonies artisans to create industries there ; to this extent we reduce the activity and the prosperity of the mother-country. Montesquieu already used this argument in his *Persian*

---

[1] We find the same criticism vigorously expressed in Rouillé d'Orfeuil's *L'alembic moral*, 1773, s.v. *Colonies*, pp. 132–3 ; cf. pp. 251–2, " colonies ruin the State ". See also Arthur Young, *Travels during the Years 1787, 1788, 1789* (1792).

Letters [1] ; we find it also in Benjamin Franklin, shortly before the French Revolution. He thundered against the luxury of European States. In his *Memoirs* he says that colonies will in time ruin the great States by encouraging excessive luxury, giving their people an unwholesome appetite for colonial products, and thus depressing their native industries and reducing the supply of necessaries which are to the advantage of the general population. Here the two arguments are linked : population and activity. Such was the principal theme of a book published half a century ago and famous in its day, Yves Guyot's *Letters on Colonial Policy*. [2] The author was a liberal economist, of the middle classes, a municipal councillor of Paris, later a deputy and finally a minister : a real " average Frenchman ". He wrote the most violent attack on colonies that has ever been made in France. " France," he says, " has no emigrants ; it is a country where the birthrate has long been declining ; [3] she has no products either, suitable for export to the colonies ; she is a country of quality, not quantity. She manufactures good and expensive things, she should export to old and wealthy countries and not at all to new countries. She has no spare capital to invest at a distance ; she is a country of ' woollen stockings ' and of small savings which should be employed without risk incurred and therefore employed at home ! " This clear-sighted man here speaks the language of every Frenchman : of the timid, anxious-minded Frenchman who has no wish to hazard either his life or his wealth. Guyot maintains that " there is danger in running colonies whether in time of peace or in time of war ". We know that the same argument is heard to-day. To colonise is to disperse strength, to fritter away resources and at the same time to ask for war ! To colonise leads to war at the same time as it reduces strength ! This is a tragic contradiction which invites condemnation ! This was the time when the deputy Georges Périn, Jules Ferry's opponent, spoke in the Chamber of " France internally collecting herself ". [4]

[1] *Lettres Persanes*, 110 and 121.   [2] *Lettres sur la politique coloniale*, 1885.

[3] The same argument recurs in E. Drumont, *La France Juive* (undated), pp. 375 f., 394 f. and 492 f. (on Tunisia and Tong-King) ; he speaks of an " insensate " colonial policy : probably the only point on which he agreed with Clemenceau !

[4] Déroulède spoke of concentrating French forces " on the continent ". For the same attitude amongst Conservatives, see de Chaudordy, *La France en 1889*, 1889, *Considérations sur la politique extér. et coloniale de la France*, 1897.—It was Napoleon III who invented the theory of " concentration " : " France, threatened," he wrote in 1841, " instead of scattering, ought to concentrate her forces, use her treasures sparingly, not squander them. Now, these distant possessions, burdensome in peace, disastrous in war, are a source of weakness." (*Nos colonies dans l'Océan Pacifique*) *Œuvres de Nap. III*, Vol. II, p. 3. Cf. J. Duval, *La politique de l'Empereur en Algérie*, 1866, p. 173.

362   PSYCHOLOGY OF EXPANSION

Increase of the country's burdens. Another argument, in the
financial domain which arouses ever-wakeful fear, is the fear of
expense. The cost is a subject on which Frenchmen—and others
too—are sensitive. In 1680 William Petty said that the principal
harm the colonies brought to England was the expenditure
entailed. Colonies were in his eyes lost capital, " frozen "
assets ! This was their mischief and their crime. Whatever
profits might appear to accrue from them, the dangers were
greater, the wastage was greater ; they were certain before long
to increase the burdens of the State. Two hundred years later
the same fear was felt. At the very moment when Disraeli's
imperialist policy was triumphing, there appeared in " Victorian "
London a book by Goldwin Smith entitled *The Empire* (1863).
The author takes up again all the arguments of his predecessors
on both sides of the Channel, and he concludes with Petty and
with Voltaire that if the liabilities exceed the assets, the deficit
must be made good, and that colonies therefore always increase
the burden on the mother-country, involving a rise in military
expenditure and a rise in financial expenditure. A well-known
Germanic ethnologist, Adolf Bastian, published in 1873 a short
essay *On Colonies.*[1] He inspired the anti-colonial party to which
Bismarck belonged, and he essayed to prove that to possess
colonies was to shoulder unprofitable burdens, or, at best, burdens
bringing very small profits. With all these thinkers, in all these
countries, the double argument recurs that the possession of
colonies imposes a tax on blood and a tax on wealth without
compensation or comfort. This is what was said in the discussion in France at the time of the conquest of Algeria. In
Parliament the speakers reverted again and again to the question
of the burdens on the country.[2] In all political parties, whether
of the Right or the Left, this argument was the weapon brandished
to stop the conquest of Algiers. Some great men, de Tocqueville [3]

[1] *Über Kolonien* (1867), reproduced in *Geographische und Ethnologische Bilder*, 1873,
pp. 307–21.
[2] See Valet's thesis, quoted above, and Tailliart, *Bibliographie de l'Algérie dans
la littérature française*, 1920, No. 1540 f.
[3] E. d'Eichthal, *A. de Tocqueville*, 1898, p. 240 ; Gobineau also pointed to the
absence of material benefit (1856), *Correspondance A. de Tocqueville et A. de Gobineau*,
1909, p. 271 f.—Stendhal, *Mémoires d'un Touriste* (1837), M. Levy's edition, II,
p. 117 f. : " The French have no colonial genius " : Volney had said the same
thing before him. Later, Lagneau objected to the too-high mortality amongst the
colonists, *Anthropologie de la France*, 1879, II, p. 101 f. For Ethiopia, Rimbaud also
spoke of " millions without profitable return ", *Lettres*, 1899, pp. 173, 176, 183, 222.
An armchair colonial, Arthur Girault, similarly said in the Chamber that the Sahara
was not worth the sacrifices, but " what is done, is done, there can be no going
back . . ." *Principes* . . . : *l'Algérie*, 5th Ed. 1931, p. 54.

and Berryer, were against the occupation. Better still : in 1840 General Bugeaud, who was a deputy, mounted the tribune and proposed that Algiers should be abandoned because the dangers were greater, vastly greater than the advantages ! The French Parliamentary discussions of fifty years later on the conquest of Tunis in 1881 and the conquest of Tong-king in 1885, are worth reading. In both cases the speakers, to whatever party they belonged, were opposed to occupation of any kind, on the ground that conquest would increase the burdens on the country. In 1881 just at the moment when the regency of Tunis had surrendered to France, Jules Delafosse, a speaker of the Right, was bitterest of all in a passionate attack on the project of a Protectorate ! He joined Jules Guesde in the chorus ! [1]

Neither to acquire colonies, nor to preserve colonies, that was the idea. To give them up, either by *restoring* them—but restoring to whom ? That is the question—or by *selling* them. In France the suggestion has been made, not once but many times, to quit the colonies, not by restoring them to their original owners, who have often disappeared, but by selling them to foreign countries. After the 1914–18 War there were writers, notably José Germain, who started a campaign the object of which was to pay off France's debts by disposing of the colonies by sale to foreign countries.[2] These proposals were made with the concepts of ownership and property in mind, not the concepts of partnership or friendship ! It was self-interest on the material plane, either in the future or in the present, which prompted these thoughts of abdication.

[1] A. Zévaès, *J. Guesde*, 1929, p. 78 f.
[2] In the *Ère Nouvelle*. See C. Guy's reply : *Doit-on vendre nos colonies ?* (*Comité Dupleix*) 1926 ; and the speech of the minister Perrier. In 1914 there was already a proposal to *exchange* Indo-China for Alsace-Lorraine : G. Espé de Metz, *Par les colons*, 1914, p. 247 f.

CHAPTER XXXIV

DEMOCRATISM OR THE PRINCIPLE OF DEMOCRACY

Liberalism plus utilitarianism is thus a road to abdication. But other roads, too, lead to the same goal ; the second is the *principle of democracy* (*démocratisme*) which might well be called emancipatory democracy : the application and transplantation of Democracy to the overseas peoples.[1] Democracy is administered in two forms, in two degrees, in two doses, so to speak : *radicalism* and *collectivism*. If, as I have pointed out, they tend to promote simple equality, they tend much more to promote the granting of freedom.

There is no shadow of doubt that this emancipatory democracy is religious ; since it is a policy, it is both dogma and faith. Socialism is a religious phenomenon with its dogma and its cult, and finally, for the last twenty years, with its god and a tomb where the faithful can repair to pray to the medicine man of the new brotherhood. Radicalism is also a faith and a hope, even if it be also covetousness . . . like every policy. These are therefore doctrines of a militant type ; when you believe yourself in possession of Truth and Good, propaganda is a duty ; you must teach, you must convert all nations. Dogma and cult are therefore exported to the colonies ; for they tend always towards the universal.

The propagation of the principle of democracy in both its forms, radicalism and collectivism, is thus a process of conversion. In distant countries it has been possible to do propaganda amongst the natives. Millions of men throughout the world have in our day pinned their faith to the new dogmas : Equality and community amongst the peoples. These are the two ideas—equality and community—which teaching and preaching have spread abroad in every clime ; radicalism stands for equality and collectivism for community. How have these two forms of Democracy led subject peoples to yearn for liberty ?

[1] See in general : H. Rolin, *Les droits de l'homme aux colonies*, *Rev. Univ.*, Brussels, 1905-6, pp. 161-73.

Radicalism leads there.[1]   At bottom, what is it?   In every place it is three things : *individualism, equalitarianism* and *nationalism*.

Individualism.   First and foremost, radicalism is generalised individualism.   It consistently pleads the cause of the individual and seeks to secure the rights of the individual.   A moment then comes when people dare to maintain that the individual, though he be coloured, has always the rights of the individual, and that he may then under every sky claim liberty, the fundamental right of every human being, proclaimed in France in 1789 by the Declaration of the Rights of " Man ", conceived of always as an individual.   The Constitution of Pennsylvania in 1776—more explicit on this point than the Declaration of Independence —held that the bond linking the colony to the sovereign was *contractual* :   the King having failed in his duty to afford protection, the bond is broken ;   this spells liberty.[2]   This is the individualism of the *Social Contract* which lays the foundation on which the option of secession is based.   Coloured men will take the argument up anew.

Equalitarianism.   Radicalism is also generalised equalitarianism.   Democracy means equality, both between men and between peoples ;   both within groups and without, both inside every " race " and between " races ".   For neither freedom nor dignity can exist without equality.   A free man, a free people, is an equal man, an equal people.   Domination is a murderous attack on the rights of nations.

Nationalism.   Finally, radicalism is also generalised nationalism, for Democracy is national dogma ;   it is patriotism, as they said in 1789.   The conception of a man's own country—which the Europeans have in very truth bestowed on the inhabitants of the colonies—is republican in essence, since the native country is a possession held in common.   The liberals of 1789, and still more the Jacobins of 1793, had already laid it down that liberty and equality could have no virtue save in the *nation* ;   that every people should be a nation, controlling its own fate, and living out its own destiny.   This vision leads men to wish an end to all domination.   It is anti-conqueror and anti-dominator :   such is indeed the spirit of republican radicalism if it is pushed to the limit and plumbed to the bottom.

Thus understood, radicalism in the colonial sense is of some

---

[1] You would even find—and that without surprise—an anti-colonial *Catholicism* at a time when these ideas are being pushed to the extreme limit.   See the review *Esprit*, Dec. 1, 1935 : *La colonisation, son avenir, sa liquidation.*
[2] F. Alengry, *La Déclaration des Droits de l'Homme*, p. 52 f.

age. Its evolution had two phases and two agents : the *fore-runners* and the *proclaimers*.

The *forerunners* have, for over the last hundred years, in the name of the three principles of Democracy, contested the right to conquer, and disputed the right to govern, overseas peoples. Volney railed against the conquest of the Nile country.[1] Blood will be shed, the Egyptian will have had only a change of Mameluks, profits will go to a few ; the French people will be frustrated ; audacity and licence, family disorders and insolent luxury will be the real fruits of the Occupation. Volney's arguments are those of our own day ! In one of his writings, *Philosophic Plan for Perpetual Peace*, the philosopher Kant [2] proposed that no State should be allowed to conquer or acquire another State, large or small, near or far, by any means whatsoever : " a society is not a thing, but a person," who ought to decide his own fate. Kant thus postulates nationalism, autonomism for every country in the world. To-day, we should call it " humanism ".

A little earlier, Morelly and Diderot in France had formally denied the right to conquer ; they contended that it was wrong to seize a distant country in order to rule over backward tribes and clans. Morelly, particularly, the author of a Utopia called *The Basiliade, or the Shipwreck of the Floating Islands*,[3] indulged in bitter criticism of all dominations. In a short pamphlet which still finds imitators—*Supplement to Bougainville's Voyage*,[4] he called it—Diderot brings a Tahitian (or an Otahitian as they then said) who addressed the European conqueror as Chief of Brigands and eloquently denies his right to settle in Tahiti. When, fifty years later, the Monroe Doctrine was proclaimed in the United States there was nothing new about it. Monroe was at the time President, and his Doctrine was inspired by a work of Jefferson's which he had consulted. This Monroe Doctrine is simply Anti-conquest Radicalism. In 1823, the date of its promulgation, the Holy Alliance was conducting an intrigue for re-establishing the Spanish Empire in the New World, reviving the doctrine of the right of conquest. It was against this that Monroe was

---

[1] *Voyage en Syrie et en Egypte*, II, Year VII (1799), p. 459 f. *annexe* (first published in 1789). But the first forerunner is really La Fontaine. We remember how his Peasant spoke : " What law has made you masters of the universe ? Why come disturbing an innocent life ? " Cf. Godchot, *L'esprit colonial de La Fontaine*, *Revue Mondiale*, Jan. 15, 1929.

[2] *Zum ewigen Frieden*, 1795.

[3] *La Basiliade ou naufrage des Iles flottantes*, II, 1753, pp. 57, 114.

[4] *Supplément au voyage de Bougainville*, republished in the *Bibliothèque Nationale*, *Mélanges Philosophiques*, I, 1893, pp. 149–50. See also Bolingbroke's *Reflections*, 1749, which speaks of " usurpers."

protesting when in that well-known letter he says that the Republic of the United States will no longer tolerate that Ancient Europe, that den of despotism, should dare to enslave any American country, the New World being " the land of liberty ". Here was a public document which fundamentally disputed the rights of States to colonise and stigmatised any attempt to do so as despotism and a violation of liberties.

These forerunners of anti-colonial Radicalism were followed by the *proclaimers*, those who built it up and planted it securely on its foundations ; setting forth in their full comprehensiveness the fundamental principles of this new dogma.   It is the French Constitution of 1848 to which we must look for the proclamation and promulgation of Democracy in the colonial system.   Article 5 of the Constitution lays down that " the Republic respects foreign nationalities, undertakes no war for purposes of conquest, and never employs its forces against the liberty of any people ". This is the first time that such a document of public nature uses the phrase " *Any* people ", thus affirming the liberty of *all* established peoples.   One of the actors in the 1848 Revolution in France, Félix Pyat, supplies a decisive commentary on this Article 5, in his *Letters to the Proscribed*,[1] published in London in 1855 : " All peoples," he says, " are in the position of masters, free to dispose of themselves,"—Here is the Woodrow Wilson formula : before Wilson—" France seeks neither conquest nor tribute . . . she makes war on oppressors for the sake of the oppressed, but not on the oppressed for the sake of the oppressors." This vision made headway and was soon the guiding light of the " militant " republicans.   It was to be the doctrine of Jules Simon :[2] no conquest, therefore no standing army either : " fraternity of men and of peoples ".

Freemasonry, a liberal and international body, also played its part, but one not easy exactly to define.[3] Dr. Guépin was a Freemason ; in a letter to Jean Macé in 1867, he proposed that the colonies should be surrendered, but to the benefit of a Europe consortium.

A " pacifist " Congress was held in Geneva in 1872 by the *League of Peace and Liberty*.   One of its resolutions expressly condemned annexation by conquest, and formally proclaimed the right of every people to belong only to itself.   This formula tried

---

[1] *Lettres aux proscrits.*   [2] *La politique radicale*, 1869, p. 37 f.
[3] Some notes by the Roman Catholic G. Goyau in *L'idée de patrie et l'humanitarisme*, 1902, pp. 31, 37, 242, etc.   For Turkey, see Bérard, *La mort de Stamboul*, 1913, p. 284 f. Bolivar, the Liberator, had also been a Freemason in Cadiz.

its fortune also at that other Peace Congress familiar to us all. A sailor of the French Republic, Admiral Réveillère noted in 1875 the incompatibility of democracy and colonisation on the principles of 1789.[1] It was in 1881, ten years later, that radical liberalism found definite expression in the famous debate in the French Parliament about intervention in Tunisia.[2] Two great orators, Pelletan and Clemenceau, in this debate proclaimed for France that growth by annexation was prohibited, in virtue of the right of all peoples to make their own laws for themselves. Camille Pelletan, a recently elected member, made his maiden speech on December 1st, moving draft laws to provide " supplementary credits " to defray the cost of the two expeditions to Tunisia and South Oran. While it is quite true, he said, " that we are not thinking of immediately abandoning Tunisia, which we could do only when we had made arrangements to secure the interests and the honour of France, we certainly do not wish to encroach on the autonomy and the independence of the Tunisian people." —For people were already talking of that purely fictitious entity " the Tunisian people " just as, quarter of a century later, we shall hear Jaurès on " the Moroccan people ". Georges Clemenceau also thundered, with characteristic vehemence and bitterness, as a true Radical. Liberty and equality make distant peoples, whether great or small, taboo—if I may so express it— the French have not the right to occupy Tunisia, for this occupation would violate the liberties of the Tunisian people, which are the liberties of all peoples.[3] Here are the words he used in the session of July 20 :

It is the genius itself of the French race to have generalised the theory of right, of justice, to have understood that the problem of civilisation was to eliminate violence from the relationships of men in the same society, and to aim at eliminating violence in the unknown future from the relationships of nations to each other. Do not let us try [he says later] hypocritically to clothe violence with the name of civilisation. Let us talk neither of right nor duty. The conquest which you are applauding is the pure and simple abuse of the power which scientific civilisation possesses over rudimentary civilisations, in order to enslave and torture man, to extract all the

---

[1] G. Goyau, op. cit., last note above, p. 272 f. and the whole of Chap. IV.

[2] See Jammy Schmidt, Les grandes thèses radicales (undated) p. 205 f. And the party's doctrine has not changed : See the Nancy Programme (1907) Art. 25, in F. Buisson, La politique radicale, 1908, pp. 54 f. and 258 f. : no adventures, no expeditions ; but preserve existing acquisitions and develop them " respecting all the rights of humanity ". Keep, but don't increase !

[3] Clemenceau's great speeches on this subject are those of Nov. 10, 1881 (Tunisia), July 19 and 20 (Egypt), Nov. 3, 1883, and March 29–31, Dec. 26, 1885 (Tong-King).

strength that is in him for the benefit of the civiliser. It is not right, it is the infringement of r.ght. To talk of civilisation in this connection is to add hypocrisy to violence.

These phrases crystallised anti-conquest radicalism [1] in France. The same phenomenon was to be seen in England at the same time, just when Victorian "colonialism" was displaying itself throughout the world. Gladstone was the English Clemenceau. As a doctrinaire partisan he opposed imperial enterprises, denouncing them as a crime against liberty. In the House of Commons, he condemned the conquest of the Sudan, carried out against a "people" justly fighting for its liberty—I am by no means sure that the Nubians of the Egyptian Sudan had in their minds any conception of a native country or its freedom !—Let us greet with surprise the fact that we meet, both in England and in France, the same vision, the same fiction that an agglomeration of Tribes constitutes an organised People ! We know how Gladstone forsook Gordon in his expedition, and how the relieving column, despatched at the urgent personal request of Queen Victoria, reached Khartum two days after the death of the defeated conqueror. [2]

Liberating Radicalism was only the herald of Liberating *Collectivism*, which has two phases or two forms : *Socialism* in its older, *Communism* in its newer form. *Socialism* proclaims equality and community between individuals and peoples. *Communism* is the idea of the domination or dictatorship of the proletariat. In both these forms collectivism has exercised influence in the Colonies. Nationalist movements which have arisen amongst the natives, or been organised by the natives, have to a large extent borrowed their watchwords from collectivism. Collectivism stirred them up and roused them to rebel against the power of their rulers. In itself and by itself collectivism has the appearance of a more pronounced "system of democracy" : it is better suited than radicalism for the unconditional, unrestricted liberation of the "oppressed" peoples. This is democracy pushed to its ultimate conclusion, two phases of which are to be distinguished : socialism, the old phase ; communism, the new phase.

At the beginning, socialism did not think of being anti-colonial. With Fourier and with Enfantin, it was imperial, or

---

[1] See, in our own day, the radically anti-colonial F. Challaye, *Impressions sur Java*, Cahiers Quinzaine, 4th Series, 13th Cahier, 1904. *Souvenirs sur la colonisation*, 1935.

[2] See Lytton Strachey, *Eminent Victorians*, 1918.

perhaps more exactly pro-colonial socialism.   Père Enfantin was in favour of occupying Algerian territory.   He proclaimed the civilisation of the universe by means of its colonisation through methods of partnership, but no gleam of emancipation entered his mind.   Enfantin was an imperialist long before the word existed.   After his day, both in France and Germany, there was a colonial socialism.   Andler was fully justified in alluding to " German imperial socialism," and what might be called conquering socialism.   Socialism in the colonial field has gone through three phases in turn : approval of the colonies, reformation of the colonies, condemnation of the colonies.   All these phases are recent : the last the most recent of all.   When the working man's newspaper *La Fraternité* spoke in 1848 of " our brothers of the black race ", it was to advocate the abolition of slavery, but nothing more.

Approval of the colonies.   In the Congresses and notably in the Workers' Congresses [1] the resolutions at first preserved complete silence on the colonial problem.   The resolution which in France founded collectivism, and which marked the penetration of Marxism into France, was the Marseilles Resolution of 1879 ; it breathes not a word about colonial abuses.   Was this due to intentional omission or to ignorance ?   We do not know.—We have to wait till somewhere about 1900 before we find the French Socialists, whom Karl Marx somewhat contemptuously dubbed " Utopists ", criticising colonial methods.

The next phase was no longer approval, but at first a demand for *reformation* of expansionist procedure : a criticism of method, but not of aims.   It was a renegade or dissident Marxist, Bernstein, who published in 1900 an article which endowed socialism with a colonial doctrine.[2]   " Socialism," he tells us, " is first and foremost equality between men, and in course of time equality also between groups and races.   It ought to combat exploitation arrived at by violence and conquest."   Socialism therefore should direct its attention to the colonial problem to demand that the conquerors should reform their procedure so as to respect and guarantee equality between peoples.   Colonisation, he contends—and here he unconsciously takes up Girardin's idea—

---

[1] For what follows, see L. Blum, *Les Congrès ouvriers* (*Bib. Social.*), 1901 ; *Les Congrès social. internat. Ordres du Jour et Résolutions* (Bureau Social. Internat. Brussels) 1902 ; L. Gravereaux, *Les discussions sur . . . le militarisme dans les Congrès Socialistes*, 1913 (thesis) ; Seligmann, *Encycl. of the Social Sciences*, VII, p. 613 (bibliography).

[2] E. Bernstein, *Le socialisme et la question coloniale* (French trans. of the *Sozialist. Monatsheft* of Sept. 1900, in *Pages Libres*, 1901, p. 485 f.).

ought to mean civilisation, and that is to say increase of population. You cannot claim to have brought civilisation to backward peoples unless you have given them the security and the prosperity which make them more numerous. Thus, according to Bernstein the sign of progress in a colonial country is increase of population. But, if this be so, the conquering peoples surely have the right and the duty of imposing themselves on inferior peoples. Civilisation by increase of population is a task which should be carried out throughout the entire universe. Here Bernstein agrees with Enfantin. The multiplication of the whole world's inhabitants cannot be achieved without conquest and domination ! For land, he says, belongs not to the people who chance to occupy it, but to humanity in general ; it is the property of all the inhabitants of all the continents. Thus, if there be distant lands, not yet opened to the new progress—and this is a 16th-century idea already to be found in Sir Thomas More—they must be seized. The superior peoples have the right to conquer and the right to develop the entire globe, to render fertile the soil, the value of which has not been utilised by inferior peoples who are incapable or, as they would say in the United States, incompetent.

Thus, in 1900, Socialism, certainly on the German side of the Rhine, was pro-colonial.[1] Bernstein resists the temptation—I quote his own words so as not perchance to misrepresent him—" of letting himself be carried away by romantic sentimentalities about the weak ". The doctrine of self-interest, the will to power, claim that the human race has the right to see the entire globe organised by the efforts of the better peoples, even if this should entail compelling the backward peoples to collaborate in the great work ! I fully realise that this writer lays restrictions on the right of conquest. Conquest must find justification in the needs of humanity since this, as we have said, is the basic reason for it. It is justified, too, only if it benefits the working man, and it must not be allowed to entail excessive expansion causing a depopulation of the Western countries which would react unfavourably on the standard of life of the working population. In short, the conquerors must pass laws to protect all their subjects. The methods of colonisation must be *reformed*, but colonisation itself is not condemned !

To arrive at *condemnation*, the third phase of socialism in the old sense, we must pass on almost to 1907. As an isolated case,

---

[1] See C. Andler, *Le socialisme impérialiste dans l'Allemagne contemporaine* (*Action nationale*), Dec. 10, 1912.

Paul-Louis, in France, and later Jules Guesde, condemned expansion as a fatal effect of capitalist over-production : a conquest of markets, a brutal remedy which would not be able to delay the end.[1] At the Paris Socialist Congress of 1900, the German Rosa Luxemburg got a resolution carried condemning expeditions. At the 4th Congress of the French Socialist Party, held in 1902 in Tours, Gustave Hervé ventured to exclaim that all colonial wars should be renounced ; the colonies should pass from the domination of missionaries, and the military government to the authority of the civil power ; whose first duty would be to study and ensure the greater happiness of the original inhabitants. In 1902 Hervé thus thought along the same lines as Bernstein : the time has not yet come to abandon the colonies ; but we must insist that no more missionaries be sent ; and we must withdraw the military [2] and place the colonies under the civil power to be administered—in the interests of the ruled. But we have already had all this in Enfantin ! In 1907, however, we hear a new note : a resolution which is a formal condemnation of colonies. It is of course true that in 1893 at the Zurich Congress, Domela Nieuwenhuis, a Dutch socialist delegate, had spoken as follows : " The invasion of Barbarians is not always an evil, the little civilisation which we possess would not exist if the Barbarians had not mingled their new blood with the thin and vitiated blood of a dying world." Perhaps this may be called a figure of speech, but not precisely a condemnation. In 1896 in London, the worker and pacifist George Lansbury defined colonisation as " an extension of the field of capitalist exploitation " : a formula, but nothing more. At the Paris Congress of 1900 Van Kol with Hyndman passed a resolution to combat " by every means " imperialism and capitalism with their " crimes " and their " shames ".[3] It was at the Stuttgart Congress of 1907 that the Marxist doctrine was definitely formulated and Jules Guesde, a French Marxist, moved a resolution in favour of " the refusal of all credit for war, the navy and the colonies ". The fruit of anti-militarism had ripened, and the fruit was anti-colonialism. Explicitly and publicly, colonial " adventures " are condemned. At the same Congress a resolution was moved by a French

---

[1] P. Louis, *La colonisation sous la 3ᵉ République, Revue Socialiste*, 1897, I, pp. 24 f. and 155 f. ; and *Le colonialisme*, 1905.

[2] Pacificism is thus unfavourable to colonies which are almost always won by fighting. See J. Dumas, *La colonisation, essai de doctrine pacifiste*, 1904.

[3] The text will be found in Dubois and Terrier's *Un siècle d'expansion . . .* 1902, p. 434 f.

delegate, the Blanquist Vaillant, and seconded by Jaurès and passed by the Congress which condemned " capitalist and colonial piracies ". The evolution of socialism was then complete, though very belated. It was in the same year, 1907, that Jaurès, in a speech on Morocco, spoke of " the liberties of the Moroccan people ".[1] Though he expressed indignation at the occupation, he did not go so far, and notably in the collected speeches known as *The Moroccan Hornets' Nest*,[2] he did not dare to go so far as unreservedly to condemn all dominations.[3] At this period Mussolini was more radical ; about 1910, in a newspaper called *La Folla*, he aired the most violent anti-Libyanism.

It was rather *communism*, in its recent sense, which returned a verdict from which there was no appeal, against " colonial imperialism ". It did so, much more by its tactics than by its doctrine.[4] By fighting expansions it hoped to shake the foundations of " capitalism " ; and it is in its procedure rather than in its principles that it is so strongly anti-colonial. All this is quite recent, a matter almost of yesterday ; for the first sign of this phobia showed itself only twenty years ago.[5]

It was in 1915, to be exact, that communism in the new sense proclaimed what it called the " stigmatisation " of overseas " adventures ". In the so-called Zimmerwald Declaration of September 8, we find these words : " After such a massacre the definitely imperialist character of the war has become more and more marked ; there is the proof that its causes lie in the imperialist and colonial policy of all the governments." [6] Not until Lenin's writings of 1917 did something like an " anti-imperial " thunderstorm break forth ; he denounces an indissoluble connection between imperialism and capitalism. If it is necessary to liberate the subject peoples by revolution, that is because Colonies are a sin of Capital ; the white working-class and the black working-class are jointly " exploited " ;

---

[1] *Œuvres de Jean Jaurès*, edited by M. Bonafous, 1933.

[2] *Le Guêpier marocain*, 1906–8.

[3] For the anti-colonialism of the " Young " Socialists see *Revue des Vivants*, Feb. 1930.

[4] See in general : G. Gautherot, *Le monde communiste*, 1927 ; *Le Bolchevisme aux colonies*, 1930 ; J. Doriot, *Les colonies et le communisme*, 1929 ; X. *Le Bolchevisme et la politique coloniale*, *Rev. Deux-Mondes*, May 15, 1930 ; J. Blomberger, *Le communisme aux Indes Néerland.*, 1929 ; L. Jalabert, *Une campagne anticoloniale*, *Études*, Oct. 5, 1934.

[5] [Written in 1936. EOL]

[6] It was an American, H. Ingram Priestley, who asserted that " colonialism " and the " exploitation " of the blacks by the whites " is the basic cause of the recent war " ; *The White Knight and the Black Pawn*, Proceedings Pacific Coast Branch Amer. Hist. Assoc., 1929, pp. 10–20. See another American, T. Sunderland, *L'Inde enchaînée*, abridged Fr. trans. 1931.

consequently, without imperialism, capitalism would be incomplete. To bring about the downfall of capitalism, you must put an end to imperialism. To achieve the destruction of the " bourgeois " régime, you must rob it of its weapon and its power which lies in exploiting distant countries. Lenin loved to repeat these words : " Polish off the West by means of the East." This meant attacking from outside inwards ; destroy the masters by drilling the subjects for Revolution.[1] It was a matter of tactics and technics rather than of dogmatics.

There was nevertheless a dogma, and one which leads to the absolute condemnation of all expansions as a violation of " the fraternal order which ought to reign between peoples rightfully equal ". This is the very phrase inscribed on the Official Programme of the Communist International of 1928. From it may be formally deduced, by pushing it to its logical conclusion, the right of the colonies to secede by every means : insurrection or revolution, so that one day these distant countries may be socialised.

We in France well know—for we are free in this place to speak frankly—the lengths to which some adherents of this doctrine have dared to go, even in our own country. In the months of March, 1925, at the tragic moment when Abd al Karim was threatening Fez, a French deputy, Doriot, wrote thus in the Polish paper *Pravda* : " From the moment that our party entered on the path of systematic Bolshevisation, we have taken organised action in view of the struggle for independence of the colonies, ours and our neighbours', especially Spanish Morocco." Further on, he added : " Now that the French Communist Party has seriously taken charge of these regions, no one can say that they will save the home country ; on the contrary, it is they who will slay France, bourgeois and imperialist France." And on September 20, 1924, after the French forces had suffered a setback, the parliamentary group of the Communist Party sent a telegram of congratulation to Abd ul Karim, which M. Briand read aloud in the Chamber on June 18, 1925 ! This was anti-colonialism savagely unleashed : the fruit of a communism not so much European as Eur-Asian ! It is a new Dogma ; a new Religion, for Lenin is God. He has his tomb, he is worshipped like a Buddha. In a certain country of the

[1] *Bureau colonial international* (The Hague) *Rapport sur la prépar. par le Gouvern. Soviétique des révoltes coloniales*, 1929 ; J. Bonin, *L'institut de propag. colon. de Moscou, Acad. Sciences Colon.* X, 1929. See the recent *Libération, Revue . . . de propag. contre l'impérialisme*, April 1936.

Near East he bears the title of a Spirit and a Hero ; he is called Lena bin Uzair ; he is a jinn, escaped from the Underworld, who in order to win the favour of Allah destroys the Unbelievers and establishes equality among the Faithful. Amongst the Persians he is believed to be the reincarnation of Ali, worshipped in Iran as the son-in-law of the Prophet !

Thus communism means conversion. A dogma has been formed, a Religion set up amongst millions of men ; as in ancient times amongst the Romans, a whole religious *syncretism* has been created. The inhabitants of the French colonies who have been converted to the new creed have evolved an indefinable blend of different conceptions. There is particularly a fusion, and confusion, of tribalism with fatalism. Tribalism is inborn in the tribal peoples, socialists by choice, communists in the spirit of their traditions, all prepared to welcome a rejuvenated communism which is a travesty of tribalism. This is aggravated by fatalism ; the new doctrine leaves no room for free will ; the destinies of nations are determined by the laws which govern history, and which have superseded the jinns and the gods. There are " saints, successors of the gods " ; there are also laws, successors of the gods ! Mechanics and mechanisation rule the world ; fatalism still and fetishism still, for which the tribal peoples are prepared. A skilful return to the primitive succeeds in reaching and stirring primitive man.

CHAPTER XXXV

AUTONOMISM—MOTIVES AND AIMS

Liberalism and collectivism pave the way to the *principle of autonomy* [1] (*autonomisme*).

We shall consider the principle of autonomy as being distinct and self-sufficient and having its own motives ; a universal phenomenon of the present time which floods the colonial empires. It is an agitation, a fermentation, manifesting itself amongst peoples far and near, to attain autonomy and the right to legislate for themselves and control their own administration : to become a Nation, to attain Statehood. We are therefore not talking of sudden *rebellions* provoked by a gesture or an abuse : such explosions have no future and from them emerges no " movement " of permanence. Such were the Sepoy mutinies of 1806 and 1857 : they were provoked by the troops being compelled to use leather and grease derived from pigs ; [2] the Cuban revolt of 1868 or that of the Kanakas ten years later ; or, lastly, that of the Filipinos in 1896.

Let us use the term " autonomy " in preference to the more commonly used " nationalism ". For it is both more than nationalism—and less.

It is much *more* : in the first place it is religious. It implies the aspiration to conquer or re-conquer religious power, to regain authority, for the Church or for the Sect which is confused with the Nation. When Algerians, Tunisians or Moroccans talk to us of " nation " they always use a qualifying adjective, " Arab Nation " or " Muslim Nation ". Islam rules in their dreams and breathes in their desires : Religious liberty and religious dignity first, as much or more than national dignity and liberty.

It is much *less* : the aspiration for independence does not imply the formation of a national group. They want to form a State without being first a true Nation. When the tribes cry out for autonomy, they are not necessarily such large, comprehensive groups as nations are, having the same conception, the same traditions and living under the same laws. *Unity of language,*

---

[1] See in general, Lothrop Stoddard, *The Rising Tide of Colour*, 1920.
[2] [The English reader will be well advised to seek the facts about the Indian Mutiny, *Ency. Brit.*, 14th Ed., Vol. 12, p. 242 f., and the authorities there listed. EOL]

unity of law create a nation ; these tribes are states which have not up to the present attained any considerable population. Common speech, common power, ruling over common territory, that is what makes the nation, out of which is born the State. Yet we see nowadays that a group may wish to be a State despite the fact that it is only a Tribe or even a Clan, or a heterogeneous agglomeration of tribes without identity, without community, bound together at most by a sultanate ruling only for a time. Such was Algeria before the coming of the French. Such was Ethiopia. Let us therefore say the principle of autonomy, or let us perhaps say separatism : the claim, the goal for which these groups are striving is the right to separation.

A confused writer, Oswald Spengler, in his *Decline of the West*, had a glimpse of how what he called " the colour revolution " is inevitable, and is not adequately explained as the result of propaganda and intervention.[1] For the desire of subjugated classes and races to break their yoke is, he says, a phase of " capitalist evolution ", the fruit of a new industrial order. The Liberation of enslaved classes ; the Liberation of enslaved races ; these are two parallel currents which have in fact the same motives. If, more than a century ago, there was in England a " world-wide white revolution ", there will soon be—nay, there already is—a " world-wide coloured revolution ". It began about 1905, soon after the Russo-Japanese War which taught the yellow Asiatic that the white warrior could be defeated ! " To-day," he says, " we are directly menaced by this coloured revolution, because France has forcibly initiated the Negroes into the secrets of armaments, technique and diplomacy, as of old Egypt taught the Libyans and the Mediterranean peoples, and Rome the Germanic peoples."

It is our task to trace the general pattern of this evolution and more particularly to indicate its principal motives or, to speak more accurately, its main driving forces. Let us say " driving forces " rather than " motives ", for these forces are very frequently unconscious. These protestations and aspirations are often obscure, and badly expressed and ill defined ; they are repulsions rather than impulses ; disgust with the present, nebulous dreams. But these motive forces are themselves phases ; when we enumerate them we see them succeeding each other. They did not come into action simultaneously, but each in turn. There are three such phases. The effects of contact which

[1] *Der Untergang des Abendlandes*, 1918, Revd. Ed. 1922, Eng. trans. C. F. Atkinson.

invariably took place in the colonies between human beings of all colours : interaction between rulers and subjects ; transformation of inferior by the superior, and vice versa ; above all the permeation of the dominated by their contact with the dominating peoples.

These, then, are the three activating phases in the change of mental attitude amongst the French subject races : revolution, education, imitation. These are Results, often intended, often unintended, effects of the conquest, which ultimately act against the conquest !

Revolution, created by the French themselves in colonial countries by bringing profound and radical change—whether intentionally or not, matters little. The native conceptions and traditions were abrogated, or adulterated. Those were the two results of the Frenchman's coming : the abolition sometimes of many traditions ; above all the distortion of many traditions.

Abolition of traditions. Willingly or unwillingly, the French brought with them to their subjects what they believed to be two benefits—which were perhaps in fact the exact opposite—*secular law* and *written law*. *Secular law*, regulating everything, valid for everyone whatever his religion, was territorial residential law to which all dwellers in the country were subject. *Written law*, edited and codified, is necessary to French tribunals. These brought two real revolutions into native life, for almost everywhere native law had been religious law and at the same time customary law : a law which each man knew and recognised, because it tallied with his religion, whatever that might be, and with his tradition, whatever that might be. Native societies were shaken to their very foundations when one common, written law put an end to and superseded their religious and their customary law. By the mere fact of their occupation, in the desire for security and for prosperity, the French were obliged to establish " public order " and put an end to " superstition ". Religion and magic had to yield, or will have to yield—for the end is not yet !—to the requirements of a new State.

Adulteration of traditions. In every case where it was thought, rightly or wrongly—documents are many—that it was wise to maintain and respect native traditions, the French did so, but in the process they distorted and adulterated them. For they inevitably caused two fundamental changes in the position of their subjects ; they compelled them to pass from the *tribe* to the *nation*, from the group to the individual. From *tribe* to *nation* since they promulgated a territorial law, that is to say, a common law valid for all without distinction of religion,[1] or of condition. If we are now able to speak of an Algerian law, a Tunisian law, a Moroccan law, an " Aofian " [2] law, this is a profound innovation ! Unity of legislation merging the tribe into the nation—this fundamental phenomenon has not been sufficiently appreciated in the colonies —had the direct effect on French native subjects of substituting the *individual* for the *group*. Before the arrival of the French, they were familiar with collective rights, village rights, family rights. This is not to deny that in many cases there existed also personal or individual rights. It is an over-simplification to speak, as people sometimes do, of primitive " communism ". There was always to a certain extent a conception of the individual and the recognition of his rights. Tribal or family or communal law was, however, always over-riding : the individual was always subordinate to the community, the personal to the collective. This being so, the French in their colonies have emancipated and revealed the individual. They are entitled to say, without the slightest exaggeration, that they have created the individual in the legal sense. They have given him, as an individual, powers and duties, they have detached him from kinsmen and neighbours. They have inspired in every individual two new sentiments which are in truth the mainspring of his aspiration towards liberty : these two sentiments are the emancipation of the individual and the assertion of the individual. Emancipation, since henceforward every individual is subject to law, has powers and tasks as an individual, is legally distinct from his father or his chief, who have heretofore represented and symbolised his grouping. Personal emancipation thus leads to the claim for personal rights. The idea of privileges to be claimed and demanded by each single person thus wove itself into the tissue of native thought. The mere fact of French occupation produced a revolution : in two directions and with two aspects.

Having created individuals, the next thing was to count them by organising a *census* : a census of persons, no longer of fires or hearths, of tents or households. French enumerators go into the houses : they dare to ask the father of the family " How many wives have you ? How many boys ? How many girls ? " —a disturbing question, an indiscreet question. King David was seriously punished for having ventured to count his subjects.

---

[1] R. Maunier, *La Nation et l'État* . . . , in *Coutumes algériennes*, 1935, p. 144 f.
[2] [A.O.F. stands for Afrique Occidentale française = French West Africa. EOL]

For by counting men instead of families, calculating the number of living persons and not only of fighting men, he invented the individual, detached the individual, gave the individual publicity. The unity of the family group was broken. Census and registration were the announcement of a new status. Even in Roman times a Jewish revolt was provoked by the census which a progressively-minded legate, Quirinus, carried out.

Education too. Knowledge of French ways was spread both by the spoken and the written word. Education was either deliberate or unintentional, but more often the former. From the very start the French ideal was to convert the natives spiritually, morally, politically and socially. To spread French opinions and French feelings by instruction ; to Frenchify the natives, to assimilate them, as we say nowadays, thus approximating their mental attitude to the French. Napoleon's expedition to Egypt was, as we have seen, not only an ethnographic but also a democratic expedition ;[1] its formal object was to reform and educate the inhabitants, to teach French manners and customs to the Egyptians.

Preaching thus began very early in the French Empire, and produced in varying degrees a transformation in the natives' natural modes of thought. Possibly this was also a factor in leading them to make claims. Preaching—that's the very word ! —was carried on in two ways, by two sets of agents : by the rulers themselves and by enemies. There were the rulers who blindly indoctrinated their subjects ; and there were the enemies too, both internal and external, who were hostile to the occupation.

Education by the *rulers*. In France, and even elsewhere, to colonise is to teach. Resident colonists are all missionaries of " progress " ; they always think of themselves as educators. Officials, notably in the French colonial empire, are missionaries and converters, converting if not to our faith at least to our tastes. Officials discoursing in palavers and *shikayahs*, official preachers in assemblies and meetings : that's what they are. From one meeting they go to another indoctrinating the natives. Then comes the book and the newspaper. It was men of religion who started the very first newspapers in the colonies. In India in 1818,[2] a little later in Tahiti, protestant pastors printed vernacular

[1] [The English reader will of course note that there was in it no trace of ambition or military strategy ! EOL]

[2] R. Chatterjee, *Origin and Growth of Journalism among Indians, Annals Amer. Acad. Polit. and Social Science*, Sept. 1929.

papers ; so similar are the methods of education and conversion. Sometimes they had to invent the scripts—the Quoc-ngu, for instance, was in very early days invented by the Roman Catholics in Annam—the better to instruct their converts. More than that : those who are developing the country, who are nowadays called the exploiters—all the colonists—are also missionaries, but without intending and without knowing it. Always, albeit unwittingly, they are propagandists for the French spirit. They are always aiming, obviously aiming, at modelling the natives to their own pattern, to their own instructions ; at " waking them up ", rousing them from their apathy, polishing the rust off them, curing them of their follies ! The first word, or one of the first words which the colonist learns to say, whether amongst Muslims or natives of Tong-King, is " Quick ! " Colonists are of their very nature instructors. Without seeking to do so, they have brought a great change in the " mentality " of the natives. Imprudently they have jostled them out of the attitude of resigna-tion. They have given them the taste for liberty : in their conversations on the café terrace, they hold forth eloquently on the subject of liberties ; publicly they allow themselves liberties they would never have taken if they had stayed at home. Thus they give the native both the conception and the example of taking liberties ! In the colonies the French are actors " before the footlights ", they play comedies, sometimes tragedies : pro-viding the natives with a show gratis !

Education which at first was the act of the rulers may become later the act of *enemies*. In our day, these enemies are the anti-colonials who go abroad to the colonies to preach love of liberty to the inhabitants, exciting them, driving them to extremes, kindling in them the idea of their claims. This teaching may proceed either from *internal* or from *external* enemies.

Internal enemies. There have always, and at all times, been in every State opponents of expansion. Colonisation has been opposed from the point of departure. Lyautey has well expressed it : " it is the rule of the game that the conqueror must first conquer . . . public opinion at home ". You must resign your-self to finding foes in your own country!

External enemies. Sometimes friends prove enemies in this connection. There is in this nothing new. To grow greater is to shock your friends ; to grow richer is to embarrass your neighbours. More than one founded settlement has met destruc-tion at foreign hands, through European friends or enemies and

not, as in Greenland, at the hands of earlier-established natives !
Brazil and Florida and many other places bear witness. In our
day every expansion by a colonial power is obstinately opposed
by other colonising peoples . . . and by non-colonisers too. The
liberation of the first inhabitants could not have been achieved
but for European assistance. If the Germans have to-day [1] a
base of expansion in the Canaries so as to stir up the French and
Spanish Moroccans against their rulers, this is no new phenomenon ; it has its precedents ; rivalries have been unleashed,
and are not yet ended.[2] More than one far-off people owes
them its liberty.

Imitation. This is the last factor making for liberation.
French ways and customs are accepted and spontaneously
borrowed by the native of his own free will without persuasion
or inducement. This is the transmission, or as the English say,
diffusion, by borrowing pure and simple. It is the result of no
preaching. It is imitation which takes place without us, or even
in spite of us ; by *contagion* proper which mayhap we would
sometimes even fain prevent. We are copied even against our
will ! Imitation is also *distortion*, for there is never imitation in
the true and strict sense which would mean pure transmission,
simple diffusion with no modification : a perfected copy such as
can sometimes be met in industrial processes. There is always
transmutation, distortion, not perfect reproduction, the imperfect,
always incomplete, adoption of an altered model. When seen
from afar the new product resembles the old, but not when seen
at close quarters. Such has been the fate of the conceptions of
liberty and equality which the natives have acquired through
contact with the French. These are exports which cannot be
stopped, which cross the seas to reign . . . or rage . . . and for
which the French have only themselves to thank !

This imitation has its *types* and its *agents*.

There are two types which we might call *imitation-by-acceptance*
and *imitation-by-opposition*. It is particularly the latter which has
contaminated the natives and incited them to make claims.

Imitation-by-acceptance. This is of course the imitation which
spontaneously, eagerly, accepts and adopts, because people are
attracted by French ideas and customs. It is sometimes an
impulsive enthusiasm : the natives begging that they should be
given, and that quickly, the means of living and thinking like

---

[1] [1936. EOL]
[2] J. Darcy's classic, *Cent années de rivalité coloniale, Anglais et Français*, 1904.

Frenchmen. We may also speak of *imitation-by-adaptation* : imitation for the sake of imitating in order to become similar to Frenchmen. This is particularly obvious in the matter of dress. A mode of dressing sometimes spreads like lightning, partly from a desire to rise in the world or from the need to indicate a real position ; for dress is always a symbol and an indication of rank. Living conditions and food are copied later for the same reasons. When these "outward signs" of "advancement" or of "evolution" are exhausted, the next step is to copy French conceptions and traditions, even French prejudices, which it is thought an honour to display ! Then the moment has come to read and translate French writings. The Bible isn't the only book to gain currency in many languages ! Is it generally known that Rousseau's *Social Contract* has been translated into Turkish as well as Arabic, as well as Chinese ? And some day perhaps into Quoc-ngu,[1] into Bantu, into Moi ? [2] For the Moi now rejoice in a script quite recently bestowed on them by the Administration. As in Japan, and for the same purposes, the French colonies are doing a great deal of translation from French into the local vernacular. Democracy was thus able to enter by the basketful. Let us note that this also is nothing new. It is more than a hundred years since a young Hindu, Ram Mohun Roy, hoping to awaken the Indian spirit, turned eagerly to the various forms of European progress ; he preached the West without fear of any excesses resulting. Against this the leaders of the Indian world later reacted.

Imitation-by-opposition is another story. It is imitation not in order to copy but to criticise and to attack. This is the master-Idea of Pan-Islamism. You must imitate the Europeans in their inventions, but in order to fight them and be able one fine day to kick them out ! You must copy the enemy's methods to protect yourself against him and free yourself from him. This is a first principle of tactics ! Khalil Pasha, the real founder of Pan-Islamism in Turkey in 1865, sought to collect into one all the forces of Islam to oppose the expansion of the Christian peoples.[3] Hostile, deliberate, premeditated imitation, questing after the very latest, and passionately seizing on it. We note the same phenomenon in India and in Turkey and elsewhere, the

---

[1] See p. 381.
[2] [Spoken by the Hill Tribes of Tong-King in Indo-China. EOL]
[3] See B. Bareilles, *Les Turcs*, 1917, p. 207 f. Seligman, *Encycl. of the Social Sciences*, s.vv. *Panislamism, Pan-movements*, Vol. XI (Bibliography).

study more especially of all war-like lore with a view to turning it against the teacher.

Imitation has also its *agents*. These are those who have promoted and encouraged it—often unwittingly—the " bearers of culture " and " envoys of the West ", all who by their mere comings and goings have left behind the footprints of the European. The agents of diffusion have been men and women, travelling in both directions, from France to the colonies, from the colonies to France. The most important of these have been the men who left their native country to come to France : students, workmen, soldiers. Before he died, Lyautey would have liked to see every one of them packed home.[1] Unsuspectingly, these men have often been messengers of Western " culture " when they returned to their home country. Influenced by France, they passed on to their neighbours and to their children some fraction of the spirit of France, like the Indians of whom Kipling wrote.[2] As early as 1785, there came to France, " a number of Indians, they say, of both sexes ", to weave Indian textiles : the forerunners of many others in more recent times.

Men came of course, but women too; this is a big innovation of our own day. Native women are no longer sheltered from every breath of the outside world. In schools, convent workrooms, factories and workshops they have been exposed to a new atmosphere.[3] A hundred thousand of them are at work in India, spinning and weaving jute and cotton. In Arab countries great influence is exercised by French women. Social intercourse, permanent contact, casual relationships, have combined to produce reciprocal imitation. French fashions long ago penetrated the harem ; newspapers and novels gained entrance too, often unknown to the master of the house. If there is any " feminism " in India, in Egypt and even in Tunisia, it is due to the Frenchwoman's attractions. Many a governess, introduced into the harem by its master's wish, has there sown the seed of a " rebellious spirit " which he had not anticipated. Women's clubs for political agitation have been formed in Indonesia and in Hindustan.

---

[1] P. Catrice, *L'emploi des troupes indigènes . . . en France. Études*, Nov. 20, 1931.

[2] R. Kipling, *Les yeux de l'Asie*, 1920, p. 40 f.
[This French selection from Kipling's work does not appear exactly to correspond to any English collection. EOL]

[3] Mme de Duras's *Ourika* is the story of the " uprooted " Negro woman. For Algeria, Abd-el-Kader Hadj, *Zohra*, 1926 ; Lucienne Favre, *Orientale*, 1930. All these are novels.

In these ways, and by these agents, the French have awakened aspirations and pretensions in their subjects. They have been perhaps not wholly willingly " bearers of culture ". It is their own action which has quickened a greater desire for liberty. We shall have henceforward to look on, and see how the natives seek emancipation, whether in the future or in the present, whether by evolution or by revolution.

CHAPTER XXXVI

YELLOW AUTONOMISM

Even if autonomy is everywhere conceded, it shows infinite diversity. We ought really to speak of various autonomies. They differ in their *motives*, in their *actors* and, finally—for we must come to this—in their *objects* and results. Subject peoples claim autonomy in two different directions ; in the direction of *progress*, in the direction of *regress* ; for advance or for retrogression.

For *progress*, that is to say, with eyes fixed on the future. If they are demanding autonomy it is as a step towards nationhood, in order to found a nation. The peoples under French rule want then to emerge from the condition perpetuated, they assert, by the French—not without ulterior motive—the barbarous and primitive condition of the tribe which, they allege, has been consolidated by the preservation of customary law. They want to be Nations ; they believe themselves capable of forming States. It is in order to march forward that they dream of gaining their liberty.

For *regress* too, that is to say with eyes fixed, not on the future, but very much on the past. They want to return of their own good will to their ancient condition, not to move towards nationhood, but to slip back again into the tribe. They want to recreate and re-invigorate their traditions, which the French have impaired, and to obey the call of their ancestors.

We have thus two aims, two spirits, two missions. Broadly speaking : the idea of retrogression tends to prevail amongst the Asiatics, black or yellow ; it is the idea of progression which tends to prevail amongst the Africans, white or black.

In the black world, they pursue innovation, evolution ; they want to be free in order to ape the white man. The Negro is a Futurist. The Yellow Man is a By-Gone-ist, who turns to the past and sighs for the vanished days of yore ; we see this most markedly in Mahatma Gandhi.[1] This is *reaction* against the present : a march to the rear, not to the van.[2]

[1] [It is questionable whether the Indian would enjoy being classified as " Yellow ". And what of the Japanese and Chinese ? See footnote 1, p. 47. EOL]

[2] This is true also of the Amer-Indian Redskins ; they have had their prophets preaching return to tradition and the end of the White Man's oppression. F. W. Hodge, *Handbook of Amer. Indians*, II, 1907, p. 309 f. Cf. Dr. Montezuma (Apache) : *Let my People Go, Congress Record*, May 12, 1916, Vol. 53, p. 8888 f.

Let us first take a look at the Asiatics, and in particular the Indians and the Indo-Chinese.[1] They grew restless as early as 1904 ; this was the result of the great Russo-Japanese conflict : a costly warning to the White Man's pride. They began to set forth their claims. From the very beginning of their agitation, they enlisted foreign sympathies. The Japanese and Chinese " supported " the Indo-Chinese demand for autonomy with finance and with agents. The Americans also approved and encouraged the new-born agitation against the White Man ! In 1927, an astounding book appeared in America, the *Revolt of Asia* by Upton Close. Upton Close is the pseudonym of Professor Hall of the University of Washington. He maintains that the revolt of Asia is legitimate and right ; it is the retort to injustice and tyranny : its aim is to punish the " bluff of the West ".[2]

The Chinese also came to the help of the Indo-Chinese. The China of to-day has been largely Americanised and Protestantised in the persons of many of its protectors ; it has been " Rousseau-ised " [3] and " Communised " in the persons of many of its leaders. Chinese brains have been soaked in equalitarianism, under the influence of Protestant clergymen. Sun Yat-sen was the son of a Protestant pastor ; he lived for a long time in the United States, he married a Wesleyan Methodist, and he had, finally, gorged himself on Rousseau, whose books have been in any case translated into Chinese. Chiang Kai-shek is also a Protestant : his austere doctrine of the " New Life " is an avatar of American Puritanism.

Round about 1900 there had of course been amongst the Yellow peoples of Asia a movement totally different in spirit ; a religious movement grounded in extremely archaic ideas, directed towards the past and not the future ; the movement known as *Pan-Mongolism*. Russia encouraged and protected this agitation in order to promote the spread of Buddhism and to profit by exploiting the good relations which up till 1904 had existed

---

[1] I do not want to touch on Oceania. For Indonesia see Semaoen, *L'Indonésie a la parole* ; A. Vandenbosch, *Nationalism in Netherlands East India, Pacific Affairs*, IV, Dec. 1931, and Blomberger's book already quoted. For the Philippines, G. M. Dutcher, *The Political Awakening of the East*, 1925. For New Zealand, W. Macmillan Brown, *Peoples and Problems of the Pacific*, I, 1927, p. 200 f. For Tonga, E. W. Gifford, *Journal Polynesian Society*, XXXIII–XXXIV, 1924, p. 281 (the birth of nationalism from mere contact with the English). For Tahiti, H. Mager, *Le monde polynésien*, 1902, p. 233 (the collective plaint of the Tahitians in 1889).

[2] *The Revolt of Asia : the End of the White Man's World Dominance*, 1927. See also other American writers already cited.

[3] On Rousseau in China : Avesnes, *En face du soleil Levant*, 1909, p. 11 f. ; J. Woo, *Le problème constitutionnel chinois*, 1925 (thesis).

between her and the Grand Lama. The Dalai Lama, the sacred and holy Pope-King who lives in Tibet and controls the lives of millions, had, very probably, concluded an alliance with the Tsar. Pan-Mongolism and Pan-Slavism were bound together for the benefit of Greater Russia. All that is now ancient history, the history of a very dead past ! If archaism has survived amongst the Yellow peoples of Asia, it is now coloured with ever-increasing modernism. This is so in India and in Indo-China.

In India the principle of autonomy is an old phenomenon ; it is a mistake—let us insist on this—to imagine that it is a new manifestation of to-day ! It is in some places a full hundred years, and not less than fifty, since the Indians began to clamour for their liberty. After Ram Mohun Roy with his passion for the West, came Dayananda Sarasvati, who preached return to the ancient Sacred Books. There were protests amongst both men and women. The National Congress was founded in 1885 [1] and has since then met every year.[2]   Indian feminism had been able to establish itself; it was championed by an Indian Princess Pandita Ramasbai Sarasvati who as early as 1888 published a daring plan for the emancipation of Indian women. She wanted to see an end to degrading practices : female infanticide, the compulsory marriage of young girl-children and the cruel power of father and husband.[3] The spirit of reform presaged a movement of protest which soon took shape in the foundation of a new type of University at Aligarh, where modernism and archaism sought to harmonise. Thus Aligarh plays the same part in India as Al Azhar plays in Egypt. From 1885 onwards various Congresses have been held to " ameliorate " the position of the Indian subject. This is a movement of reform or of transformation but not of communism. Reformers and transformers have so far usually been champions of the Indian " people " if this word has any meaning in so vast a country. About 1890 Malabari represented this movement : he demanded that the most educated Indians should have some share in the government.[4]

It was, however, a curious type of reform movement, focussed

---

[1] [Founded by an Englishman to encourage Indians to take more interest in politics.   EOL]

[2] See in general : Piriou, *L'Inde contemp. et le mouvement national*, 1905 ; Seligman, *Ency. of the Social Sciences*, VII, p. 674 (Bibliog.) Tarakhnat Das (Hindu), *Indien in der Weltpolitik*, 1932.

[3] On the women's unions : Janet Kelman, *Labour in India*, 1923, p. 236 f.

[4] D. Menant, *Malabari*, p. 207 f. He was strongly supported by an Englishman, Sir William Wedderburn ; S. K. Ratcliffe, *Sir W. W. and the Indian Reform Movement*, 1923.

on the past, seeking " reaction ", desiring the re-introduction of ancestral custom, preaching return to simplicity, to the bliss of the golden days . . . before the English came. Théophile Gautier in *La Belle-Jenny* has pictured this mood : " He will drive out the English, these coarse barbarians who profane the waters of the Ganges, who speak to outcastes, who prevent widows from burning themselves to death as decency demands, who make their belly the sepulchre of life . . ."—We may be very sure that Gandhi [1] is not the only representative of this reforming conservative spirit in India, nor Tagore either. Yet Gandhi is an anglicised Hindu, he studied law amongst the Anglo-Saxons and practised as a barrister in South Africa ; yet, modernised in mind though he is, he remains a reactionary at heart in love with the past. What he would like to see is a return to the men of old, a rebirth of pure Buddhism which is Contemplative Thought, which is the Rule of Resignation ; yet on the other hand he draws inspiration from the religions of the West, he embodies the teachings of Christ and invokes the Sermon on the Mount, weaving out of it all a curious *syncretism*. He has read the Old Testament and the Gospels, but he has also read Tolstoi. [2] Gandhi-ism is a curious mixture, a cross between Buddhism, Christianity and Tolstoi-ism. This is why Gandhi's reform movement, rooted in the past, presents three elements to our view : asceticism, mysticism and archaism.

First comes *Asceticism*. For Gandhi believes that suffering is good : the dream of Buddha, the dream of Tolstoi. He believes that we should therefore renounce our comforts, renounce our work ; we should cultivate the taste for poverty and for purity ; we should despise effort, and view possessions with disgust. One of the vows which his disciples must take, and which was taken by the young Englishwoman who followed him, is the vow of non-possession, the renunciation of property and the renunciation of activity. Refusal to possess, means radical refusal to progress. Thus the Mahatma preached a re-born asceticism, condemning all the strivings of the West. Let us turn our backs on fake progress ; let us flee from false desire ; for only through suffering can Man attain God.

Secondly, *Mysticism*, which is the fruit of asceticism. Why must we refuse to possess ? Why must we refuse to progress ?

---

[1] [These passages were of course written in 1936, 12 years before Gandhi's assassination. EOL]

[2] R. Rolland, *Mahatma Gandhi*, 1923 ; C. Freer Andrews, *Mahatma Gandhi's Ideas . . .* , 1930 (selected extracts) ; M. Markovitch, *Tolstoi et Gandhi*, 1928.

For a religious reason. Buddhism is the core of Gandhi-ism. Poverty is only a path to purity ; it is a taboo, an interdict, which we ought to impose on ourselves ; in all religions it is the road to holiness. Comfort is impure, and luxury is defiled. It is the foreigner with his imported pleasures who has perverted the Indian people by introducing degrading needs. All the products of our Western factories are kneaded of misery and woven of woe ; they are steeped in immorality. To recapture the purity of ancient Indian Buddhism, we must place them all under a strict taboo. He feels therefore a contempt for, rather than a hatred of, progress.

Lastly, *Archaism* : a worship and glorification of the past. Gandhi preaches a return to the procedures and regulations of olden times. He wants to draw his blue pencil through progress. Shut the factories, smash the machines, throw out the tools ! Get back to the old handicrafts, get back to the spinning wheel, an object in company with which Gandhi is frequently and willingly photographed—thus making use of at least one of our Western inventions ! It is manifest that this doctrine reverts to the long-distant past. By thus making the apologia for primitive hand-labour, making one tool only into a tradition, eulogising simple work performed in the bosom of the family, under peaceful patriarchal rule, Gandhi teaches us that the Indian is pure and the Englishman impure : he is invoking the prehistoric dread of the foreigner ! In the name of the ancient *dharma*, the law of the true Hindu, in accord with the spirit of the Lawgiver-King Manu, return to the ancestors ; through them recapture once again the Faith and the Law of the People of Saints. If he wishes his people to abstain from *co-operating* with the English, this is a matter of tactics and battle technique to prevent their buying English products ; but it also has its source in a revulsion from the impure foreigner. How can the pure associate with the impure without being defiled ? It is therefore in the name of the prehistoric taboos against strange peoples that Gandhi preaches contempt for the English. Indian autonomism is of a religious nature. If there is an anti-English movement in India it almost always has its face turned towards the past. It is reaction against progress : a homesick yearning for pristine happiness.[1]

---

[1] [For up-to-date information about India, the student may be referred to three invaluable books by Professor R. Coupland, published by the Oxford University Press : *The Indian Problem, 1833–1935* (1942) ; *Indian Politics, 1936–42* (1943) ; and *The Future of India* (1943) ; also to *India and Democracy*, by George Schuster and Guy Wint. EOL]

In Indo-China things are different [1] if we can judge of a movement very imperfectly known except to those with access to confidential reports and information. [2]

What original element is there, then, in the Indo-Chinese autonomy movement ? It is the fact that we already see definite organised *parties* with written regulations and statutes : Fluid parties, lasting sometimes . . . a whole forenoon ; reformed, transformed, as in a game of chess to gratify jealousies which overthrow their chiefs ! Yet there are parties and they preserve a local colour and a local spirit. They are, in fact, or were at any rate in the beginning, *secret* societies with rites and oaths, with dogmas and statutes, the revelation of which to the new member constitutes initiation. They still pay homage to blood relationship. [3] They are, at one and the same time, *parties* and *sects*, national groups and religious groups, in the heart of which East and West are blended. This is why these parties are more *multiple* and more *unstable* than in France. In France, when they speak of a large party, they mean a numerous and extensive group with ramifications throughout the whole country ; a group of some duration which will live for some years, not merely a few months. This is not the expectation of all these parties which the Indo-Chinese form, and dissolve, and reform. Their multiplicity and their instability are their two great weaknesses. For they are very numerous and they very quickly die. There are only a few which have survived for a few years. It is they we shall discuss. The bulk of the others have lasted a few weeks or months only. Like the Dragon of Annam in the old-time legend, they change their skin, they change their name—that would not greatly matter—they change their head, they change their idea, they change their mind. They have no unity, no solidity. [4] There are some among them which might be called

[1] [Written in 1936. EOL]

[2] Varet, *Au pays d'Annam* . . . , 1923 ; L. Roubaud, *Viet Nam*, 1931 ; J. Dorsenne *Faudra-t-il évacuer l'Indochine*, 1932 ; L. Villemotier, *Le patriotisme . . . en Indochine*, *Mercure de France*, Oct. 15, 1934 ; *Cahier des vœux annamites* . . . , 1926 (Saigon). Above all : *Indochine française, Direction des Affaires polit. et de la Sûreté générale, Documents*, 4 fasc., undated (description of the parties by P. Marty)—On the " abuses " and their relation to the movement, P. Monet, *Les Jauniers* ; and Andrée Viollis, *Indochine S.O.S.*, 1935 (contains some truth, but material is unsifted and facts are inadequately checked).

[3] The leaders of the preceding *revolts* were, as in India, saints and heroes, invested with mysterious powers and fed by winged tigers sent them by the Emperor of Heaven. Jules Boissière, *Fumeurs d'opium* (1896), New Ed., p. 148.

[4] Similarly, many small newspapers flourished, some in Quoc-ngu, some in French ; some in Annam, some in Paris. *L'Ame annamite*, for instance, in 1927, the *Bulletin d'informations du Comité d'amnistie* . . . , 1933, in which some French writers collaborated.

privileged or pre-eminent, that have some continuous doctrine or at best continuous tendency. They have their members and their chiefs ; for in Annam an idea is nothing without a chief. A party cannot be established unless men have founded it and carried it on. The problem is, where did these men appear from, and who trained them ? How did party leaders emerge from the midst of a population which is always attached to its traditions ? The answer is simple ! These leaders were trained in France, taught in France ; they would never have arisen if French propaganda and French education had not been unfurled amongst the inhabitants ! Who then are these chiefs ? We can check their history by documents. In almost every case they are the *Young*. The Indo-Chinese party is an *age-group*, a generation ; they are the New versus the Old ! Like Hitlerism and Fascism, you cannot understand the first thing about them, unless you know that they represent a reaction against the Elders. This was the case in Annam. There was no country where the Elders had more power or where greybeards were more respected than Annam, and consequently none where the arrogant demand of the Young to seize the reins of parties was more rudely felt. Who are these Young ? They are students, reporters, officials, or . . . teachers. The students are the most numerous, the reporters are numerous too, I meet some in my own historic Paris ; the state officials form another element, and the personnel of factories and shops. Lastly the teachers, who under every sky are protest-mongers—that is a natural law ! The best known of them, and justly well known, is Nguyen-ai-Quoc; his story is worth comment.[1] In studying his life you note the contagion of French parties. The son of an educated man, he felt the new spirit that was abroad. He left his family and wanted to earn his livelihood ; he thus became one of the uprooted. He became a sailor, and got a " navigator's " certificate in the Messageries Line. He served many years with them ; and it was on board ship that he became indoctrinated by some exponent of Marseilles Socialism. There are always a lot of Indo-Chinese on the French liners. He went to England and then to America and finally to Paris, where he lived for many years. It was there that he read Marx. So, many cross-influences combined to create this specimen of an agitator, the man whom French schools first awakened, who having quitted the shelter of the family and freed

---

[1] Nguyen-ai-Quoc, *Le procès de la colonisation française*, 1926. From 1918 he had edited a *Cahier de Revendications* which he circulated in Versailles.

himself from paternal control—which in Indo-China had remained all-powerful—thus became uprooted and rebellious, and was obliged to betake himself to a far country to receive the revelation.

If these parties have had their creators and their actors, they have also had their objectives, they have had their hopes, ill-analysed, ill-worked out and not free from self-contradiction. If you read the many statutes of all the parties this will suffice to show you that you cannot talk of doctrines, but at best of un-defined tendencies. Nevertheless, you can trace some distinc-tions and discover two different mental attitudes : reformation, revolution.

Reformation. Most of the Indo-Chinese agitators are reformers only ; they are " thirsting for reform " and they " denounce the abuses ". Many would like to revert to the past ; for them the only *progress* would be a *return*. The only thing they want, how-ever, is reform. This desire expresses itself, very differently, in two separate movements : caodaïsm and radicalism.

Caodaïsm [1] is a synthesis of the old and the new. Reform, but to what end ? To restore the ancient tradition, to re-establish the ancient religion, but endowing both with new youth and richer content by blending the Buddhism of old with the religion of the conquerors. Synthesis is a need of troubled times. In the last ten years it has won half a million adherents. It takes the form of the worship of a new god : the God Caodai is an invented god, abstract and impersonal—though he is graphically represented—in no way anthropomorphic after the fashion of the gods of Chinese Buddhism. Caodai is nothing but an Eye in the middle of a Triangle ! But he has his followers, and his altars are hospitable to other gods : Buddha and Confucius, and Lao Tse, too, and even Jesus Christ. Many Caodaïsts have added others, including Joan of Arc and the Curé of Ars ! [2] We have here living testimony to the fecund influence of the White man on the Yellow, stimulating anew the diffusion of the ancient gods. Some Frenchmen have moreover joined the cult : a sign of the times. The disturbances and unrest which the French occasion in all these countries create strange composite beliefs. Faith seeks to live again and tries to renew its youth by a synthesis that links past and present by pouring the new rice-alcohol into the ancient jars !

[1] See *L'Illustration*, May 5, 1928 ; and in particular the files of the *Revue caodaïste*, to which both Annamites and French have contributed.

[2] [Saint Jean-Baptiste-Marie Vianney, the Curé of Ars, was canonised in 1925. Ars is now a place of pilgrimage. EOL]

Radicalism is a newer phenomenon. In Tong-King, as in France, a radical spirit appeared, a desire for liberty and equality which tends to apply the French principles of 1789 for the Indo-Chinese. This reforming radicalism is not focussed on the past, it is " progressive " ; it aims at *free partnership* of Annamites and French. The rôle of the French in this country is not played out. Collaborating with the native they will be able to bring fresh progress. This doctrine was accepted in the Section of the *League of the Rights of Man* at Hanoi which counted seventy-six members in 1931 : another importation of a French product.[1] Let us enquire what the reformers of Tong-King were thinking. It is the same as is thought by the Constitutionalist Party of Hanoi, founded there by an old pupil of mine, Duong van Giao—nowadays outstripped, as is the special fate of pioneers—and afterwards transferred to Paris.

It is wiser and more sensible, they said, to accept facts as they are. Since the French are in the country, let us not drive them out. Let us be just and take note of all the benefits—these are complacently enumerated in the Rights of Man discussion at Hanoi—we have derived from French rule. Let us nevertheless claim our rights, let us request the French, who have preached liberty to the whole world, to apply the Rights of Man to our country. Let us ask of them—these are the three main demands —more *education*, the *protection* of the workers and, finally, a *Constitution* with liberties. This means, in every country, even in Annam, a Constitution with Assemblies chosen by universal suffrage, a Parliament and Elections. They want to elect, and they want to be elected !

Their idea is, however, that the Constitution-creating Parliament should be set up after a lapse of time, not suddenly and overnight, but gradually and by transition stages, the privileges of the inhabitants being increased little by little. They feel, in fact—but a discreet mist hangs round the subject—that a day will come at some distant date when the voters can be completely emancipated, having fully mastered their duties and responsibilities. Then Liberation will follow, but will not put an end to French collaboration. As partners, the French will be able to serve the future interests of Annam. In a reforming rescript of 1933, His Majesty Bao Dai would seem to foreshadow a Constitution of the Empire of Annam.

[1] *Ligue des Droits de l'Homme.* *Le Congrès National de 1931*, p. 344 f. (Declaration of the Hanoi Section.)

If some want reformation, others want *revolution*. Particularly in the last ten years, various Revolutionary parties have been founded, claiming affinity with oriental communism. Their only slogan is : Drive out the French ! They differ from each other in the way they envisage the national future after the " flight " of the French. They agree, however, especially the three predominant parties among them, on driving out the French. This is explicitly proclaimed in no measured terms and is writ large into their statutes. There are three main parties taking this line.

First *The Revolutionary Party of Young Annam.* When it was started, round about 1918, it was a secret society with a whole initiation ritual involving some rough horse-play at the expense of new recruits. We need not be surprised to find that it was composed not of working " proletarians " but of educated and middle-class folk. They were mostly students, still in their college days, scarcely more than children ! They had heard talk of the rights of oppressed peoples. Some of their professors had lectured on the Fourteen Points which the President of the United States was just then proclaiming. It was at College, under the inspiration of unsuspecting French professors that these boys, scarcely yet students, for they were only fourteen or fifteen years old, set up secret societies amongst themselves, which societies merged—the members having meantime grown up !—into this Party of Young Annam. Most of these college lads had ultimately become teachers ; and the party thus continued its recruitment mainly from teaching circles. Thus, amongst the educated and the semi-educated, was born the hope of a Revolution which should put an end to French rule.

Another party also arose vowing its intention to be absorbed in Communism ; it was the latest-comer among the parties, the *Indo-Chinese National Party* founded in Tong-King in 1927. Three years later it sprang to life again in China after the organisers of the 1930 rebellion had taken refuge there, especially after the Yenbay murders of which the Party was the chief instigator. As exiles in China the principal leaders were able to re-form their association. They drew their inspiration from, or rather, they imitated the Chinese Kuomintang in their ideas, and their methods were also Chinese. It was they who put the expression Viet-Nam into currency, the name by which the Annamite country is known, *Viet-Nam*, namely the Country or the Kingdom of the South—it might also be called *Dai-Nam*. It is the Nation

whose duty it was to free itself by revolution from the tyranny
of the French State.   This party also ran a whole semi-secret
initiation ritual, especially a sort of religious oath which new
members were obliged to take " in full view of the rivers and the
mountains of the country ".   But it was organised according
to the revolutionary " technique ".   It contained a group of
" bravos ", to carry out its death sentences !   The French
Governor, Pasquier, was formally sentenced to death in the
name of the party.   There was a woman's section too ; in Lower
Tong-King a considerable number of *nhaqué* women came in
from the villages to take their share in the national movement.

The last party is still flourishing, the *Indo-Chinese Communist
Party* which has absorbed the first party of which I spoke, the
party of Young Annam.   It is communist in every sense of the
word, in structure, doctrine and technique, in its constitution,
in its thought and in its acts.

It is organised in *cells* of little groups scattered through villages
and factories.   These cells are called *chi-bo*.   In a country that
is almost without a working class, except in a few towns, especially
Nam-Dinh, it is remarkable that these cells have proved successful,
thanks to poverty and the effects of famine, and have been
successful not only amongst the teaching classes but amongst the
peasants, the *nhaqué*.   There is a peasant communism in Tong-
King which up to now has thriven amongst the women.   Over-
population, which in this country is extremely grave, is the real
reason.   In Lower Tong-King one native eats 100 kilogrammes
of rice a year.   That is 300 grammes (or approximately 10½ oz.)
a day supplemented by a little fish.   Such is the poverty, and
this is the key to the situation.   It is a tragic problem and it
will take time to find a solution for it.   What would be needed
is . . . a Tong-King Malthus !

As to its *thought* : the party teaches an almost unadulterated
Marxism, but tinged with asceticism and steeped in mysticism,
as is always essential in an oriental country.   They want to set
up a Dictatorship of the Proletariat, but putting the emphasis on
a spirit of devotion and of abnegation even unto death, on heroism
and asceticism, which are of course the laws of all the parties but
which here are placed in the very forefront as in some religious
sect.   Some devotees of this party have been known deliberately
to court death !

In the matter of *action*, it was Lenin and not Karl Marx who
was their guide.   When, on the instigation of the new party,

revolts broke out, the attempt to adapt the tactical procedures of Moscow was obvious. Murders and tortures in the old Asiatic tradition were not enough. What the Moscow communist jargon calls " encircling by numbers " was employed : tactics and strategy aiming at surprise and seeking to prevent help arriving in time.

There is a new spirit and a new will in this party which, though in law completely abolished, is—I venture to assert—by no means dispersed in fact. It is revolution carried out by the agents and the methods of the West. It is a plan for the near future to overthrow French power by an insurrection. There is no room here for talk of partnership or collaboration ; emancipation is wanted, to enthrone the proletariat : liberation which demands suffering and devotion ; preparation through asceticism and heroism for the catastrophe which will usher in the era of salvation and of happiness. This is another synthesis of the Eastern and the Western spirit. Happiness and Salvation are comprised in the one single hope ... Revolution is the Apocalypse. The old dragon of Annam whose spiny back upholds the universe, will with a sudden movement cause it to crumble when by a better and supreme effort his faithful ones have attained that purity and holiness which is felicity.

CHAPTER XXXVII

WHITE AUTONOMISM

The Africans, especially those of the Maghrib, also display very diverse mental attitudes.[1] These Africans are White men, closely akin to the French, they are chiefly people of the Maghrib (otherwise, the West), the Barbaresques, as they used to be called not a hundred years ago ; there are also Berbers, Arabs, Turks and people of mixed blood, who have been overtaken by autonomism.[2] Two attitudes of mind prevail amongst them, both of ancient date. There are on the one hand the Conservatives, advocates of retrogression, champions of the past, and on the other the Reformers, advocates of progress, champions of the future. The former are known in the vernacular as the *Salafi* and chief among them are the *'Ulama*, or the learned men (the word is the plural of *'Alim*, which means a man of learning), who take the place of clergy in Muslim countries. The latter are the *Islahi*, who are strongly opposed to the *Salafi* ; they are the advanced, who have become adapted or what is called " evolved ".

The fact is that thanks to French influence the most marked possible change of a social nature has taken place. Since the occupation the inhabitants, at least in the towns, have been obliged to alter their grouping ; they have passed from the tribe or the craftsman class into the trade union or the party. They were men of the tribe or of the handicraft ; in the towns they were men of the corporation, a professional group of a religious nature, at once a guild and a brotherhood, under the authority and control of the government. Now, in our day, what do we find ? We see these same people, in the towns but also in the

---

[1] Amongst many other authorities let me quote in general : J. Desparmet, *L'œuvre de la France en Algérie jugée par les indigènes*, Bulletin Soc. Geogr., Algiers, 1910, Nos. 55 and 7 ; P. Azan, *L'avenir indigène nordafricain*, 1925 ; G. Gautherot, *Le monde communiste*, 1927, p. 100 f. ; P. Catrice, *En Terre d'Islam*, Jan. Feb. 1932 ; E. Ghersi, *I movimenti nazionalistici nel mondo musulmano*, 1932 ; L. Roubaud, *Moghrab*, 1934 (reportage) ; *Les Cahiers du Redressement français, La Crise de l'Afrique du Nord*, 1935. A fuller Bibliography in the series of articles by P. Jalabert, *L'inquiétude nord-africaine* (Études, Aug. 20, 1934, and Aug. 5, 1935) ; R. Montagne, *L'évolution moderne des pays arabes*, Annales Sociolog. Series A, fasc. 2, 1936, pp. 29–76 ; J. Mélia, *Le triste sort des indigènes* . . . , 1935.

[2] [To classify all these very mixed and miscellaneous people as " white " seems odd to an English mind. EOL]

country, quit their tribe, quit their craft, quit their birthplace, thus evading the traditional authority of the father or of the chief (*abu* or *amin*) which was burdensome to them ; freeing themselves in this way from the old controls. But they do not by any means achieve complete liberty, they merely become members of a new herd in new surroundings and fall under other powers, when they affiliate themselves to parties or trade unions, these inventions imported from France. From the tribe or the guild to the union or the party, such is their " evolution ", or better the " mutation " which abruptly takes place, very often without any transitional phase, not a mutation in a general sense, but one which has at least overtaken a fair number of individuals. There thus arises a divorce, often very marked, between two " environments " in which the population live. There are the folk of the old school and those of the new ; those who have remained in tribe or guild, subject still to the traditional author-ities, in a word, the *backward*, and those who have joined union or party and ranged themselves under new authorities, in a word, the *advanced*. These regressives and progressives are often in opposition and sometimes in actual conflict. From this point onwards, according to rank and position, there will be opposition on the one hand and acceptance on the other in relations with the French.[1] Thus the occupation has cloven a gulf between the olden and the modern times. When we speak of Musulmans in Algeria—this applies much more in Algeria than in Tunisia or Morocco—we are no longer speaking of a single element or a single group. The opposition amongst them all is very marked, the backward or " retarded " are opposed to the advanced or the " evolved ", the people of the old school to the people of the new. Everywhere in the colonies we have to distinguish between the people who cling to their own institutions, who are unreceptive and resistant to French manners and customs, and those who on the other hand have broken away from their traditions, who accept and adopt French ideas and tastes, who follow their new rulers sometimes with enthusiasm and exaltation, " more royalist than the king ", more French than the French. These are two parties which have come into being through the influence of the French.

Thus, by the contact of the Maghrib people with the French,

[1] A good observer, Le Glay, in *La mort de Rogui* (1926, p. 115 f.), noted that the French are more readily accepted amongst the artisans and middle classes than amongst the people or the chiefs.

the centuries-old contrast between Musulman and Christian was vigorously renewed. About 1850 an Arab shaikh was speaking to that famous student of Algeria, General Daumas and quoting some Muslim proverbs, maledictions which an Arab may utter against himself : [1] " May Allah condemn me to make water standing as the Infidels do ! "—" May Allah condemn me to leap in the dance (that is to prance about unceasingly for no reason) as the Christians do ! "—" May Allah cause me to carry burdens like the Christians ! " Such are the curses they invoke as a punishment for their sins ! This opposition has been increased as we well know by the revival of Muslim fanaticism when contact with the Unbelievers became closer.

It was nevertheless inevitable that the contagion of French manners should come into play, sometimes speedily, sometimes suddenly. This contagion acted in two directions.

First, as of old, in the days of the Greeks and Romans, it came from the East to the West, from the Orient to the Occident. Coming from the Near East, " modernism " spread to the Maghrib from Turkey,[2] from Syria and from Egypt. These had long been reforming countries, more advanced than those further West, and they thus served as instructors to the Maghrib people. This was propaganda for European ways—through an interpreter. French ideas, current for more than a hundred years amongst Ottomans and Egyptians, came from them to the Tunisian and the Algerian. Western contagion, making a détour, struck by ricochet, through various ways and various agents. It came through brotherhoods and mosques ; particularly through the brotherhoods which are strong bonds in Muslim countries, above the tribes, above the regions. The Senussi Brotherhood boasts members from Nanking to Dakar ! By their preaching and by their teaching, these tariqa created a unity highly favourable to French penetration. They have been, at one and the same time, agents of retrogression and agents of progress.—More recently the printing press has taken a hand, books and newspapers, notably those printed in Cairo. Cairo publishes Arab books and Arab newspapers which circulate throughout Islam. Let us examine a bookshop in Fez ; there you will see printed matter from Cairo tightly stacked. In this way Egyptian influence has penetrated the Maghrib, always

[1] E. Daumas, La vie arabe et la société musulmane, 1869, p. 99 f.

[2] J. Desparmet, La turcophilie en Algérie, Bulletin Soc. Géogr., Algiers, 1916, p. 1 f. ; 1917, p. 1 f.

acting in two directions, conservative or reforming, for retrogression or for progress. The "Arab Press" extends from Tunis to Morocco [1] and the Arab language has undergone a veritable renascence.[2] Finally, the theatre and the film have more recently begun to play their part. For some time there has now been ocular propaganda for Western fashions and methods, always through Egyptian channels, in the Arab theatre and the Arab film. A famous singer has devoted himself for the last two or three years to awaking by poem and song a new spirit in the Maghrib. He is Mahi ud Din, a happy blend of Eastern and Western tastes. He presented the comedy *Phaco*, which "treats of the present-day life of the Algerian Arab, his ignorance, his atavistic apathy, his fanaticism and his greatest curse . . . alcohol". The Egyptian film has also made its appearance. There are now Egyptian film studios, where Arab actors, speaking Arabic, excite and stir up the "patriotisms" of subject peoples.— The gramophone and the wireless also make their contribution. There is a radio transmitter at Abu Zabal, quite near Cairo, which carries far !

There is also contagion from North to South directly from America and Europe to North Africa across the sea.[3] This is straight contagion, not through the medium of an interpreter. Propaganda has also acted through the French, who are the representatives, in every sense of the word, of the French spirit. Be they officials or colonists, merchants or soldiers, they are missionaries in speech and act. By their gestures, by their talk, they transplant their manners and customs, often without suspecting it. They are propagandists in word and deed. Thus in the Maghrib the contagion works directly. Better still : it works through organised parties deliberately and with premeditation. Centres, reviews, newspapers (the *Maghreb*, for instance, a review suppressed over there, but which continues to circulate . . . under the *bournous*) make it their expressed aim to emancipate the Arab peoples from the French. The violent pamphlet, *Martyred Tunisia* [4] in 1920 had no authors other than Tunisians ! We need feel no surprise at meeting from now on in

---

[1] For Tunisia, see *La presse destourienne, Afrique française*, Sept. 1930. An analysis of the Arab Press in the Review, *Oriente Moderno*, and by the Paris Institute of Islamic Studies. Other extracts are confidential.

[2] J. Desparmet, *La réaction linguistique en Algérie, Bulletin Soc. Géogr.*, Algiers, 1931, p. 1 f. ; Le Thomel, *La question des langues . . .*, *Afr. franç.*, June, 1935.

[3] Thus always the effect of Woodrow Wilson's ideas. See *Les revendications du peuple algéro-tunisien*, a memorandum presented in 1919 to the Peace Conference in Geneva. [4] *La Tunisie martyre.*

these countries the same two attitudes of mind which we found
in Indo-China.   In a subtle book,[1] the novelist Robert Randau
has skilfully brought on the scene North Africans representing
the two points of view regarding the French : from the resigned
accepters to the protesting opposers.   We note particularly these
two mental attitudes : *reformation, liberation.*

Up to the present the advocates of *reformation* are, I think,
much, infinitely, the more numerous in Algeria.   They want
domination reorganised in the interest of the Algerians.   They
are numerous, those inhabitants of the Maghrib who have
accepted French domination—not perhaps in the bottom of their
hearts : don't let us plumb so deep !—at least, and this is enough,
on the surface of their skin !   In the days of Abd ul Qadir there
was even a *fatwa* (an expression of opinion by an important
leader of Islam) issued at the request of his French secretary-
interpreter, Léon Roches, a *fatwa* according to which French
rule was legitimate and the inhabitants were advised to submit
to French authority ! [2]   Such is the normal attitude of mind
amongst the Algerians.   For the moment they are resigned and,
as true Believers, convinced that it is the Will of Allah !   In
conversation—as I have very frequently myself observed—they
willingly admit all the benefits and all the advantages which
they have derived from French rule.   At the same time they
often say that they liked the old times better, when danger
stimulated " vitality "—just as Stendhal would have said in
France.   Peace and security imported by the foreign conquerors,
has for them less value than their own values of long ago !   I
remember that in talking one day to a Kabyle, I said to him :
" You know very well that nowadays you don't need to carry a
gun on your saddle when you go to market ! "   Lightning
flashed from his eye as he jerked out : " It was better far when
men were able to fight unto death ! " . . .   Don't let us deceive
ourselves into believing that the natives are grateful for French
law and order with all their advantages.   They accept the
French, however, but they demand progress.   They wish most
particularly that they should be given a more generous measure
of two things : prosperity and equality.

First *prosperity*, since security is already attained.   They are
fully aware that under the French there are fewer of those famines

---

[1] *Les Compagnons du Jardins*, 1933.
[2] The text is to be found in L. Roches, *Trente-deux ans à travers l'Islam*, II, 1887
p. 239 f.

that are the scourge of Allah, than there used to be in olden days. But much progress is needed. The French have too readily backed with their power the exactions of the chiefs, and the exploitation of the humble *fellah* by the *qaïds* and the *marabuts*. They have consolidated the powers of all these by the " policy of the big chiefs " pursued by every successive régime of the occupation in Algeria. It has also been adopted in Morocco. Hence arise abuses, supported by the French, aggravated by the French, which the people most rightly demand that the French should abolish. They also demand the right to develop land and forest. The restrictions which in the interests of their colonists, the French impose on the extensive and destructive use of land and forest, are most galling to the natives. It is the old conflict between the cultivator and the grazier ! The French are the cultivators and they absolutely must put an end to the use of the land for destructive grazing. The natives ask that less harshness and more flexibility should be shown in defending progress, they ask that the transition should be more considerate and that the new and the old should make mutual concessions.

Above all, *equality*. This is a subject on which they are highly sensitive. Those reformers who accept French rule or are at least resigned to acquiescing in it, want more dignity and more equality, and they want to see wider rights than at present granted to the natives. Bin Jallul, a native of Constantine,[1] the " agitator ", who was so much talked of, always asserted that he was a partisan, not an enemy, of the French. Here are two documents, amongst others, in which it is possible to see how the spirit of reform is in fact an aspiration towards dignity and equality. They are by two Algerians, one of whom was a pupil of mine, and they express different longings.[2]

Counsellor-General Ferhat Abbas would like to see pauperism brought to an end, but also and above all he wants Arabs and Frenchmen to be placed in the same rank, on the same level and on a footing of complete equality—this idea all the time obsesses him—by raising the social standing of the Algerians.[3] The achievement of brotherhood between French and Algerians ought thus to be approached by various ways. First, the Algerians ought to be enriched, so as to reach the same material standards as the French, and then they ought to be educated

---

[1] [One of the *départements* of Algeria. EOL]
[2] Ferhat Abbas, *Le jeune Algérien*, 1931 ; H. Hesnay Lahmek, *Lettres algériennes*, 1932.
[3] Another Algerian also insists on this, the retired native teacher, S. Faci : *L'Algérie sous l'égide de la France contre la féodal. algér. . . .* , 1936.

up to the same level. He wants especially to see fuller education both in Arabic and in French. The proletariat which the French have created in Algeria must be got rid of. Government should be in the interest of the peasant and the natives should be gradually emancipated for a future—a distant future, he admits—by immediately giving them suitable teaching and more training and education. He does not at all think that it is necessary to assimilate Algerians and French; nor necessary to frenchify the Algerians—he is firm on this point—but they must be uplifted and raised by offering them teaching so that they may enjoy the spiritual benefits of French culture. This shows faith in the virtue of French culture.

Hesnay Lahmek, a liberated Kabyle and a French citizen, has drawn a portrait in dialogue of a very hide-bound colonist, too much colonist by half, over-simplified in his failings and sins, who conducts an interesting controversial discussion with some Algerians. There is a Berber in particular who holds forth, not so much against the French as . . . against Islam. We thus see that in the Maghrib the reformers are very far from being always at one, or sharing the same hopes and the same visions. Amongst the *'Ulama*, in the mosques and the *Zawia* there are great numbers passionately attached to the past, who long to recapture the purity and the holiness of the Islam of early days. On the other hand, there are others more modern-minded and up-to-date who have broken loose from Islam. They hold no brief for the Musulman versus the Christian. Of these Hesnay Lahmek is one : " Islam," he says, " is a death-factor ; we must therefore secularise." What he would like to see prevailing in Algeria is the French spirit in its secular form. Let the Berber country become another Europe ; let the contact and union between Kabyles and French be made close and intimate. He then criticises French administration ; he would like numerous abuses to be abolished, and above all he would like—and on this point all reformers in the colonial countries are agreed—training and education for all natives. " Out of the Church !—Into the School ! " that is the slogan of all the freed natives. They may not be legion, but they do count ; and it is well to listen to them.

The dream of the future is thus intellectual equality on the one hand, and material equality on the other ; *de facto* equality and *de jure* equality. Let us not be, they say, people " eternally disqualified ". What are the claims of the reformers in this connection ? Let us emphasise one important point. The *de jure* equality which Bin Jallul demands, is not exactly, nor wholly, equality in the French sense ; equality in public and private law. In clear language, such as the French rejoice in, equality on every legal plane is implied ; in the public sphere it is the right to obey completely the same laws, to be entrusted with the same powers, and subject to the same duties. Bin Jallul's Equality is therefore Identity. Not all the reformers would acquiesce in what this implies : *the unrestricted submission of all Algerians to French law* ; the application of this law without modification to all natives without exception : assimilation, frenchification, on the legal plane ! Now, we know that there is no question of the frenchification of private law ! Does the native wish to renounce his personal status, his polygyny, his easy divorce, and no longer exclude women from the right to inherit ? No ! That would mean a break with tradition, laid down by the Quran, guarded by the Sunna ; it would mean abjuring Islam in becoming French citizens. · This is not at all what Bin Jallul wants ; what he looks for is equality . . . by half ; identity under public, but by no means under private law : he wants " citizenship in the constitution ".[1] Let the French give the Algerians the privileges and liberties of a French citizen : let them abolish the status of Native Citizen (*l'indigénat*), so derogatory to common law, which puts the natives too much at the mercy of the administration. For under the *Indigénat* the administration may inflict exceptional penalties on the natives. Let the same rights be granted to Algerians and French. As for taxes, they are already assimilated and frenchified. In 1918 the Muslim taxes were abolished. In Algeria—but not in Tunisia or Morocco—natives and French are legally subject to the same taxes : French taxes. On the other hand, the natives do not wish to see private rights frenchified. A Frenchman, H. Bernier, in Algiers is clamouring for this, but he is radically at fault in talking of " equiparity of rights and duties ". It is extremely easy nowadays for an Algerian to become a French-man ; since the law of 1919, he has in certain specified cases a right to do so by merely making a declaration before a tribunal ; if the procedure is thought too cumbrous, it can be simplified and cut down. This request is however always subject to one condition : the would-be Frenchman must renounce his native status and as a Frenchman be subject to French law in his actions

[1] The problem was early discussed by J. Vinet, *Le droit commun pour les indigènes en Algérie,* 1869.

and relationships ; [1] he must renounce *the whole* of his native status, to accept the whole of his French status. This is why there are very few cases in which an Algerian has been able to make up his mind to be a Frenchman. We must get this clear : they want a semi-French status not full French status ; they want *privilege* not common law, inequality not equality. At any rate they do not want separation ; they talk of " fusion " and of " common destiny " ; they dream of a " Franco-Musulman " people and they appeal to sociology. They say : " Community is less a question of blood than of will." [2]

Amongst those therefore whom we might call " the moderates", those who are resigned to French rule, we find diversity and contradiction of desires. This is still more the case amongst those excited fanatics whose aim is *liberation* or revolution. They are fairly numerous in Algeria and Tunisia and even in Morocco, these men who want to drive out the French either immediately or in the future. Liberation by revolution is the aim of what are called the Young Algerians and the Young Tunisians—while any day may give us Young Moroccans too. This impulse originates from two very different motives, between which there is the same distinction as we noted in Indo-China. Some of the revolutionaries desire revolution in order to restore the customs of long ago, others in order to introduce new customs, to progress towards the future but without, not with, the French. So we might speak of two types of emancipation : *liberation-for-restoration* and *liberation-for-change* or liberation by revolution to establish a new order whether slowly or suddenly, whether by evolution or revolution.

Liberation-for-restoration. This is the aim of the 'Ulama, and the Tullab, the mob-leaders of Islam, of the teachers and preachers who would like to drive out the French in order to restore their shattered power. This was the vision which inspired the foundation in 1931 in Algiers of the Council of the 'Ulama whose aim is to restore the Muslim religion in its ancient purity. [3] People

---

[1] (P. Bourdarie) : *Revue indigène* (replies), 1911 ; P. Chauveau, *Les citoyens qui s'ignorent ; L'accession dans le statut est-elle admissible* (Extracts, *Revue africaine*, Trim. 1 and 2, 1935.)

[2] The paper *La Justice* (Algiers), No. 1, Oct. 31, 1934. A Spaniard who collaborates in the review *Maghreb* hopes to re-awaken " the community of Spanish-Arab blood ", and talks of the two " brother peoples ", the association, not the separation, of Spaniards and Moroccans.

[3] J. Desparmet, *Les guides de l'opinion algérienne, Afrique française*, Jan. 1933, p. 11 f. E. F. Gautier, *Menaces sur l'Afrique, Rev. de Paris*, Sept. 1, 1934. These two authors are admirable informants. Another excellent authority is P. Giacobetti, *Effervescence et chaos dans l'Islam algérien, Études Missionnaires*, I, 1933, p. 251 f.

have talked of a Musulman Renaissance which through privation would achieve true purity. One hundred and fifty years ago Abd ul Wahhab, who preached religious asceticism and started an Islamic revival, is now reborn in Algeria and a Neo-Wahhabism has sprung to life. Such is the meaning of the sermons, very popular in the mosques, of Al Taiyyib al Uqbi. The 'Ulama would fain be restorers, not only in the field of dogma but in the field of politics. Following the inspiration of Abd ul Wahhab they would like to drive out the French and re-create the autonomy of ancient Islam. Their mind is also concerned with legal matters. They would like to preserve the traditional law, the religious precepts revealed by Allah and written down in the Quran ; they would like to return to the *Sunna* which the French have modified or abolished. They have therefore protested against the obligation laid on the Algerian Musulman to abandon his personal status if he wishes to become a Frenchman. They would like well enough to be French while keeping their personal law which to them is a religious law. *Muslim* Law, this word says everything. Thus in Morocco some years ago, there was a protest, whose echoes resounded loudly in Egypt— where I happened at the time to be travelling—against the decision of the Sultan of Morocco whose famous decree of 1930 recognised and sanctioned Berber customs and set up Berber tribunals. The Muslims saw in this—or professed to see—a deadly attack on Islam ; for the Berbers being Muslims (extremely half-hearted ones !) could not be withdrawn from Quranic jurisdiction. By protecting Berber law, the Sultan was attacking Islam ! He was compelled to revoke this decision, at least in part.[1] In Syria there have been protests against French laws touching *waqfs* and *hubus*, religious endowments protected against alienation and intended to guarantee the foundations of religion. We might here speak of a Musulman awakening, both dogmatic and juridical. A campaign which still continues bears witness to its reality. The " World Congress of Islam " which met in Jerusalem in 1931 categorically condemned colonisation as contrary to law and to religion.

Liberation-for-change. This is a new spirit which has gained ground under two forms, in two ways : through *modernism* and through *communism*. The advocates of these are the *islahi*, diametrically opposed to the *salafi*.

[1] See H. Bruno, *La réorganisation de la justice séculière au Maroc. Questions nord-africaines*, I, June 25, 1935. See the criticism of the 1930 decrees by Mouslim Barbari (pseudonym), *Tempête sur le Maroc*, 1931.

Modernism is spread throughout the whole of Mediterranean Islam.[1] From Egypt in the first place, and then by contagion in the Maghrib, there has grown up amongst the Muslims a whole reforming spirit, a religious modernism in two directions, the dogmatic and the juridical.[2] *Dogmatic* modernism seeks to change the faith, *juridical* modernism to alter the law. Some thirty years ago a great reformer appeared among the Egyptians, the famous Shaikh Abdu who died in 1905. He inspired a new ideal.[3] He was Professor at the Flowery Mosque, the famous Al Azhar ; in these countries, " mosque " and " university " are often synonymous. It was he who founded Muslim modernism. He had read Guizot . . . in Arabic ; he had lived in Paris. He preached in favour of monogamy ; in one of his writings he also admits the lending of money at interest. He thought he could prove that, if carefully interpreted, and not according to the blunders of the Commentators, the Quran could be reconciled with feminism and monogamy. At the beginning of his career Shaikh Abdu thus supported the demands of Egyptian women. " The Quran," he used to say, " is a book of progress. It is thus possible for a True Believer to be an advanced person, a man of the Future and not of the Past. A careful search will disclose Constitutional Government in the Quran. Return to Islam is therefore the real progress."

There is *Communism* too, but it is more recent : in Algeria, in Tunisia and in Morocco. It was through Communism more than anything else that the hope of liberation made headway.

Socialism has changed greatly in Algeria in the last hundred years. Over there, the followers of Enfantin and Fourier were seeking equality and wanting partnership, but had no desire for emancipation and even less for revolution. The followers of Lenin, and already there are some, dream of downfall and collapse, and long for destruction. The ambition of Communism is to set the "oppressed peoples" free. Its actors and its leaders

---

[1] H. Carra de Vaux, *Les penseurs de l'Islam*, Vol. V, 1926.

[2] For Tunisia, see an early work, Khérédine, *Réformes nécessaires aux États musulmans*, Fr. trans. 1868, and in general, R. Maunier, *Loi française et coutume indigène en Algérie*, 1932, Chap. V (Bibliog.). For Morocco : L. Brunot, *Congrès . . . Société indigène* (1931 Exhibition), 1931, p. 546 f. For the Near East : E. Jung, *Le réveil de l'Islam . . .*, 1833 (pro-Arab) ; L. Jovelet, *Évolution sociale et politique des pays arabes*, 1933 (extr. *Revue Études islamiques*, Cahier IV) ; L. Jalabert, *Syrie et Liban*, 1934. See the petitions of the Syrian groups in Paris and Geneva in the Annual Reports of the Mandates Commission (e.g. Session XXVI), 1934, Appendix. The Turks had submitted their claims about 1910 ; B. Bareilles, *Les Turcs*, 1917, p. 262 f.

[3] He was thus opposed to Shaikh al Saiyid Jamal ud Din, al Afghani, who died in 1897. He was anti-West and preached return to the True Tradition.

are not the '*Ulama* and the *Amirs* nor even the doctors—I mean the physicians—assimilated and frenchified as they are, and trained at the Algiers University. As elsewhere, the Communists are always the teachers, the workers and the sailors. In Algeria the militant champions of Bolshevik Communism are the teachers and the sailors. Many natives are employed in sailing the French ships and they have been indoctrinated by the master-experts. At night, while the passengers dance on deck, down below in the holds the teaching goes on ! The stevedores and dockers also hear the Communist gospel. Fifteen years ago they began forming unions and cells. Particularly in the ports, at Algiers and Oran, there have been cells organised for the battle ; from now on the yearning for the Dictatorship of the Proletariat is openly admitted. The party newspapers and pamphlets denounce " exploitation " not only by the French, but by the *qaïds* and *marabuts* : the " bourgeoisie " as they are called in speech and writing. The " Arab bourgeoisie " is " stigmatised " together with the French. No rule of any kind is to be tolerated except the Dictatorship of the Proletariat. This is a sign of profound disturbance in Islamic countries, especially in Algerian lands. As far as the outskirts of the desert, in the towns of the M'zab, the Communists carry on their preaching campaign whose ideal is the eviction of the French.[1] The Mozabites, purest of the pure, these dissident heretics, these segregated ascetics, have been infected and contaminated ; a blast has swept into the heart of the M'zab !

[1] See *La cause du peuple mozabite* by K. E., Mozabite, 1924 (Algiers).

CHAPTER XXXVIII

BLACK AUTONOMISM

Let us now come to the *Black Man* whom for two reasons it has been wise to keep to the last.[1]

First, because it would seem as if they were the last to develop a spirit of making demands. It is only since the war [2] that they have made themselves heard. The American and African Negroes had had occasional *revolts* ; momentary outbursts such as may occur anywhere and which have no long-term results. These were usually quickly repressed without much trouble. Here and there some White Men were massacred ; this often was because they had, perhaps unwittingly, violated some serious taboo. There was for instance shortly after 1700 the murder which Bosman reported, of two Europeans in the kingdom of Guinea because they had slain a fetish-serpent.[3] In this case it was the fetish-worshippers or the sorcerers who stirred up the rebellion in defence of tradition and of their own interests. The White men shocked the Black and galled them at the same time. Similarly, in Haiti revolts were prepared by secret Voodoo séances and the crowd excited by women's dancing and worked up to a frenzy by the sacred symbol brandished by the chief ; it was . . . a bull's tail.[4] In 1733 in the island of Guadeloupe a Jesuit said in a sermon : " Men are revolting against God ; the Blacks are revolting against the Whites and they are thereby avenging God ; the time is not far off." This was a prediction of Toussaint L'Ouverture's [5] appearance !

The second reason is that, though beginning late, the Black Man developed more strongly than others a universal sense. Whether the movement was first American or first African, it tended at once to overflow continental boundaries. It resounded throughout the world, and in our own day we see it in Ethiopian

---

[1] See in general : Alain Locke (Negro), *The New Negro*, 1927 (Bibliog.), T. L. Schoell, U.S.A., *Du côté des blancs et du côté des noirs*, 1929 ; M. N. Work, *Negro Year Book*, 1931–2 (Tuskegee. Bibliog. for 1925–30 at the end) ; B. Schrieke, *Alien Americans*, 1936 (Bibliog.).

[2] [1914–1918. EOL].

[3] C de Brosses, *Du culte des dieux fétiches*, 1760, p 32 f.

[4] G. d'Alaux, *L'empire Soulouque*, 1856, p. 13 f.

[5] [L'Ouverture (1743–1803) led the San Domingo insurrection of 1796–1802. EOL]

affairs. Harlem, the Negro quarter of New York, is stirred. Race does not enter into the question : the Ethiopians are Hamites, not Sudanese or Bantus. It is colour, and colour only, which unites them all. Where things are so, the movement is really a " Colour Movement ". The early insurgents in the " American Islands " believed that the souls of their dead went off to Africa and that those slain in battle against the Whites would there be happily reborn ! Having come from Africa, Africa was in their thoughts. The slave-transports thus prepared a common feeling between Black Men.

If a Pan-Negro movement thus arose, it was only an extension of a Pro-Negro movement. The first to plead the cause of the Non-Whites have always been White people. We remember the whole Anti-Slavery campaign ; we know how a movement for *alleviation* may be the prelude to a movement for *liberation*.[1] Yet more . . . it was White Men who long ago proclaimed the superiority of the Black. In 1813, Schopenhauer advanced the theory that Man in his original state was black, and lived in the Tropics, and that White men made their appearance only when Man was able to live in cold climates and the pigment of his skin grew faint. He also held that the Black Man was the first to become civilised and that the movement of progress had been from Black to White. Even Gobineau, the eulogist of the White Races, took notice—and this was long before the American mania for the tunes of Louisiana—of the exceptional gift for music of every kind which the Black Man appears to possess . . . The White Man the technician ; the Black the musician. In the ethnology of to-day sympathy for the Black Races holds the field.[2] Backward they may be, people say, but degraded—NO.

Nevertheless, to provoke the " Negro Awakening " in America a great contemporary event was needed. This was the *migration* of black workers from South to North in the States. Penned at first into the Southern States, sometimes lynched[3] or at least persecuted, they came in numbers into the Northern towns into factories and offices. They became *urbanised*. They quitted the plantation to become imprisoned in the skyscraper ! The town Negro was an unprecedented phenomenon in the long, long history of the black labourer. In consequence, they became *civilised*. Though their ideas probably changed less than their

---

[1] Above, Chap. XXVII.
[2] This is striking in Maurice Delafosse's book, *Les nègres*, 1927.
[3] E. Cutler, *Lynch Law* . . . , 1905 ; M. N. Work, *Negro Year Book*, 1931, p. 293 f.

ways, the inward less than the outward man, they have nevertheless become very obviously "americanised" : living in the same quarters, wearing the same clothes, eating the same food as the full-blooded Yankee : attending the same church, frequenting the same cinema ! None of these things would have been possible in a Southern State. Going down Fifth Avenue on the top of a tall bus you find yourself all at once without any transition in the City of the Blacks. Nothing is different—except the faces ! Harlem is the capital of a Black Empire ; half a million Negroes are there gathered together. They are thus assimilated both to the Whites and to each other. Coming from all directions, scattering to all directions, in an incessant ebb and flow, the Negroes are brewed and re-brewed in this sinister crucible. Natives of the Antilles or of the Congo, they live together and think together. Being mobilised by the French during the War, they made contact with the Negroes of the French Sudan. They have not lost touch : the bond is preserved both by *travel* or by emigration, for the Harlem Negroes travel as far as the Sudan ; and by *education* or preaching, since the Negro of Segon sometimes reads the Harlem papers or hears the echo of them. *The Negro Press* [1] is a very important and quite recent phenomenon. It is a great influence for unity throughout the whole Black World. The Negro *school* and *college* form another phenomenon, less influential perhaps, because of less extent, but one without which the newspaper could not have thriven. The foundation by the celebrated Negro, Booker Washington,[2] of a Negro University at Tuskegee, proved by its results to have been a great event. Booker Washington was the first Negro to be received at the White House ; it was Theodore Roosevelt who welcomed him. The educated Negro, and the Negro writer publishing in English or "American ", met with success : Claude Mackay, for instance. Abbé Grégoire would not have thought it possible ! Nor would he have foreseen the bourgeois Negro or the wealthy Negro ! From slavery to salaried service, from poverty to property-owning ! : such is the transformation that has taken place in less than fifty years. The American Negro of to-day is often lawyer, doctor and even business man. Whatever people's feelings, there is inevitable social contact of White and Black,

---

[1] List in *Negro Year Book*, p. 533. Analyses used to be given fortnightly by the French *Comité* of the *rue d'Ulm*, but have now ceased, with the *Comité*.

[2] Booker Washington, *The Future of the American Negro*, 1899 ; *Up from Slavery* (an autobiography), 1901.

a dual contamination or assimilation, such as we are familiar with, working in two directions : Black to White, White to Black. A similar contact soon took place in France, for Montparnasse also is a melting-pot.[1] Another has been the packet-boat, in the bowels of which black men work, Americans and Negroes mixed together ; another, the factory and the trade union, where workers of both colours lodge their claims. These things have created the unity of the Black World, now no longer in the stage of a mere draft. And unity is made for liberty.

That is why the "Negro Awakening" was, more than any other, the awakening of everything new. It stands for progress not retrogression ; it is essentially modernist. We must realise that everything is confused ; the old feelings have in Africa been re-awakened amongst the tribal Negroes ; barbarism has drawn new nourishment from the new spirit ; the old primitive rites, re-quickened and rejuvenated, have taken a line of protest and developed a liberating power. It was a recoil that could have been foreseen. Cults and sects have spread ; fetish-worshippers have discovered prophets for themselves in their own country . . . Thus *Kibangism* sprang up in the Belgian Congo [2] and became *Ngounzism* in the French Congo.[3] The Negro Kibangu had been a Protestant catechist : about 1918 he began to preach against the Whites ; having become a "modernist" and having broken with the fetish-worshippers, he fought against statues, drums and dances, in the name of a brand-new god. He was condemned to death, but reprieved and transported. In a more backward spirit, charms are being sold to protect rebellious Blacks against the White Man's weapons ; almost everywhere in the Belgian Congo secret societies have taken a new lease of life.[4] These are all revivals ; revivals of tradition, of religion, of local or regional archaisms, like Caodaïsm in Indo-China ; but there is about them nothing national or international like the present Pan-Negro movement, which bears witness to the unity of the Black Man's spirit.

After having first met by accident, the "evolved" or emancipated Blacks deliberately planned to meet each other : for the first time in 1921, for the second time in August 1922, in Brussels,

---

[1] List of "*Negro Balls*" in *Les guides parisiens. Bals nègres et bals pittoresques.* For the U.S.A., see the curious novel, *Dinah Miami*, by Pierre Mac Orlan.

[2] P. Salkin, *Le problème de l'évolution noire*, 1926 ; *Congo*, Feb. 1936, p. 238 f.

[3] C. Joffre, *L'Afrique aux Africains : le "Ngounzisme" au Congo belge*, *Études*, March 5, 1934.

[4] E. de Jonghe, *Formations récentes de sociétés secrètes au Congo belge, Africa*, Jan. 1936.

in Paris and in London. This was the *Pan-African Congress* or
the " All Black " Congress.[1] It had its fourth meeting in Paris
in 1927. It was the American Negroes who initiated it ; they
had acquired practical experience in their " meetings " ; groups
of them financed the expenses of travel and publications. An
Indian and a Chinese also attended ! There were both men
and women present, women reporters, women aviators . . . Black
Modernism, I should say Black Futurism, thus asserted itself.
Up to the present there has been nothing like it, either in the
Magrib or in Tong-King. · In the contributions of the various
speakers there was manifest the clash of the two points of view
we already know : *reformation* and *emancipation*. Some—the
French deputies Diagne and Candace elected by the Black
citizens of the colonies—preached *partnership* between Black and
White ; " no more pariahs ", but equals remaining in collaboration for human happiness. " France," they said, " is the mother
of the Blacks. They owe her too much to cast her off ! " This
is the attitude of mind—let us repeat it—which remains the
normal one amongst French " subjects ". Others, however,
wanted *separation* through liberation. Some disciples of Marcus
Garvey, a man whom we shall speak of presently, demanded
" Africa for the Africans ", and wanted to see the whole continent
a sanctuary for Black Men, what might be called a Liberia of
infinite proportions. In their mystical exaltation they did not
stop to reflect whether the Liberian experiment had shown
results to encourage large-scale imitation ! [2] Recover a home-
land, expanded to the whole of a continent ! A strange dream
and very American . . . in its vastness. Even Du Bois, of whom
also we shall be speaking presently, holds that separation must
come, and if the Whites were obstinately to refuse the status of
free equality, revolution would be inevitable. This was not the
conclusion arrived at by the Congress Declaration, the " Charter
of the Black Race ". It aims at reform and " solidarity ". It
borrows from the Whites the White Man's Idea that it is a duty
to educate the Blacks and to " assist backward and oppressed
races to attain to the fulness of life ". White and Black could
then live in " mutual respect ". The black peoples should
govern themselves through their own agents and by their own
means ; they should control their own fate and resume possession

[1] F. Challaye, *Cahiers des Droits de l'Homme*, 1922, p. 420 f. ; de Warnaffe, *Le
mouvement pannègre. Congo*, May 1922. Cf. *Revue de Paris*, 1929, p. 160 f.
[2] On Liberia, see N. Azikiwa, *Liberia in World Politics*, 1935, and the instructive
reportage of P. Bénard, *Malikoko* (undated).

of their land which the Whites would restore to them ; but they would collaborate with the Whites who would remain their friends. This is what I have called " *equalised partnership* ". Meanwhile they want teaching, welfare measures and assistance ; the protection of the workers by such methods as are authorised by the I.L.O., finally they want an International Institute to study the ways and means of emancipating the oppressed Blacks. A modest programme ! A very anti-colonial French writer bitterly remarks that the French Negroes have remained . . . " too prudent in their desires and schemes : it is the Negroes of Africa who put the brake on the radical spirit of the American Negroes."

The Pan-Black movement has verily its own *doctrine* which is regulated by two theorists, Dr. Du Bois and Marcus Garvey, both of them a hundred per cent Negro.

W.–E. Burghardt du Bois [1] is the pioneer of the new movement. He has been writing this forty years. He is a Protestant, therefore a democrat ; hence his success in the United States. He has preached equality, basing it on two grounds—the *theological*, which we have already analysed : [2] the unity of Man by the Creation. Negroes and White Men are alike the work of God ; they are relatives by origin ; let them be treated fraternally as relatives !—secondly, the *democratic* ground. This is entirely logical ; there is nothing pre-logical in the argument. It is, he says, the majority which confers authority ; if in any place the Blacks are the more numerous they should rule by electoral law. In Africa therefore they should be masters in their own house. Africa for the Africans . . . for they represent Number invested with Power. But Dr. Du Bois ventures to hope that the change will come peaceably by evolution ; that the Whites will educate the Blacks, associate them with Government and to begin with, tide over the transition period by entrusting them with local government. If the French wish to keep the colonies let them give the Blacks the same rights as the Whites. Otherwise . . . the Blacks will take them !

More recently, Marcus Garvey has been more clamant. It was he who launched the slogan " Africa for the Africans ", and he has been the preacher of what I should call *Pan-Melanism*. He is a Jamaican Negro who has travelled as far afield as Berlin

---

[1] *The Souls of Black Folk, Essays and Sketches*, 1903 ; and particularly *Dark Water*, 1920.
[2] See above, Chap. XXIV.

and Paris. He has founded the paper called *The Negro World*. In it he defends Schopenhauer's theory that the Negro is superior to the White Man by reason of his valour and his virtue. Let the Black Men then shake off the White Men's tyranny ; let them flow back into Africa and there establish—first in Ethiopia !— the Republic of Forty Million Men. Let them bid the Whites get out ! "The Blacks," he says, "to whom the White Man has taught the art of slaying", and who have "won the war" for him, will assuredly in the future know how to win the war for the Blacks !

Up to the present Garvey's voice would seem to have found few echoes. But this idea of equality, shared by Du Bois and Garvey, prevails already in South Africa,[1] thanks in the first place to the White Man, as is the case also elsewhere. There have been the *Koffervriends*, the Friends of the Kaffir who have been called *Negrophils* and who go about preaching equality from mainly religious motives : the Bible is always on the horizon and the missionary is in the front rank.[2] They aim at equality in partnership, and this is the spirit of the *South African Institute of Race Relations* founded in South Africa in 1929 "for peace and for goodwill", which labours most enthusiastically to improve the lot of the natives by discussing their just desires in European-Bantu Councils.[3] This is the partnership policy.

We must, however, recognise that Communism has contrived here and there to affect the Negroes, especially the industrial workers. The first *International Congress of Negro Workers* met in 1930 ; the idea of class was there superimposed on the idea of *colour*. All this is very European . . . or perhaps, rather, Eur-Asian. For Moscow is playing its own game in this ; and the paper *The Negro Worker* is a Soviet product as is also *The Cry of the Negro*. Negro Clubs have been founded in Cuba ; no white members are allowed and the clubs are practically Soviets.[4] The trade unions, sometimes mixed Black and White, sometimes only Black, have provided the soil in which this microbe has been able to flourish. So far, however, its influence is limited and it is gaining little ground.

One great fact must at least henceforward be recognised, a

---

[1] Brookes, *The Colour Problems of South Africa*, 1934, pp. 79 f., 153 f. ; J. Weulersee, *Afrique noire*, 1934.

[2] This is the spirit of Basil Mathews, *The Clash of Colour*, 1924 (Church Missionary Society) ; cf. J. H. Oldham, *Christianity and the Race Problem* (Student Christian Movement).

[3] See their *Sixth Annual Report*, Johannesburg, 1935.

[4] A. Fabre Luce, *Révolution à Cuba*, 1934, p. 110 f.

unity of feeling amongst the Blacks such as the Japanese imperialists hoped to arouse in the future amongst the Yellows. There is a *mystiqne* of colour, and colour only, not of race or of class ; the Negro feels himself a Negro whether he is an American or an African, whether he hails from the Antilles or the Sudan. This unity was recently demonstrated when the Guiana Negroes of Surinam ordered numerous photographs of Mussolini (five thousand, it was said !) They were wanted for the Voodoo sorcerers who claimed that by the aid of these portraits they could work Black Magic against the enemy of the Ethiopians ! This pleasing phenomenon shows the ancient past linking with the present, the savagery of earliest times harnessed to modern progress. The whole of the Black World feels itself affected when one of the Black peoples is attacked. The law of To-morrow is the Universal.

CONCLUSION

In the attitudes of mind which we have been examining and pondering, which range from one extreme to the other, from one pole to the other : the acquiescent and the protesting ; the resigned and the rebellious ; the conservative, the reformative and the destructive ; in them all, we have been able to trace in all overseas countries, two fundamental phenomena : syncretism and reformism. Both are tinged with, or, better, dyed in religion. Always and everywhere they are " mystiques " : authority, utility, equality are aspirations of a religious nature,

Syncretism in which every new spirit appears as a product of that blending of ideas which even in ancient times was the result of colonisations. Desired or not, intellectual syncretism comes to saturate the ruled ; all expansion entails a mixing of souls ; the subjects are inevitably and compulsorily conditioned to be infected by the dreams and hopes of their rulers. This fact has brought the spread of all the French ideas of equality.

Reformism in which change is desired either with or against French concurrence. The natives of the French colonies, more especially the Musulmans, were for a long time resigned : " It is the Will of Allah," they said when good or evil fortune overtook them ; " it is written " (*maktub*). If a plan was made, if some step forward was suggested, they would say *Inshallah !*, "if God so will ! "—a lesson perhaps for the impatient European. In this respect a change has come over them, a profound change, under our very eyes. Fatalism has given way to a passion for reform : to aspiration for happiness, aspiration for importance ; a craving for new possessions, for new rights. The subject races, particularly the Muslims of North Africa, are thus no longer as of old resigned and acquiescent people leaving their fate in the hands of Allah ; but through French influence, French contagion, French inspiration, they have learned to protest and to lay claims.

For progress consists in exchange and blending. The French have been able to give the inhabitants of their colonies, both in law and in practice, prosperity and security. They gave at the same time the desire for more humanity, more equality. They taught their subjects to reform themselves, to separate themselves. Converting the tribes into nations, the French directed their subjects' hopes and wishes against themselves. For to enlighten people is to set them free. This is the tragedy of all expansion.

For Product Safety Concerns and Information please contact our EU
representative GPSR@taylorandfrancis.com
Taylor & Francis Verlag GmbH, Kaufingerstraße 24, 80331 München, Germany

www.ingramcontent.com/pod-product-compliance
Lightning Source LLC
Chambersburg PA
CBHW060130280326
41932CB00012B/1478